MODERN HUNGARIAN HISTORIOGRAPHY

STEVEN BELA VARDY

EAST EUROPEAN QUARTERLY, BOULDER
DISTRIBUTED BY COLUMBIA UNIVERSITY PRESS
NEW YORK AND GUILDFORD, SURREY

1976

EAST EUROPEAN MONOGRAPHS, NO. XVII

The publication of this book was made possible by a grant from the Hungarian Cultural Foundation

Steven Bela Vardy is Professor of History
at Duquesne University

Library of Congress Catalogue Card Number 75-27773
ISBN 0-914710-08-7

Printed in the United States of America

EAST EUROPEAN MONOGRAPHS

The *East European Monographs* comprise scholarly books on the history and civilization of Eastern Europe. They are published by the *East European Quarterly* in the belief that these studies contribute substantially to the knowledge of the area and serve to stimulate scholarship and research.

1. *Political Ideas and the Enlightenment in the Romanian Principalities, 1750, 1831*. By Vlad Georgescu. 1971.

2. *America, Italy and the Birth of Yugoslavia, 1917-1919*. By Dragan R. Zivojinovic. 1972.

3. *Jewish Nobles and Geniuses in Modern Hungary*. By William O. McCagg, Jr.

4. *Mixail Soloxov in Yugoslavia: Reception and Literary Impact*. By Robert F. Price. 1973.

5. *The Historical and Nationalistic Thought of Nicolae Iorga*. By William O. Oldson. 1973.

6. *Guide to Polish Libraries and Archives*. By Richard C. Lewanski. 1974.

7. *Vienna Broadcasts to Slovakia, 1938-1939: A Case Study in Subversion*. By Henry Delfiner. 1974.

8. *The 1917 Revolution in Latvia*. By Andrew Ezergailis. 1974.

9. *The Ukraine in the United Nations Organization: A Study in Soviet Foreign Policy, 1944-1950*. By Konstantin Sawczuk. 1975.

10. *The Bosnian Church: A New Interpretation*. By John V. A. Fine, Jr. 1975.

11. *Intellectual and Social Developments in the Hapsburg Empire from Maria Theresa to World War I*. Edited by Stanley B. Winters and Joseph Held. 1975.

12. *Ljudevit Gaj and the Illyrian Movement*. By Elinor Murray Despalatovic. 1975.

13. *Tolerance and Movements of Religious Dissent in Eastern Europe.* Edited by Bela K. Kiraly. 1975.

14. *The Parish Republic: Hlinka's Slovak People's Party, 1939-1945.* By Yeshayahu Jelinek. 1976.

15. *The Russian Annexation of Bessarabia, 1774-1828.* By George F. Jewsbury. 1976.

16. *Modern Hungarian Historiography.* By Steven Bela Vardy. 1976.

17. *Values and Community in Multi-National Yugoslavia.* By Gary K. Bertsch. 1976.

18. *The Greek Socialist Movement and the First World War: The Road to Unity.* By George B. Leon. 1976.

This book is dedicated to my former professors:

Robert F. Byrnes
Robert H. Ferrell
Charles Jelavich
C. Leonard Lundin
Michael S. Pap
Denis Sinor
Ferenc Somogyi
Piotr S. Wandycz

PREFACE

The aim of this study is to present a comprehensive view of the development of Hungarian historical sciences from the eleventh to the middle of the twentieth century. But while summarizing and analyzing the events of the earlier periods of Hungarian historiography, its emphasis is undoubtedly on our own century. This is so partially because of the greater significance of twentieth-century developments; but perhaps even more so because of the author's intention of elaborating and analyzing the developments of the earlier centuries in greater detail in a companion volume to this work.

Although the aim is comprehensiveness, there are in fact several areas of Hungarian historical sciences that this work does not cover. The most glaring omissions are proto-history and oriental studies (including Byzantinology, Turkology, Central Asiatic studies and Semitic studies), all of which had outstanding representatives among Hungarian scholars (e.g. A. Vámbéry, I. Goldziher, A. Stein, G.J. Németh, G.J. Moravcsik, L. Fekete, A. Alföldi, L. Ligeti and others). The reason for this omission is primarily the lack of space. Simultaneously, however, one can also make a case for their exclusion on the basis that these subdisciplines are at least as much a part of linguistics as history. This consideration also affected the coverage of East European studies in this volume, where many noteworthy achievements remained untreated primarily because they are really part of Hungarian linguistic, rather than historical sciences.

The idea for this work was conceived and the research undertaken in the course of the academic year 1969-1970, while the author was an IREX (International Research and Exchanges Board) Fellow and Visiting Scholar in Hungary. More specifically, it was begun because of the realization (also pointed out by a number of colleagues in Hungary) that the achievements of Hungarian historical scholarship are not only unknown, but they are even misunderstood in the Western World. This was demonstrated recently in a work by an otherwise respectable British scholar who — although unable to read Magyar — characterized the whole Hungarian historiography as "naive" and disfigured by "disputatious patriotism"(1) — a judgment based undoubtedly on a few English language works of questionable scholarly value. Yet, almost with the same breath, he praised the works of the Hungarian positivist historians V. Fraknói and F. Salamon as the products of "the best traditions of nineteenth-century German Scholarship"(2) — unaware that he was praising a few of the translated works of these Hungarian historians, and thus in effect the achievements of nineteenth-century Hungarian historical scholarship.

Knowing how difficult it is to treat the achievements of scholars who are still active, the original aim was to exclude all living historians from considerations in this study. But however desirable, this aim proved to be unrealistic. To have left E. Mályusz and his Ethnohistory School out of interwar Hungarian historiography — to cite just one example — would have made it virtually impossible to cover the historiography of that period. And there are several other cases as well.

In the course of my research and writing I have received the intellectual and moral support of numerous scholars and the help of several institutions both here and in Hungary. While it would be impossible to list them all, I would like to mention a few of them by name. Thus, I am particularly grateful to the Institute of History of the Hungarian Academy of Sciences, headed by Academician Z.P. Pach, where I spent much of the year during my stay in Hungary, and to a number of colleagues at that institution, including Drs. F. Glatz, T. Kolossa, E. Niederhauser, G. Ránki and A. Várkonyi. No less am I grateful to Drs. G.G. Kemény and K.Cs.-Gárdonyi of the National Széchényi Library, to Dr. Cs. Csapodi of the Library of the Hungarian Academy of Sciences, to Professor A. Csizmadia of the Institute of Legal History of the University of Pécs, to Dr. A. Degré, formerly of the University of Pécs and now Director of the Zala County Archives in Zalaegerszeg, to Professor E. Mályusz, formerly of the University of Budapest and of the Institute of History of the Hungarian Academy of Sciences and the "father" of the Hungarian Ethnohistory School, as well as to numerous other colleagues of the University of Budapest, the Hungarian National Archives and a number of other scholarly institutions.

I also wish to thank some of my colleagues and friends here in the United States, notably Professor James F. Clarke of the University of Pittsburgh, Dr. T.L. Szendrey of Gannon College, Professor J. Értavy-Baráth of the Hungarian Cultural Foundation, Dr. E. Bakó of the Library of Congress, and especially my former professors Dr. Robert F. Byrnes, Director of the Institute of Russian and East European Studies and Dr. Denis Sinor, Chairman of the Department of Uralic and Altaic Studies of Indiana University, and Dr. Ferenc Somogyi, formerly of the

University of Pécs and Western Reserve University. Their encouragement and help at various stages of this work was of great significance.

My appreciation also goes to the International Research and Exchanges Board of New York and to its Hungarian counterpart in Budapest *(Kulturális Kapcsolatok Intézete)* for their financial support and courteous help; to Dr. G. Grosschmid, Academic Vice President, Dr. F. Gross, Dean of the Graduate School, Dr. J. McCulloch, Dean of the College of Arts and Sciences, and Dr. S.J. Astorino, Chairman of the Department of History of Duquesne University for their help during the preparation of this manuscript; and to my always helpful wife, Dr. Agnes Huszar Vardy of Robert Morris College, for her inspiration and criticism. Moreover, I should also like to thank Professor S. Fischer-Galati, Editor of the *East European Quarterly,* for undertaking the publication of this work, and the Hungarian Cultural Foundation for the generous grant that made the publication possible.

Because many geographic names in the Carpathian Basin have several variants, it was decided to use the spelling that was "official" at the time under consideration, but at critical junctures also giving the other variant or variants in parentheses.

The manuscript was read by the following scholars: F. Glatz (Budapest), E. Niederhauser (Budapest), D. Sinor (Bloomington), F. Somogyi (Cleveland) and A. Várkonyi (Budapest). While I have profited much from their comments, the final interpretation is mine; and — needless to say — they may not necessarily agree with all the views expressed in this volume.

Spring, 1975

Steven Bela Vardy
Duquesne University

TABLE OF CONTENTS

PART I

Chapter I

THE DEVELOPMENT OF MEDIEVAL HISTORIOGRAPHY

The course of Hungarian historiography during the past millennium was basically identical with its West European counterparts. Like the latter, it too started with various heroic legends based on long-surviving oral traditions. These legends usually dealt with gods and pre-Christian tribal and national heroes, born on the lips of the people, and preserved, shaped and transmitted to posterity by minstrels, bards, as well as family and clan elders. The role of the latter was particularly important during the earlier phase of the development of these legends.(1)

In light of their pre-Christian origins and pagan mythological contents, these heroic legends of the Magyars (like those of their predecessors and many contemporaries) came under the attack of the Christian clergy immediately after the introduction of Christianity to Hungary in the late tenth century. Those that survived, did so only in a mutilated form, as incorporated parts of the national chronicles of the early Christian age. Even so, many of these legend-fragments managed to retain some of their original flavor, as well as the essence of the historical or mythical event around which they were formed.

Based on their content, these heroic legends of the Magyars can be divided into at least three different categories. Thus, there are those that deal with the origins and ancestry of the conquering Magyars of the ninth century, those that concern themselves with the conquest itself, and those that deal with the deeds of the national heroes of the post-conquest period. Among the first of these, mention can be made of the "Legend of the Mythical Stag," which deals with the origins of the two sister nations, the Magyars and the Huns; the "Legend of the Sword of God," which centers on the divinely ordained mission of Attila, the emperor of the Hunnic Empire — generally regarded by Magyar traditions to have been an ancestor of the conquering Árpád; and the "Legend of Álmos" on the origins and destiny of the Árpád dynasty, the founder of medieval Hungary. The most important of the legends on the Magyar conquest of Hungary is the "Legend of the White Stallion," which tries to justify the Magyar occupation of the Carpathian Basin not only by virtue of military conquest, but also by its alleged symbolic purchase by Árpád from Svatopluk, the next to last ruling prince of the nearly defunct Great Moravian State. Among the post-conquest legends of the tenth century, the several legends of "Lél" ("Lehel"), "Botond" and "Bulcsú" are perhaps the best known. Their aim is to depict and to idealize the incessant struggles of the Magyars — a relatively small nation — in their effort to retain their newly conquered lands against the joint efforts of the German, Bulgarian and Byzantine empires.(2)

Subsequent to the Christianization of Hungary, legends were also born in connection with various Christian national heroes. Some of these were clearly simple adaptations of pagan legends to the new Christian circumstances and surroundings. As an example, there is the "Legend of the Mythical Junior Stag" on King St. Stephen, the founder of the Christian Hungarian Kingdom. Others, however, were new creations and reflected many elements of Christian miracles. Thus, there is the "Legend of Csanád," who was one of St. Stephen's generals and helped to subdue the rebellions of various pagan princes, as well as numerous legends on some of Hungary's eleventh-century Christian kings, including those of Andrew I, Béla I, Salamon, Géza I, and particularly St. Ladislas — whose role as a Christian ruler is exceeded only by the role of St. Stephen.(3)

Parallel with the birth of these post-Christian heroic legends, the second half of the eleventh century also witnessed the birth of the first Hungarian annals, *gestas (res gestae* —deeds done) and hagiographies, including *acta* (deeds), *vita* (lives) and *legenda* (legends).

The oldest among the annals or yearbooks were the *Annals of Pannonhalma* which had been started in 998. But there were a number of others as well, usually connected with one of the newly founded monasteries or cathedral chapters. These annals were generally simple chronological accounts of events, which reflected a Christian view of the world, but did not as yet serve the political, social and dynastic interests of the recently reorganized Hungarian state.

The situation was totally different with the gestas of the late eleventh and twelfth century, which were written with such goals in mind. These goals included the desire to consolidate and to perpetuate the new social, political and religious order, as well as to ensure the permanency and relative unlimitedness of the powers of the Árpád dynasty. But they also reflected the continued pride in the Magyar national past, even though the large majority of that past was inseparable from the pre-Christian pagan traditions of the nation.

According to Hungarian historiographers, the first Hungarian gesta, the so-called "Ancient Gesta" *(Ősgesta)* was written around the middle of the eleventh century. Later it was amended, altered and expanded to suit the political, social, religious and dynastic needs of the times. Its late eleventh-century version is known as the *Gesta Ladislai Regis* (Gesta of King Ladislas). This, in turn, was followed by several twelfth-century versions — some of them perhaps independent creations. All of them dealt with one or another aspect (and version) of Magyar origins, conquest and foundation of the Hungarian state, but none of them survived, except as sections of subsequent compilations. Thus, we don't even know their exact number, although at least three are believed to have existed. The first fully surviving Hungarian gesta is the late twelfth-century *Gesta Hungarorum* by an unknown author ("Anonymus" — P. dictus magister), who in all probability was an employee of the Chancery of King Béla III (1172-1196)(4)

Simultaneously with the appearance of officially sponsored gestas the late eleventh century also witnessed the development of legends of saints or hagiographies whose purpose appears to have been to hold up the lives of Hungary's early Christian saints as examples for the newly Christianized nation. The oldest of these hagiographies were written around 1060, and they deal with such non-Hungarian saints as St. Zoerard and St. Benedict. Much more important are the legends of the first Hungarian saints, for these also contain details about contemporary Hungarian history. The latter include the two St. Stephen legends *(Legenda Maior* and *Legenda Minor);* the legends of St. Emeric, St. Stephen's son; the so-called *Hartvik Legend,* which combines the two St. Stephen legends; St. Gerard's legend, on the first important martyr of Hungarian Christianity; and the legend of St. Ladislas, Hungary's second canonized ruler of the eleventh century. All of these legends were produced around the turn of the eleventh and the twelfth century, and they all reflect not only the Christian ideals of the relatively newly Christianized Hungarian state, but also its consequent economic, social, cultural and political composition.(5)

Thirteenth-Century Travelogues and Gestas

Following the birth and development of Hungarian gestas and hagiographies in the eleventh and twelfth centuries, the turn of the twelfth to the thirteenth century saw the rise of a number of different types of historical writings, including descriptive travelogues and chronicles. The most important of the former are Frater Ricardus's *Relatio* (1237), which describes Frater Julianus's travels in the Volga region in search of *Magna Hungaria,* and Magister Rogerius's *Carmen Miserabile* (1243-1244), which portrays Hungary's destruction by the Mongols in 1241-1242.(6) Even more significant than these descriptive travelogues, however, were the new type of gestas and chronicles that began to appear following Anonymus's late twelfth-century *Gesta Hungarorum* and produced a sudden flowering of Hungarian chronicle literature that lasted right into the fifteenth century.

Next to Anonymus's celebrated *Gesta Hungarorum*, which combines semi-mythical and historical traditions with the social, economic, ethnic and political realities of his own day (and which thus has to be used with caution), we have such other thirteenth-century gestas as the *Gesta of Magister Ákos* (1260's), an anonymous chronicle composition of the age of Stephen V (1270-1272), and Simon de Kéza's (Simon Kézai's) *Gesta Hungarorum* (c. 1283). The first two of these represent the economic and social interests of the great oligarchic families of the late thirteenth century, while the last tries to point out the community of interest between the lesser nobility and the king in their respective struggles against the oligarchs. All of these gestas, therefore, relate the history of the Magyars from the vantage point of the special interests of these two camps, but the eloquent Kézai places a considerably greater emphasis on the pre-conquest period than either Magister Ákos or the author of the anonymous gesta of the age of Stephen V. Moreover, in line with Magyar national traditions, Kézai regards the Huns and the Magyars as basically identical people and discusses the Árpádian conquest of Hungary simply as "the second coming of the Huns."(7) (Interestingly enough, some current research appears to substantiate at least part of this theory.)(8)

The Anjou Chronicles

Following the extinction of the Árpáds in Hungary, the next ruling dynasty came from Italy. They were the Italian Anjous or Angevins, who initiated a new great age in Hungarian history, and who had an especially close relationship with the Franciscan Order. This relationship perhaps supplies the reason why fourteenth-century Hungarian chroniclers all came from the ranks of the Franciscans, and why the *chronicle* displaced the *gesta* as the primary form of historical literature in fourteenth and fifteenth-century Hungary. (It should perhaps be noted here that while it is impossible to draw a clear distinction between a gesta and a chronicle, the former is generally a chronological account of the nation's history as a whole, while the latter is usually a monographic compendium of a series of great events connected with a specific period of history or with a great historical personality. In Hungary, eleventh to thirteenth-century histories were generally called gestas and fourteenth to fifteenth-century works chronicles. The latter were an improvement over the former, for they tended to give a more complete picture of a chronological segment of Hungary's past.)(9)

The first of the Hungarian historical works to appear under the title of chronicle was the *Chronica Hungarorum* by a certain Johannes, Provincial of the Hungarian Franciscans between 1323 and 1331, and generally referred to in historical literature as the "Anonymous Minorite." In its introductory section, up to the year 1272, this work is basically a compilation, based on Kézai's *Gesta Hungarorum* and on the anonymous gesta of the age of Stephen V. For the period between 1272 and 1332, however, it is the original work of the Anonymous Minorite. As portrayed in this work, the author of this first known Hungarian chronicle was not a man of great conceptions, but he was a good writer who was particularly apt in depicting historical details and in relating interesting anecdotes.

The *Chronica Hungarorum* of Johannes, the Anonymous Minorite, was followed three decades later by the famed "Viennese" *Illustrated Chronicle* (c. 1360), the most beautifully executed of all medieval Hungarian chronicles, which previously had generally been attributed to Márk Kálti (c. 1300-1360's), the Archcanon of Székesfehérvár. The *Illustrated Chronicle,* in turn, was followed by the chronicle fragments of Johannes Kétyi (mid-fourteenth century) who — contrary to the author of the *Illustrated Chronicle* — continued the traditions of the earlier gestas. Finally, there came the Chronicle of Johannes Apród of Tótsólymos, (1320-1394) the archpriest of Küküllő (János Küküllei), whose work is basically a descriptive account of the life and deeds of Louis the Great (1342-1382), the greatest of the Anjou kings of Hungary.

Based largely on such earlier histories as the *Gesta Ladislai Regis* of the late eleventh century, on the twelfth-century gesta of the age of Stephen III (1161-1172), and most importantly on the *Chronica Hungarorum* of the Anonymous Minorite, the author-compiler of the *Illustrated Chronicle* had put together some of the best pages of Hungarian medieval gesta literature, placing St. Ladislas into the very center of medieval Hungarian history. His ideal appears to have been the wise and able philosopher king, selected by God to rule in the best interest of the nation as a whole. And in line with the values of that age of Hungarian chivalry, apparently it was St. Ladislas who came closest to that ideal.

Next to the *Illustrated Chronicle,* the chronicle-fragments of Johannes Kétyi appear much less impressive. His coverage of the second half of Charles Robert's rule (1308-1342), however, is most detailed. In a way, it appears to be a continuation of the *Chronica Hungarorum* by the Anonymous Minorite.

Much more important is the work of Johannes Apród of Tótsólymos (1320-1394) or János Küküllei, even though his work is closer to a *vita* than to a summarizing chronicle. This work is in a way a boundary stone, for it represents the end of the line for the chronicle literature imbued with the spirit of medieval chivalry. But in dealing with the spirit of chivalry (and basically all of king Louis the Great's deeds are described in such terms) Johannes Apród of Tótsólymos does not turn to St. Ladislas as the ideal, as did the author of the *Illustrated Chronicle,* but rather to Alexander the Great, who is reshaped in this chronicle into a medieval knight. Johannes Apród is undoubtedly the last Hungarian historian of the medieval chivalric school. Moreover, like Kézai a century earlier, he too represents the views and aspirations of the king and the lesser nobility against the aristocracy.(10)

''Secular Latin Culture'' of the Hungarian Lower Nobility

By the fifteenth century, the medieval chivalric culture that had produced the chronicles of the Anjou period had come to an end. Its place was taken by the ''secular Latin culture'' of the Hungarian lower nobility; a culture that represented the transition between the chivalric culture of the late Middle Ages in Hungary and the humanist culture of the Renaissance. In Western Europe this secular Latin culture was the culture of the emerging urban classes — be they burghers or members of the intelligentsia. In Hungary, on the other hand, this culture was carried by the Latin speaking *literati* and bureaucracy who came from the ranks of the lesser nobility.(11) There, it was this secular Latin culture that produced the major fifteenth-century works of history, including a number of unoriginal compilations, as well as a significant original synthesis of Hungarian history. The most notable of the first of these are the *Buda Chronicle* and the *Dubnic Chronicle,* while the second type is represented by Johannes Thuróczy's *Chronica Hungarorum.*

Fifteenth-Century Compilations

For about a century after the death of Johannes Apród of Tótsólymos, there appears to have emerged no historian to continue the rich traditions of the Anjou chroniclers. This is all the more unexplainable, as starting with the reign of Sigismund in Hungary (1387), and continuing throughout the fifteenth century, Hungary became the primary adversary of the expanding Ottoman Turkish power; and these Turkish-Hungarian encounters could and should have served as sources of inspiration for contemporary chroniclers.(12)

This lack of initiative on the part of fifteenth-century Hungarian historians is also evident from their apparent unwillingness to reinterpret the views of earlier chroniclers on their nation's history. This unwillingness is explainable by the absence of a need for such a reinterpretation. More specifically, the rising social and political prominence of the lower nobility, coupled with the burgher class's inability to rise to such prominence, made the class interests of the lesser nobility the most decisive factor in influencing the orientation of historical thinking and writing in contemporary Hungary.

The class interests of the Hungarian lower nobility, however, had already been expressed by Simon Kézai in his thirteenth-century *Gesta Hungarorum,* which contained the seeds of the doctrine of the political pre-eminence of that class. Moreover, this doctrine had also infiltrated into several fourteenth-century chronicles and gesta fragments. Thus, fifteenth-century Hungarian historians did not need to rewrite their history to suit the needs of the emerging lower nobility. They could simply go on "copying and contaminating" various earlier works that portrayed their own conception of Hungarian history.(13)

The most famous and worthwhile of these fifteenth-century compilations is the *Buda Chronicle,* which has the honor of being the first printed book in Hungary, published in 1473 under the title *Chronica Hungarorum.*(14) Sponsored by László Kara, the Royal Vice Chancellor and a provost of Buda, and printed by András Hess, the pioneer of Hungarian book printing, the *Chronica Hungarorum* is based essentially on Kézai's *Gesta Hungarorum* and on various fourteenth-century copies thereof.(15) But it had also been expanded by the addition of Johannes Apród's (Küküllei's) description of the life and deeds of King Louis the Great, as well as by a few original cursory chapters on the period after 1382, probably written by Hess himself with the help of one of the clerks in the Royal Chancellory of Buda.(16)

The last of these fifteenth-century compilations is the *Dubnic Chronicle* (1479), prepared six years after the *Buda Chronicle,* with the apparent intent of improving it.(17) After his initial enthusiasm, however, the anonymous compiler of the *Dubnic Chronicle* gave up his original intention and produced an awkward compilation for which he borrowed freely and unevenly from such sources as the *Illustrated Chronicle,* the chronicles of Johannes Kétyi and Johannes Apród (Küküllei), and even from the *Buda Chronicle (Chronica Hungarorum)* itself. Thus, the *Dubnic Chronicle* contains very little that is new, and its most important claim for notice is its compiler's willingness to criticize a reigning monarch, Matthias Corvinus (1457-1590). This is the first instance of such criticism in the history of Hungarian historical studies; and it was undoubtedly a daring act.(18)

Thuróczy's Chronica Hungarorum

Following these late fifteenth-century compilations, which had little new to offer, Thuróczy's *Chronica Hungarorum* (1488), written only a decade or so after the latter, appears quite refreshing.(19) It may be regarded as the first independent synthesis of Hungarian history since the *Illustrated Chronicle* of the mid-fourteenth century. While naturally relying on various earlier works, it is substantially different both from twelfth and thirteenth-century gestas, as well as from the chivalric chronicles of the Anjou period. In addition to being more synthetic, it also differs from the former in its orientation. Thus, contrary to its predecessors, it displays neither dynastic, nor oligarchic interests. Nor does it contain any of the chivalric characteristics of the Anjou chronicles. Thuróczy appears to stand only for the interests of the "noble communitas" — the nobility as a whole — without acknowledging any of the existing differences between the higher and the lower nobility. Yet, by doing so, he obviously represents primarily the class interests of the latter.

Structurally Thuróczy's *Chronica Hungarorum* is divided into two parts. The first part summarizes the history of the Magyars in the Hunnic-Scythian traditions right up to the death of Louis the Great (1382); and the second part contains Thuróczy's fully original contribution and brings the story up to Thuróczy's own time.(20)

Thuróczy's *Chronica Hungarorum* became a success almost immediately. This success was due at least partially to the timeliness of this first real synthesis of Hungarian history since the *Illustrated Chronicle* in the mid-fourteenth century. But Thuróczy's ability as a writer must also have played a part.(21) Although his prose lacks the rhetorical solemnity of some of the contemporary early humanist works, Thuróczy has a good literary style, ample humor, and more than average ability to synthesize. For these reasons, his *Chronica Hungarorum* was not only an immediate success, but it also became the standard handbook of Hungarian history for well over a half century. Not until the 1530's and 1540's did Antonio Bonfini's great humanist work, the *Rerum Ungaricarum Decades,* began to displace Thuróczy's work; and even then it took several additional decades before the shift from Thuróczy to Bonfini became fairly general. Moreover, by the eighteenth century, Thuróczy's *Chronica Hungarorum* again gained ascendancy over Bonfini's work, and remained in that position until the birth of the first "modern" syntheses at the turn of the eighteenth to the nineteenth century.(22)

Chapter II

HUMANIST HISTORIOGRAPHY

The foundations of modern scholarship, including historical scholarship, were laid down during the period of the Renaissance. In line with the demands of the new secular culture of the rising urban classes new areas of scholarship were born and others were renewed. The new ideal human being became the *homo doctus* (scholar) as opposed to the pious *homo religious* (religious man) of the Middle Ages. *De fide* ceased to be an accepted form of argument in scholarly circles.(1)

This change in European mentality and outlook also had an impact on Hungarian historical scholarship, even though the needed center of a true humanist scholarship, the national university, was missing. It is true that in earlier times Hungary had several universities. But the universities of Pécs (1367) and Óbuda (1389) have both ceased to exist by the early fifteenth century, and the short-lived *Academia Istropolitana* of Pozsony (Pressburg, Bratislava), which was founded by Matthias Corvinus in 1467, had never really developed into a center of learning comparable to the contemporary Italian universities.(2) Thus, while the demand for the rewriting of Hungarian history in line with the expectations of the rising humanist spirit grew progressively in the late fifteenth century, there were no Hungarian scholars for such a major project. (As we have seen, although completed as late as 1488, Thuróczy's *Chronica Hungarorum* was a product of the late medieval Latinist culture, and thus failed to meet the requirements of humanist scholarship.) Consequently, the first truly humanist elaboration of Hungarian history had to be done by an Italian, Antonio Bonfini (1427-1503), one of the numerous Italian humanist scholars at the brilliant Renaissance court of Hungary's king Mathias Corvinus (1458-1490).(3)

Humanist historiography of that period was basically the product of the Italian mind, and it was in Italy where this scholarship had reached the highest level of development.(4) In historiography it was characterized by a return to the annalistic form of writing first developed by Livy during the last decades of the pre-Christian era; by the elevation and rhetorization of certain dramatic and clearly visible events of history (such as wars, revolutions, invasions and the like); by placing an undue emphasis upon the deeds of great men, as opposed to historical developments and their interaction; and finally by an attempt to Romanize everything and everyone through the application of classical forms and characteristics to events and personalities of the post-Roman period of European history. Thus, humanist historiography may have displayed more literary than scholarly characteristics, although the overall picture it drew was considerably more encompassing and sophisticated than the picture drawn even by such advanced fifteenth-century chroniclers as Thuróczy in Hungary.

Antonio Bonfini's Hungarian history *(Rerum Ungaricarum Decades Quattuor et Dimidia)* was written during the late 1480's and early 1490's, and it displays all of the positive and negative features of humanist historiography that one finds in the works of Bonfini's own master, Flavio Biondo (Flavius Blondus) (1388-1463).(5) About three-fifths or twenty-eight of the forty-five books of the *Rerum Ungaricarum Decades* is devoted to the summary of Hungarian history up to the reign of Mathias Corvinus; while the remaining two-fifths or seventeen books deal with the reign of the great king (1458-1490) and with the years of confusion that followed (1490-1496).

In writing the first part of his work, Bonfini relied largely on Thuróczy's *Chronica Hungarorum.* For the Christian period, however, he also relied on the legends of the Hungarian saints, as well as on a number of Western sources. Outside of his flowery and rhetorical style characteristic of the humanist school, Bonfini's only original contribution to the first part of this work was his Romanization of Hungarian history and historical personalities. His real contributions came in the second half of his work, where he relied heavily on information collected verbally, as well as on his own experiences in Hungary.

The end result of Bonfini's labors was a Romanized and partially idealized Hungarian history, in which the center of the stage is occupied by Mathias Corvinus, the great "Renaissance ruler" of Hungary, who clearly enjoyed Bonfini's admiration. This is even more evident in the last section of the work where — in light of the chaos that followed the great king's death in 1490 — Bonfini's admiration became even more expressed.

As an historian Bonfini is best in his description of court life and Renaissance mentality, which best suited his own mentality and rhetorical style and which consequently brought the most out of him. But he was also good as a synthesizer in the humanist sense of that term. His *Rerum Ungaricarum Decades* was a beautifully written piece of humanistic history, and it was bound to displace Thuróczy's somewhat medievalistic *Chronica Hungarorum* as the *opus magnum* of contemporary Hungarian historiography. But as his work remained in a manuscript form until the middle of the sixteenth century (it was printed partially in 1543 and fully in 1568),(6) it did not become the standard handbook of Hungarian history until a half century after Bonfini's death. Once it did, however, it remained fairly unchallenged until the eighteenth century, when Thuróczy's *Chronica Hungarorum* made a surprising comback.

Humanist Memoires

In light of the ultimate success of Bonfini's *Rerum Ungaricarum Decades,* for a considerable time there appears to have been no need for the rewriting of the whole of Hungarian history. The post-Corvinus (1490) and post-Mohács (1526) collapse of Hungarian society and state, however, produced a need for the examination of the calamities-filled immediate past of the Magyars. The result was the birth of the so-called "humanist memoire literature," based largely on the personal experiences of the respective authors. Thus, the letter-like memoire of the thirteenth century now grew into the "historical memoire," which became an important form of expression for sixteenth-century historians. The majority of the latter were either highly placed priest-diplomats, or various other members of the higher or lesser clergy.(7)

The most notable among these priest-historians were István Brodarics (c.1470-1539), Miklós Oláh (1493-1568) and Antal Verancsics (1504-1573) — the first of these being the chancellor of Louis II of Mohács fame, and the latter two the archbishops of Esztergom and primates of Hungary in succession.(8) These three were followed by a number of lesser lights, who wrote their memoires and memoire-fragments primarily at Verancsics's insistence.

Brodarics's great work is his description of the Battle of Mohács (1526) and of the fall of the Hungarian state *(De Conflictu Hungarorum cum Turcis ad Mohatz Verissima Descriptio,* 1527) that he wrote on the basis of personal experiences in a style reminiscent of Livy and thus conforming to some of the conditions of humanist historiography. Structurally, Brodarics's work is a little masterpiece. His realistic descriptive scenes, his constant search for logical explanations, and his relatively objective judgments make his *De Conflictu Hungarorum* into a valuable historical source. These positive features are further augmented by Brodarics's attention to geography and by his description of the general conditions in contemporary Hungary.

In his experimentation with the historical memoire, Brodarics did not remain without imitators. He was soon followed by Miklós Oláh, the learned head of the Catholic Church in Hungary, who devoted two major studies to the Hungarian past and present. His *Hungaria* and his accompanying *Attila* (1536-1537) combine the characteristics of the historical memoire with conventional descriptive history. Oláh's whole theme in these two works centers on the desire to contrast the sorrowful present with the glorious past (the latter represented by Attila and by Mathias Corvinus), and to urge his countrymen to work for the restoration of the past greatness of Hungary.

Another of Brodarics's major disciples was Antal Verancsics, Oláh's successor as Hungary's primate. After producing an archeological description of the Roman remains of Transylvania and of the two Danubian Principalities *(De Situ Transsylvaniae, Moldaviae et Transalpinae,* 1530's), Verancsics decided to write a sequel to Bonfini's *Rerum Ungaricarum Decades.* It was for this reason that he urged many of his contemporary humanist-oriented countrymen to prepare memoires on the notable events of the recent past in which they have personally participated. Even though his plan did not materialize, Verancsics was responsible for the birth of several Magyar and Latin language historical memories, a number of which remained intact in his collection.

The most notable of these Verancsics-sponsored works is György Szerémi's (c. 1490-1538+) *Epistola de Perditione Regni Hungarorum* which, while written in a very bad Latin, gives a vivid description of the collapse of the Hungarian state and Hungarian society during the first half of the sixteenth century up to 1543. Like most of his predecessors and contemporaries, Szerémi too tended to emphasize the contrast between the great age of Mathias Corvinus and the disintegrating, chaotic world that followed. Others in this group include Tamás Bornemisza (16th c.), Ferenc Zay (1505-1570), and Gábor Mindszenthi (16th c.). None of their works, however, came up to the quality level and importance of Szerémi's memoires, let alone to those of his greater predecessors.

The great mid-sixteenth-century philologist and polyhistor János Zsámboki (Johannes Sambucus) (1531-1584) was also urged by Verancsics to write down his reminiscences of the age. Zsámboki, however, never managed to complete this undertaking. Thus, his most important contribution to Hungarian historiography consists of his editing and publishing of Bonfini's *Rerum Ungaricarum Decades* in 1568, to which he added both his own summary on the period between 1496 and 1526, as well as Brodarics's description of Hungary's fall at Mohács.(9)

Historiography of the Hungarian Reformation

Faithful to its original social content, when Reformation came to Hungary, it caught the attention of all of the urban elements whose mentality and class interests rhymed best with its doctrines. It also produced a rapid growth of literacy and a flurry of new literary pieces. Yet, contrary to the situation in the Western and Northern countries where Protestantism advanced the cause of the native languages, in Hungary its linguistic-cultural influence was two-directional — splitting further the largely German-speaking burghers of the walled Royal Cities and the ethnically and linguistically Magyar citizens of such semi-urbanized ''agricultural towns'' *(mezővåros)* as Pest, Szeged and Debrecen. Whereas the Reformation of the Royal Cities expressed the class interests and advanced the cause of the German language and culture in Hungary, the Reformation of the agricultural towns did the same for the Magyar townsmen and for their language and culture. The ranks of the latter were also increased by the national realignment of such originally German cities as Kassa (Kaschau, Košice) and Kolozsvár (Klausenburg, Cluj) which — due to their economic interests within the context of sixteenth-century Eastern and Northeastern Hungary — were soon Magyarized and came to support the cause of the ''Magyar Reformation.''(10)

By the mid-sixteenth century, this ''Magyar Reformation'' had become a nationally-based dynamic socio-cultural-political movement, which was directed largely against the post-Mohács anarchy in Hungary. Soon it grew into a dynamic anti-oligarchic ideology of the socially and economically oppressed classes — an ideology that was carried throughout the country by the wandering Protestant preachers of that period. These self-appointed and dedicated spokesmen of righteousness moved from town to town to enlighten the masses and to give them hope. The most notable among them were Mátyás Dévai-Biró (?-c. 1545), Imre Ozorai (?-?), Gál Huszár (?-1575), Péter Méliusz-Juhász (c. 1536-1572) and Ferenc Dávid (?-1579), the founder of Unitarianism. They also had a number of friends and disciples who contributed not only to Hungarian Protestantism and Magyar literacy, but also to Hungarian historiography of the period.(11)

One of the most noted of these Protestant preacher-historians was István Benczédi-Székely (c. 1510-c.1563), the author of the *Chronicle of the Outstanding Events of the World (Chonica a világnak jeles dolgairól,* 1559), which came in wake of a number of similar, but lesser works. These included András Farkas's *On the Jewish and the Magyar Nations* (1538), András Batizi's *History of the Past and Future Events from the Creation to the Day of Judgment* (1544), and András Dézsi's

The Events from the Beginnings of the World (1548).(12) Like those of his predecessors, Benczédi-Székely's conception of world history rhymed fully with the Biblical conceptions, and he too equated "Magyar Protestantism" with Magyar patriotism. His aim was to demonstrate a parallel between the Roman Church's abandonment of the principles of original Christianity and the Magyar nation's abandonment of the ideals that had once made her into a great and prosperous nation. The result in both instances was disintegration and suffering. Benczédi-Székely's answer to these problems was obvious: A return to the original ideals of Christianity and a simultaneous return to the former ideals and virtues of the Magyar nation, last practiced during the reign of the great Mathias Corvinus.

While an important work of Hungarian historiography, Benczédi-Székely's work was not nearly as significant in its impact as Gáspár Heltai's (1490 1510-1574) *Chronicle about the Deeds of the Magyars* (1575), which is generally regarded to be the first Magyar language version of Bonfini's *Rerum Ungaricarum Decades.* In point of fact, Heltai's work is much more than that. Not even the section on pre-sixteenth-century developments is a simple translation of Bonfini's work. In general, Heltai cleansed Bonfini's *Rerum Ungaricarum Decades* of all of its Romanizing qualities and made it into a truly Magyar history. Moreover, he eliminated most of its Catholic features (derived from the legends of the Magyar saints) and replaced Bonfini's rhetorizing humanist style with his own direct and Magyar style. Heltai also reorganized the whole inner structure of Bonfini's work, changing its periodization to conform to the sequence of Hungarian rulers. As to the sixteenth-century section of Heltai's *Chronicle,* it is wholly his own compilation — based partially on Brodarics's and Zsámboki's earlier works, and partially on his own research and experiences.(13)

Heltai was the first to apply the philosophy of "Magyar Protestantism" to the whole course of Hungarian history. Moreover, as opposed to Benczédi-Székely, who stood for the semi-urbanized Magyar townsmen, Heltai represented the interest and culture of the truly urbanized burghers of Hungary — and did so in the Magyar language. And this is all the greater achievement as Heltai was born a Transylvanian Saxon who became assimilated only in his adult years.

Historical Ballads

Before the publication of his *Chronicle about the Deeds of the Magyars,* Heltai had also published his *Cancionale, A Book of*

Historical Ballads (1574), which contained historical ballads by six different sixteenth-century Hungarian bards.(14) With this publication Heltai became the first literary propagator of this new form of historical literature.

The "historical ballad" *(historiás ének, krónikás ének),* in its Hungarian context, was a typical sixteenth-century form of historical literature, created by the new frontier conditions brought about by the Turkish conquest of a large segment of Hungary. This type of historical ballad was not identical with the naive epic literature of the Middle Ages where myth and fancy mingled freely with elements of historical truth, but rather a new form of oral history (soon to be written down). These historical ballads were composed with the dual aim of preserving the historical events of the recent past, and of making these events known to the inspiration-hungry Magyar masses through the wandering bard historians of that period.

The most noted of these bard-historians of the sixteenth century was Sebestyén Tinódi (Lantos) (c. 1505/1510-1586), who wrote perhaps two dozen such historical ballads — many of them based on his own personal experiences as a frontier fighter against the Turks. Tinódi had numerous followers during the second half of that century, including Péter Ilosvai-Selymes (? - ?, active during the 1540's to 1570's), András Valkai (1540-1587), and perhaps over a dozen others. None of them, however, could match Tinódi's fame as a creator and propagator of the Hungarian historical ballad.(15)

The Climax of Humanist Historiogaphy

Hungarian humanist historiography, that began with Bonfini in the late fifteenth century, came to full flowering only at the turn of the sixteenth to the seventeenth century in the works of the secular humanist scholars associated either with the court of the Báthori princes in semi-independent Transylvania, or with the Habsburg court of Royal Hungary. These scholars — the most notable among whom were Ferenc Forgách, István Szamosközi and Miklós Istvánffy — were all products of Italian humanism and more specifically of the University of Padua.

The University of Padua in the second half of the sixteenth century happened to be both the center, as well as the battleground of two distinct schools of history. One of these schools, represented by Francesco Robortello, believed that the obligation of an historian is simply to relate the facts of history, without adding any explanations and value judgments. The competing school, lead by Francesco Patrizzi, on the other hand, demanded that historians engage in value judgments in their works so as to make them more useful to contemporary statesmen and more relevant to the needs of the people in general. Given the chaotic circumstances of Hungary of the sixteenth century, all Padua-educated Hungarian humanists became the followers of the second of these schools. Consequently, most of their works contained some tendentiousness, and they also produced political tracts in which they advocated specific political goals.(16)

The earliest of these late-humanist scholars was Ferenc Forgách (c. 1530/1535-1577), a pro-Habsburg statesman-diplomat, who subsequently shifted alliances and became the chancellor of anti-Habsburg Transylvania. In the course of his political activities, Forgách also authored several historical works, including his *Commentary on the Conditions of Hungary (De Statu Republicae Hungaricae . . . Commentarii).* Written between 1568 and 1573, this work is basically a humanist history of mid-sixteenth-century Hungary (c. 1540-1572), with extensive flashbacks to the period of Mathias Corvinus. Forgách's picture of contemporary Hungary is that of a country in a state of total social and political collapse. Like so many of his predecessors, Forgách also attributed this collapse to the loss of ancient Hungarian virtues and discipline. His ideal stateman was likewise Mathias Corvinus. But contrary to many of the previous historians, Forgách had already discovered a number of new idols as well, and in his *Commentary* he had put forth several of the struggling frontier captains (Szondi, Dobó, Zrinyi, etc.) as examples of heroic selflessness.(17)

Parallel with Forgách, several Transylvanian humanists were also active at the ducal court of Stephen Báthori (1533-1586), the future king of Poland (1575-1586). Besides Báthori himself, these humanists included Márton Berzeviczy (1533-1590), Farkas Kovacsóczy (1540-1594), Pál Gyulai (c. 1550-1629), Ambrus Somogyi (1564-1637), Lestár Gyulafi (1557-1605), János Gálfi (? -1593), János Baranyai-Décsi (? -1601), as well as the Italian Gian Michele Bruto (János Mihály Brutus) (1517-1592)(18). All of these wrote historical compendiums or historical memories. None of them, however, produced works comparable to Forgách's *Commentary,* not to speak of the works of the two greatest exponents of Hungarian humanist historiography, István Szamosközy (1570-1612) and Miklós Istvánffy (1538-1615).

Szamosközy is rightfully known as the most outstanding exponent of Hungarian Transylvanian humanist historiography. He was the first to take note of the growing cultural and political divergence that began to emerge between the Magyars of Royal Hungary and those of his narrower homeland Transylvania. As his writings reveal, Szamosközy was a conscious Transylvanian Magyar, who was very fond of the little independence that Transylvania was able to gain and preserve amidst the gigantic struggles between the Habsburg and Ottoman empires. Thus, he has the tendency to judge historical events and personalities primarily from the vantage point of Transylvanian politics.

As an historian, Szamosközy is a conscientious scholar. He relies heavily on written sources, but he examines these with a critical mind. Moreover, contrary to many of his contemporaries, he is also aware of many other history-shaping forces in addition to the role of personalities. Thus, in examining historical evolution, he does so in light of the existing economic, social, cultural, geographical and ethnic factors and forces of the period. Consequently, although less of a literary artist than Forgách, Szamosközy is a greater master in re-creating the atmosphere of past ages.

Szamosközy wrote extensively, though none of his many works came down to us in their entirety. The most important of these include his *Rerum Ungaricarum Libri IV (Four Books on the Deeds of the Magyars), Rerum Transylvanarum Pentades (Five Books on the Deeds of Transylvania),* and *Hebdomades (Seven Books).* The first of these is an attempt to reproduce the history of Hungary in the second half of the sixteenth century (1558-1586); while the latter two deal with the history of Transylvania around the turn of the century (c. 1600). Szamosközy also authored several shorter works, including a study on the origins of the Magyars *(De originibus Hungaricis).*(19)

If Szamosközy represented the climax of Hungarian humanist historiography in Transylvania, his counterpart in Royal Hungary was undoubtedly Miklós Istvánffy, the successful continuer of Bonfini's Hungarian history. Although a product of the same school that produced Szamosközy (Padua), Istvánffy's path took him into the Habsburg camp of divided Hungary.

Istvánffy wrote his great *History of the Magyars in Thirty-Four Books (Historiarum de Rebus Ungaricis Libri XXXIV)* during the latter part of his life, after having produced a number of lesser works. His history covers the period between 1490 and 1606, and thus it is a direct sequel to Bonfini's *Rerum Ungaricarum Decades.* In its first part it is based largely on such earlier works as those of Brodarics, Tinódi, Forgách, Brutus and others, and in the second part on the personal source collections of the author. As evident from this work, Istvánffy's political goal was united Hungary. Contrary to Szamosközy and other Protestant Transylvanian historians, however, he could conceive of this unity only under Catholicism and under the rule of the Habsburg emperors.

Istvánffy's monumental work, running into 900 folio pages, was first published in 1622 and soon rivalled the popularity of Bonfini's *Rerum Ungaricarum Decades.* Thus, like Bonfini's work for the earlier history of Hungary, Istvánffy's history became the standard work for sixteenth-century Hungary, and remained so for the next century and a half.(20)

With Istvánffy's death in 1615, the main line of the great Hungarian humanist historiography came to an end. Certain minor humanist histories were still being written as late as the third quarter of the seventeenth century, but not until the turn of the eighteenth to nineteenth century (following the political memoire writers and the eighteenth-century source collectors) did a new synthesizing school arise, which ultimately made Bonfini's and Istvánffy's histories obsolete.

The most noted of the late humanist historians were Gáspár Bojti-Veres (1595-1640+), János Bethlen (1613-1678), Farkas Bethlen (1639-1679) and János Szalárdi (1601-1666)(21) — all of them Transylvanian Magyars and all of them concentrating on the history of their more immediate homeland. Of these four historians, particularly important was Szalárdi, whose *Sorrowful Hungarian Chronicle (Siralmas magyar krónika)* (1662) — contrary to standard humanist works which appeared in Latin — was written in Magyar and reflected the emotional and pessimistic mood of the author. Szalárdi's work thus represents a transition between classical humanist historiography and the Baroque memoire literature that followed. Moreover it deals with Hungarian history in a Transylvanocentric fashion, and thus in its ideological orientation it foreshadows the so-called *kuruc* (anti-Habsburg) historiography of the nineteenth and early twentieth centuries.

Chapter III

BAROQUE HISTORIOGRAPHY: POLITICAL MEMOIRES

The relatively peaceful period that saw the emergence of Hungarian humanist historiography to full bloom during the second half of the sixteenth century was soon displaced by a period of violent confrontation between the Habsburg and the Ottoman empires. This confrontation took the form of the so-called Fifteen Years War (1593-1608), and it was already during this conflict that many of Szamosközy's and Istvánffy's works were completed.

One of the most significant results of this confrontation from the Hungarian point of view was the further enlargement of the cleavage that had been created between the social, political economic, but especially cultural and intellectual developments of Transylvania and Royal Hungary. The result was a growing dichotomy in Hungarian culture that became particularly significant in the course of the seventeenth century in consequence of the confrontation between the lingering humanist influences and the slowly penetrating Baroque culture and spirituality — a confrontation that occurred later in Transylvania than in Royal Hungary. During the transitional period in the first half of the seventeenth century, the relationship of these two tendencies was further complicated by the presence of a number of other ideological-cultural trends, including stoicism, mannerism and Orthodox Calvinism. Moreover, the second half of the same century saw Hungary made into the battlefield of the retreating Ottoman armies and of the often even more destructive armies of Christian Europe — which certainly hindered the normal evolution of culture and scholarship. Thus, not until after the Peace of Szatmár of 1711 — which terminated the desperate Rákóczi Revolution against the growingly insensitive Habsburgs — did things begin to return to normal and could the Magyar literati again turn to the peaceful examination of the Hungarian past. In the meanwhile, whatever history-writing occurred, it manifested itself largely in the already mentioned few late-humanist works of Gáspár Bojti-Veres, János Bethlen, Farkas Bethlen and János Szalárdi, and most of all in the birth of a new form of political memoire literature.

The latter was the product of the new Baroque culture that utlimately, although belatedly, triumphed in all of reunited Hungary and put an end to all humanist influences.(1)

The political memoire literature of the late seventeenth and early eighteenth century was indeed the product of the triumphant Baroque culture and spirituality. Although memoires had already been written during the Renaissance period, they were used primarily for the recording of public events, rather than personal feelings and reminiscences. Thus, the memoires of the Baroque Age brought the personality of the author to the fore. His deeds were presented in a rather subjective manner, and they generally occupied the stage. The authors of Baroque memoires wrote with posterity in mind. Their goal was to justify their personal and political actions and the actions of those close to them before the court of history.

Although the Baroque spirituality that produced the Hungarian memoire literature of the seventeenth and the early eighteenth century penetrated first into Royal Hungary, the center of Hungarian memoire literature was Transylvania. The reasons for this may be sought partially in the relatively greater emphasis on *belles lettres* in the West, and partially in the less willingness on the part of the of the Habsburg aristocracy and intelligentsia to expose their true feelings about contemporary political events. To these may be added the less cosmopolitan and consequently stronger Magyar national character of the aristocracy and the educated classes in Transylvania.(2)

The Greatest Memoire Writers

Not counting Mihály Veresmarti's (1572-1646) earlier autobiography-like Baroque memoires *(The Story of my Conversion)*,(3) the first and one of the most important political-personal memoires are those of János Kemény (1607-1662). Kemény was the gifted but tragic prince of Transylvania (1660-1662) who assumed the leadership of the principality after György Rákóczi II's irresponsible rule (1648-1660), but then fell victim to the chaos unleashed by his predecessor. He wrote his soul-searching *Autobiography (Önéletírás)* during one of the darkest periods of his life, while in the captivity of the Crimean Tartars (1657-1659). It certainly reflects his resignation and disillusionment both with his own fate, as well as with the fate of his country. Kemény was a man of deep perception, and his personal sketches of some of his contemporaries are invaluable — even though his tone is often satirical and biting.(4)

With his exceptionally successful *Autobiography* Kemény became the father of the Hungarian historical memoire literature of the Baroque period. He had several good imitators and successors — including Gáspár Kornis (? -1683+), Prince Mihály Apafi I (1629-1690) and Imre Thököly (1657-1705)(5) — but none of these were able to rival Kemény as a memoire writer, and even less the greatest Hungarian Baroque memoire writer of all times, Miklós Bethlen.

Miklós Bethlen (1642-1716) was one of the most cultured individuals among contemporary Hungarian men of letters. His social and political ideals included a middle class oriented Western society and an independent Transylvania. Like Kemény before him, Bethlen too wrote most of his political and historical works during the darkest period of his life, after 1704, while in the political captivity of the Habsburgs in Vienna. Thus, he wrote his *Autobiography (Önéletirás)* for the purposes of clearing himself from the charge of high treason. It turned out to be an exceptional work — great both in the area of history, as well as literature.(6)

Before turning to writing, Miklós Bethlen was an able statesman in the general category of Gábor Bethlen (1580-1629) and Miklós Zrinyi (1620-1664).(7) He was a man of honesty, responsibility and bravery, and displayed a cosmopolitan culture that always shined through his patriotism. In addition to his *Autobiography* — which he wrote in the form and style of St. Augustine's and Petrarca's autobiographies — Bethlen also authored numerous other political and religious works, none of which, however, compare to his *opus magnum.*

The only other examples of memoire literature in the same class with Bethlen's *Autobiography* are the two major works of Prince Ferenc Rákóczi II (1676-1735) — his *Memoires* and his *Confessions.* Like Kemény's and Bethlen's memoires, Rákóczi's works were products of personal and political afflictions and distress, following the collapse of his prolonged struggle against the Habsburgs (1703-1711). He began his memoires in Latin in 1716, after already having fallen under the pietistic, stoical and spiritual influences of the Jansenists of Grosbois. When describing his anti-Habsburg struggles, however, he switched to French for political reasons. In his *Confessions,* which deals mostly with the personal miseries of his emigration, Rákóczi again switched back to Latin, the language in which most of his writings were done. Subsequently, Rákóczi also authored a number of studies in philosophy and political philosophy, but none of them could rival his *Memoires* and his *Confessions* in historical importance.(8)

Some Late Baroque Memoires

Besides Bethlen's and Rákóczi's analytical autobiographical works — both of which have historical, as well as literary significance — a number of other similar works were also written during this period. These were usually authored by men who had played some role in the anti-Habsburg *kuruc* movement of the late seventeenth and early eighteenth century, connected with the names and activities of Imre Thököly and Ferenc Rákóczi II. When undertaking to write their memoires, they generally wished to portray their roles in these events in light of the new realities that followed the collapse of the *kuruc* movement (1711) and the subsequent compromise between the Habsburgs and the conservative nobility of Hungary (the *Pragmatic Sanction* of 1723).

The most notable of these political figures and memoire writers were Sándor Károlyi (1668-1743), Rákóczi's former commander-in-chief; György Ottlyk (1656-1723+), an associate of both Thököly and Rákóczi; Mihály Teleki (1671-1720), the son of the powerful chancellor of Transylvania of the same name; Dániel István Vargyasi (1684-1774), a Transylvanian nobleman; and Kata Bethlen (1700-1759), the wife of Mihály Teleki's brother, József Teleki. While all of their works have considerable historical significance, the most distinguished both from the historical and the literary point of view is Kata Bethlen's *Autobiography (Önéletírás)*(1751), generally regarded as the last of the significant Hungarian Baroque memoires. In its content, composition and lyrical tone Kata Bethlen's works is perhaps closest to Rákóczi's sentimental and emotional *Confessions.*(9)

With Kata Bethlen's *Autobiography,* the memoire literature of the Hungarian Baroque came to an end. By that time, however, Hungarian historiography, in the more traditional sense of that term, was also on the upswing. In fact, it reached one of its early climaxes immediately after Kata Bethlen's *Autobiography,* in the great source collecting schools of the eighteenth century.

Chapter IV

THE SOURCE COLLECTING HISTORIOGRAPHY OF THE EIGHTEENTH CENTURY

Following the relative decline of Hungarian historical scholarship in the seventeenth century, the eighteenth century saw the rebirth of historical studies, as well as the birth of several so-called source collecting schools.

As mentioned earlier, the incessant internal and external struggles connected with the period of Hungary's trisection were not conducive to systematic historical research. With the expulsion of the Turks and the reunification of the country (1699), and the subsequent compromise with the Habsburgs (1711,1723), however, the situation changed altogether. Hungary was still not free from internal struggles, but these new struggles took the form of religious and intellectual conflicts between the Catholics (supported by the Habsburgs) and the Protestants (who now lacked the support of the once powerful principality of Transylvania). This religious conflict, in turn, turned the attention of scholars toward the history of their respective religions, which resulted in a growing need for the systematic examination of the history of these religions. But, as they soon found out, such an examination proved to be impossible without the prior systematic collection of historical sources. Thus, following the Peace of Szatmár of 1711, Hungary's internal consolidation was paralleled by the rise of the great historical source collecting schools.(1)

The collection of historical sources, of course, was not a new phenomenon. Classical, as well as medieval historians had already engaged in it. But they did so mostly without a systematic and conscious effort. Moreover, they had made no effort to criticize the collected sources and to try to eliminate obvious misstatements and contradictions in their content.

Contrary to their predecessors, the historians of the Renaissance had recognized the importance of source research and source criticism. Thus, their source research was already the result of a conscious effort. Yet, their research and collecting activities were far from systematic. Nor were they sufficiently critical to satisfy the needs of true "critical historical scholarship."(2)

Source research and source criticism was given a major boost in the sixteenth and the seventeenth centuries by the intellectual ferments connected with the Protestant Reformation and the Catholic Counter Reformation of that period. Protestant scholars had hoped to utilize the consciously collected historical sources to prove the validity of their position against Catholicism and the Papacy. Simultaneously, Catholic scholars began to use the same weapon as an instrument of defense and counter-offensive against Protestantism.

These intellectual ferments eventually resulted in the birth of a new type of historian, who henceforth devoted his whole life to the study and examination of specific historical problems and who was generally a member of the clergy of one of the religious orders. One of the most important centers of such new type of historical scholarship in Europe was the Jesuit monastery of Antwerp where — under the leadership of Johann (Jean) Bolland (1596-1665) — the Jesuit masters established the great Jesuit Source Collecting School.(3) Founded in the first half of the seventeenth century (they began to publish the *Acta Sanctorum* in 1643), the influence of this school soon spread into France, Germany, Italy, and by the end of the seventeenth century into Hungary, where it came to center on the Jesuit university of Nagyszombat (Tyrnavia).

Hevenesi and the Beginnings of Jesuit Source Collecting in Hungary

The initiation of systematic source collection and source criticism in Hungary is connected with the name of Gábor Hevenesi (1656-1715), the rector of the *Pázmáneum,* a seminary in Vienna founded in 1623 expressly for the education of Hungarian priests. Keeping the counter-reformational activities and examples of the Dutch Bollandists in mind, Hevenesi decided to undertake the documentary elaboration of Hungarian church history. His *Modus Materiae Conquirendae pro Annalibus Ecclesiasticis Regni Hungariae* (Source Collection Directive for Hungary's Ecclesiastical Annals) (1695) called specifically for a concerted national effort for the collection of sources on Hungarian ecclesiastical history. These were to include even sources on political history with relevance to religious matters.(4)

Hevenesi's efforts were supported by Cardinal Leopold Kollonich (Kollonitsch) (1631-1707), Hungary's pro-Habsburg primate who immediately recognized the significance of Hevenesi's undertaking in his effort to strengthen the position of Catholicism. Upon Hevenesi's and Kollonich's urging, a number of Jesuits went to work in several

Hungarian and foreign archives and initiated a collection process that continued almost unabated for over two centuries. Hevenesi's own collecting efforts ultimately resulted in 140 unpublished volumes, which subsequently became a mine of information for some of the synthesizing historians who came after him. Moreover, while Hevenesi was never able to complete his intended documentary history of the Hungarian Catholic Church, several of his followers and disciples did emerge into the top ranks of the Hungarian Jesuit Source Collecting School (e.g. Timon, Kaprinay, Pray, Katona) and ultimately completed much of the work envisaged by the founding master.

Debreceni-Ember and the Beginnings of Protestant Source Collecting

Only a few years after the appearance of Hevenesi under the flags of Catholicism, the Protestants also went to work to prepare the ground for their own version of Hungarian church history. The first sign of this work was the publication of a brief history of the Hungarian Evangelical Church *(Historia Diplomatica de Statu Religionis Evangelicae in Hungaria)* and a history of Transylvanian Protestantism *(Brevissimum Compendium Principatus Transylvanici Historiae)* in 1710. These works of an anonymous author were paralleled by the activities of Pál Debreceni-Ember (1660-1710), the author of the first great history of Hungarian Protestantism and the pioneer of Hungarian Protestant church history. Debreceni-Ember, however, died before he could publish his work (finished in 1706). Subsequently it was published in Utrecht by the university professor Adolf Friedrich Lampe, to whom Debreceni-Ember's manuscript was transmitted by his brother-in-law. Lampe, however, published it under his own name, with the title *Historia Ecclesiae Reformatae in Hungaria et Transylvania* (1728).(5)

Debreceni-Ember was followed by several younger Protestant scholars who also attempted to write histories of Hungarian Protestantism, but did so without the benefit of extensive new source collections. The situation changed completely with the appearance of David Czvittinger (1676/1680-1743) and Mihály Rotarides (1715-1747) on the Protestant Hungarian scene. Both of these scholars engaged in an extensive collection of sources on the history of the whole of Hungarian intellectual, cultural and religious life. In point of fact, Czvittinger became the author of the first Hungarian scholarly encyclopedia *(Specimen Hungariae Literatae,* 1711); while Rotarides authored one of the first literary histories of Hungary *(Historia*

Hungaricae Antiqui, Medii et Recentoris Aevi Lineamenta, 1745), based partially on his own, and partially on Czvittinger's source collections.(6)

Bod and the Protestant Source Collecting School

The foundations laid down by Debreceni-Ember, Czvittinger, Rotarides and others soon produced visible results. By the mid-eighteenth century, the Protestant Source Collecting School had also come into its own. This was evident, among others, in the works of Péter Bod (1712-1769), who was perhaps the greatest polyhistor scholar of the Hungarian late Baroque — eclipsed only by the slightly older and yet to be discussed founder of the Hungarian *Staatenkunde* School, Mátyás Bél.

Like his predecessors, Bod was a product of Hungarian, German and Dutch Protestant learning, and he devoted his whole life to the study of Hungarian Protestantism and to the examination of the cultural and political traditions of Transylvania. For these purposes he conducted an up-to-then unparalleled source collecting activity, which eventually extended from Transylvania to the whole of historic Hungary, and came to encompass the whole of Hungarian cultural traditions.(7)

Bod's scholarly research and activities were so manifold that they ultimately included such widespread disciples as theology, canon law, religious history, *Staatenkunde* (the study of the state), political history, linguistics and literary history. Besides dozens of lesser works, Bod's most important publication is his four-volume *Hungarian Church History (Historia Hungarorum Ecclesiastica)* (1788-1790), which — although published posthumously — had already been finished in 1756. For a long period this work has been the most important publication in Hungarian Protestant church history.

In his secular historical studies Bod was a follower of the *Staatenkunde* School (the study of the state in all of its possible aspects) which was introduced into Hungary from Germany by Mátyás Bél (1684-1749), the greatest polyhistor scholar of eighteenth-century Hungary. In this category belong many of his unpublished works, including his *Short History of the Transylvanian Vlachs (Brevis Valachorum Transylvaniam Incolentium Historia),* and his *Hunno-Dacian Land of the Szeklers (Siculia Hunno-Dacia).* His goal in this area was to prepare a comprehensive *Staatenkunde* type description of Transylvania's past and present, but he was able to complete only fragments of his great projected work.

Bél and the Hungarian Staatenkunde School

The origins of the *Staatenkunde* School (which had considerable impact on eighteenth-century Hungarian scholarship) reached back to seventeenth-century Germany, and more specifically to the desire on the part of the German ruling princes to introduce centralism (monarchical absolutism) and a centralized economic system into their respective states. This goal naturally required a detailed description of the geography and of the economic conditions and potential of each of these states. Subsequently, matters relative to their historical, political, constitutional, legal, administrative, etc. developments and conditions were also added to the list of desired information. Thus was the new discipline of *Staatenkunde* born, which found expression first in the writings of Hermann Conring (1606-1681). It was this discipline that Mátyás Bél transplanted to Hungary during the post-Szatmár period (1711). He did this, however, not so much in the interest of monarchical absolutism (as was the case in Germany), but rather in the interest of the Hungarian burgher classes. This was so even though Bél was not necessarily an enemy of Habsburg centralism.(8)

As a student of the University of Halle, and more specifically of Christopher Cellarius (Keller) (1638-1707) at that university, Bél decided to imitate his master and to prepare a thorough description of Hungary — past and present — including its history, geography, ethnography, as well as its political, economic, social and administrative development, in the best traditions of *Staatenkunde.* During his productive life Bél wrote scores of works (many of them still unpublished) on such diverse topics as history, linguistics and even ancient Hungarian runic writing, but he was never able to complete his intended *opus magnum,* except in fragmentary form. One of these "fragments" was his five-volume *Historical-Geographical Description of Modern Hungary (Notitia Hungariae Novae Historico-Geographica)* (1735-1742) which contains the statistical description of ten of historic Hungary's northern counties.(9) Bél also managed to complete the manuscript for the Transdanubian counties, but — with the exception of Moson county — this material remained unpublished.

As a byproduct of his *Notitia,* Bél also initiated a systematic collection of Hungarian historical sources, which he planned to publish in thirty volumes. Ultimately, however, he was able to publish only twelve important narrative sources which appeared in his incomplete *Sources on Hungarian History (Adparatus ad Historiam Hungariae)* (1735-1746). Subsequently he also aided his student, the Austrian

Johann Georg Schwandtner (1716-1791), in the latter's publication of his *Ancient and Genuine Writings on Hungarian History (Scriptores Rerum Hungaricarum Veteres ac Genuini)* (1746-1748), which contained some of the most significant narrative sources of early Hungarian history.

Mátyás Bél's scholarly production was of such extent and quality that his name soon became known and respected throughout Europe. He was elected to the membership of numerous scholarly societies (London, Berlin, Jena, etc.), and in general none of the other eighteenth-century Hungarian scholars could match his accomplishments. Moreover, in one or another way, most of the scholars of the second half of the eighteenth century were his disciples. These included such members of the Protestant Source Collecting School as the already discussed Péter Bod, as well as the somewhat younger Miklós Sinai (1730-1808), Daniel Cornides (1732-1787) and Pál Wallaszky (1742-1824).(10) But indirectly Bél influenced even the greatest members of the Jesuit Source Collecting School, including Timon, Kaprinay, Pray and Katona. The latter, however, were more the carriers of the traditions of the Dutch Bollandists than the traditions of the Protestant Bél and of his *Staatenkunde* School.

The Jesuit Source Collecting School

The first of the Jesuit scholars who continued Gábor Hevenesi's Bollandist traditions and developed into a respectable historian, was Sámuel Timon (1675-1736), a professor at the University of Nagyszombat, and subsequently at the Jesuit Theological College of Kassa. In his earlier works Timon concentrated on giving descriptive accounts of contemporary Hungary's urban centers (e.g. his *The Topography of the Notable Cities and Towns of Hungary — Celebriorum Hungariae Urbium et Oppidorum Topographiae,* 1702). Later, however, he turned to the study of Hungary's historical chronology. After several earlier versions, Timon finally published his definitive *Chronological Abstracts of Hungarian History (Epitome Chronologica Rerum Hungaricarum)* (1736) which covered Hungary's history up to the year 1676. Subsequently, this work was updated in the mid-eighteenth century by Tamás Rost (1695-1765), one of Timon's many disciples. During the latter part of his life Timon also published a two-volume geographical description of Hungary under the titles *The Image of Old Hungary (Imago Antiquae Hungariae)* and *The Image of New Hungary (Imago Novae Hungariae)* (1733-1734), respectively.(11)

By the middle of the eighteenth century the activities of the Jesuit source collectors — originally initiated by Hevenesi and continued by Timon — had grown into a full-fledged historical school. Soon it was represented by such noted Jesuit scholars as Kaprinay, Pray and Katona.

Of these three historians, István Kaprinay (1714-1786) was the last member of the purely source collecting generation. His activities, therefore, represented a transition from simple source collecting to the more critical and somewhat more synthetic oriented scholarship of Pray and Katona.

Kaprinay was also the most open-minded of the eighteenth-century source collectors. Even though he was a Jesuit, he is known to have sought out the help of Protestant scholars. This helped him in his source collecting activities, but it also reflects on his attitude toward the study of history.

Among Kaprinay's greatest achievements is the reorganization of Hevenesi's 140 volumes into a systematic source collection and of gathering together the haphazard collections of several other Jesuit scholars into the fifty-four-volume *Collectio Kapriniana in Folio.* Following this monumental achievement, Kaprinay began his own collecting activities with the help of a number of fellow Jesuits (e.g. János Terstyánszky, Károly Wágner, etc.) and ultimately copied and collected an additional 102 volumes of documents called *Collectio Kapriniana in Quarto.* To this collection he subsequently added twenty-seven more volumes containing critical essays and various mixed notes. By the time Kaprinay had finished his work, there were over 300 volumes of organized source collections in his possession.

Kaprinay had hoped to publish his collection with appropriate scholarly annotations. To the eternal sorrow of Hungarian historical scholarship, however, he was unable to publish more than two sizable volumes which deal with the age of Matthias Corvinus in Hungary *(Hungaria Diplomatica Temporibus Mathiae de Hunyad,* 1767-1771). The forcible dissolution of his religious order in the course of 1772 and 1773, and the subsequent termination of the Jesuit centers of learning in Hungary prevented him from achieving this goal.(12)

The work of Kaprinay and of his predecessors, however, was not in vain. His collection — which was transferred along with the University of Nagyszombat to Buda (1777) and then to Pest (1784) — was subsequently utilized and partially published by a number of Hungarian historians. These included his younger contemporaries Pray, Katona and Kollár, as well as the early nineteenth-century historian György Fejér.

Although a product of Hevenesi's traditions within the Jesuit Order, Kaprinay's oldest noted contemporary, Ferenc Ádám Kollár (1718-1783), had left the order much before its dissolution. Ultimately he became the director of the Viennese Court Library (the predecessor of the present *Nationalbibliothek),* where he soon fell under the influence of German publicistic historical scholarship and enlisted his pen into the service of Habsburg imperial interests. Yet, Kollár remained faithful to the Hungarian Jesuit traditions of collecting sources on Hungarian history. The most notable of his publications, however, deals with the history of Vienna and of the ruling dynasty *(Analecta Monumentorum Omnis Aevi Vindobonensia,* 1761-1762). But Kollár was also responsible for the publication of the works of the great sixteenth-century Hungarian humanist scholar Miklós Oláh.(13)

Perhaps the greatest member of Kaprinay's and Kollár's generation, and simultaneously of the great Jesuit Historical School, was György Pray (1723-1801) who is generally known as the initiator of the true critical orientation in Hungarian historiography. Pray's historical scholarship is too extensive and varied to be treated here, but it is fair to say that he was equally at home in religious and secular history. In the field of religious history he produced numerous works on the lives of Hungarian saints and ultimately also wrote a major synthesis of Hungarian church history entitled *An Attempt at the (History of) Hungarian Hierarchy (Specimen Hierarchiae Hungariae)* (1777-1779). In the area of secular history, he published both on Hungarian and European history. He was particularly interested in the question of Magyar origins and he argued vehemently against János Sajnovics's (1735-1785) new theories on the alleged relationship between the Lapps and the Magyars. Like most Hungarian historians, Pray too held on to the belief of Hunnic-Avar-Magyar continuity contained in most Hungarian chronicles — a tradition that is gaining renewed creditability today.(14) His important works on Magyar origins include *The Ancient History of the Huns, Avars and Magyars (Annales Veteres Hunnorum, Avarorum et Hungarorum)* (1761) and the *Historico-Critical Studies on the Ancient Story of the Huns (Dissertationes Historico-Criticae in Annales Veterum Hunnorum)* (1774). Pray's *opus magnum,* the five-volume synthesis of Hungarian history *(The History of the Kings of Hungary — Annales Regum Hungariae,* 1763-1770) was a direct continuation of his earlier studies on Magyar origins, and it carried the history of Hungarian developments up to 1564.(15)

As professor of diplomatics and director of the library of the University of Pest (1777-1790), Pray was also instrumental in keeping the large Hevenesi-to-Kaprinay source collection basically intact and of making the University Library into the main center of Hungarian historical research. In light of the dissolution of the Jesuit Order and the disintegration of the Jesuit centers of higher learning and scholarship, the latter was a particularly significant achievement. Among the scholars who congregated around Pray at the University Library we find both Protestants and Catholics. These included the Protestant Dániel Cornides (1732-1787) — a student and follower of Mátyás Bél; as well as the ex-Jesuit István Katona (1732-1811), who used the Hevenesi-to-Kaprinay collection perhaps more than anyone else, and who next to Pray became the greatest member of the Jesuit Historical School.(16)

Katona was a professor of history at the University of Buda-Pest for over a decade (1773-1784), during which period he began the publication if his *Critical History of the Hungarian Kings (Historia Critica Regum Hungariae),* which ultimately reached forty-two volumes (1779-1817). Katona based this work almost exclusively on the 300 odd volumes of the Hevenesi-to-Kaprinay collection; although later he also became engaged in some source collecting himself.(17)

Although lacking the unusual critical acumen of Pray, Katona managed to clarify many of the outstanding questions about the authenticity and meaning of significant historical sources. Moreover, precisely because of the published nature of his sources, most of the great nineteenth-century synthesizing historians from Engel and Fessler in the first part of the century, to Szalay and Horváth in the middle of that century, relied first of all on Katona.

The Great Synthesizers of the Early Romantic Period

With the passing of Timon, Pray, Cornides, Katona and others, the great eighteenth-century source collecting schools came virtually to an end. The only exception to this rule is constituted by the activities of Márton György Kovachich (1744-1821) and of his son József Miklós Kovachich (1798-1878).(18) Their source collecting work, however, concentrated largely on legal and constitutional developments and paralleled the new synthetic orientation in Hungarian historiography represented by the German language works of J.K. Engel (1770-1814) and I.A. Fessler (1756-1839), and the Magyar language syntheses of Benedek Virág (1754-1830), Esiás Budai (1776-1841) and others.(19)

Of the synthetic works of the early nineteenth century, Fessler's ten-volume *Die Geschichte der Ungern und ihrer Landsassen (The History of the Hungarians and their Conquest)*(1815-1825) is not only the last, but also the best and most reliable work. Although based almost solely on the Jesuit and Protestant source collections of the previous century, it had already broken away from eighteenth-century traditions and reflects some of the ideological transition from Enlightenment to Romanticism.(20)

This transition is less evident in Engel's earlier works, such as his *Geschichte des Ungarischen Reiches und seiner Nebenländern* (History of the Hungarian Empire and of its Neighboring Lands) (1797-1804) and his *Geschichte des Ungarischen Reiches* (History of the Hungarian Empire) (1813-1814), but much more evident in the Magyar language works of Budai and Virág. Of the latter two, Budai's *History of Hungary (Magyarország históriája)* (1805-1812) is more traditional and less inspiring. Virág's *Hungarian Centuries (Magyar századok)* (1808-1816, 1862), on the other hand, tends to go overboard in its glorification of medieval and pre-Christian Hungarian history.(21)

Conclusions

The Hungarian histories of Engel, Fessler, Budai and Virág were the first, and for a while also the last noteworthy syntheses based on the great collections of the eighteenth-century source collecting schools. Following these works, the spirit of Romanticism and the political activism of the Hungarian Reform Period (c. 1825-1848) had a growing negative impact on the quality of Hungarian historical studies. The result was the birth of a number of interesting, but mostly unreliable works. Perhaps the best known among the so-called "mirage-chasing" national romantic historians who authored these works were Ádám Pálóczi-Horváth (1760-1820) and István Horvát (1784-1846). The latter was particularly well known for his over-romanticized view of Hungarian history, and his *Sketches on the Most Ancient History of the Hungarian Nation (Rajzolatok a magyar nemzet legrégibb történeteiből)* (1825) is generally held up as an extreme example of the influence of romantic nationalism on the historiography of the Reform Period.(22)

In the area of source collection and publication, this romantic view of history, and the consequent relative scholarly laxity that it produced, was best represented by the librarian-historian György Fejér (1766-1851) and his huge *Collection of Hungarian Ecclesiastical and Secular Documents (Codex Diplomaticus Hungariae Ecclesiasticus ac Civilis)* (1829-1844), which ultimately numbered forty-three volumes. Although an often used work, Fejér's *Codex Diplomaticus* contains many of the shortcomings associated with the influence of the spirit of

Romanticism on scholarship. These include erroneous copying, uncritical inclusion of all sources or alleged sources, as well as innumerable typographical errors — which combine to make this work difficult and even dangerous to use, especially to the non-specialist.(23)

Chapter V

THE DEVELOPMENT OF "SCIENTIFIC" HISTORIOGRAPHY IN THE NINETEENTH CENTURY

As can be inferred from the above summary, Hungarian historiography of the first quarter of the nineteenth century was still very traditional and displayed characteristics which have been labeled, among others, dynastic, clerical, feudal and over-patriotic. This is less evident from Fessler's major ten-volume synthesis, than from some of the commonly used textbooks. But then Fessler's *Die Geschichte der Ungern und ihrer Landsassen* was not as widely read as Esiás Budai's *History of Hungary,* or the numerous textbooks of the even more popular Glycer Spanyik (1781-1850).(1)

If the situation of Hungarian historiography in the first quarter of the nineteenth century was far from ideal, it was even worse in the second quarter of the century when Hungary's most popular historian appears to have been the "mirage-chasing" István Horvát — generally regarded to be the most extreme exponent of national romanticism. Whatever one's views about Horvát's contribution to the Magyar national revival of that period (and there are many who value it very highly), his works in history represent a definite qualitative decline of Hungarian historiography.

As mentioned earlier, this qualitative decline stemmed partially from the anti-rationalism of Romanticism and partially from the overheated patriotic emotions of contemporary Hungarian intellectual and political life.(2) On the one hand, Romanticism gave a free hand to the imagination, previously bound by the rationalism of the Enlightenment; on the other, the feverish political atmosphere of the Reform Period captivated the majority of the Hungarian minds and transferred their loyalty from the realm of quiet scholarly labors to the field of higher national politics.

From the vantage point of historical scholarship, the greatest positive achievement of the Hungarian Reform Period was the foundation of the Hungarian Academy of Sciences (1825) which subsequently also became involved in historical research on the highest level.(3) The establishment of the Academy of Sciences was followed in importance by the quiet scholarly labors of a number of unheralded historians and literary scholars, including János Mailáth (1786-1855), József Péczely (1789-1849), József Teleki (1790-1855), Antal Gévay (1797-1845), József Bajza (1804-1858), as well as the still rather young Mihály Horváth (1809-1878) who subsequently emerged as one of the two greatest synthesizing historians of the National Liberal School.(4) While the majority of these scholars were not very well known to their contemporaries, they have produced a number of significant works which subsequently proved to be more valuable than the much heralded works of their national romantic counterparts. In their time, however, many of them had little impact on the contemporary Hungarian mind — occupied as it was with the feverish political events of the day.(5)

Post-Revolutionary Revival of Historical Studies

While the promising Reform Period of Hungarian history represented a decline in the qualitative level of Hungarian historical scholarship, paradoxically enough the absolutistic period that followed the defeat of the Hungarian Revolution of 1848 (1849-1867) saw the total renewal of Hungarian historical studies. This paradoxical situation was due to the fact that — while during the Reform Period, the best minds in Hungary were occupied with the question of Magyar national revival — amidst the gloom of post-revolutionary absolutism, most Hungarian intellectuals turned to the study of Magyar national history. They did this partially out of the desire to escape from the oppressive atmosphere of the present, and partially to find a way out of the national catastrophe by learning from the experiences of the past.(6)

The best examples of this turning to the past, while brooding over the fate of the Magyar nation, are the lives and works of Joseph Eötvös (1813-1871) and László Szalay (1813-1864). Eötvös's *The Influence of the Dominant Ideas of the 19th Century upon the State* (1851-1854) and Szalay's *History of Hungary* (1852-1859) — both of them written mostly in emigration — are classic examples of great intellectual works by scholars and statesmen who — while obviously pained by the unfortunate fate of their country and nation — were able to stay above petty party politics, national antagonism and mutual recriminations, and were able to think in European perspectives.(7)

Notwithstanding Hungary's oppressive political atmosphere of the 1850's, therefore, in light of the mass expulsion of Hungarian intellectuals from political activity and their consequent return to the study of Hungarian culture and civilization, Hungarian historical scholarship began to bloom anew. This happened partially in the form of the appearance of such great syntheses of Hungarian historical evolution as those of László Szalay and Mihály Horváth — the two greatest representatives of the largely synthesizing National Liberal School of that period.(8) But perhaps even more important was the initiation of a number of major source collections by the Hungarian Academy and several other scholarly organizations, including the newly founded Hungarian Historical Association. Established in 1867 — the year of the Austro-Hungarian Compromise — the Historical Association was particularly significant for the profession, for it gave a totally new orientation to the whole historical scholarship in Hungary.(9)

The first important institution to become involved in giving support and direction to Hungarian historical scholarship, however, was not the Historical Association, but the Hungarian Academy of Sciences. This came in 1854, in the form of the establishment of the Academy's Historical Commission *(Történelmi Bizottság)*, which soon became the most important forum for organized historical research.(10) Among its most significant actions was the initiation in serial form of the *Monumenta Hungariae Historica*, which is still the largest collection of medieval and early modern sources on Hungarian history. Initiated in 1857 in two series *(Diplomataria* and *Scriptores)*, to which subsequently two additional series were added *(Monumenta Comitialia* and *Acta Extera*, 1874), the Hungarian *Monumenta* was modeled more on the *Fontes Rerum Austricarum* (1849-) than on its namesake, the *Monumenta Germaniae Historica* (1826-). Paralleled with the *Monumenta Hungariae Historica*, the Academy's Historical Commission also initiated the *Hungarian Historical Repository (Magyar Történelmi Tár)* (1855-1877) for the publication of smaller historical sources. Subsequently this series was taken over by the Historical Association, and published for three decades under the slightly altered title *Historical Repository (Történelmi Tár)* (1878-1911).(11)

During the 1860's this renaissance in Hungarian historical scholarship continued unabated, and soon the members of a new generation (those born during the 1820's and 1830's) also joined the ranks of Szalay's and Horváth's generation. By 1867, several members of this new generation had already played a significant role in the foundation of the Hungarian Historical Association. Moreover, during the next decade, the most outstanding members of this generation — such as Arnold Ipolyi (1823-1886), Frigyes Pesty (1823-1889), Károly Szabó (1824-1890), Ferenc Salamon (1825-1892), Sándor Szilágyi (1827-1899), Károly Ráth (1829-1868), Nándor Knauz (1831-1898) and others — generally took over the leadership of the whole Hungarian historical profession.(12) Thus, by 1875 — the year of the birth of Kálmán Tisza's (1830-1902) Liberal Party, which dominated much of Hungary's politics during the last quarter of the nineteenth century(13) — the leadership of Hungarian historical scholarship also fell into the hands of the new generation. The remaining members of the Horváth-Szalay generation all faded into the background; and to a lesser degree this was also true for the much younger national romantic, Kálmán Thaly (1839-1909), who up to 1875 had been in the very center of the historical profession. Subsequently Thaly became the founder of the *kuruc*-oriented new National Romantic School of the early twentieth century, which drew its inspiration largely from the Transylvanian and Protestant-based anti-Habsburg struggles of the late seventeenth and early eighteenth century.(14)

Simultaneously with the emergence of the first post-Horváth-Szalay generation to dominance in Hungarian historical studies, the older members of the future great "positivist generation" — including Imre Hajnik (1840-1902), Gyula Pauler (1841-1903), Vilmos Fraknói (1843-1921) and Ignác Acsády (1845-1906) — also began to emerge.(15) They in turn were followed by their younger colleagues, born during the Age of Absolutism (1849-1867), from among whose ranks came the greatest historians of the Hungarian Positivist School. Outside of the most outstanding *Geistesgeschichte* historians of the interwar period, this generation produced perhaps the greatest names in Hungarian historiography. They included such scholars as Sándor Márki (1853-1925), Árpád Károlyi (1853-1940), Lajos Thallóczy (1854-1916), Henrik Marczali (1856-1940), Dávid Angyal (1857-1943), László Fejérpataky (1857-1923), Károly Tagányi (1858-1924), Remig Békefi (1858-1924), Lajos Szádeczky-Kardoss (1859-1935), Sándor Takáts (1860-1932), Antal Hodinka (1864-1946), László Erdélyi (1868-1947) and Antal Aldásy (1869-1932).(16) Parallel with them, there were many others who represented various shades and levels of the National Romantic School that enjoyed unabated mass popularity during most of the dualist and interwar periods. The most outstanding adherents of this orientation during the dualist age, next to Thaly himself, were the legal-constitutional historian Ákos Timon (1850-1925), and the political historian Aladár Ballagi (1853-1928) — the holders of chairs of legal and world history, respectively, at the University of Budapest.(17)

The Hungarian Positivist School

While recent research has established the presence of positivism in Hungarian historical thinking as early as the 1830's and 1840's, traditional Hungarian historiography held that the positivist ideology had not been transplanted to Hungary until the early 1870's, when it came through the conscious efforts of G. Pauler.(18) Whatever the case, by the last third of the nineteenth century positivism became the dominant orientation in Hungarian historical scholarship. Its influence among professional historians was greater than that of any other philosophy, with the possible exception of *Geistesgeschichte* in interwar Hungary. (Marxism as a philosophy of history is purposely left out of this comparison, for its all-pervasive influence is derived at least partially from its position of being the only officially acceptable philosophy of history in Hungary of the post-Second World War period).

Contrary to the yet to be discussed *Geistesgeschichte* orientation, and thus to some degree similarly to Marxism, positivism is a philosophy of history that believes in a systematic and rational historical evolution. Thus, in its theory of historical evolution, positivism distinguishes among three distinct stages of development. These include the so-called theological, metaphysical and positivist (or scientific) stages through which human society allegedly proceeds in its progress toward perfection. In consequence of this evolution — so claims the positivist theory — human society moves progressively away from the influence of religious, mystical and emotional factors, and comes gradually more and more under the influence of science and rationalism. The positivists naturally expected historical scholarship to take cognizance of their philosophy of history and to examine historical developments in light of that philosophy.

While Comte's positivism was basically a philosophy of historical evolution, within the context of practical historical scholarship, it also meant a specific scientific method of historical research, developed first of all in Germany. In point of fact, in nineteenth-century historical studies, positivism was perhaps more of a methodology than a philosophy of history.(19) This was so both because of the lack of sufficient critically evaluated sources that could be used in the application of the positivist philosophy to European history, as well as because of the scientific, and thus anti-metaphysical tendencies of the contemporary European mind.

If the insufficient application of the philosophy of positivism to the study of history was true for positivist European historical scholarship in general, it was even more true for Hungarian historiography, where positivism came to be equated basically with the critical-philological method of source criticism developed and perfected by German historical scholarship. This method attempted to collect, select, evaluate and utilize historical sources with the precision of natural and physical sciences. It came to Hungary primarily via the Institute for Austrian Historical Research *(Institut für Österreichische Geschichtsforschung),* founded and directed by Theodor Sickel (1826-1908). This institute had served through much of the dualist period (along with the Austrian National Archives) as one of the most important centers of continued training for some of Hungary's greatest historians.

Although the influx of the critical-philological method into Hungary began during the 1860's and 1870's, not until 1895 did it become a regular part of the education of prospective historians. The greatest merit in this connection belongs to H. Marczali and L. Fejérpataky, both of whom were appointed to professorships at the University of Budapest in 1895; and to A. Károlyi, who resided mostly in Vienna, was a founder of the so-called "Károlyi-Thallóczy Circle" or the "Viennese School" of Hungarian historiography and by the early twentieth century became the director of the Austrian National Archives. With the collaboration of Sándor Mika (1859-1912) — a professor at the intellectually exclusive Eötvös College of Budapest, where the majority of the great twentieth-century Hungarian historians had received their education — Marczali and Fejérpataky produced several generations of young historians, including the most outstanding members of the *Geistesgeschichte* School. Károlyi, on the other hand, furthered and broadened the education of the best of these historians, first at the Austrian National Archives, and then after 1921, at the Hungarian Historical Research Institute in Vienna.(20) Thus, the majority of the greatest historians of the interwar period were wholly or at least partially the products of this rigorous schooling centered in Budapest and Vienna. These included Sándor Domanovszky, Imre Szentpétery, Tibor Gerevich, Gyula Szekfű, Bálint Hóman, József Holub, Ferenc Eckhart, István Hajnal, Elemér Mályusz and several others, many of whom eventually founded their own schools during the interwar period.

The climax of the Hungarian Positivist School came in the last decade of the nineteenth century, when several decades and hundreds of source publications after its birth, the positivist historians of Hungary undertook the synthetic elaboration of the whole course of Hungarian history. The most imposing result of their effort was the ten-volume *History of the Hungarian Nation* (1895-1898), the so-called "Millennial History," edited by Sándor Szilágyi, the "dean" of

Hungarian historians, for the occasion of the first millennium of the Magyar conquest of Hungary.(21) This multi-authored work on Hungarian history was paralleled — but not rivalled in significance — by the twelve-volume *Great Illustrated World History* (1898-1904) under the editorship of Henrik Marczali, who himself authored the last six volumes on the early modern and modern periods.(22) Some of the other great contemporary syntheses included József Szalay's and Lajos Baróti's *The History of the Hungarian Nation* (1896-1898), Ignác Acsády's *The History of the Hungarian Empire* (1903-1904), Ákos Beőthy's *The Development and Struggles of the Hungarian State* (1900-1906), Gyula Andrássy's *The Development of the Hungarian State and its Constitutional Liberties* (1901-1911), and H. Marczali's classic *History of Hungary* (1911), which is based on the great master's university lectures. Of these works, however, Beőthy's and Andrássy's syntheses contain more nineteenth-century liberalism than positivism, and are not the efforts of professional historians.(23)

Although all of these syntheses are impressive in their own way, and certainly reflect the commendable achievements of Hungarian positivism, they tell us at least as much about the flaws and failures, as about the strengths and achievements of the Positivist School. In light of these works, the most significant achievement of this school was the development and effective application of the critical-philological method of source research and source criticism in Hungarian historiography. Its most evident weakness, on the other hand, was its relative inability to synthesize. Undoubtedly, it was this lack of real shythesizing ability — combined with the new ideological trends of the early twentieth century — that ultimately undermined the pre-eminent position of the Positivist School in Hungarian historiography and permitted the rise of several new orientations. Thus, by the turn of the century, the hitherto relatively uniform Hungarian historiography was in the process of splitting into several new orientations. And this disintegration was equally reflective of the Positivist School's inability to adjust to the new needs of Hungarian historical studies, as well of the fragmentation and polarization of the contemporary social and political order in Hungary.

Disintegration of Positivism and the Rise of New Schools: The Economic History School

Among the new schools of history born during the period of declining positivism, the first in time was the Economic History School that grew up around the *Hungarian Economic History Review (Magyar Gazdaságtörténelmi Szemle)* (1894-1906). Its founder and guiding spirit was Károly Tagányi, already mentioned among the ranks of the great positivist historians of the late-dualist period. The chief merit of this school was that — following the ephemeral attempts of Mihály Horváth during the 1840's(24) — it turned the attention of Hungarian historians for the first time toward the study of economic and social problems and the everyday life of the masses. One of its main goals was to produce a major synthesis of Hungarian economic history for the occasion of Hungary's Millennium (1896) — a goal that turned out to be irrealistic. Their journal, however, did publish many essential sources, as well as numerous preliminary studies toward that end.(25)

Tagányi's main collaborators in the Economic History School were Ignác Acsády, Sándor Takáts and the young Ferenc Kováts (1873-1956), the latter of whom succeeded Tagányi as the editor of the *Hungarian Economic History Review* during the last few years of its existence (1901-1906). Of the other two historians, Acsády was the author of the first and in many ways still indispensible *History of Hungarian Serfdom* (1906);(26) while Takáts is known for his hundreds of delightful and informative socio-economic and cultural essays on the everyday lives of the masses, particularly during the age of the Turkish conquest of Hungary.(27)

The Hungarian Civilization (Kulturgeschichte) School

Almost parallel with Tagányi's Economic History School arose the Hungarian Civilization or *Kulturgeschichte* School. Modeled on the works and ideas of Jakob Christopher Burckhardt (1818-1897), Karl Lamprecht (1856-1915) and on the German *Kulturgeschichte* School in general, the Hungarian Civilization School was initiated by the priest-historian Remig Békefi, who was basically positivist in his approach and who held the first chair of Hungarian Civilization at the University of Budapest (1899-1911).

Békefi's Hungarian Civilization School concentrated primarily on the cultural and educational aspects of the history of Hungarian society. Békefi's younger contemporary at the University of Kolozsvár (1911-1918) and Szeged (1919-1938), László Erdélyi, on the other hand, dealt more with the social, legal and administrative institutions of medieval Hungary.(28)

The main line of the Hungarian Civilization School after Békefi's retirement in 1911 was carried on by Sándor Domanovszky (1877-1955), his successor at the University of Budapest, who — as we shall see in a subsequent chapter — tried to combine the goals and aspirations of Békefi's Hungarian Civilization and Tagányi's Economic History School. Domanovszky soon emerged as one of the towering historians of interwar Hungary. The somewhat eccentric Erdélyi, on the other hand, remained largely isolated from the main stream of interwar Hungarian historical studies — his influence extending hardly beyond his small chair of Hungarian Civilization at the University of Szeged.(29)

The Organic Sociological School

Among the newly emerging early twentieth-century schools of history, the school that was most reflective of the disintegration of traditional Hungarian society and traditional values was the so-called Organic Sociological School that drew its inspiration from Darwinian, Spencerian and partially Marxian ideas, and whose followers congregated around the progressive scholarly journal the *Twentieth Century (Huszadik Század)* (1900-1918). The latter were generally sociologists, philosophers and historically oriented publicists who sympathized with socialism, and who generally went under the name of "bourgeois radicals." Their most important spokesman was the learned sociologist-publicist Oszkár Jászi (1874-1957), who subsequently achieved some fame in the United States with his penetrating, if perhaps overly critical diagnosis of the causes of the disintegration of the Austro-Hungarian Empire *(The Dissolution of the Habsburg Monarchy,* 1929). But their ranks also included Péter Ágoston (1874-1925), Pál Szende (1879-1934), as well as Ervin Szabó (1871-1918) — the latter of whom was the first noteworthy philosopher and scholarly spokesman of Marxism in Hungary. With the collapse of dualism, however, this school also came to an end. Moreover, due to the triumph of a conservative system in interwar Hungary, its influence on interwar Hungarian historical studies was only indirect and rather limited.(30)

PART II

Chapter VI

THE END OF THE OLD ORDER AND THE SEARCH FOR THE NEW

The period of "declining positivism," which coincided with the *fin de siècle* period and its decadent cultural manifestations, had produced — as we have seen — a number of new historical and philosophical orientations. These included the Tagányi-lead Economic History School connected with the *Hungarian Economic History Review* (1894-1906), the Organic Sociological School which centered on the periodical *Twentieth Century* (1900-1918) and was lead by the bourgeois-radicals with a sprinkling of some Marxist oriented publicists, the Civilization or *Kulturgeschichte* School connected with the scholarly activities of R. Békefi, L. Erdélyi and later S. Domanovszky, as well as the slowly regenerating but hardly visible Positivist School based on the silent but scholarly labors of H. Marczali and L. Fejérpataky at the University of Budapest, of S. Mika at the university's Eötvös College, and of the Károlyi-Thallóczy Circle in Vienna. Yet, notwithstanding the appearance and functioning of these schools and orientations, the most visible and dominant orientation of the period of late dualism (1900-1918) was the mirage-chasing and mostly dilettante National Romantic School of K. Thaly and of his enthusiastic disciples.(1) Their views, based on a considerable degree of subjectivism and superficiality, apparently rhymed best with the ideological and cultural appetite of the relatively shallow intellectual world and sonorous nationalism of the general reading public. The latter (like their teachers and idols) saw Hungary's modern history only in terms of the Hungarian-Habsburg conflict of the previous four centuries — interpreting it as an unceasing struggle between the forces of good and the forces of evil.

This national romantic orientation became so dominant in popular historiography (particularly after S. Szilágyi's death in 1899, when the "Great Compromiser's" passing removed all restraints from the irreconcilable *kuruc* extremists) that its criticism and the criticism of its prophet K. Thaly was generally regarded as equivalent to a professional suicide. "Weakness, fear, (and) dread of controversy prevented everyone from speaking up against Thaly,'' declared the prominent literary critic A. Schöpflin in 1914,(2) in conjunction with his review of the first major attack against the self-proclaimed ''court historians'' of Prince F. Rákóczi II and his National Romantic School.

The Rákóczi Controversy

This attack appeared in the form of a monograph entitled *The Exiled Rákóczi* (1913),(3) and it came from the pen of the young and as yet unknown archivist-historian G. Szekfű (1883-1955), the product of the Marczali, Fejérpataky and Mika-seminars of Budapest, a member of the Károlyi-Thallóczy Circle of Vienna, and subsequently Hungary's greatest synthesizing historian of the *Geistesgeschichte* School. The publication of Szekfű's work (which was primarily a detailed and pedantic study of Rákóczi's life in exile (1711-1736), and only secondarily a post-mortem criticism of the scholarship of his ''court historian'') produced one of the greatest and most bitter controversies in the history of modern Hungarian historical scholarship. Known as the ''Rákóczi Controversy,'' it continued bitterly even during the interwar years, dividing historians into pro- and anti-Szekfű camps — generally, but not always, coinciding with the former *labanc* (pro-Habsburg) and *kuruc* (anti-Habsburg and pro-Turkish) orientations. In fact, some of the resonance of this bitter debate is still with us today.(4)

Under normal circumstances the Rákóczi Controversy could and should have remained on the level of a scholarly debate. Given the heated political and decadent cultural and scholarly atmosphere of the late dualist period, however (an atmosphere that demanded the continued exclusive dominance of the National Romantic School even after K. Thaly's death (1909),) the Rákóczi Controversy grew into a political debate of unusual proportions and bitterness.(5) As such, it reflected perhaps more on the cultural decadence, ideological intolerance and national bigotry of that age (of which it was a symptom), than on the participants themselves. The latter were perhaps only accidental tools in this affair. Whatever the case, this controversy placed the young, but extremly gifted Szekfű into the limelight of national notoriety and hatred. It left on him a lifelong psychological scar, but simultaneously it also pushed him on upon the road of almost unparalleled scholarly achievements. Moreover, almost as a byproduct, this controversy also saved Szekfű's rather superficial and vain opponent, the professor-historian A. Ballagi (yet to be discussed below) from sinking into total anonymity — although at the expense of acquiring an unenviable notoriety for himself.(6)

On the eve of the Rakoczi Controversy, Szekfu was but one of several young historians who "were preparing to break . . . with . . . the heavy legacy of the past," and who "were yearning to say something new."(7) Although they were ready to accept the advice and guidance of their masters, the best scholars of the great "positivist generation," they did not wish to duplicate the latter's achievements. In light of their Viennese experiences, they had already formed a rather well-founded and homogeneous picture of the relative "cultural backwardness of the Hungarian public in general."(8) They were also aware of the ideological shallowness of Hungarian party and parliamentary struggles, which were tearing at the very fabric of Hungarian society, as well as of the superficiality and dillettantism of national romantic historiography, whose dictums were accepted blindly by the provincial-minded "educated public" of Hungary. "The current conditions are such," wrote Szekfű just before the First World War, "that construction (of something new and better) is possible only at the expense of the total restructuring of the old."(9) It was with this goal in mind that Szekfu undertook to write *The Exiled Rákóczi* and to examine the two and half decades of emigré life of the leader of Hungary's struggle against Leopoldian absolutism during the early eighteenth century. The result was a totally new picture of Rákóczi, which was refreshingly different from the glorified "prince of liberty and of Christian virtue" image painted by Thaly and his disciples and spiritual successors. Contrary to Thaly's etherial and unreal Rákóczi-image, Szekfű produced a thoroughly documented, realistic picture of a rejected and bitter political exile, who had fallen from the position of a celebrated and idolized ruling prince into the "weightlessness of private life," and who consequently — notwithstanding his great and glorious past — had become but another hopeless "claimant to a throne" — a simple "chunk of the petrified past."(10)

As a byproduct of his research on Rákóczi, Szekfű also detoured briefly to pass judgment on Thaly's superficial historical methodology and on his blantantly biased ideological outlook; and he did so without much consideration for the reverence in which Rákóczi's late "court historian" still stood with the general public.(11) As summarized so well by Thaly's latest biographer, A. Várkonyi, in almost a single breath Szekfű pointed out all of the objectionable features of the old "court historian's" scholarship. These included the unreliability of his factual information, the tendentiousness and erroneous nature of his source criticism, the naiveté of his philosophy of history, the surprising laxity of his scholarly ethics, as well as his custom of preventing all scholarly criticisms of his works through intellectual terrorism exerted via the uncritical reading public.(12) The result was — so Szekfű claimed — a general retardation of Hungarian historical studies and the emergence (at least in the eyes of the same uncritical reading public) of Thaly's own dilettante National Romantic School as the ultimate arbiter of historical truth in Hungary.

In the course of the ensuing controversy, Szekfű was subjected to the most vicious and concerted attack ever experienced by an Hungarian scholar. He was branded a traitor and a paid political agent of Habsburg interests. But as usual in such instances, "his attackers did not even read his work. Newspaper articles threw misconstrued statements around . . . (while) . . . hurling the unsubstantiated charge of 'high treason' (of being a traitor to his nation) into the author's face."(13) Only the staunch support of some of his friends and sympathizers, including a number of great scholars of the old positivist generation (e.g. Angyal, Békefi, Károlyi, Tagányi, Takáts, etc.), the bourgeois radicals of *The Twentieth Century* (who supported him because of his iconoclastic aims), and above all the backing of the influential aristocratic statesman and scholar, Count G. Andrássy Jr., prevented Szekfű from a total collapse,(14) or perhaps from following the example of his less fortunate predecessor, B. Grünwald (1839-1891), who was driven to suicide following the appearance of his critical study of eighteenth-century Hungarian society *(Hungary of Old,* 1889).(15)

Szekfű tried to defend his scholarly integrity and fidelity to his nation in a number of articles and pamphlets, which demonstrated further his capabilities as a critical scholar, while also sharpening his skill in his future secondary role as a political and cultural publicist of the interwar period.(16) All in all, Szekfű had emerged from this bitter contest a different man. While retaining and even sharpening his scholarly skill, he was thoroughly frightened by the provincialism and bigotry of the so-called "educated public" of contemporary Hungary. This in turn made him a rather fervent champion of "Europeanism," and in particular of the so-called "Christian German Civilization," of which he regarded Hungary and Hungarian Civilization as an extended part. In championing the German Christian Civilization idea and the objective, critical and broad "European" spirit that it allegedly contained, however, Szekfű emerged in the eyes of most of his compatriots, and in particular in the eyes of those with the provincial *kuruc*-oriented mentality, as a "Habsburgianer" or a pro-Habsburg historian. He was and is still regarded so by many educated Hungarians (including some historians), even though Szekfű himself had always denied this allegation.

Szekfű's "Europeanism" and the Geistesgeschichte School

In Szekfű's mind, his own personal trials somehow merged with the trials of his country and of his nation, which — rightly or wrongly — he attributed to the triumph of the same mentality that ultimately led to the fall of Austria-Hungary and to the dismemberment of Hungary itself. This soon led to his re-examination of the whole Hungarian past, and in particular of the "Age of Liberalism" since the first half of the nineteenth century. He undertook this task under the influence and with the aid of a new philosophy of history, the Dilthey-inspired *Geistesgeschichte,* of which he became the first and most accomplished master in Hungary.(17)

The two initial works which grew out of this re-examination were *The Biography of the Hungarian State* (1917) and the much more influential *The Three Generations: The History of a Declining Age* (1920).(18) The former was the first attempt in Hungary to apply on a modest scale the *Geistesgeschichte* philosophy to Hungarian history; while the latter was a clinical analysis and a scathing criticism of the Hungarian version of liberalism of the post-*Ausgleich* (1867) variety, as well as of the spirit of provincialism, dilettantism, and superficiality which it had fostered. In Szekfű's estimation it was this alien spirit of pseudo-liberalism and its impact upon the fallible Magyar soul which led to the prostitution of scholarship, art and politics, and to the virtual disappearance of self-criticism. Moreover, it was also the pseudo-liberalism of that period which led to the collapse of the whole dualist order, along with historic Hungary's territorial and political integrity.

Whatever its faults or merits, Szekfű's *Three Generations* had rightfully been called a "spiritual and intellectual catharsis", both from a personal, as well as from a national point of view.(19) It may be regarded as a kind of watershed between two distinct intellectual and spiritual worlds: The world of positivism and national romanticism, on the one hand, and the world of *Geistesgeschichte* historiography and its various offshoots, on the other. Its fuller description, however, belongs to a later section of this study.(20)

The Search for a New Order: Szekfű, Eckhart, Mályusz and Hajnal

While the roots of Szekfű's rebellion against the "Old Order" reach back to the pre-World War I period, his open proclamation of the birth of the "New Order" appeared only in 1920 in the form of his abovementioned *Three Generations.* But, as we have seen, this proclamation came largely in consequence of the cataclysmic events of the years 1918-1920, which resulted in the disintegration of Austria-Hungary, the dismemberment of historic Hungary, and in the crushing and inglorious end of the whole traditional world. The post-war revolutions and the ensuing counter-revolution only added to the chaos and pain caused by the collapse of the old world. This chaos and pain was further increased by the birth of a new, physically dazed and bewildered world, represented by the neo-Baroque atmosphere of little rump Hungary's conservative regime.(21)

As a result of this almost unparalleled cataclysm in its history, the Magyar nation had lost its sense of direction and destiny, and the Hungarian society as a whole became derailed. The exponents of every ideological, political and scholarly orientation were dazed, and they were personally as well as collectively lost in the new chaotic world. Some waited passively for fate to take its toll; others grabbed frantically in every direction, hoping to find the straw of redemption. Still others turned their countenance to the past, either for solace, or in order to examine the road that had led to this inglorious end. Finally, some went to work immediately to prepare themselves and their nation for the ultimate and — in their view — inevitable resurrection of the already idealized past. To the last two groups belonged the great path-making historians of interwar Hungary: G. Szekfű, the transplanter of the German *Geistesgeschichte* orientation into Hungarian historical studies; F. Eckhart (1885-1957), the partially *Geistesgeschichte*-oriented demythologizer of Hungarian legal and constitutional history; E. Mályusz (b. 1898), the father of the similarly *Geistesgeschichte*-influenced Hungarian Ethnohistory School; and I. Hajnal (1892-1956), the founder of the new Sociological School that emphasized the role of social interrelations in history.

Szekfű and his *Geistesgeschichte* followers viewed history primarily as the product of the universal (and thus mostly non-Magyar) human spirit, and saw historical evolution as the recognition of and constant search for basic human goals. Moreover, contrary to traditional historiography, they assigned a dominant role to "intuition" and "re-living" in their attempt to re-create the past, and thus, in a way, they represented the early twentieth-century version of psycho-history.(22)

To a lesser degree this was also true for Eckhart, although — as a dedicated deromanticizer and demythologizer of history — he was less prone to creating new myths, like Szekfű and his followers. Moreover, Eckhart had also recognized the significance of economic and social forces in historical evolution, and thus he tried to examine Hungarian legal and constitutional developments in light of current socio-economic developments.(23)

While accepting the basic tenents of *Geistesgeschichte* philosophy, Mályusz moved in a direction that appeared to place him into a rival position with the emerging *Geistesgeschichte* School. In reality, however, Mályusz was also a *Geistesgeschichte* historian, and his opposition was not against this idealist philosophy of history, but rather against the way Szekfű and his followers applied this philosophy to Hungarian historical evolution. The result was that Mályusz soon developed his own school of history (the so-called Ethnohistory School), which, on the one hand, rejected Szekfű's tendency to interpret Hungarian history primarily in light of the role of alleged Western influences, and on the other, placed an unusual emphasis on the role of the indigenous "Magyar spirit" in Hungarian historical evolution. Moreover, breaking with the state-centered (etatistic) and socially elitist traditional historiography, Mályusz turned the attention of interwar Hungarian historiography toward the study of the life and role of the Magyar masses *(Volk)* in the shaping of Hungarian history(24)

Hajnal, the fourth member of the interwar path-makers also started out under *Geistesgeschichte* influences but contrary to Szekfű, Mályusz and Eckhart, he gradually moved from a basically idealist to a partially materialist philosophy of history. In his rather eclectic philosophy, Hajnal emphasized "technological progress" and the "spread of literacy" as the most significant factors of social and historical evolution. At the same time, he also believed that mutations in historical evolution are caused by the incessant flux of interrelations among the individual members and groups in human society. Ultimately, Hajnal ended up with the theory of progress that rejected both the pre-eminence of *ideas (Geistesgeschichte),* as well as *economic forces* (historical materialism), and made the fluctuations in social interrelationships into the foundations of historical evolution.(25)

Next to these path-breaking and innovating historians of interwar Hungary, most other significant and influential historians were adherents of one or another of the more traditional schools of history (i.e. positivism, *Kulturgeschichte* and to a lesser degree national romanticism). Some of the remaining scholars, on the other hand, either did not represent professional historical scholarship (i.e. the populists), or they could not function openly due to their political convictions (i.e. the Marxists).

Chapter VII

THE REORIENTATION AND REORGANIZATION OF INTERWAR HUNGARIAN HISTORICAL RESEARCH

As we have seen, the cataclysmic events of 1918-1920 have brought forth a number of innovating and interesting new orientations in Hungarian historical studies. These same events, however, also caused a total reorientation and reorganization of interwar Hungarian historical research. Much of this reorientation and reorganization was carried out under the leadership of the dynamic Count K. Klebelsberg (1875-1932), and to a lesser degree under that of B. Hóman (1885-1951), who jointly served for over two decades as interwar Hungary's ministers of culture and education.(1)

The Emergence of Klebelsberg

As one of the most agile and untiring of all Hungarian cultural politicans, Klebelsberg's name is connected with the total reorganization of the Hungarian educational system from the elementary schools through the universities and research institutes.(2) He was also one of the authors of the almost superhuman effort to raise the dejected spirit of his defeated nation from a point of despair to a level of hope, pride, expectation, and belief in a new destiny. This goal was to be achieved through the ideology of "neo-nationalism" which — contrary to traditional Magyar nationalism that had rested on the politics of power — was to be based on the alleged cultural and intellectual pre-eminence of his nation in the Carpathian Basin.(3) Klebelsberg believed in this cultural pre-emience, just as much as he believed in the unifying power of the "ancient Hungarian Constitution," as well as in the unique "state-forming capacities" of the Magyars. Moreover, he was convinced that the combination of these factors would ultimately restore to his nation both its shattered unity, as well as its position of leadership in the territories of historic Hungary.

Although not an historian in the strict sense of that term, Klebelsberg was a lover and ardent supporter of the historical discipline. Furthermore, due to an intimate link between historical studies and national politics (a phenomenon that was universal in East Central Europe), and due to the nature and structure of the Hungarian Historical Association (which had both scholarly and socio-cultural goals to fulfill), (4) Klebelsberg rose rapidly in prominence, and by 1917 he became the Association's president. As president of the Historical Association during perhaps the most critical period of the nation's history, Klebelsberg had forged an even closer link between the historical profession and his new cultural policies based on neo-nationalism.(5) While perhaps questionable from a pure scholarly point of view, this trend was a natural byproduct of the situation in which the Magyars have found themselves after the First World War and of their desire for the restoration of historic Hungary. Thus, the Hungarian learned public became even more history-conscious than before, and the support of the historical profession became a matter of national priority.

The Historical Association versus the Historical Commission

The leadership of the Hungarian historical profession in the nineteenth century was essentially in the hands of two organizations: The Historical Commission of the Hungarian Academy of Sciences established in 1854, and the Hungarian Historical Association founded in 1867. During the 1850's and 1860's the Historical Commission had a near-monopoly in the ideological and administrative leadership of historical studies. By the 1870's, however, the Commission was obliged to share this position with the Historical Association, and later even to relinquish its number one position to its younger rival.(6)

During the interwar period, the pre-eminence and significance of the Historical Association over the Academy's Historical Commission increased even further, and it soon reached a point where the Historical Association became almost the exclusive "frame" within which the historical profession functioned.(7) There are also indications, however, that the two groups followed a policy of division of labor, according to which medieval history remained primarily within the competence of the Historical Commission, whereas the Historical Association concentrated largely on the modern period.(8) Yet, the Association's pre-eminence was rather evident. It was evident, among others, from the disproportionately larger funds made available to the Association as compared to the Academy's Commission; from the Association's sponsorship and control of most of the noteworthy new institutions and publications in the area of history; as well as from the composition of the respective leadership groups of the two organizations. Thus, the Academy's Commission was manned primarily by the representatives of the old school, the exponents of positivism, such as L. Fejérpataky, D. Angyal, A. Áldásy, etc. The Historical Association, on the other hand, had already fallen into the hands of a new generation of scholars, several of whom were apostles or at least partial exponents of the *Geistesgeschichte* philosophy in historical studies (e.g. B. Hóman, S. Domanovszky, G. Szekfű, I. Lukinich, F. Eckhart, I. Hajnal, E. Mályusz, etc.).(9) From the mid-1920's onward, these younger scholars dominated all major orientations and schools in interwar Hungarian historical studies.

Klebelsberg and the Organization of Interwar Historical Studies

The acquisition of power and the dominance of the Historical Association by the young generation of historians in interwar Hungary was due to two factors: First to Klebelsberg himself, who — as president of the Association (1917-1032), and as minister of religion and public education through most of the first half of that period (1922-1931) — made the Association into the basic forum for the propagation of his partially politically motivated cultural and educational policies; and secondly, to the triumph of the *Geistesgeschichte* philosophy. While understood and absorbed by many of the younger scholars, this philosophy remained incomprehensible and alien to the old positivistic scholars of the Academy's Historical Commission.

Klebelsberg's culturo-political activities were too numerous and too manifold to be here detailed. But, as related specifically to the historical discipline, the most important among these was his goal and desire that Hungarian historians "should work in an organized and planned manner in line with the spirit of our new goals." In other words, realizing that in "this age of large corporations," the heroic age of the individual scholar (the "period of the California Gold Rush" in Hungarian historical studies, as he called it) was over, he pointed to the need for the organized and collective effort of numerous scholars to carry out the huge task that confronted Hungarian historiography. This involved, on the one hand, the organization of several historical research institutes (the need of which had already been pointed out by several young positivists at the Hungarian Historical Congress of 1885), and on the other, the mass publication of the hitherto virtually untouched sources on the modern period of Hungarian history.(10)

The historical institutes were intended to serve two purposes: First, the post-university training of young research scholars, and second, the utilization of their collective efforts and talents in the production of "half-finished goods" (i.e. source publications and small caliber, but reliable monographs). These goals require an up-to-date knowledge of historical methodology, archival research, source criticism and source analysis, but require no real synthesizing ability. According to Klebelsberg's plan, major "finished products" or summarizing syntheses were to be left specially to gifted mature scholars, who would base their syntheses on these lesser works, unearthed, analyzed and compiled by the research scholars of the newly founded research institutes.(11)

Klebelsberg's efforts were unusually successful even in the mutilated and economically destroyed post-Trianon Hungary, where funds were scarce, or simply unavailable even for the most essential social, let alone cultural and scholarly programs. He managed to re-establish the Hungarian Historical Institute in Rome (originally established by the priest-historian V. Fraknói in 1888, and placed under national control in 1913); helped to make the nascent Hungarian Institute of the University of Berlin (1916) into a viable center for Hungarian studies which, in addition to the *Ungarische Jahrbücher* (Hungarian Yearbooks, 1921-1944) published numerous monographs on Hungarian topics; and most importantly, he established the Hungarian Historical Research Institute of Vienna (1920). In view of the lack of a native historical institute in Budapest until 1941, and in light of the importance of the archives of the former imperial city for Hungarian historical writing, the Viennese institute became for a while perhaps the most important center of Hungarian historical research. In these three major centers of European learning, Klebelsberg also founded government-sponsored study and residence centers ("Collegium Hungaricums") to aid the continued education of Hungarian youth (Vienna and Berlin in 1924, Rome in 1927). Moreover, his tenure in the Ministry of Religion and Public Education also saw the establishment of four other, though less active institutes, attached to the universities of Stockholm (1920), Helsinki (1926) and Paris (1927), and the Papal Court of Rome (1927), as well as several university chairs (Amsterdam, Nymwegen and Utrecht, all in 1927) and lectureships for Hungarian studies (Sofia-1925, Helsinki-1926, Vienna-1927, and Munich-1929). Following Klebelsberg's death, his successor B. Hóman continued to establish additional Hungarian institutes (Rome-1934, Ankara-1935, and Sofia-1939), university chairs (Vienna-1935, Rome-1935, Bologna-1935, Paris-1938, Nizza-1939), as well as lectureships (Leipzig-1935, Rome-1935, London-1937, Lille-1937,

Geneva-1937, Torino-1937, Milan-1937, Naples-1937, Pisa-1938, Pavia-1938, New York-Columbia-1939, Padua-1940, Trieste-Fiume-1940, etc.).(12) But in doing so, Hóman was simply executing Klebelsberg's grand scheme for the univeral dissemination of Hungarian culture and learning.

Naturally, not all of Klebelsberg's institutional plans materialized; and those that did, did not necessarily live up to the full expectations of their founder. Thus, he was unsuccessful in his efforts to re-establishing the ephemeral Hungarian Research Institute of Constantinople (Istanbul), which had functioned during the last two years of the existence of the Austro-Hungarian and Ottoman Turkish empires (1917-1918). His desire to create a major domestic historical research institute also failed, for not until 1941 did the first such domestic research center come into being as a section of the Teleki Institute.(13) Funds were simply too limited in the small, mutilated and impoverished country. Thus, notwithstanding his overall success, many of Klebelsberg's ambitious plans never came to be realized. Others, such as his yet to be discussed ambitious publication projects, slowly lost their initial impetus during the 1930's.

Publication Projects

In addition to establishing the impressive chain of foreign centers for Hungarian studies, and his equally heralded domestic cultural and educational reforms and university building program (all of which had some impact on Hungarian historical studies), Klebelsberg's most lasting achievements relative to the discipline of history were connected with his sponsorship of a number of major publication projects. These included the most extensive Hungarian source publication series relating to modern and early modern Hungarian history, the two so-called *Fontes* series on the Turkish and post-Turkish periods; the projected forty-nine volume *Handbook of Hungarian Historical Sciences;* as well as several major syntheses in the so-called "Hungarology" series. The latter was planned to include several mostly multivolumed syntheses on Hungarian ethnography, ethnology, folklore, geography, anthropology, art history and history — all of which were to be executed in the spirit of the new *Geistesgeschichte* philosophy.

The Fontes Series

The purpose of the two *Fontes* series was twofold: First, to fill in the period-vacuum left by the medieval-centered source publications of the dualist period; and secondly, to counterbalance their heavy political orientation by concentrating on the social, economic, cultural and artistic aspects of modern Hungarian history.(14) Of the two series, the *Fontes . . . Aevi Turcici* (Sources on the Turkish Age) was intended to concentrate on the sixteenth and seventeenth centuries (1526-1686), and the *Fontes . . . Aevi Recentoris* (Sources on the Recent Period) on the eighteenth and nineteenth centuries (1686-1918).(15) At the end, however, only the latter proved to be a viable undertaking. For various reasons (not the least of which were the insufficiency of funds, and the greater need for sources on the more recent period), the *Fontes . . . Aevi Turcici* never got beyond the first volume, which was an annotated and introduced diary of a prominent citizen of Pozsony (Pressburg, Bratislava) during his captivity in the *Yedikule* (Seven Towers) of Istanbul in 1664.(16)

The specific plans for the *Fontes* series were elaborated in detail in the course of 1918-1919.(17) A master plan was essential because Klebelsberg and the Historical Association wished to avoid the arbitrariness of selection that characterized most previous source publications. "We will be especially careful," declared Klebelsberg, "that the volumes should not appear haphazardly . . ., but . . . according to the importance of the topics."(18) Moreover, as most of the archival research (particularly in connection with the *Fontes . . . Aevi Recentoris)* was to be conducted in Vienna, the Historical Association also prepared a detailed plan for systematized archival research, geared specifically to the conditions in the former imperial city.(19) At the same time provisions were made for the publication of the finished volumes. The Hungarian Historical Research Institute of Vienna was a direct outgrowth of the Historical Association's Viennese plans and activities.

Between 1921 and 1944 altogether forty-four volumes appeared in the *Fontes . . . Aevi Recentoris* series; with seventeen additional volumes appearing (to date) in the period after 1948. The interwar volumes were published under ten separate sub-headings, including eight broad topical and two specific categories. The latter included Count I. Széchenyi's works (of which thirteen volumes appeared, yet it remained unfinished), and the sources of the history of the Hungarian National Theater (2 vols.). The topical categories included personal letters (1 vol.), official papers and letters (5 vols.), memoires (3 vols.), the national minority question (8 vols.), social and economic history (1 vol.), diaries, autobiographies and other historical works (1 vol.), governmental and administrative papers (6 vols.), and the history of political emigration of 1848-1849 (4 vols.). The seventeen post-Second World War volumes of this series appeared in three separate categories, including the papers of the Hungarian Jacobins (3 vols.), the anti-revolutionary role of the Hungarian landed aristocracy in 1848-1849 (3 vols.), and a new critical edition of L. Kossuth's papers (11 vols. to date).(20)

Needless to say none of the interwar topical categories received adequate treatment, with the probable exception of the national minority question. In point of fact, a number of categories remained very under-represented despite the declared goals of Klebelsberg. The most outstanding example of this lack of fulfillment is the single volume under social and economic history, which is a direct violation of the original goals of the conceivers of this series. On the other end, the best represented categories are Széchenyi and the national minority question, both of which rhymed well with interwar Hungary's ideological orientation. Thus, Hungary's dismemberment at Trianon, and the consequent staunch revisionisms of both the political regime and of interwar historiography made the study of the national minority question the number one problem of contemporary historical scholarship. This political expediency factor also holds true for Széchenyi's papers; for — in light of the cataclysmic failure of the "liberal experimentation" of the dualist period — Széchenyi's "conservative reform program" became the guiding spirit of interwar political ideology. Széchenyi's influence, however, was present in an unprostituted form only in the reform activities of such moderately conservative intellectuals as the historian G. Szekfű and his followers. To many of the arch-conservatives with their neo-Baroque mentality, Széchenyi's ideas represented simply a convenient facade for the concealment of their reactionary views.(21)

In addition to political and ideological considerations, the two other factors that played a role in the relative under or over-representation of some categories in the *Fontes* series were economics and the lack of sufficient number of well-trained research scholars willing to devote several years of their lives to one or several of these basically documentary volumes.

In view of the scarcity of funds, Klebelsberg and his supporters were often forced to find financial sponsors among the members of the well-to-do classes (mostly aristocrats). While in itself commendable, the influx of these outside funds added an undesirable factor to this whole undertaking, namely pressures in the area of what should be published. As an example, the papers of Palatinate Joseph and Alexander Leopold of the Habsburg family were published in the category of "Governmental and Administrative Papers" with the financial support of the Hungarian Habsburgs — probably at the expense of other categories. On the other side, another proposed work by the legal historian B. Baranyai on Cardinal Leopold Kollonich's so-called *Einrichtungswerk,* a late-seventeenth-century attempt on the part of the Habsburg's to amalgamate Hungary into their empire, remained unpublished. Had it appeared, it would have proven the treasonable behavior of Palatinate Prince Paul Esterházy, one of the most illustrious ancestors of contemporary Hungary's most powerful and richest feudal family — which neither Klebelsberg, nor the Hungarian Historical Association dared to antagonize.(22)

The problems stemming from the scarcity of funds were augmented by the scarcity of trained historians who were willing to forgo the possibility of rapid advancement for the mixed-glories connected with one of the *Fontes* volumes. The keen competition for academic positions which created the pressure for rapid publication, usually turned the attention of young aspiring scholars away from the slow and laborious archival research needed for the preparation of a *Fontes* volume. They usually opted for easier projects, which promised quicker and easier rewards.(23) While understandable from a personal point of view, this tendency had certain negative impacts both on Hungarian historical research, as well as on the *Fontes* series.

As to the methodological execution of the *Fontes* volumes? They represented a qualitative improvement over all previous source publications, including the venerable *Monumenta* volumes. Contrary to the latter, the *Fontes* volumes did not aspire at completeness; that is, they were not intended to contain all available documents relative to a specific historical problem. (Such completeness was feasible only in the medieval field). At the same time, however, the method of reproducing the documents was far superior to all previous attempts. The text was verbatim, scientifically precise (even errors were reproduced), and always in the original language. In case of the less familiar languages (e.g. Slavic and Greek), however, Hungarian translation was also provided. Moreover, all of the published sources went through a much more rigorous process of source criticism than most earlier similar publications. They were also accompanied by detailed historical and critical annotations; and all of the volumes were preceded by unusually lengthy historical introductions, equivalent to a thorough monographic elaboration of the problem involved.(24) These studies usually amounted to between one-third to one-half of the rather sizable volumes. In case of multivolumed works (of which there were several) this "introduction" usually took the form of a separate volume (or volumes), which usually appeared last following the publication of all of the documentary volumes.

The Handbook of Hungarian Historical Sciences

Although prepared under various pressures, and only partially completed, the *Fontes* series was still very successful, and it had considerable impact on interwar Hungarian historical studies. This was also true about Klebelsberg's and the Historical Association's second major undertaking, *The Handbook of Hungarian Historical Sciences,* even though of the projected forty-nine (later forty-seven) parts only thirteen appeared in print.(25)

According to the original plan elaborated in 1920 by an editorial committee composed of a number of prominent interwar historians (S. Domanovszky, J. Holub, B. Hóman, I. Lukinich), the purpose of the *Handbook* was twofold: "On the one hand, to pave the way toward a new synthetic elaboration of Hungarian history, while supplying guidelines for planned basic research in the future; on the other hand, to provide a guidebook for the practitioners of history, as well as for secondary school teachers and university students." In line with these goals, the declared intention of the editors of this project was "not so much to establish new theories and hypotheses, but rather to provide objective summaries of the results of the research efforts of the past decades." Moreover, where the preparation of such summaries were as yet impossible due to the inadequacy of preliminary studies (e.g. legal history and historical statistics), they hoped to provide at least "schematic elaborations" intended to point out the desirable direction and goals of future historical research.(26)

The proposed *Handbook's* original plan foresaw three separate series (called incorrectly "volumes"), each to be composed of several parts and still more *fasciculi.* In effect the *Handbook* was to be composed of forty-nine separate publications, varying in size from modest pamphlets to large volumes. The first of these series ("volumes"), entitled "The Philosophy and Sources of Historical Scholarships," was itself to be composed of eight parts in twenty-seven *fasciculi.* These were to include a separate publication each on the philosophy of history, historical methodology, source research and criticism, bibliography of Hungarian source publications, as well as over twenty analytical volumes on the various types of native and foreign sources of Hungarian history. The second series bore the title "The Auxiliary Sciences of History" and it was scheduled to include works on such topics as the history of the auxiliary sciences, paleography, diplomatics, papal diplomas, chronology, heraldry, genealogy, epigraphy, numismatics and monetary history, historical geography and ethnography, historical statistics, linguistics and on the Latin dialect of medieval and early modern Hungary.

As opposed to the first two series of the *Handbook,* its third series was not meant to contain methodological or philosophical volumes, nor even a description of sources. Rather, it was to be composed of eight new major syntheses on the Hungarian past on such diverse topics as constitutional and administrative developments, legal history, Catholicism and Protestantism in Hungary, economic and social developments, literature, the arts and music. Moreover, a separate, but never fully elaborated part of the *Handbook* was also to include a new synthesis on the totality of the Hungarian past.(27)

The plan of the proposed *Handbook* was an unusually ambitious one, and it reflects well the planned and centralized aspects of Klebelsberg's cultural policies. Had it been completed, it would undoubtedly have turned out to be one of the most ambitious and influential projects of twentieth-century Hungarian historical studies. As in the case of the two *Fontes* series, however, the *Handbook* also proved to be beyond the financial and manpower capacities of interwar Hungary's historical profession. At the end, of the forty-nine projected volumes or *fasciculi* only thirteen appeared in print; with one exception, all during Klebelsberg's ministry in the 1920's. The single exception was G. Moravcsik's *The Byzantine Sources of Hungarian History* (1934), which appeared two years after Klebelsberg's death and signalled the *de facto* termination of this worthy undertaking. Of the other twelve published volumes of the *Handbook,* six were in the category of "philosophy and sources," five in the category of "auxiliary sciences," and one in the area of synthesising summaries. All of these works were written by the best authorities on the subject and all of them are still useful today. In view of the pre-eminence of Marxist philosophy in current Hungarian historical studies, however, this is much less true about the volumes on the philosophy and methodology of history, which — contrary to the other volumes — have lost much of their usefulness in Hungary of today.(28)

Although initiated by an editorial committee, the *Handbook* was in fact edited by B. Hóman, Klebelsberg's successor in the ministry and in the presidency of the Historical Association. Strangely enough, however, the *Handbook* progressed only until Klebelsberg was at the helm of Hungarian cultural and scholarly life. Once Hóman took over, not only the *Handbook,* but all other major serial publications, which have flourished under his predecessor, came to a grinding halt. Even the major new synthesis of Hungarian history (co-authored by Hóman and Szekfű) was finished only belatedly in 1934, after Szekfű had assumed some of the obligations on the late fifteenth and early sixteenth century originally assigned to Hóman. Thus, while an excellent medievalist, Hóman was much less able and farsighted as a cultural politician than Klebelsberg.(29) And there is no question that without the latter's unusual dedication and administrative ability, Hungarian historiography of the interwar period would have achieved far less than it did.

The Hungarian "National Collection University"

As already implied above, in its institutional and administrative aspects, Klebelsberg's cultural policy was based on two seemingly contradictory principles: Autonomy and centralization. More specifically, Klebelsberg was in favor of a strong autonomy for Hungary's scholarly and cultural institutions so that they be able to preserve their integrity against political pressures. At the same time, however, he hoped to coordinate their efforts and activities through a centrally planned cultural policy which would point out the direction they ought to take toward the common goal of national resurrection.

The policy was best examplified by Klebelsberg's organization of the "Hungarian National Çollection University" *(Országos Magyar Gyüjteményegyetem)* in 1922, which functioned for twelve years, and which ultimately included most of Hungary's scholarly and cultural institutions, except the universities and the Academy of Sciences (e.g. museums, archives, research libraries, research institutes, all foreign-based centers of Hungarian learning, etc.). In effect, the "Collection University" was a federation of Hungary's most prominent scholarly and scientific centers for the purposes of co-ordinating their scholarly efforts in the direction of the nation's single most important goal in accordance with a grand national plan embodied in Klebelsberg's cultural policy. The universities and the Academy of Scienes were not included because of their position of leadership in the intellectual life of the nation. Moreover, their inclusion would have been interpreted as the termination of their highly respected autonomy.(30)

While Klebelsberg's policy of co-ordination contained political motivations and implications, under his leadership this policy was pursued with moderation and on a high scholarly and ethical level. He did not deny the presence of Hungarian nationalism and at least partially justifiable revisionism as a prime motivating factor behind his cultural policy, but he refused to permit this policy to be made into a tool of contemporary day-to-day politics.(31) His successor, Hóman, was less cautious in this regard. Consequently, during the 1930's there was a growing politicization of Hungarian cultural policy, which — unfortunately — also affected Hungarian historical studies.

Chapter VIII

THE EMERGENCE OF SZEKFŰ AND THE *GEISTESGESCHICHTE* SCHOOL

Although the politicization of historical studies was an undeniable reality in interwar Hungary, it was neither a uniquely Hungarian phenomenon, nor was it limited to the interwar years. It had been an acknowledged part of East Central European and Balkan historiography ever since the national revival period of the previous century; although perhaps never as intense and coordinated as during the emotion-packed interwar years.(1)

Its new interwar intensity stemmed from the events following the collapse of the old order in that part of Europe. More specifically, it was connected both with the revolutions and counterrevolutions of the immediate post-war years, as well as with the harshness of some of the post-war treaties and the subsequent revisionist aspirations of the defeated states and dismembered nationalities. To these may be added the emergence of the new idealist *Geistesgeschichte* philosophy in historical and related humanistic studies whose emphasis upon the subjective and the irrational made it easier for scholarship to mix with nationalistic political movements. The hard-to-define *Geistesgeschichte* undoubtedly became the dominant philosophical orientation in interwar Hungary; just as its transplanter and most successful applicator, the historian G. Szekfű, became perhaps the most noted ideologist of that period.

The Philosophy of German Geistesgeschichte

Geistesgeschichte (which defies translation into English) is an idealist philosophy of history, inspired by the writings of W. Dilthey (1834-1911) in the late-nineteenth century, and subsequently amended by E. Troeltsch (1865-1923), H. Rickert (1863-1936), M. Weber (1867-1920), E. Spranger (1882-1963) and others. It believes that human history is essentially the history of the manifestations of the human soul, and contrary to positivism and Marxism, it rejects the contention that there are objective laws which govern historical and social evolution.(2)

Dilthey divided "sciences" (fields of knowledge) into two distinct categories: Natural sciences *(Naturwissenschaften)* and spiritual sciences *(Geisteswissenschaften),* and claimed that laws and objective reality existed only in the former. Categorizing the discipline of history into the spiritual sciences, he defined human history as "the sum total of unique and singular phenomena," and claimed that "the task of an historian is to perceive them and to describe them artistically."(3)

In continuing to develop these ideas, Dilthey's noted disciple, Troeltsch, went even further in his denial of the presence of laws and objective reality in the progress of history. This was also true for a number of his other disciples, even though they tended to disagree on several basic issues. Among them Spranger was particularly emphatic in the rejection of all predetermined regularity in the historical process, claiming that human existence was basically an indeterministic, but incessant strive toward "the timeless, the absolute and (the) highest of values."(4) No less was this true for Rickert and Weber, both of whom emphasized the singularity and uniqueness of every single phenomenon in history, even though Weber rejected the Rickertian idea that each of these singular phenomenon must be measured in terms of a certain, absolute and transcendent value system.

In a way G. Simmel went even further than Rickert and Weber. For him "facts of history" did not even exist. These were simply "relics" from which historians had to reconstruct the "facts". And because Simmel saw history as "an affair of the spirit," an historian could reconstruct the past only by virtue of his own spirituality.

Methodology and Historical Process in Geistesgeschichte

While the basic methods of research and source criticism of the *Geistesgeschichte* historians were essentially identical with those of the positivists (i.e. the critical philological source criticism and analysis developed in nineteenth-century Germany), their instrument of comprehension was quite different. Contrary to the more fundamentalist positivists, they relied heavily on the process of re-living *(nacherleben)* and thus re-creating the past through the historian's power of intuition. Thus, they disagreed with those who tried to comprehend human history and social evolution through logical mental categories. They regarded the use of such categories as appropriate only to the natural and physical sciences. In the discipline of history, these were necessary only to the less-elevated minds for comprehension purposes. Men of loftier intellect — they believed — should attempt to comprehend the past only through intuition based on the available facts. In their view, it was this capacity of intuition which separated the great historians from the unimaginative mass man and placed them into the category of the aristocracy of the mind.(5)

Looking at it from the point of view of the philosophy of history, therefore, *Geistesgeschichte* was a specific manifestation of German idealist philosophy of the *fin de siècle* period, which found expression in the works of a number of philosophers and historians, and which soon made itself felt throughout the German-influenced lands of East Central Europe. From another vantage point, however, *Geistesgeschichte* can also be viewed as a reaction against various nineteenth-century materialist or materialistically-inclined philosophies of history, including positivism, Spencerian organic sociology, as well as Marx-inspired historical materialism. All of these orientations or philosophies expressed at least some attachment to scientific materialism, and all believed in some kind of objective laws which allegedly guide and govern the progress of human history.

This difference between the idealist and materialist philosophies of history was also there in reference to the "force" or "forces" that moved history forward, whether in a rational or irrational manner. Thus the eighteenth-century idealist-oriented G.B. Vico (1668-1744) spoke of a vaguely defined "Absolute Spirit" as the mover of the historical process. The materialistically inclined nineteenth-century positivists, on the other hand, believed in an irreversible and unimpedible progress from the primitive "theological," through the higher "metaphysical," to the lofty "positivist" or scientific stage, and cited the analogy of biological growth — as did the adherents of the Spencer-inspired organic sociologists. Simultaneously, Marx and his followers emphasized the all-importance of material and economic forces and the forces of production as factors which allegedly move the historical process along a dialectical path.(6)

Contrary to these materialist oriented philosophies, and in the traditions of Vico, the *Geistesgeschichte* philosophers went to the other extreme. They rejected the claimed pre-eminence of material and economic forces, and either denied the very validity of a question relative to alleged "forces" which supposedly move history forward (just as they denied the existence of objective laws), or simply pointed to some vague and never fully defined "spirit" (perhaps the "spirit of the age") which may play that role. As defined by a self-proclaimed Hungarian ideologist of this school (B. Hóman), they believed that "human history is nothing but the history of the human soul," and "Hungarian history is nothing but the history of the Hungarian soul, i.e. the description of those forms in which the Hungarian soul had manifested itself for many millenniums."(7)

Definition of Hungarian Gesitesgeschichte

While interesting, the above definition gives us little help in understanding the historical process. Yet, it is only one of innumerable such definitions of *Geistesgechichte,* most of which are so vague and misty that they are virtually meaningless. No wonder that one of its most prominent idealist critics, E. Mályusz — who criticized Hungarian *Geistesgeschichte* largely because of the high pressure tactics and alleged pro-Habsburg, pro-Western and pro-Catholic bias of some of its over-enthused advocates — was unable to find a simple "clear (and) sensibly constructed definition as to what constitutes *Geistesgeschichte.*" As Mályusz observed, "it is not an exaggeration to claim that there are no two protagonists (of this school) who could agree as to its meaning."(8) Thus, while bound together by their general anti-materialist beliefs, their constant reference to the decisive role of some unknown and ill-defined "spirit" (often described as a *Zeitgeist* (spirit of the age), "absolute spirit," and even "folk spirit"), their tendency to use cultural and artistic terms to identify ages of history (e.g, Gothic, Renaissance, Baroque, Rococo, Romantic, etc.) and their dislike of basic research and preference for large synthetic overviews, Hungarian *Geistesgeschichte* historians produced such a broad and ill-defined conception of their ideology that "it could include just about everything that went beyond spiritless factography — formerly incorrectly called 'positivism'."(9) And here Mályusz, the author of this statement, was again correct. He was also right in his claim that the hazy philosophical foundations of the *Geistesgeschichte* School and the rapid influx of droves of opportunist dillettantes under its victorious flags during the interwar period made it difficult to study the essence of its ideological orientation, except perhaps from an evolutionary point of view; that is from the vantage point of its practical application to, and manifestations in Hungarian historical studies. This is the road we shall follow. Before doing that, however, let us look briefly at a rather compact Marxist definition of this orientation.

As summarized by G. Mérei, the main characteristics of the *Geistesgeschichte* philosophy of history are: "Indeterminism versus determinism, free will and voluntarism versus laws and causality, extremist subjectivism versus objectivism based on the material reality of history, irrationalism versus rationalism, God instead of the subconsciously existing material reality and history-shaping activity of man, (and) spiritual self-development instead of progress-furthering class struggle."(10) Although written from the vantage point of an opposing philosophy of history, the above characterization is basically correct. In its philosophical aspects, *Geistesgeschichte* is undoubtedly an irrational school of history. Its protagonists, however, regard this "irrationalism" not as a negative, but as a positive feature. As adherents of an idealist philosophy of hisory, they believe in the spiritual-versus material dualism of reality, profess the pre-eminence of the spirit over matter and are convinced that the history-shaping "spirit" acts completely independently from any and all allegedly "scientific" laws, patterns or systems acclaimed by various materialist or perhaps "objective" (versus "subjective") philosophies of history.

The Beginnings of Hungarian Geistesgeschichte

While one may or may not agree with the *Geistesgeschichte* philosophers' conception of historical evolution, one would be hard put to deny that the historical syntheses produced by the historians of this school are among the most interesting, challenging and masterly summaries ever written under the aegis of any philosophy of history.

As previously mentioned, the *opus magnum* of Hungarian *Geistesgeschichte* historiography is the multivolmed *Magyar History* by B. Hóman and G. Szekfű, which gave birth to innumerable lesser syntheses and which had a profound and still persisting effect on Hungarian historical thinking.(11) The "Hóman-Szekfű," as it is commonly known, however, had been preceded by several other lesser works of synthesis which pointed in that direction. Moreover, it was also preceded by a general effort on the part of a number of intellectuals to belabor the philosophical aspects of the *Geistesgeschichte* ideology, and to adapt it to the needs of contemporary Hungarian historical studies and other so-called "spiritual sciences."

The main credit for these efforts must go to the brilliant and indefatigable historian Szekfű, aided by the work of such other intellectuals as the literary critic T. Thienemann, literary historian J.

Horváth and social philosophers G. Kornis and I. Dékány. Their work in this area was particularly momentous during the 1920's.(12) But even they had their predecessors, as manifested in the largely anti-positivist and idea-oriented philosophical experimentations of such philosophers and social philosophers as K. Bohm (1846-1911), B. Alexander (1850-1927), O. Prohászka (1858-1927), G. Hornyánszky (1869-1933), A. Pauler (1876-1933), and others. A number of their important treatises of the late dualist period dealt with the connections between history and philosophy, and in particular with the impact of ideas upon historical evolution. As such, they may be regarded as forerunners of the Hungarian *Geistesgeschichte* School, which assigned an almost exclusive position to the role of ideas in the historical process.(13)

G. Szekfű, the Apostle of the Geistesgeschichte School

But to return to the main protagonist of *Geistesgeschichte* philosophy and approach in Hungarian historical studies, G. Szekfű, he too started out as a positivist historian. He wrote most of his research monographs in the pre-*Geistesgeschichte* period (prior to 1918), all of which are basically products of the Positivist School — although with growing attention to the philosophical and psychological factors as shapers of history. Szekfű's early positivism, however, should not come as a surprise. After all, he was the product of such great positivist masters as Marczali, Fejérpataky, Mika and Károlyi. Not until 1918 did he publish his first brief synthesis (a form which lends itself better to *Geistesgeschichte* treatment). This was his already mentioned *The Biography of the Hungarian State*, which was the first Hungarian work of historical synthesis that broke with the positivist tradition (the last major work of which was Marczali's *History of Hungary,* 1911) and tried to apply the more complex ideas-oriented approach to the examination of Hungarian historical evolution.(14)

In writing this synthesis for the series *Politische Bücherei* ("Political Library") edited by Erich Marcks in Berlin, Szekfű was still more influenced by the traditionalists L. Ranke and F. Meinecke than by Dilthey. Yet, by this time he had definitely turned away from positivism and he had also purged himself from the influences of such great romantics as J. Michelet, F. Mignet, T. Carlyle and T. Macaulay, or the Hungarian M. Horváth. Instead, he came to accept permanently Ranke's theory on the universality of ideas and of their impact and began to examine Hungarian developments primarily in terms of their relationship to external ideological developments.(15) Szekfű also accepted Ranke's views regarding the pre-eminence of diplomatic and political forces in the shaping of national histories and consequently — in light of the traditional German political and cultural dominance of East Central Europe — he came to treat Hungarian developments largely within the context of the so-called "Christian German Cultural Community," emphasizing the importance of Hungary's role in this Germanic cultural world.(16)

Yet, while Ranke's influence was all important in Szekfű's makeup as an historian, by the time he wrote his *Biography of the Hungarian State* he was also under the influence of Dilthey and his ideas-oriented view of history. Thus, for the first time he began to use such difficult-to-define concepts in his work as the "eternal" and "unchanging" "moral forces of Magyardom," which allegedly moved the Hungarian state through its millennial struggles for existence and pre-eminence in the Carpathian Basin.(17) These and similar concepts, which first appeared in his *Biography of the Hungarian State,* were only a step away from many other hardly more definable concepts which increasingly dotted his subsequent writings. These include such phrases as "the misty forces of the (Magyar) blood," the "racial strength" of Magyardom, the "collective spirit," the "folk spirit," the "collective and moral attitude," and the "eternal moral strength" of the Magyar nation, etc.(18) In Szekfű's view, these concepts, as applied to and manifested in the Magyars, were unique and quite distinct from all similar manifestations of all other nations.

Szekfű's Three Generations

Szekfű's views about the psycho-spiritual, but not necessarily biological uniqueness of the Magyar nation, as well as his *Geistesgeschichte* "methodology" became even more developed and more explicit in his most popular work, the *Three Generations* (1920).(19) This most influential of all interwar historial syntheses was prepared as Szekfű's own "spiritual and intellectual catharsis" following the collapse of the old order in 1918. "This book had to be written. This book is my personal experience," — wrote Szekfű in his introduction to the *Three Generations.* "In the midst of those trying conditions into which the catastrophe of October 1918 (the collapse of the Dual Monarchy) had thrust us, (and)the misery of which is felt first of all by us Hungarian intellectuals, I felt . . . that I would never be able to recover my strength and inclination for work until having taken account of the (causes of that) decline which had led us to this catastrophe; that is, until having confronted myself with the forces which had dragged my nation out of the stream of healthy evolution. Thus did I come to write this work, and . . . thus did I redeem my soul *(salvavi animam meam)*.'(20)

In light of the above, Szekfű's *Three Generations* cannot be regarded simply as just another narrative and analytical account of Hungary's nineteenth and early twentieth-century developments. It is different from a straight historical synthesis both in its motif and in its method of execution. It reflects the impressionistic features characteristic more of great creative works than of standard scholarly compendiums. Thus, it emerges as the first true *Geistesgeschichte* synthesis of a phase of the Hungarian past, with all the orchestration of ideas and other manifestations of the human spirit that only the greatest of *Geistesgeschichte* synthesizers could attain. For this reason, "it cannot be read with cool objectivity," but, as one of its recent critics had observed, "only with enthusiastic approval . . . or with an emotional disdain."(21) And so it was read during Szekfű's time, making it into one of the most influential ideologically potent works of the interwar period.

Szekfű's coverage, approach and ideological orientation are fully revealed in the subtitle of his work: "The History of a Declining Age." He understood the "Declining Age" to be the epoch between the Hungarian Reform Period, starting with c. 1825, and the collapse to the dualist system and of historic Hungary in 1918. He divided the epoch into three sub-periods, coinciding with the functioning of three distinct generations of Hungarian intellectual and political leaders. The period of the First Generation (c. 1825-1849) coincided with the Age of Reform, and was characterized by a gradual social, political and national progress. It was best portrayed and represented by the father of Hungarian national revival, Count István Széchenyi (1791-1860) and his "conservative reform program." As Szekfű said, the "eternal" and "unchanging" spiritual and intellectual forces of Magyardom, "which for a thousand years had carried on their shoulders the Hungarian state, came to be manifested in the person of Széchenyi." The only dissonant and disturbing voice in this general progress by the First Generation, in Szekfű's view, came from the direction of Lajos Kossuth (1802-1894) and his somewhat uncompromising followers who, with their well-meaning but rush demands and actions, hindered and ultimately frustrated the success of Széchenyi's wise and rational reform program. This reform program, according to Szekfű, consisted of an attempt to improve the social, economic and political conditions of his nation, and also of a desire to reform the "Magyar soul" and thus to alter the "whole inner subjective world of Magyardom."(22) With this interpretation, Szekfű turned basically against the rational (anti-idealist) interpretation of history and began to view Hungarian historical evolution more and more simply as the manifestation of the "Magyar national soul."

As to the basic cause of Hungarian decline? Szekfű identified this cause as "revolutionary liberalism" and the Magyar soul's inability to adjust itself to this alien phenomenon. While recognizing the merits and commending the ideas of classical liberalism — particularly as represented by such great Hungarian exponents of this ideology as J. Eötvös (1813-1971) and his "Centralist Circle" — Szekfű still regarded it as ultimately detrimental to Hungarian national evolution. He believed this to be so partially because of the "revolutionary and rational origins of liberalism," and even more importantly, because in his view this ideology unavoidably led to radicalism and revolution.(23) He correctly assessed these as inimical to Széchenyi's reform conservatism based on the idea of gradual change. What was even more significant, however, was the fact that Szekfű viewed radicalism and revolution as fundamentally contradictory to the needs of the "Magyar soul."

After praising the First Generation connected with the Age of Reform in Hungary,(24) Szekfű also commented favorably on the outstanding members of the Second Generation,(25) responsible for the Austro-Hungarian Compromise of 1867 and for restoring Hungary into a position of reasonable dignity and national independence (e.g. F. Deák, J. Eötvös, J. Andrássy). In his view "the Compromise had guaranteed our (Hungarian) independence to the greatest possible degree; much more so than (the constitution of) 1848."(26) He believed this to have been the result of the "temperate" and as yet "non-radicalized" liberalism that governed the hands of the makers of the Compromise.

In Szekfű's estimation, their death or departure from positions of leadership soon after the completion of the Compromise was one of the greatest misfortunes of Hungarian national life. They were then succeeded by their younger counterparts in whose hands liberalism soon "shallowed into materialism." The ensuing "materialistic liberalism" was simply not suited to the special Hungarian conditions. "It purged all conservative thought, all new idealism and all positive, gradual (and) corrective cultural orientation in the name of patriotism,"(27) but failed to provide the type of climate and leadership best suited for the special Hungarian conditions and the "Magyar soul." Yet, not until the period of the Third Generation (1890's-1918) — characterized by social and political chaos, the rule of mediocrities and such occasional heroes as the tragic Count István Tisza (1861-1918) and the brilliant but decadent poet Endre Ady (1877-1919) — did this process lead to a situation where "materialisitic liberalism" gave birth to various revolutionary orientations and movements, including bourgeois radicalism and Marxist socialism.(28)

If, as Szekfű asserted, liberalism was basically inimical to the "Magyar soul" even in its classical form, in its radicalized form it became totally unacceptable and contributed much to the downfall of the nation. It did this by helping to undermine the position of the Magyars vis-a-vis the national minorities; by contributing to the denationalization (cosmopolitanization) of the Magyar culture and national life through superficial assimilation of alien ethnic and cultural elements; and by reorienting the thinking of the Hungarian urban elements (largely of alien origins) and thereby making them easy preys of various revolutionary thoughts and movements.

In Szekfű's view, therefore, the "Magyar soul" was basically traditional, moderately progressive and anti-revolutionary. Thus, any theory that espoused radicalism and revolution was fundamentally alien to it. Therefore, the acceptance of any radical or revolutionary ideology (even in the form of radicalized liberalism) could only lead to catastrophe — as it did in 1918.

As we have seen, Szekfű's views on historical evolution were truly in line with the *Geistesgeschichte* philosophy of history, and he did make the allegedly unique spiritual attributes of his nation (as supposedly manifested in the "Magyar soul") a constant element in his historical synthesis. He also spoke of "Magyar race" and "Magyar ethnicity" almost as frequently as about the "Magyar soul," making these terms often interchangeable. Yet, Szekfű was not a racist in the conventional sense of that term. He was basically a tradition-oriented patriot, but with a powerful attachment to "Europeanism" and even cosmopolitanism. Thus, he rejected Gobineau's and Chamberlain's conceptions of a "race" with allegedly unique biological and intellectual attributes, regarding it simply as an historical-cultural-spiritual phenomenon, the result of a long historical-cultural evolution.(29) Consequently, while effusing belief in his nation's special destiny and role in the Danubian Basin, Szekfű's ideas were free from the ethno-mythical conceptions of some of his contemporaries, such as Dezső Szabó (1879-1945) and the various Turanists and Right Radicals. To Szekfű, a nation had no ethno-mythical only historical, cultural, moral and emotional identity.(30)

Chapter IX

THE "MINERVA CIRCLE" AND OTHER PROPHETS OF *GEISTESGESCHICHTE*

The post-*fin de siècle* philosophical experimentations by B. Alexander, V. Bőhm, O. Prohászka, G. Hornyánszky, A. Pauler and others, and Szekfű's path-breaking historical syntheses of the post-1918 period gave a firm foundation to the *Geistesgeschichte* orientation in Hungarian historiography, while also establishing the latter as the "father" of the Hungarian version of this orientation. Szekfű, however, was not alone in his aim to lift the Hungarian *Geisteswissenschaften* ("spiritual sciences") out of the unimaginative shallowness into which they had sunk during the late positivist period connected with his "Third Generation." As already mentioned, he was aided in this goal by several other scholars, working in related fields, such as the literary critic T. Thienemann, the literary historian J. Horváth, the philosopher G. Kornis, the social-philosopher I. Dékány, as well as others.

Thienemann and the "Minerva Circle"

The most important among these by far, from the point of view of spreading and popularizing this philosophical trend, was T. Thienemann (b. 1890), the founder of the "Minerva Society" (1921-1944) and the editor of the society's official organ of the same name (*Minerva,* 1922-1940) — both of which were dedicated to the cause of the Dilthey-inspired *Geistesgeschichte* orientation.(1)

The Minerva Society came into being in May of 1921 with the self-proclaimed goal of "cultivating this history of Hungarian spiritual life."(2) This was soon followed in 1922 by the establishment of the journal *Minerva,* which thus became Hungary's first and most theoretical forum of the Hungarian *Geistesgeschichte* ideology and — strangely enough — predated even its leading German counterpart, the *Deutsche Vierteljahrschrift für Literaturwissenschaften und Geistesgeschichte* (German Quarterly for Literature and *Geistesgeschichte).*(3)

Most of the society's founding members came from the professorial staff of Eötvös College in Budapest, and in particular from the faculty of the Royal Elizabeth University. Founded just before the First World War in 1914 at Pozsony (Pressburg, Bratislava), with Hungary's territorial losses following the war the Elizabeth University had to spend several years in exile in Budapest. Not until 1923 did it finally find a permanent home at Pécs, the site of Hungary's first medieval university (1367), which also meant in effect the relocation of the Minerva movement to that city.(4)

Thienemann remained the intellectual leader of the Minerva movement throughout its existence, even though the founding membership included such noted exponents of the *Geistesgeschichte* School as the philosopher Kornis, the literary historian Horváth, and the medievalist Hóman (Szekfű's co-author of the great *Magyar History),* not to mention Szekfű himself. Simultaneously, however, the membership also included several other great scholars who, while toying with *Geistesgeschichte* ideas, were never fully captivated by this philosophical orientation (e.g. the linguist J. Melich, the Turkologist G. Németh, the constitutional-legal historian F. Eckhart, the socio-cultural historian S. Domanovszky, etc.).(5)

Although the movement was founded in Budapest, with the shift of the Elizabeth University to Pécs, the Minerva Circle's center of gravity also shifted to that ancient center of Hungarian higher learning; and with it perhaps also the center of Hungarian *Geistesgeschichte* studies. While in some ways beneficial, this shift contained the seeds of the Minerva movement's future decline — the most important being its inevitable isolation from the center of Hungarian intellectual and cultural life, Budapest. Thienemann naturally tried to retain his journal's national profile, but despite his efforts, after 1923 the *Minerva* increasingly became the forum of the so-called "Pécs group" of the Minerva movement. Initially this group included the majority of the illustrious founding members. But as their numbers shrank — primarily through transfer to the more prestigious University of Budapest — so did the influence and effectiveness of the Pécs-centered *Minerva* and of the whole Minerva movement. This was particularly true after Thienemann's own promotion to Budapest in 1934, when the *Minerva* ceased to appear as a regular journal and continued only in the form of irregular issues until 1940.(6) (The "Minerva Books" initiated in 1924, which contained dissertations and reprinted studies from Thienemann's journal, however, appeared right up to the end of 1944.)(7) Moreover, in view of Szekfű's and Hóman's continued presence in Budapest throughout the interwar period, and in light of the foundation of Szekfű's own less theoretical *Hungarian Review (Magyar Szemle)* in 1927 in Budapest,(8) one may even question whether the center of Hungarian *Geistesgeschichte* movement had really ever left Budapest, despite the Minerva movement's relocation to Pécs. This is particularly questionable with respect to the discipline of history, as Thienemann's *Minerva* was always primarily a literary and a theoretical journal. Its area of interest was first of all Germanistics, followed by the study of Romance and Latin humanistic literature.(9)

In its philosophical orientation, the *Minerva* had three distinct goals: The *Geistesgeschichte* elaboration of the Hungarian past, the description and interpretation of the most current German philosophical orientations for the Hungarian reading public, and the establishment of the philosophical basis of "new Hungarian idealism."(10)

The first of these goals was by far the most successful, particularly in the area of the history of ideas, where such related disciplines as history, literary history, cultural and art history touched one another. And here the *Minerva* did publish, as well as inspire numerous pioneering and worthy studies and monographs. This was also true in the area of transmitting and interpreting German philosophical trends to the learned Hungarian public. Not so, however, in the third of its goals, where — discounting a few attempts — the philosophical foundations of a "new Hungarian idealism" remained unfounded. All of the attempts in that direction were simply "too eclectic and artificial."(11) This is true even for the much debated *The Wanderer and the Fugitive* (1934) by L. Prohászka (1897-1963), a professor of philosophy and pedagogy at the University of Budapest (1930-1948).(12)

This attempt at producing a philosophical portrait of Magyar spirituality did not lack philosophical depth and intellectual comprehension. But it was so pessimistic about the past attainments and future potentialities of Magyar spirituality — which the author regarded simply a pale copy of its German counterpart — that not even the generally pessimistic Szekfű could bypass it without admonishing the author. As such, Prohászka's work was certainly not fit to serve as a foundation stone of the much sought after "new Hungarian idealism."(13)

While perhaps not in the mainstream of Hungarian thought, mention should also be made of a similar work by K. Pap (1897-1945), a self-conscious, messianic chronicler of the tragic fate of Hungarian Judaism. In his *Jewish Wounds and Sins* (1935), Pap had re-lived the "destiny," "doom," and "suicidial spirituality" of his people in a "gigantic mythical vision," and if anything, displayed a pessimism about their fate that exceeded even Prohászka's pessimism about the Magyars.(14)

Thienemann's Relationship to Szekfű

According to a recent able analyzer of Hungarian *Geistesgeschichte* ideology, "one of the most characteristic distinguishing features of Hungarian *Geistesgeschichte* was that it appeared not as a philosophy of history, (like its German counterpart), but as an applied philosophy of history."(15) Thus, from its very birth, it had certain specific ideological and political goals and functions, even though it refused to get involved in "immediate political questions." Its overall program, therefore, was closely linked to the "conscious worldview-forming purpose of *Geistesgeschichte,*" according to which it aimed to redraw Hungary's historical past "into one of the component elements of our present."(16)

Apparently, this was also one of Thienemann's and the Minerva Circle's goals; and it was certainly identical with Szekfű's purpose in his re-examination of Hungary's "Declining Age". This is best exemplified by Szekfű's attempt to sort out the "corrupting forces" of "radicalized liberalism," and to make the "true Magyar traditions" of Széchenyi into the seeds of resurrection for the present and the future. Thus, while approaching this question from two different directions (Szekfű's historical versus Thienemann's "purer theoretical" position), "the directions of their ideological conclusions were similar."(17) The Szekfű-drawn view of the Hungarian past — as elaborated in his *Magyar History,* as well as on the pages of the *Hungarian Review* — generally pervaded also the works of the *Minerva's* literary historians.

This unity of view between the *Minerva's* and the *Hungarian Review's* respective "circle of friends" was also true with respect to the Szekfű-inspired ideas on the nature of the Hungarian "national character," his concept of the "spiritual race" (as opposed to biological race) and his views on the "Europeanness" and the "cultural pre-emenince" of the Magyars in the Carpathian Basin. No less did the Thienemann-led Minerva Circle accept Szekfű's overall *Geistesgeschichte* approach to the treatment of the "spiritual sciences" which — contrary to various social, economic or other approaches — "made great social changes float and drift on a stream of ideas."(18)

Horváth, Kornis and Dékány in Hungarian Geistesgeschichte Studies

Thienemann's contribution to the Hungarian *Geistesgeschichte* School consisted largely of his having created a forum (the *Minerva)* for the elaboration, clarification and dissemination of the philosophical view of that school, as applicable to Hungarian literature and aesthetics. However, he had also contributed in the area of "pure theory," both in his highly praised *Basic Concepts of Literary History* (1930), as well as in his chapter "Literary History" in the oft-mentioned handbook of Hungarian *Geistesgeschichte* historical studies, *The New Paths of Hungarian Historiography* (1931).(19)

Outside of these purely theoretical and methodological studies Thienemann wrote very little. Not so J. Horváth (1878-1961), Szekfű's contemporary and close friend, and possibly the greatest of Hungary's modern literary historians.(20) Horváth was a prolific writer and excellent synthesizer, though perhaps not quite in the same class as Szekfű. His name is almost as closely connected with the re-evaluation of Hungarian literary developments, as is Szekfű's with the re-evaluation of Hungarian history. They both broke with the "liberal-positivist historical scholarship of the *fin de siècle,* as well as with the language boundaries and emotional hero-worship of the nationalist conceptualization of the past."(21) Thus, contrary to the nineteenth-century Hungarian approach, which excluded the study of all literary works written in other than the Magyar language and Magyar spirituality, Horváth made all of these works part of Hungarian literature, even if not of the *belles lettres* variety.

In line with his *Geistesgeschichte* orientation, Horváth also regarded the spirit as basic in social and economic developments and pointed to a "common spiritual form" as the chief collective achievement of national and social evolution. Yet, while stressing the primacy of the spirit, Horváth did not quite disregard the role and importance of social forces — as did many of the *Geistesgeschichte* synthesizers. Thus, he would tend to disagree with an historian who, when discussing the seventeenth and eighteenth-century relationship between the Hungarian landlords and their peasants, would assign primacy to "Baroque spirituality," as opposed to the "political oppression and economic exploitation" as the decisive factor in this relationship.(22) Or to put it more explicitly, while Szekfű and his *Geistesgeschichte* followers placed the influence of the undefinable spirit over that of all material and economic forces, Horváth was less convinced of the primacy of this spirit.

Although not as one-sided in his preference of the influence of the spirit over socio-economic forces as many others in the *Geistesgeschichte* school, Horváth was still basically an adherent of the ideas-dominated philosophy of history. Moreover, as most of the great minds of that period in Germanic Central Europe, he was also drawn to *Geistesgeschichte* by his antipathy toward "exact scholarship, scientific determinism and the unceasing fact-collecting" that characterized positivist historical scholarship, as well as by his preference for a panoramic and synthetic view of the past to which the *Geistesgeschichte* approach lent itself so well.(23)

This preference for the panoramic, idea-governed synthetic approach — as opposed to the positivistic, fact-gathering compendiums — had also characterized the views and works of two other important exponents of Hungarian *Geistesgeschichte,* the philosopher G. Kornis (1885-1958) and the social philosopher I. Dékány (1886-1965). Their approach, however, approximated more that of Szekfű and Thienemann than that of Horváth. This was so both because of the greater philosophical content of their work, as well as their almost exclusive emphasis on the history-shaping role of the spirit — to the exclusion of the primacy of the social and economic forces. This was particularly true about Kornis and his eclectic philosophical system, put together from the conservative elements of various contemporary German philosophical orientations, including the neo-Kantian dualist value philosophy and Diltheyan irrationalism. Kornis was also influenced by the contemporary crisis philosophies of Spengler and Ortega y Gasset and spoke up strongly against the frenzy of social ascendancy and "the diseased desire for social mobility," which allegedly characterized the turbulant masses of the day. In his view, "the rise of the masses" — to quote Ortega — could only lead to the dilution of the higher culture and to the universal ascendancy of mass mentality.(24)

Like his fellow *Geistesgeschichte* historians and philosophers Kornis too hoped to reconstruct and to understand human cultures in their entirety — a phenomenon that was unique to *Geistesgeschichte* historiography. But he was convinced that it could not really be attained through the traditional methods. He argued that the information available to us about the past is largely illusory and it has no rational relationship to what actually happened. Thus, this information has to be filtered through the historian's intuition; who then must "re-live" the past spiritually to be able to reconstruct it comparatively faithfully.(25)

As a social philosopher, Dékány was basically a proponent of contemporary Western sociological orientations, but with a heavy infusion of *Geistesgeschichte* spirituality.(26) And thus, he too was an opponent of anti-spiritualist (materialist) trends. This is evident both from his noteworthy attempts at an original, if ultimately eclectic, social philosophy (e.g. *The Fundamental Concepts of Social Philosophy*, (1933), *Today's Society*(1943), etc.), as well as from his *Methodology of Historiography* (1923), a volume that he contributed to *The Handbook of Hungarian Historical Sciences*.(27)

Both Kornis and Dékány wrote extensively, both held prominent social and cultural positions and both were influential in the shaping of the philosophical and historical thinking of interwar Hungary. Neither they, nor anyone else, however, wielded an influence that rivalled Szekfű's impact on the historical profession of that period.

Chapter X

TRIUMPH OF THE *GEISTESGESCHICHTE* SCHOOL

However important the work of the "Minerva Society" and of the literary and philosophical scholars who gathered around it, and however momentous the shadow-hunting elaboration of the *Geistesgeschichte* philosophers on a metaphysical level, the fate and future of the *Geistesgeschichte* historiography in Hungary was still basically in the hands of historians, and in particular in the hands of G. Szekfű.

In his early synthesizing works, Szekfű had established the desirability to transfer the foundations of Hungarian historiography from the once useful but now outdated positivistic to the more complex and sophisticated *Geistesgeschichte* orientation. Then he undertook to carry out this aim on two different levels: On the level of a scholarly, but popular journal, and on that of a major new scholarly synthesis of Hungarian history.

The Hungarian Review Society and the Hungarian Review

The scholarly-popular journal in question was the already cited *Hungarian Reivew (Magyar Szemle).* It was basically Szekfű's creation, and it soon emerged as the most sophisticated exponent of the ideas-oriented historical thinking in Hungary. (Thienemann's *Minerva* was too theoretical and abstract to achieve similar popularity.) Founded in 1927 as the most important publication of the Hungarian Review Society *(Magyar Szemle Társaság),* the *Hungarian Review* was sponsored by Hungary's prime minister, Count István Bethlen. Its ideological leadership, however, came from Szekfű.(1)

As expressed by Szekfű himself, the aim of the society and of its journal was "to bind the souls of several (Hungarian) generations together and to lead them toward better, more Magyar, and more human ideals."(2) On a less esoteric and more prosaic level, the *Hungarian Review* had three aims. The first of these was to lead the Hungarian reading public out of the stuffy self-contained world of "*extra Hungariam non est vita*" (there is no life outside Hungary) and to make them realize that their fate is intimately linked with the fate of Europe and of the surrounding nations. Secondly, the *Review* was intended to diagnose the internal maladies of Hungarian society, and then to suggest cures for these maladies. Finally, it was to keep a constant watch over the fate of the separated Magyar masses in the "Succession States" and overseas who — in Szekfű's view — had an important role to play in the hoped-for reconstitution of Hungary and of the Hungarian future.(3)

Although nationalist in purpose, these goals were to be fought for and partially attained within the context of a broader European frame of mind and with the ultimate goal of making the somewhat provincial-minded and Hungarocentric Magyars into broader-horizoned Europeans. Szekfű himself was an all-out "European" in the traditions of the great nineteenth-century thinker J. Eötvös whom he idealized, and his ideal civilization was the "European Christian Civilization" put forth by Eötvös as an example for the inward-oriented Magyars. Like Eötvös before him, Szekfű too regarded that civilization as "our greatest and only treasure, not to be sacrificed . . . for any (other) strange orientation (e.g. Turanism.)" The Hungarian version of that civilization, he added "was created by the Magyar ethnic stock here in Europe, in a thousand year old country, in close association with the eternal European spirit." The true Hungarian civilization ("eternal Hungarian culture") in Szekfű's view, therefore, was the product of the collective effort of Magyar ethnicity and of the "eternal European spirit," and to him it was "the only way of life within which we Magyars can hope to approach the eminence of the human spirit."(4)

In light of the *Hungarian Review's* goals (which included the hoped-for triumph of both the "eternal European" and the "eternal Hungarian" spirit), and in light of its quality (having the active support of many of Hungary's top intellectuals devoted to progressive national reform),(5) Szekfű's journal soon emerged as the number one scholarly-popular journal of the 1930's. Its impact on the young educated intellectuals was immense, and certainly more extensive than that of the older and more theoretical *Minerva* or of the younger *Vigilia,* founded in 1935. (The latter was the Catholic version of Szekfű's *Hungarian Review).*(6) Throughout its existence, the *Review* represented basically Szekfű's conception of the Hungarian future. This remained true even after 1938, when after thirteen years and 135 issues, Szekfű relinquished its editorship to S. Eckhardt. The latter continued to edit the *Review* right up to the end, which came in March 1944, in consequence of the German occupation of Hungary.(7)

The Hungarian Review Society's Other Publications

While the *Hungarian Review* was undoubtedly the most important of the Hungarian Review Society's publications which spread the belief in a better Hungarian future on an intellectual level, within the context of the ideas-dominated philosophy of history it was not its only publication. Thus, in 1929 and 1937, respectively, it was joined by three separate book series. These included the scholarly "Books of the *Hungarian Review*" (1929-1942), the popular "Treasurechest" paperback series (1929-1942) and the literature-oriented "Classics of the *Hungarian Review*" (1937-1942).(8) Of these three series, the first two were considerably more significant than the third, although their relative significance is difficult to assess. The "Books" and the "Classics" were directed more to the "learned public", while the popularly written small volumes of the "Treasurechest" more to the general public.

The seventeen volumes of the "Books" represented the work of twelve highly respected scholars of contemporary Hungary and contained some of the most influential works of that time. These included the still-to-be discussed *New Paths of Hungarian Historiography* under Hóman's editorship (1931);(9) two volumes of J. Horváth's epoch-making *Geistesgeschichte* synthesis of medieval Hungarian literature, *The Beginnings of Hungarian Literary Culture* (1931) and *The Diffusion of Hungarian Literary Culture* (1935); G. Farkas' great, if controversial study on Hungarian late romanticism, *The Age of "Young Hungary"* (1932); G. Gratz's two-volume synthesis, *The Age of Dualism* (1934); as well as Szekfű's own two theoretical works on the national and spiritual evolution of the Magyar nation, namely his *What is a Magyar?* (1939) and his *State and Nation: Studies on the Nationality Question* (1942).(10)

On the popular level, the hundred odd volumes of the "Treasurechest" were equally important. Advertised as Hungary's "only inexpensive book series with the aim of popularizing scholarship," it was indeed an encompassing and authorative series which presented "a short, yet thorough and enjoyable overview of virtually every branch of knowledge," both of Hungarian and non-Hungarian interest. As all of its select contributors (most of them well-known scholars in their fields) were adherents of the ideas-oriented philosophy of social evolution, this series also contributed much to the diffusion and popularization of the *Geistesgeschichte* orientation in Hungary.(11)

Of the Hungarian Review Society's three book series, the "Classics" were undoubtedly the least known and also the least influential. This was so both because of their late start (1937), as well as of the very nature of the series. While similarly ideologically motivated as the other two series, of the seven published volumes (really four works) only one, S. Eckhardt's *The Unknown Bálint Balassi* (1943), was of interpretative nature. The rest of them were anthologies or collections of early Hungarian prose writings, with little or no introductory studies.(12)

Hóman's and Szekfű's Magyar History

Whatever its faults or ommissions, the Hungarian Review Society and its various publications under Szekfű's idological leadership had contributed much to the spread, popularity and eventual triumph of the *Geistesgeschichte* ideology in Hungary. Yet, while the Society's impact was considerable, what was really needed to make this triumph a thorough one, was a new major synthesis of Hungarian history, written in the belief of the primary history-shaping role of the randomly manifested "human spirit." And this was precisely the work that Szekfű undertook during the mid-1920's conjointly with his duties at the University of Budapest and his work on the *Hungarian Review* and in collaboration with the distinguished medievalist B. Hóman (1885-1951). The result of their common effort was the celebrated and envied, praised and castigated, demeaned yet unparalleled multivolumed *Magyar History* (1927-1934) — commonly known as the "Hóman-Szekfű."(13) Notwithstanding its unavoidable errors, some questionable judgments and perhaps faulty spiritual, ideological and political orientation, and notwithstanding its quarter century of official dethronement by post-1945 Hungarian Marxist historiography, this work is still unsurpassed today. It is the most vibrant and inspiring synthesis of Hungarian history; and it will always remain one of the great classics in its field.

The Motivating Forces Behind the Magyar History

Like Hungarian *Geistesgeschichte* philosophy itself, Hóman's and Szekfű's *Magyar History* was also connected with the series of catastrophies arising out of World War I. The subsequent political and social disorganization created a need for the re-examination of the Hungarian past. Out of this need was born Szekfű's *Three Generations*, and it was this same need that produced the *Magyar History*. As expressed by Hóman's preface to this work: "Our generation had experienced so much that its interest in the past could not be satiated any more by the historians of a by-gone age — even if only of thirty years ago."(14) And here he was referring primarily to the great positivist historians, whose synthetic works had in fact been written for readers of a quite different world and mentality. Be it the Szilágyi-edited ten-volume "Millennial History" *(The History of the Hungarian Nation,* 1895-1898) or any of the smaller works by such historians as J. Szalay *(The History of the Hungarian Nation,* 1873-1883), I. Ácsády *(The History of the Hungarian Empire,* 1903-1904) or H. Marczali *(History of Hungary,* 1911), these works had been written for a different generation, living in a totally different social and intellectual world. Contrary to the postwar generation, they were interested almost exclusively in political and constitutional questions, particularly as related to Hungary's relationship to Austria. The interest of the postwar generation, however, had been turned largely to "social, economic and spiritual-historical problems."(15)

Finding themselves confronted with a multitude of new problems, the generation of the interwar years tended to view even old questions from different perspective. Thus, with the collapse of Austria-Hungary and the dualist system, many previously acute political and historical questions had lost their original meaning and currency (e.g. Habsburg-Hungarian relations) and could now be examined free from everyday political pressures. Even more importantly, however, interwar Hungarian historiography had "much more perfect means at its disposal relative to the usefulness and validity of sources than (the historiography of) a generation earlier." Moreover, its scholarly goals have also changed radically. Thus, contrary to the old positivistic method of compartmentalized synthesizing, the new aim was "to conceive the whole of history as a single organic process." For, just as they believed that "human history is nothing but the history of the human soul," the *Geistesgeschichte* historians were also convinced that "the soul cannot be partitioned into sections." In writing their new synthesis, therefore, the two authors of the *Magyar History* knew that each of the major epochs of the Hungarian past must contain "the soul of all Magyardom, (as well as) the whole of the Magyar Soul."(16)

Hóman as a Geistesgeschichte Historian

Without going into a discussion of co-author Hóman's prior achievements as an historian, and without trying to demean his undoubtedly enviable contribution to the *Magyar History,* it must be pointed out that there does exist an evident quality and readability difference between Hóman's and Szekfű's respective contributions to this major compendium — to the distinct advantage of the latter. This seems to be due partially to Hóman's lack of adequate philosophical preparation and understanding and his consequent inability to integrate fully the *Geistesgeschichte* conceptions into his synthesizing works.(17) But it is due perhaps even more to Szekfű's enviable philosophical comprehension and synthesizing ability. Unable to master thoroughly the complex synthesizing methodology of the *Geistesgeschichte* School, Hóman's section of the *Magyar History* appears slightly forced wherein the *Geistesgeschite* orientation is exhausted largely in the use of relevant, but mostly pompous and bombastic terminology. Moreover, contrary to the more somber Szekfű, Hóman became much more entangled in Hungarian "great power dreams," which he projected generously into his treatment of several medieval epochs of Hungarian history (e.g. the periods of St. Ladislas, Béla III and Louis the Great). Thus, his work on the medieval period of Hungarian history is probably more "myth-seeking" and "myth-creating" and intellectually less inspiring than that of Szekfű on the early modern and modern periods. Undoubtedly, in his strive to keep up with the high philosophical demands of the synthesizing, ideas-dominated *Geistesgeschichte* School, Hóman often over-exerted himself and then tried to hide his bewilderment in the sonorous phraseology of his adopted, but not fully digested historical ideology.(18)

For this same reason (coupled with his growing involvement in politics), Hóman was never able to complete his originally assigned share of the *Magyar History.* Thus, it was Szekfű who — after completing his own share — had to go back to write also the section on the late-fifteenth and early sixteenth century (1458-1526) originally assigned to Hóman. This in turn, allegedly led to some periodization dislocations in Szekfű's original plan from the vantage point of the *Geistesgeschichte* philosophy. This dislocation is best examplified in his assignment of the Hungarian Renaissance to the age of Matthias Corvinus in the second half of the fifteenth century, even though in terms of the society as a whole (which in Corvinus's time still retained a "Gothic world view"), it should have been assigned to the sixteenth century.(19)

Problems of Periodization in the Magyar History

Although many objections have been raised against its approach, periodization and ideological orientation, few would deny an element of brilliance in Szekfű's section of the *Magyar History*. In addition to its captivating brilliance, due largely to Szekfű's unique capacities as a "born writer" and synthesizer, there are two factors which most characterize his synthesis. The first of these is the presence of several noticeable, though understandable dislocations in his periodization (one of which we have already alluded to). The second is his interpretation of Hungarian history from the sixteenth through the twentieth century, largely within the context of a perpetual struggle between the so-called "Little Hungarian" and the "Great Hungarian" ideas.

The periodization dislocations are particularly evident in connection with the Hungarian Renaissance and the Hungarian Baroque periods. As already mentioned in an earlier section of this work, the terminology of *Geistesgeschichte* periodization has been borrowed by historians from areas of cultural and literary history, wherein the various succeeding epochs are all characteristic of a specific type of spirituality, attitude, world view and life style. Thus, this system tends to speak of the Romanesque spirit and life style, followed by the Gothic, Renaissance, Baroque, Enlightened, Romantic, etc. spirit, attitude, world view and life style — with perhaps only certain regionally meaningful sub-periods and dislocations in time. These dislocations in time are particularly evident in the case of East Central Europe which — as the eastern most section of the Latin Christian World — was usually the last to feel the impact of the successive waves of new spiritual-cultural forces. Thus, the Italian Renaissance of the fifteenth and early sixteenth century, the Spanish-French Baroque of the late sixteenth through the early eighteenth century, and the French Enlightenment of the late seventeenth and the eighteenth century naturally reached East Central Europe somewhat later than it did the neighboring states of Western Europe. It also took longer for these trends to develop in these borderlands of Western Civilization. Moreover, initial Western influences usually affected the outlook and life style of only the ruling classes. Thus the impact of these movements among the masses in general was considerably delayed. But however delayed, the sequence of these trends and influences never changed. Moreover, while certain local sub-epochs may have been interjected here and there, these basic spiritual-cultural-historical trends could hardly be separated from one another by two centuries in time — as in the case of Szekfű's "Hungarian

Renaissance'' (second half of the fifteenth century) and ''Hungarian Baroque'' (eighteenth century). He simply placed the former too early, and the latter too late.(20)

Szekfű's misplacement of the Hungarian Renaissance can be explained, at least partially, by the cited technical problems which obliged him to deal with the question of the Renaissance after he had already completed the post-1526 history of Hungary. Even more important, perhaps, is the fact that at the time when he composed his scheme for sixteenth-century developements, his *Geistesgeschichte* views on the evolution of Hungarian history were still in a state of flux. Apparently, he saw sixteenth-century Hungarian developments more within the context of the Ottoman-Habsburg clash than in the light of the dominance of the Renaissance spirit and life style. Moreover, in his subsequent treatment of the late-fifteenth century, he was misled by the truly Renaissance life style of the Royal Court of Matthias Corvinus (1458-1490), at the time when ''the masses were still the followers of the Gothic world view'' and life style.(21)

As to Szekfű's misplacement of the Hungarian Baroque into the eighteenth century, apparently this too was the byproduct of certain outside factors, among them the embryonic state of contemporary Baroque studies. In point of fact, Szekfű's composition of his volumes on the sixteenth and seventeenth century in the late 1920's went virtually hand-in-hand with the maturation of European Baroque studies. Thus, not until his volume on the eighteenth century was he sufficiently up-to-date intellectually to attempt a treatment of a portion of Hungarian history within the context of the Baroque spirit and life style.(22)

While perhaps somewhat out of place, Szekfű's placement of the Hungarian Baroque to the eighteenth century is at least understandable. Although the Baroque spirit in Western Europe had already relinquished its place to that of the Enlightenment, it was still important in the Habsburg Empire of that period, even though it had to share its influence with the growing spirit of the Enlightenment. But as Szekfű's staunch critic, E. Mályusz had pointed out in a number of polemical studies against Szekfű's views, the persistence of certain Baroque influences in the eighteenth century did not necessarily make that into ''the Baroque century in Hungary''. In point of fact, as Mályusz asserts, the Baroque spirit and life style had already reached Hungary in the early seventeenth century and — displacing the Renaissance outlook of the sixteenth century — it had become the dominant spiritual and historical force at least in two sections of the trisected country: Habsburg Hungary and Transylvania. (Turkish Hungary remained basically unaffected by these trends of West European origin.) Mályusz also believes that had Szekfű had the energy and spiritual strength to rewrite his work thoroughly, in all probability he would have made a number of significant changes in the construction of his scheme of post-Renaissance Hungarian history. Without such a strength, however, he was forced to defend his position, perhaps even against his own better sense.(23)

"Great Hungarian" versus "Little Hungarian" Views in the Magyar History

In addition to his unorthodox periodization scheme, the most evident feature of Szekfű's work is his interpretation of post-fifteenth-century Hungarian history within the context of the "Little Hungarian" versus "Great Hungarian" ideas. Superficially, this appears to be simply a refined version of the old "*kuruc* versus *labanc*" (anti-Habsburg versus pro-Habsburg) conception that had characterized Hungarian historiography of the dualist period. At closer look, however, it becomes rather evident that Szekfű intended it to be something else: He hoped to view and evaluate the modern history of the Magyars not in terms of petty factionalism and fratricidal internal struggles, but rather by pitting universalism against provincialism and by looking at events of history from the vantage point of long-range national goals and universal human values.(24)

As summed up by Szekfű himself in an essay written parallel with his great synthesis of Hungarian history, the traditional *kuruc* or "Little Hungarian" concept of history was essentially a simplicistic view which saw Hungary's history within the Habsburg realm simply in terms of good versus evil. In the popular *kuruc* view, good was always represented by the anti-Habsburg and the evil by pro-Habsburg forces. Such a view, however, in Szekfű's estimation was not only unscholarly, but it also produced a completely distorted picture of Hungarian historical developments. Its most important flaw was that it con-condemned certain developments, events and individuals outright without attempting to evaluate the specifics involved, while at the same time praising others simply on the basis of their political alignment.(25)

In Szekfű's view, one of the direct results of the influence of the "Little Hungarian" concept was that Hungarian historiography "placed the study of a series of freedom ideas into the very center of historical interest." This alone produced a "distortion of perspectives," however, for — not being a nation of slaves — there were several extended periods in the history of the Magyars "wherein the freedom question played little or no role whatsoever." The historians of the "Little Hungarian" concept, however, paid no attention to these periods and virtually eliminated them from the history of the nation.(26)

One of the direct consequences of this attitude — as represented by *kuruc* historians — was a distorted view about the role and relative importance of "Royal Hungary" (Habsburg Hungary) and of Transylvania during the two centuries of struggle for the resurrection of unified Hungary. Thus, in the light of this view, "every move by the Principality of Transylvania was portrayed as a struggle for freedom, and the state of Transylvania itself emerged as the symbol of Hungarian liberty and consequently as the sole foundation of Hungarian history."(27) As opposed to this, the role of Royal Hungary and of the pro-Habsburg nobility was constantly demeaned and castigated by these historians. At the best, their role was looked upon with suspicion; but most of the time simply as treasonable. Their "quiet, unceasing work, their self-sacrificing role between the Turks and the Germans and their political wisdom devoid of extremism — none of which could fit into the freedom-oriented historical concept — were usually left unmentioned by 'Little Hungarian' historiography." The result was generally the "crude demeaning of the Western Magyars in Royal Hungary."(28)

What Szekfű hoped to achieve with his new synthesis of Hungarian history was to restore the balance of the distorted picture of the Magyar past by giving justice to these unheralded heroes of Hungarian history, and by elevating their more "universal" approach to historical and political questions to a position of respect. In trying to achieve this goal, however, he may have overdone his "balancing," tilting the picture in the other direction. The reasons for this may be sought partially in the political realities of the day, and partially in his own relatively traditional political orientation.

The Political Realities Behind Szekfű's View of Hungarian History

The political realities which dictated Szekfű's reorientation of Hungarian historical studies all stemmed from Hungary's political and geographical mutilation at the Treaty of Trianon in 1920. However imperfect the dualist system (Austria-Hungary) may have been, and whatever Hungary's real or imagined disadvantages within that system from the point of view of Magyar nationalism, the country's pre-1918 position was still far superior to her position following the dismemberment of Austria-Hungary and with it historic Hungary itself. It was only natural, therefore, that many Hungarians should turn with nostalgia to the formerly castigated dualist period and to view even the role of the Habsburgs and of the Habsburg Empire in a more positive light than previously. And Szekfű was no different. This was especially so in light of his general political and ideological outlook, which was always more European and German oriented than those of most of his contemporaries. To this must be added his so-called "conservative reformist" ideas, which he had borrowed from the great nineteenth-century pioneer of Hungarian political and social reform, Count István Széchenyi, and which had already dominated his *Three Generations*.(29)

Szekfű's conservative reformist outlook was based essentially on his attachment to the idea of gradual reform as opposed to revolution; on his conviction that religious faith is an essential ingredient of a healthy social order and social progress; and on his rejection of all violent revolutions and of all ideologies which were contrary to peaceful, gradual and ordered social progress. On top of this — as mentioned earlier — Szekfű was also an apostle of the idea of a unitary European Christian Civilization (as developed by Eötvös), and he was unable to visualize a healthy Hungarian national evolution outside the confines of the so-called "German Christian Cultural Community." And it so happened that his "Great Hungarian" views were more in harmony with this idea than with any of the more nationalistic but also more provincial conceptions of Hungarian history.

As we have seen, Hóman's and Szekfű's *Magyar History* differred from its noted predecessors in a number of ways, and this difference came to be expressed in its very title. Thus, it was not entitled the "History of Hungary," "Hungarian State," or of the "Hungarian Empire" — like many of its positivistic predecessors — but rather *Magyar History,* as if to signify the shift of emphasis from statehood to ethnicity.(30) In light of the new realities (that is the destruction of historic Hungary as a political entity), the new synthesis aimed to be the history less of the Hungarian state and more of the Magyars, or perhaps the history of the manifestations of the "Magyar Soul." Whatever the merits of this goal and whatever the achievements and failures of this work, the "Hóman-Szekfű" certainly came closest to capturing the spiritual aspects of Hungarian history.(31)

The New Paths of Hungarian Historiography

Even before completing their joint *opus magnum* in 1934, Hóman, Szekfű and their allies and supporters felt ready to take account of their achievements and to outline the remaining goals of Hungarian *Geistesgeschichte* historiography in light of this self-assessment. This project was completed and published in the form of the *New Paths of Hungarian Historiography* in 1931, to which eleven prominent scholars have contributed.(32) Of these eleven scholars, however, perhaps only as few as six were unqualified devotees of the *Geistesgeschichte* view of history as interpreted by Hóman and Szekfű. In addition to Hóman and Szekfű themselves, this group included Thienemann, Dékány, Gerevich and perhaps Révész. Of the remaining five scholars, two (Mályusz and Eckhart) had serious reservations about the Hungarian version of the German *Geistesgeschichte* School, while three others (Szentpétery, Tompa, and Németh) worked in disciplines which simply did not lend themselves well to *Geistesgeschichte* treatment.

Hóman's Orientation of the New Paths

The tone of the volume was set by Hóman's introductory study, which may be regarded either as a orientation-setting study, or simply as a summary of the basic *Geistesgeschichte* views about the several disciplines represented in the volume. In all probability, both of these elements were involved for, while displaying an orientation-setting tone, Hóman's essay rested heavily on the other studies of the volume.(33)

The purpose of the *New Paths* was also twofold: To sum up the past achievements of historical studies in general, and then to direct the future orientation of Hungarian historiography toward an anti-materialist view of history. Hóman spoke strongly against all "materialist" conceptions. In his view, this category included, in addition to Marxist historical materialism, both positivism (in its philosophical aspects), as well as Spencerian organic sociology as it influenced historical studies. In denouncing materialism and all materialist conception of historical evolution, Hóman — of course — was simply reaffirming his belief in idealism and the idealist view of history. "Our path today," he said, "proceeds toward idealism and toward a more worthy appreciation of spiritual phenomena." Contrary to earlier assumptions, however, he denied that *Geistesgeschichte* was simply or even primarily a philosophical or ideological orientation. "In the definition of an historian," he explained, "it is purely a methodological conception, without any sense of content or form.'' Hóman identified this ''methodology'' as the ''application of (historical) assessments, based on the knowledge of the spirituality of individuals and of ages,'' through the intuitive ''re-living of the spirituality of past ages.''(34)

Hóman concluded his study with a brief philosophization about the new ''true nationalism which combines all national values,'' is based on ''absolute truth'' and is leading the nation toward a new moral and national resurrection. This ''true nationalism'' was undoubtedly to be a part of the new historical science in Hungary, which was to aid the Magyars in their strive for moral and national resurrection.(35)

The Pro-Geistesgeschichte Essays of the New Paths

Hóman's tone-setting essay was followed by ten topical essays on such diverse sub-disciplines and auxiliary sciences of history as literary history (Thienemann), art history (Gerevich), church history (Révész), economic and social history (Dékány), ''ethnohistory'' (Mályusz), legal and constitutional history (Eckhart), archeology (Tompa), linguistics, (Németh), auxiliary sciences (Szentpétery) and political history (Szekfű). All of these essays dealt basically with the past achievements and future goals of the respective disciplines, but only those of Szekfű, Thienemann, Gerevich, Dékány and Révész were basically of the *Geistesgeschichte* orientation.

Szekfű's study on political history had already been mentioned in conjunction with his contribution to the *Magyar History.* It certainly is one of the most successful pleas for the need of an ideas-oriented philosophy and a complex synthesizing approach to the study of history. In Szekfű's view, the commonly practiced ''political history'' had no validity in modern historical studies, for ''the state and all political phenomena were only appendices of social, economic (and) cultural momentums.'' All of these, in turn, were products of the individual and collective national spirits of the age.(36)

Similar ideas-oriented summaries were prepared by Thienemann in literary history and Gerevich in art history. Thienemann's essay was on an even higher metaphysical level than that of either Hóman or Szekfű.(37) In light of his activities around the *Minerva,* however, this was expectable. His aims were, on the one hand, to point out the importance of literary events in historical developments, and on the other, to emphasize that only through historical and metaphysical idealism can one arrive at a true understanding of the historical process.

Although on a lower philosophical level, Gerevich's essay was also an all-out *Geistesgeschichte* presentation.(38) Gerevich, however, went further than expected in claiming primacy for art history in the area of *Geistesgeschichte* orientations. Disregarding many of the claims of the late nineteenth and early twentieth-century prophets of this ideas-oriented school, he declared that "*Geistesgeschichte* is neither a new orientation, nor a new methodology in art history; but rather the not-always-attained climax of a type of methodology which had already been used before."(39) With this claim Gerevich placed art history into the role of the fathership of all "spiritual sciences" *(Geisteswissenschaften)*. He was able to do this all the more so, as most of the periodization terms, as well as much of the spirit of the new synthesizing approach — allegedly depicting the divergent attitudes and life styles at various periods — had in fact been borrowed from art history (e.g. Romanesque, Gothic, Renaissance, Baroque, etc. attitudes and life styles). Gerevich tried to demonstrate the truth in his assertion by reference to Italian artistic developments, and in particular to the Age of the Baroque in Italy. Like Hóman and Szekfű, Gerevich also displayed his dislike of materialism by speaking up strongly against all anti-spiritualist philosophies of history. As he said, "the final synthesis of all serious art history is of the *Geistesgeschichte* variety."(40)

Dékány's and Révész's essays, although similarly structured and oriented, were perhaps less important in their impact. Dékány, was simply too theoretical and abstract for the topic of his essay (economic and social history);(41) while Révész's topic (church history) was relatively inconsequential in Hungarian historical studies.(42) Not so the studies of the two prominent sceptics of the *Geistesgeschichte* orientation, Mályusz and Eckhart. Both of their contributions created quite a stir in Hungarian scholarly and political circles. But as about this time Mályusz became the founder of the so-called "Ethnohistory School," and Eckhart the re-founder of Hungarian legal and constitutional history, their essays will be treated in conjunction with the discussion of their respective subdisciplines.(43)

The Positivistic Essays of the New Paths

Of the remaining three scholars, Szentpétery was in the "auxiliary sciences," Tompa in archeology and Németh in linguistics and Turcology. At the time of the publication of their essays all three held chairs at the University of Budapest and all of them tried to adjust their philosophies of history to the triumphant *Geistesgeschichte* orientation. Due to limitations stemming from their disciplines, however, none of them were able to go beyond the occasional use of *Geistesgeschichte* phraseology.

From the vantage point of an historian, the most relevant of these three studies was Szentpétery's essay on the "auxiliary sciences."(44) As the most promising student of L. Fejérpataky (the transplanter of the German scientific methodology to Hungary) and as his successor to the chair of Heraldry and Diplomatics at Budapest (1923-1950), Szentpétery was already a man of considerable achievements. In his contribution to *The New Paths of Hungarian Historiography* he discussed the past and present status of such traditional auxiliary sciences and subdisciplines in Hungary as diplomatics, palaeography, epigraphy, sfragistics, heraldry, numismatics, genealogy and chronology, and did so basically on a traditional positivistic basis. While he did use some *Geistesgeschichte* phraseology, his topic was simply not pliable enough for a philosophical treatment. Moreover, Szentpétery was not at all convinced of the superiority of the *Geistesgeschichte* approach when it came to basic research. As he pointed out, whatever the goals and philosophical orientation of historiography, "historical scholarship cannot build a solid super-structure without a thorough knowledge of the sources."(45) He also remained unconvinced that the "comparative method" — a much heralded feature of the *Geistesgeschichte* approach — was unique to that school. In his estimation, it had already been known and used by a number of cultural historians long before the rise of the Dilthey-inspired *Geistesgeschichte* orientation. All that this new school did, he thought, was to popularize the idea and to gain wide acceptance for the methodology of historical comparison.(46)

If Szentpétery's treatment was basically positivistic, this was even more true for Tompa's and Németh's discussion of the state and goals of Hungarian archeology and linguistics, respectively, as auxiliary sciences of history. F. Tompa (1893-1945) was the first incumbent in the Chair of Pre-Classical Archeology (1938-1945) and G. Németh (b. 1890) the internationally known Vámbéry's successor to the Chair of Turkish Philology (1916-1970) at the University of Budapest. The lack of relevance of their topic in the debate over the merits and goals of Hungarian *Geistesgeschichte* historiography was rather evident in both their studies. Neither Tompa, nor Németh could go beyond describing the past contributions and future usefulness of their respective disciplines as aids for Hungarian historical research. Thus, their essays — despite their innate merits — added little to the cause of the *Geistesgeschichte* School, nor to the intent of the handbook in which they appeared.(47)

Despite the evident shortcomings of this Hóman-edited handbook of the Hungarian *Geistesgeschichte* School (e.g. the inclusion of basically positivistic essays, the lack of agreement on the meaning, content and purpose of the new orientation, etc.), one may still agree with the assessment that "*The New Paths of Hungarian Historiography* — (did) provide a theoretical base for the ever more triumphant *Geistesgeschichte* methodology." Nor can one deny that "by placing positivism on the same level with Marxism," i.e., by classifying both as materialist and anti-idealist philosophies, this work also served as a *coup de grace* to the once dominant Positivist School.(48) The appearance of *The New Paths* therefore (at the time when the great new synthesis, the *Magyar History* was also beginning to have its impact felt), signalled both the end of the old and the beginning of the new epoch in Hungarian historical studies. For all appearances' sake, henceforth the *Geistesgeschichte* orientation ruled supreme. This outward view, however, was deceptive. Underneath the apparent dominance of the *Geistesgeschichte* School, old forces had been preserved, and new forces were flexing their muscles.

Chapter XI
THE DIFFUSION AND DIFFERENTIATION OF *GEISTESGESCHICHTE* HISTORIOGRAPHY: THE RISE OF A YOUNG GENERATION

The appearance of the tone-setting *New Paths of Hungarian Historiography* (1931) and the completion of Hóman's and Szekfű's *Magyar History* (1934) produced an atmosphere of triumph for the *Geistesgeschichte* School in Hungary. This seeming triumph was made even more convincing by the publication of several large compendiums and shorter syntheses of history and literary history, all of which professed at least superficial adherence to the *Geistesgeschichte* philosophy of history.

In the field of history, these shorter syntheses included a dozen or more one-volume histories, based largely on Hóman's and Szekfű's *Magyar History*.(1) But they also included the multivolumed *Universal History* (1935-1936)(2) and the folio sized volumes of the *Saint Stephen Memorial Album* (1938).(3) The latter work combined the efforts of dozens of Hungarian scholars with the aim of orchestrating their slightly mystifying views on the special mission of the Magyars in the Carpathian Basin.

Whatever the scholarly merits of these works, most of the *Geistesgeschichte* syntheses were much more lively and readable than their positivistic predecessors. But for sheer brilliance as a synthesis of whatever orientation, none of them came close to A. Szerb's *History of Hungarian Literature* (1934). As a synthesis this work remains unequalled even today. Moreover, it contains the best short summary on the application of the *Geistesgeschichte* philosophy to literary history.(4)

The Young Generation

While significant in themselves, the importance of these new syntheses and collective works was at least equalled by the importance of the rising new generation of historians. These young scholars were generally products of the *Geistesgeschichte* School. Ultimately, however, they contributed not only to the diffusion, but also to the differentiation of the *Geistesgeschichte* philosophy. In addition to the literary historian A. Szerb (1901-1945), these young historians included T. Joó, B. Iványi-Grünwald, P. Váczy, J. Deér, G. Istványi, D. Kosáry and others. Some of them dealt with the philosophy of history, while others concentrated on various aspects of Hungarian or European history. What brought them together was that all of them started out as exponents of the *Geistesgeschichte* School. Later, however, they grew apart and gave birth to several new trends that amplified, diffused and differentiated that school. Thus, by the early 1940's, the still dominant *Geistesgeschichte* orientation was closer to a multicolored spectrum than to a homogeneous philosophy of history.

Tibor Joó: The Philosopher of the Young Generation

Being more of a philosopher than an historian, T. Joó (1901-1945) was concerned first of all with the philosophical aspects of the *Geistesgeschichte* School. But being interested primarily in the philosophy of history, his most significant goal was to apply the *Geistesgeschichte* philosophy to Hungarian historical evolution.(5)

Joó's most significant philosophical work is his *Introduction to Geistesgeschichte* (1935), wherein he summarized the essence of this philosophy of history.(6) His conclusions are self-evident: "Spirit" is the true motivating force of historical evolution and *Geistesgeschichte* is the methodology that best explains this role of the spirit.(7)

After summarizing the essence of the *Geistesgeschichte* philosophy and methodology, Joó began to apply *Geistesgeschichte* to Hungarian historical evolution. Probably the most successful of his relevant monographs is his *Matthias and his Empire* (1940), wherein he analyzed the historical role of King Matthias Corvinus (1458-1490) as perhaps the purest manifestation of the creative "Magyar spirit."(8) But his application of the *Geistesgeschichte* philosophy and methodology is also evident in Joó's works on Magyar nationalism, including his *The Concept of Hungarian Nation* (1939), *Magyar Nationalism* (1941) and *Confessions about Magyardom* (1943).(9) In these works he contrasted the historically tolerant Magyar nationalism of the pre-modern period with what he called the "imperialist nationalism" of the West. Joó attributed traditional Magyar tolerance to their paternalistic and protective Central Asiatic nomadic traditions. In his view, the problems between the Magyars and the other nationalities of historic Hungary arose only at the time of the influx of the "conquering nationalism" of the West, which created nationality conflicts in the Carpathian Basin.

Váczy, Iványi-Grünwald and Kosáry

As opposed to the philosophically oriented Joó, P. Váczy (b. 1904)(10) and B. Iványi-Grünwald (1902-1965)(11) were historians in the traditional sense of that term. During the 1930's and early 1940's they were perhaps the most significant exponents of Hungarian *Geistesgeschichte* in the traditions of Hóman and Szekfű. At the end of the 1930's, however, they were joined by a number of even younger members of their generation. Perhaps the best known among them is D. Kosáry (b. 1913),(12) a former professor of history at Eötvös College (1938-1948) whose *A History of Hungary* (1941) became one of the best known short syntheses in the English speaking world.(13) Kosáry's main scholarly achievements, however, have unfolded in the post-1945 period under the aegis of Marxism, and thus they lie beyond the limits of this work.

While ultimately Váczy's and Iványi-Grünwald's most significant works were written in Hungarian history, they both became better known initially for their work in European history. They both contributed a volume each to the multi-volumed *Universal History;* and Váczy's *The Medieval Age* (1936) and Iványi-Grünwald's *The Most Recent Age* (1936) were undoubtedly the most *Geistesgeschichte*-oriented syntheses in this major undertaking.(14)

Iványi-Grünwald's most significant work in Hungarian history is his brilliant analysis of Count Széchenyi's economic reform activities, which served as an introductory study to a new edition of Széchenyi's epoch-making work *Credit*.(15) He also authored a number of related works on the Hungarian Reform Period.(16) But as he settled in England as early as 1939, Iványi-Grünwald's role in Hungarian historical studies ceased earlier than that of any of his colleagues of the same generation.

The situation was different with Váczy who was appointed to the chair of medieval history at the University of Kolozsvár (Kluj) in 1940, whence he transferred to a similar chair at the University of Budapest (1942-1961). He soon became an influential scholar, although his influence waned gradually after 1945. Like the majority of his colleagues who held various chairs in world history, (17) Váczy's major interwar contributions were in Hungarian history. The most significant of these include *The Role of Feudalism in St. Stephen's Monarchy* (1932), *The First Epochs of the Hungarian Kingdom* (1935), and *The Magyars in the Age of the Romanesque and Gothic Styles* (1939).(18) These works are not only brilliant studies, but they also reflect Váczy's devotion to the *Geistesgeschichte* philosophy of history — both in their spirituality, and in the author's terminology. But going beyond traditional *Geistesgeschichte*, some of Váczy's works (e.g. *The Age of Symbolic State Philosophy in Hungary*, 1932)(19) also reflect his orientation toward the philosophy of state symbolism and charismatic kingship — a philosophy that was best developed by J. Deér of the same young generation of *Geistesgeschichte* historians.

József Deér: The Exponent of State Symbolism and Charismatic Kingship

J. Deér (1905-1974)(20) — who served in rapid succession as professor of Hungarian history at the universities of Szeged (1932-1940), Budapest (1940-1944, 1945-1948) and Bern in Switzerland (1950-1974) — believed that the rulers of nomadic tribal federations and empires of Eurasia assumed the rule over their people in the conviction that they had been divinely ordained to fulfill certain missions. In his view, a "nomadic ruler thus represents God on earth and rules in His name."(21) This was the reason why the ruler of the Huns, similarly to the Chinese emperors, claimed to be the "Son of Heavens," and why the Turk kagan thought of himself as "a heavenly born sage, akin to God."(22)

As elaborated in such major studies as his *Paganism and Christianity in the Old Hungarian Monarchy* (1934) and *Pagan Magyardom — Christian Magyardom* (1938),(23) Deér, therefore, believed in the "elect" nature of nomadic rulers. In his view, they were constantly shadowed by an "invisible charisma," wherefore they generally played the role of a "political Messiah" of their peoples.(24) Deér also believed that this invisible charisma was biologically inheritable and that some of this charisma also extended to the officials who surrounded the king or the kagan.(25) In his view, this was quite evident in the case of the Magyars, who became united into a nation under the leadership of such charismatic rulers as the Árpáds. Árpád's successors continued to possess some of this charisma, which later was augmented and amended by the Christian concept of "by the grace of God." Thus, St. Stephen's Hungarian kingdom united within itself both the nomadic and the Christian concepts of an absolutistic state, with all the outward manifestations (state symbolism) that the merging of these two concepts entailed. It was this charismatic kingship concept that made it impossible for the Magyars to accept anyone as their ruler who lacked the charismatic blood of the national dynasty — at least in the female line.

Deér also joined hands with the philosopher Joó in characterizing medieval Hungarian nationalism as a tolerant one that was willing to extend protection and livelihood to anyone without the goal of forced assimilation. He attributed this tolerance to the nomadic traditions of the Magyars, wherein tribes and subtribes were permitted to group and regroup freely, without losing their identity, and wherein the relationship between the ruler and the people was primarily ''dynastic and political'' in nature.(26)

Géza Istványi and the Rationalization of Geistesgeschichte

Joó's, Iványi-Grünwald's, Váczy's and Deér's growingly separate roads during the 1930's and early 1940's was undoubtedly the sign of the diffusion and the gradual disintegration of the Szekfű-led *Geistesgeschichte* School. This is also evident from the work of the youngest member of this generation, the unusually gifted G. Istványi (1913-1943), who died at the age of thirty.(27)

Although Istványi was also educated as a *Geistesgeschichte* historian, he was primarily a product of Imre Szentpétery of the University of Budapest who worked in the area of the auxiliary sciences of history. This perhaps explains why Istványi was the first among these young historians to speak up against the rapidly ''academized'' and ''dogmatized'' philosophical mystification that characterized the triumphant *Geistesgeschichte* historiography. He did this in his own program declaration (''*Geistesgeschichte,* Neo-Positivism, New Historical Realism,'' 1938), which contained the seeds of a new anti-relativist orientation, which was to be implemented on the basis of rational sociological considerations.(28) Istványi's view of history appeared to approximate closest the yet to be discussed philosophy of I. Hajnal, which emphasized the significance of social relations and the history shaping role of work and technological progress.(29)

While calling his orientation ''neo-positivism,'' Istványi's goal was not to return to the asynthetic and dry factography that characterized nineteenth-century positivism. On the contrary, he regarded the synthetic approach of *Geistesgeschichte* historiography as very desirable. All he tried to do was to cleanse that orientation from its idealism and subjectivism, and to substitute in their place realism and objective knowledge. Nor did Istványi deny the significance of the ''spirit'' in history. Contrary to the *Geistesgeschichte* historians, however, he regarded the ''spirit of the age'' not as a determining factor of history, but simply as the manifestation of the social conditions of a particular age.

Istványi was convinced that by the late 1930's the general trend in historiography was away from subjectivism and toward realism. This he thought to be true even for German historiography, despite the fact that numerous German historians have fallen under the influence of the national socialist "racial concept of history" — which he believed Hungarian historians would avoid. While in this belief he proved to be wrong (for some Hungarian historians did in fact fall under the influence of national socialism), his call for realism was well received by the members of the youngest generation. And while the rising spokesman of *Geistesgeschichte* philosophy, T. Joó immediately attacked him,(30) Istványi and his followers continued along their chosen path, studying historical evolution with the curiosity of "natural scientists in search of natural laws."(31)

Besides Istványi, Deér and the other discussed historians, there were also several others on various levels of scholarly achievements who, although starting out under the influence of *Geistesgeschichte,* by the 1930's and early 1940's have developed their own views about the future course of Hungarian historiography. These included E. Lederer (b. 1897),(32) who was one of the most accomplished, but least appreciated younger practitioner of social and economic history; Ö. Málnási (1898-1970),(33) a somewhat eccentric professor of history at the Law College of Eger, who vacillated between the Radical Left and the Radical Right, and who wrote history in the manner of a political publicist; M. Asztalos (b. 1899),(34) who was perhaps the most faithful popularizer of the Szekfű-version of *Geistesgeschichte,* mixed with a generous amount of nationalism; T. Baráth (b. 1906)(35) who, as professor of Hungarian history at the re-established University of Kolozsvár (Cluj) between 1940 and 1944, authored a new program for Hungarian historiography, which incorporated the "national socialist racial concept of history," but which he still called a "realist orientation;"(36) as well as a number of others, some of whom disappeared from the historiographical scene in 1945, and some of whom rose to prominence under the aegis of Marxist historiography.

In light of the above, it seems evident that by the late 1930's and early 1940's traditional *Geistesgeschichte* historiography did not fulfill the needs of many promising members of the younger generation of historians. Some, like Istványi and his followers, were simply disenchanted with the bombastic philosophizations and subjectivism of the *Geistesgeschichte* historians and theoreticians and wished to study historical evolution with "more concrete and more realistic methods than hitherto.''(37) Others did not object to the subjectivism of this school — and may even have added to it themselves — but simply wished to go out on their own, influenced by various eclectic views of history. The result was the birth of a number of new historical orientations, usually under the synthesizing *Geistesgeschichte* umbrella, none of which, however, had the time to develop into a recognized school. Thus, the major rival historical schools in interwar Hungary were represented either by some of the surviving traditional schools, or by those orientations that have come into being under the leadership of the great path-breaking historians of interwar Hungary: Mályusz, Eckhart and Hajnal. Of these orientations, however, only Mályusz's Ethnohistory School encompassed the whole of Hungarian history, and thus it was this school that ultimately emerged as the major rival of the Hungarian *Geistesgeschichte* School as interpreted by Szekfű, Hóman and their followers.

Chapter XII

MÁLYUSZ AND THE HUNGARIAN ETHNOHISTORY SCHOOL

In light of the above-discussed diffusion and differentiation of the Szekfű-led Hungarian *Geistesgeschichte* School, it would appear that the Hungarian Ethnohistory School — founded by E. Mályusz (b. 1898), the youngest and perhaps most gifted member of the great interwar Hungarian historians(1) — was its most significant rival. This, however, is not the correct interpretation. Despite Mályusz's growing disenchantment with Szekfű and his view of the Hungarian past, Mályusz himself always remained an idealist historian and he regarded his Ethnohistory School simply as "a complement to *Geistesgeschichte.*"(2) In other words, Mályusz's aim was not the establishment of a separate and rival school, but rather the redirection of *Geistesgeschichte* so that it would place a greater emphasis on the role of the "Magyar spirit" in Hungarian history, as opposed to the "universal spirit" — which in Szekfű's interpretation generally took the form of the "spirit of German Christian Civilization." It was, therefore, Szekfű's almost total disregard of the creative role of the "Magyar spirit" (despite his constant reference to it) that made Mályusz turn against the father of the Hungarian *Geistesgeschichte* School and pushed him toward establishing his own school, which often — but quite incorrectly — is thought to be an anti-*Geistesgeschichte* orientation.(3)

The Meaning of Ethnohistory

Ethnohistory as represented by Mályusz's views is almost as difficult to define as *Geistesgeschichte.*(4) Just like the latter, which has often been confused even by historians with intellectual history, ethnohistory has also been mistaken for population history. This was particularly so in its Hungarian context because of the similarities between the two Magyar terms *népiség történet* (ethnic or ethno-history) and *népesedés történet* (population history). According to Mályusz, the easiest and simplest way of defining ethnohistory is to draw an analogy between the terms "nationality" *(nemzetiség)* and "ethnicity" *(népiség)* as used in the composite term "ethno-history" *(népiség történet).* If nationality, at least in its Hungarian context, means among others "the sum total of the *conscious* spiritual and political aspirations and goals of a people possessing identical historical consciousness," than "within the concept of ethnicity we find compressed the *unconscious* life and cultural activities of the people as a whole."(5) In other words, contrary to most other schools of history, where the emphasis is largely on the state *(etatism),* whether of the mechanical or organic version, in ethnohistory the emphasis is shifted to the people *(ethnicism).* Ethnohistory, therefore, includes the study of all possible aspects of popular culture and all possible manifestations of the *Volk* —from the moment of its inception, through the long path of its genetic evolution into a unitary and uniform socio-cultural-ethnic phenomenon. This study cannot be limited by political frontiers, nor by the various possible stages of nation-building or statehood through which a particular people may or may not have passed in the course of its national evolution.

Elemér Mályusz

Although almost a generation younger than the chief apostles of Hungarian *Geistesgeschichte* historiography (Szekfű and Hóman) and such other great historians and philosophers of history as S. Domanovszky I. Szentpétery, F. Eckhart, G. Kornis and others, Mályusz was the product of the same rigorous system. He had studied with the great masters of source criticism Fejérpataky and Marczali, as well as with the humanistic-oriented D. Angyal, the young Domanovszky, and even with the very young Szekfű, his future opponent and rival at the University of Budapest, during the latter's tenure as a *Privatdozent* (special lecturer) at that institution. Moreover, Mályusz did so as a member of the intellectually exclusive Eötvös College, which produced the most brilliant of interwar Hungary's great scholars and intellectuals. At Eötvös College Mályusz received additional historical training at the hands of Mika's successor I. Madzsar (1878-1946), an unheralded but much respected master of historical methodology and pedagogy.(6) The combination of this rigorous training and his unusual native abilities made Mályusz into one of the greatest Hungarian historians of all times. (D. Angyal, his former professor at the University of Budapest, had characterized him as "a genuine talent'' even in his student days.)(7) Mályusz's exceptional abilities manifested themselves both in his written works, as well as in his professorial activities at the University of Budapest where his seminars and his Institute of Settlement and Ethnohistory were known for their ''unusually highly demanding standards.''(8)

As an exceptionally talented historian, Mályusz appeared on the Hungarian historical scene rather early. His work on the *Development of Thuróc County* (1922),(9) prepared in 1920 at the age of twenty-two as a doctoral dissertation, was not only a major piece of research, far beyond the contemporary requirements of a doctorate, but in its content, goals and methodology it already foreshadowed the future Ethnohistory School.

After spending some years in the archives of Vienna (1920-1922) and serving for almost a decade in the Hungarian National Archives (1922-1930); and after becoming a qualified university lecturer *(Privatdozent)* in 1925 with his already mentioned major contribution to the *Fontes* series *(The Papers of Palatinate Archduke Alexander Leopold)*,(10) in 1930 Mályusz became the youngest incumbent of the Chair of Hungarian History at the University of Szeged as successor to the old positivist and national romantic historian Szádeczky-Kardoss.(11) This in turn was followed two years later by his transfer to Budapest, where he obtained the prestigious chair of medieval Hungarian history, once held by Marczali and most recently by the *Geistesgeschichte* oriented medievalist Hóman. Mályusz's tenure in that chair (1932-1945)(12) made medieval Hungarian history into one of the most difficult, but also most highly respected fields of study. What was even more important, however, this chair provided a solid base to Mályusz for the development of his School of Ethnohistory, as well as for the education of a number of devoted disciples and the dissemination of his ideas.

The Development of Ethnohistory

The author of the most recent compendium of Hungarian historical studies, E. Lederer claims that ''it was Mályusz's essay of 1931 (in the Hóman-edited *New Paths of Hungarian Historiography)* which started this orientation (of ethnohistory).''(13) While technically correct, and Mályusz's orientation-setting essay of 1931 was indeed an important milestone in the evolution of Hungarian ethnohistorical studies (as was his subsequent essay collection entitled *Hungarian Historical Sciences*, 1942),(14) the roots of the Hungarian Ethnohistory School reach back to the early 1920's. On the one hand, they are rooted in Mályusz's own pioneering study, *The Development of Thuróc County*, and on the other, in the German *Vokstumkunde* (Folk and Ethnic Studies) of that period, represented by the works of such scholars as H. Aubin, O. Stolz, W. Goetz and others.(15)

The origins of the German *Volkstumkunde* itself go back to the nineteenth century, and more specifically to the flowering of local and regional history studies which — contrary to their politically and genealogically oriented Hungarian counterpart of that period — dealt extensively with the social, economic and cultural life of the German masses *(Volk)* and focused their attention less on politics and genealogy and more on the role of the people in the evolution of the German nation. *Volkstumkunde* was particularly interested in the role of the people's material and spiritual culture in this nation building and in the genetic (ethnic) evolution of Germandom.(16)

This trend in nineteenth-century German historical scholarship resulted among others in the realization of the importance of the people *(Volk)* in the development of a nation and in the sharing of its history. This emphasis on the role of the *people,* as opposed to the *state* represented by certain privileged classes, became even more intense after 1918, when the revisionist spirit of post-Versailles Germany threw the spotlight largely on those German ethnic elements which had been forcibly separated from the fatherland *(Grenzdeutschtum*-Border Germans), as well as on those who had lived for centuries outside the physical limits of the German State *(Auslanddeutschtum*-Foreign Land Germans).(17) With the advance of *Volkstumkunde,* therefore, we see the emergence of a type of populism, which began a slow ascendancy over *etatism* that had dominated nineteenth-century German historical studies.

German *Volkstumkunde* (which, by the way, had never developed into a full-fledged German Ethnohistory School as its Hungarian counterpart) naturally had considerable impact on ethnohistory studies in Hungary. The Mályusz-led Ethnohistory School, however, was not simply a copy of the German model. Undoubtedly, it owed much to the latter in the area of methodology, and there were also certain similarities in their respective aims. But perhaps for this very reason, they clashed violently when it came to German aspirations relative to the *Auslanddeutschtum* in the Carpathian Basin.(18) Moreover, Hungarian ethnohistory had never acquired the connotation and characteristics of biological ethnicity (racism) that became so prevalent in its German counterpart.

The Goals of Ethnohistory

As elaborated in two of his major orientation-setting and methodological studies in 1931 and 1941 respectively, Mályusz saw historical studies as having two basic goals: To reconstruct exactly and faithfully the historical past of the people *(Volk)* and to help solve the basic problems of the age.(19) As applied to Hungarian history from the vantage point of the interwar period, the first of these goals was "to learn everything about the past of the people," and the second, to retain the cultural and spiritual unity of the forcibly fragmented Magyar nation, while also examining the mutual cultural and spiritual relationships and impact of the Magyars and the non-Magyars upon one another during their millennial coexistence within the Hungarian State.

In Mályusz's view, the first of these two goals of history (reconstructing the past of the *Volk)* remains unchanged with the passage of time. Only its tools and methods change. The second goal relative to solving the basic problems of the age, however, does change in accordance with the needs of the succeeding epochs and generations. Thus, he believed that the purpose of eighteenth-century historiography was to aid the emergence of "humanity" or "humaneness" as the guiding force of human society; while that of the nineteenth-century was to advance the cause of nationalism and of the rising national state. In the first few decades of the twentieth century, on the other hand, Mályusz saw historiography pursuing several competing goals. These included the goal of internationalizing human society under the aegis of historical materialism (served by Marxist historiography), as well as the attempt to view human history simply as a sequence of the impacts of spiritual and intellectual forces, while also making history-writing into a form of art (as in the case of *Geistesgeschichte* historiography).

From the vantage point of the early 1940's, however, Mályusz doubted the viability of either one of these two prominent twentieth-century historical orientations. In his view, the real goal of the historical studies of his own age must include the effort to examine and to aid the process whereby political nations are transformed into people-oriented "ethnic nations" *(népi nemzet),* which he saw as the unavoidable fate of all twentieth-century nations. Moreoever, the goal of Hungarian historiography should also be "to struggle for the people beyond the (current) political frontiers (of rump Hungary), and to uplift those living inside (these frontiers)." Mályusz thus drew a sharp contrast between *etatism* and ethnicity. To him the political nation appeared artificial and ephermeral and the ethnic nation natural, "untouchable and inviolable."(20)

If Mályusz regarded ethnicity (which he viewed primarily as a cultural phenomenon) far more important than *etatism,* he was also aware of the deficiencies of Hungarian historiography in the area of ethnic studies. He substantiated this assertion by pointing to the lack of understanding of the terms "people" and "ethnicity". Thus, he was certain that while there were many who could define the meaning of "state" and who could discuss the various types of states and forms of government of the past, very few could give an adequate definition of the term "people" *(nép, Volk),* let along to discuss the various manifestations of its life and existence. To Mályusz this meant that the Hungarian educational system was guilty of grave ommissions. While emphasizing the study of political sciences *(Staatenkunde* — state science), the study of the people through *Volkstumkunde* (including ethnography, anthropology, etc.) was totally neglected. He regarded this situation particularly reprehensible in light of the general trend toward populism, which was bound to triumph and which thus will have to be studied. Yet, when the time arrives, neither the spiritually oriented *Geistesgeschichte* School, nor any of the other existing schools of history will be able to handle the new ethnically oriented historical studies.

In Mályusz's view, the answer to this predicament was clearly the reorientation of historical sciences in the direction of ethnohistory. In its Hungarian context this would mean that historical sciences henceforth would concentrate primarily on the study of "the Magyar *Volk* (and) on their centuries of existence spent in grueling labor," which "bears vivid testimony that notwithstanding all oppression — Turkish conquest, Mongol devastation and alien tyranny (Habsburg rule) — they still remained Magyars (and) retained their lands, customs and language."(21)

Mályusz's first major study in the area of the emerging Hungarian ethnohistory, *The Development of Thuróc County* (1922),(22) was followed in the 1920's by several appeals for the reorientation of historical studies in that direction. These included his 1924 essay on the goals and methods of Hungarian local and regional history and historical geography,(23) and his 1928 memorandum on the need to study the historical movement of the Magyar ethnic frontiers.(24) The big step, however, was taken in 1931, with the publication of his essay on ethnohistory in the Hóman-edited *New Paths of Hungarian Historiography.*(25) It was here where Mályusz came forth with a complete program for his new school, which — while unsaid in this handbook of *Geistesgeschichte* historiography — was in fact to be a rival to that triumphant school.

This did not mean that ethnohistory itself was free of *Geistesgeschichte* influences; for it was not. Moreover, both of these schools were based on an anti-materialist and therefore idealist philosophies of history. To this must be added Mályusz's approach to ethnicity, which he regarded at least as much a spiritual and cultural as a biological phenomenon. Thus, in speaking about popular or ethnic *(népi)* culture, he held that the nature of such cultures was determined basically by "certain spiritual characteristics (and) ethnic features *(alapvonások)*... which were manifest to us up to now to some degree in the language, but primarily in ethnographically describable customs — even though these are also manifested in history (e.g. in the historical role of certain nationalities or ethno-cultural entities)."(26)

This philosophical link between ethnohistory and *Geistesgeschichte* is evident even from Mályusz's subsequent criticism of the Szekfű-led school, which in the former's estimation placed too much emphasis on searching for alleged manifestations of alien (mostly Western) spiritual and intellectual trends, while giving virtually no attention to the similar and perhaps much more important manifestations of the native Magyar spirit, as embodied in the complex and exquisite folk culture and folk life of Magyardom stretching into the highest levels of Hungarian civilization. Mályusz therefore found a kind of "contempt, indifference (and even) maliciousness" among Hungarian *Geistesgeschichte* historians toward Magyar ethnic culture and toward its manifestations (most of which they attributed to Western influences), as well as toward the apostles of Hungarian ethnohistory.(27) Rightly or wrongly, he attributed this attitude of the *Geistesgeschichte* historians to their alleged conviction that "we Magyars were never masters of our own destiny (and) have lived in a kind of shadow-world, torn from our own souls, in an alien-inspired web of traditions, which have been with us from times immemorial."(28)

Mályusz's Ethnohistory School, therefore, was also an idealist phenomenon, and as such it too was the product of the same anti-materialist philosophical orientation and the same socio-political conditions that came to full flowering during the first part of the twentieth century to try to counteract both historical materialism and positivism. Yet, outside these general philosophical similarities, ethnohistory and Szekfű's version of *Geistesgeschichte* did not mix well. Moreover, because of the up-to-date methodological and philosophical training of its protagonists (as opposed to the national romantics and even some of the neo-positivists), ethnohistory was by far the most potent rival of *Geistesgeschichte* in interwar Hungarian historiography — notwithstanding the general lack of support from Hungary's official circles.

In his 1931 essay, Mályusz elaborated a detailed program for the development of the Ethnohistory School. As he pointed out, the ideal goal of Hungarian ethnohistory should be to produce a major synthesis of the history of the laborious struggles and the unceasing interaction that went on for centuries between the land and the people, as well as among the various peoples of Hungary, and which eventually produced that material, spiritual and ethnic culture that ultimately went into the making of Hungarian civilization.

Contrary to Szekfű and his followers, Mályusz saw Hungarian civilization as the result of native Hungarian efforts and struggles, and regarded it as a symbiosis of the centuries of peaceful coexistence and collaborative efforts of the Magyars and non-Magyars of the Hungarian State. The ultimate goal of his efforts was to be the synthetic description and evaluation of these efforts, leading to this symbiosis. Yet, Mályusz realized fully well — perhaps more than anyone else — that such a project could never be undertaken with any hope of success without the appropriate preliminary studies, including systematic data gathering, the writing of monographic works, and the enlistment of several allied and auxiliary sciences. Many of the latter, listed by Mályusz, had not even been regarded as such by historians of the past. Besides such traditional sub-disciplines as linguistics and cultural history, these included in his estimation such newer disciplines as ethnography, ethnology, anthropology, anthrogeography, sociology, as well as the study of settlement patterns (settlement geography). Many of these disciplines, however, were still struggling with their own internal problems of development and had no real connections with history. Moreover, to be helpful to ethnohistorians, many of their practitioners would be obliged to reorient their research efforts. As an example, henceforth linguists would have to pay considerably more attention to the development of the vernacular ("*Volk* speech") than to the intricacies of the literary language.

As to the preliminary work to an ethnohistorical synthesis of the Hungarian past? Mályusz identified this as concentrating in the area of local and regional history, but not in the traditional sense of those terms. He spoke of a genetic approach, which contentwise would include all aspects of human existence (e.g. economic, agricultural, settlement and cultural developments), and areawise would concentrate not on the political and administrative development of artificial units (e.g. counties and provinces), but rather on the genetic development of such natural units as large agricultural estates *(latifundia),* the settlement patterns and socio-economic development of certain river valleys, the rise of the productive and consumer market areas of certain free royal boroughs, the communal life of various peasant villages and agriculturally engaged communities of the Hungarian lower nobility ("sandal nobility"), etc. Such new monographs, written with this new ethnohistorical approach, then would result in a thorough knowledge about the development of these natural units of Hungary and Hungarian society. But more than this, these monographs would also serve as mosaics of a future major synthesis of the genetic evolution of the whole of Hungarian history and society — with an emphasis this time on the people, their way of life, and their material and spiritual culture; and not upon higher politics, nor upon the largely hybrid higher culture.

True to his thoroughness as an historical researcher, Málуusz wanted to start Hungarian ethnohistorical research by organizing a nationwide movement for the systematic collection of local place names (traditional names of hills, rivers, springs, creeks, woods, meadows, fields, dirt roads, areas, etc.) in imitation of the already successful German *Flurnamensammlung* movement, and on a scale that would be comparable to efforts expanded on the collection of folk literature and folk traditions during the Age of Romanticism when such treasures were saved from extinction as the Finnish *Kalevala.* This process of collecting was to be on the local, as well as on the archival level, with the enlisting of both the local intelligentsia and of trained archivists. The work was to be co-ordinated by the Hungarian National Archives, which would also become a kind of training institution for local and provincial researchers.

Mályusz also spoke of the need for the establishment of several other institutes, as well as a number of specialized journals whose efforts would be co-ordinated toward saving some of the fast disappearing millennial cultural treasures and traditions of Magyardom. He regarded this work particularly urgent in the detached sections of historic Hungary (Slovakia, Carpatho-Ruthenia, Transylvania, Banat, Bachka, Burgenland, etc.) where the politically motivated denationalization movements (including the renaming of all geographical and topographical features) could lead to the total extermination of these mute witnesses of the millennial Magyar ethnic culture.(29)

The Achievements of the Ethnohistory School

Mályusz's clarion call of 1931 was not followed by any major effort on the part of Hungary's cultural and political leadership to implement his program of ethnohistorical research. Lederer is probably correct in claiming that "Mályusz's conceptions did not rhyme well with the political goals of the leading *(Geistesgeschichte)* historians and in particular with those of Bálint Hóman,"(30) the powerful minister of religion and public education during the 1930's and early 1940's who controlled most of the purse strings for historical research. Furthermore, "the Mályusz-proposed research into details also lacked the promise of spectacular results," as was the case with the more vibrant, but also more subjective and superficial *Geistesgeschichte* studies.(31) Ethnohistory's partial anti-*Geistesgeschichte* orientation undoubedly also had a part in the benign neglect this school was subjected to, just as much as Mályusz's unwillingness to accommodate German claims of alleged cultural superiority by refusing to accept the idea of the pre-eminence of Western (largely German) influences in the makeup of Hungarian culture and civilization.

In 1934 Mályusz made another attempt to try to enlist official support for his program.(32) When no such help came, he decided to go on alone.(33) This consisted of intensifying his teaching activities in the area of ethnohistory so as to produce as many devoted disciples as possible; and of initiating several publication ventures to publish some of the results of his own and his students' and followers' efforts. One of these ventures was the series entitled *Studies in Settlement and Ethnohistory* (1938-1943) which contained the finished doctoral dissertations of his students at the University of Budapest.(34) Most of the studies which appeared in this series displayed a depth and breadth of archival and field research far beyond the requirements of contemporary doctoral dissertations in Hungary. In addition to bringing forth badly needed sources and monographic elaborations for broader ethnohistorical research, they also demonstrated the unusually rigorous demands that Mályusz made on his students at Budapest.

Of the eight dissertations that appeared in this series, six dealt with the ethnohistorical picture and evolution of six distinct counties of historic Hungary during the middle ages, all of which were lost in consequence of the Treaty of Trianon in 1920 (i.e. Nyitra in Slovakia, Fehér, Kolozs, Szatmár and Bihar in Transylvania and those sections of the Hungarian Plain which were attached to Roumania, and Máramaros in Ruthenia). Of the remaining two, one dealt with the Magyar ethnic island around Felsőőr (Oberwart) in Burgenland and the other with the migration of a group of Calvinist Magyars from the north-central section of the Great Hungarian Plain *(Jászkunság)* down to Bachka *(Bácska)* in the eighteenth century.(35) Contrary to most dissertations, the majority of these studies are still used today as reliable ethnohistorical monographic elaborations of their respective topics. This tells us much about their quality, as well as about Mályusz as a teaching historian. No less important is the fact that since their emergence from Mályusz's Institute of Settlement and Ethnohistory at the University of Budapest, many of these young scholars have risen to the rank of prominent historians in their own right. They include Professors Z. Jakó of the University of Cluj (Kolozsvár) and M. Kovács of the University of Saskatchewan, as well as É. Balázs, V. Bélay, E. Fügedi, E. Iványi (Iczkovits) and F. Maksay, all of whom are connected with various institutions of higher learning or research in Hungary.(36)

István Szabó and Ethnohistory

The other series edited by Mályusz was entitled *Magyardom and Nationality: Studies in the Area of Hungarian Ethnohistory* (1937-1946), and it was intended to contain the works of more established scholars in the attempt to collect all available ethnohistorical data on historic Hungary.(37)

The first volume of this series on Ugocsa County by I. Szabó (1898-1969) was a masterpiece of ethnohistory on a monographic level and it remained unsurpassed for considerable time.(38) But contrary to some other works, it relied only on archival research. Although Szabó had not been a student of Mályusz (they were of the same age), he was influenced by developments in the Ethnohistory School.(39) Subsequently he became one of Hungary's most eminent practitioners of settlement and agricultural history and he even founded his own school within post-1945 Marxist historiography. His major works published before that date include his already mentioned *Ugocsa County* (1937), *The History of Hungarian Peasantry* (1940), *The Biography of Magyardom* (1941), and *The Territorial Expansion of the National Minorities and the Magyars* (1942).(40) The influence of ethnohistory is evident in all of these works.

Because Szabó emerged as a major historian only after 1945, the discussion of his contributions to Hungarian historical scholarship, and in particular to settlement, agricultural and population history, falls outside the scope of this volume. It should nonetheless be mentioned that his last major works (including *The Evolution of the Village System in Hungary in the 10th to the 15th Century,* 1966 and *The Medieval Hungarian Village,* 1969),(41) along with his numerous related publications,(42) make him perhaps the most significant exponent not only of agricultural history, but also of the remaining ethnohistorical orientation in Hungarian historiography of the post-1945 period.

The other volumes in the Mályusz-edited series *Magyardom and Nationality* were all done by B. Ila, another disciple, though not a student of Mályusz. Ila came forth with his multivolumed ethnohistorical study *Gömör County* between 1944 and 1969. But the first volume, which is to contain the synthesis of his research, is still to be written.(43) Ila's volumes (the last of which was published with the special recommendation of the Slovak Academy), in conjunction with Szabó's earlier work on Ugocsa County, give a good indication as to the nature and quality of ethnohistorical research proposed by Mályusz.

Mályusz's influence may also be traced in many other comparable works written by such scholars as A. Fekete-Nagy, K. Eperjessy, I. Bakács, L. Makkai, as well as his student F. Maksay. Maksay's recent work *The Settlement System of the Medieval Hungarian Village* (1971) is a typical example of an excellent research monograph in the traditions of Mályusz's Ethnohistory School.(44)

Although launched very successfully with Szabó's *Ugocsa County*, the *Magyardom and Nationality* series soon bogged down. This was due both to the lack of financial support, as well as to the lack of worthwhile manuscripts outside of Ila's volumes. Time was simply not ripe yet for this undertaking.

Mályusz originally intended the *Magyardom and Nationality* to include a sub-series on the methodological and philosophical aspects of ethnohistory and its auxiliary sciences. But due to the two factors mentioned above, this intention came to naught.(45) Thus, the only studies on the methodological and philosophical side of ethnohistory are those by Mályusz himself, which we have discussed in an earlier section of this chapter.

The Impact of the Ethnohistory School

Although probably the most uniquely Hungarian and most research oriented of all interwar historical schools, the impact of ethnohistory on interwar Hungarian historiography was less immediate and less pervasive than that of the Szekfű-led *Geistesgeschichte* School. This was due to a number of factors, of which the lack of official support and the lack of sufficient time are only two. Perhaps even more decisive was the very nature of ethnohistory. At this early stage it required lengthy, laborous and relatively uninspiring source research and the writing of mostly uncelebrated monographs. Without such preliminary work a major snythesis could not be undertaken.

Perhaps equally significant was the fact that ethnohistory did not engage in lofty — if often cloudy — philosophizations about the alleged influence of one or another Western (mostly German) idea upon the "Magyar soul." On the contrary — and this may have been the real source of its difficulties — it emphasized native Magyar spirituality and creativity and sought the autochthonous roots of Hungarian culture and civilization; and did so at the time when all East Central Europeans were vying with one another in their acknowledgement of the pre-eminence of German influences on their culture and civilization. Thus, the aspirations of the Ethnohistory School went against the trend of the times.

Nor did some of the historical conclusions of Mályusz rhyme well with those of the *Geistesgeschichte* historians. This is evidenced among others by the Szekfű-Mályusz controversy of 1939-1941 on the existence and nature of a Hungarian minority policy during the Middle Ages. In this controversy Szekfű claimed that the medieval Hungarian monarchs pursued a policy of conscious minority protection. Mályusz, on the other hand, detected a conscious policy of assimilation through the practice of the territorial dispersal of the national minorities who were invited to settle during the age of the Árpáds.(46)

Watever the scholarly merits of their respective arguments, a controversy between these two historians was generally followed by an anti-Mályusz barrage on the part of various Szekfű-epigons and opportunists. Convinced or not of the merits of their arguments, they usually repeated Szekfű's conclusions and did not even refrain from accusing Mályusz of political opportunism and national sellout.(47) Such political and personal controversies ultimately turned the struggle between *Geistesgeschichte* and ethnohistory into a Goliath versus David duel. Despite the unfavorable odds, however, ethnohistory was gaining adherents and not even *Geistesgeschichte* historians could escape its influence; and this was true even for Szekfű and Hóman. Thus, the latter pushed himself into a nominal co-editorship with Mályusz of the series *Magyardom and Nationality* and claimed certain hardly justifiable priorites for himself in the emergence of the Ethnohistory School.(48) Szekfű, on the other hand, tried to come to grips with some of the same problems that Mályusz had been struggling with for years in a volume entitled *What is a Magyar?* (1939).(49) This collective work edited by Szekfű naturally displays a basically *Geistesgeschichte* approach. The majority of the topics, however, speak of ethnohistorical influences (e.g. Magyar character, Magyar ethnic types, Magyar language and literary styles, national characteristics in light of ethnography, Magyar music, art forms and spirituality, Magyar character in history, etc.) When reading this work, one cannot help feeling that it owed much more to Mályusz and to the Ethnohistory School than the individual authors or the editor would dare to acknowledge.

The influence of Mályusz and ethnohistory was also felt in many related disciplines, including ethnography, sociology and cultural anthropology. One of the best examples of this influence is the case of L. Mikecs (1917-1944),(50) whose work *The Csángós: The History of the Magyars of Moldavia* (1941)(51) is a masterpiece in its field. Mikecs's goal was to paint a total picture of this small Magyar speaking ethnic group of Moldavia and Bukovina by examining them as a social entity and by combining the study of their past with the examination of their present. In doing so, he combined field work with meticulous archival research. Moreover, he worked in several related human sciences simultaneously. The result was a comprehensive ethnohistorical picture of the Csángó society, which gives us an additional glimpse into what ethnohistory could have produced, had it been able to develop fully.

In addition to scholarly circles and disciplines, the influence of ethnohistory was also felt by the Hungarian populist movement of the 1930's. This was natural, for they had an identical interest (the people or *Volk),* and they were both disenchanted with the *Geistesgeschichte* School's over-emphasis on alleged Western and German influences on Hungarian culture and civilization.(52) The influence of ethnohistory on Hungarian populism, however, was more indirect than direct. As opposed to the demanding scholarly level of Mályusz's Ethnohistory School, the populists operated on an informal and publicistic level. They could also afford to be subjvctive in their writings. This was true even for the writings of the greatest populist intellectual L. Németh, who — as we shall see in a later chapter — also had his differences with Szekfű.(53) Their lack of scholarly training and official position in Hungarian historical circles conveniently exempted them from obligations of scholarly responsibility even when dealing with the scholarly theses of their opponents. Despite their own subjectivism, this was obviously not true for Szekfű and the *Geistesgeschichte* historians; and even less so for the research-oriented Mályusz and the Ethnohistory School.

Although the development of the Ethnohistory School was cut short by the triumph of Marxist historiography after 1945 and by Mályusz's simultaneous retirement at the age of forty-six, ethnohistory had already made its mark on Hungarian historical studies. Moreover, it continues to thrive — although in an amended form — both in Mályusz's works, as well as in the works of a number of younger scholars who write in the area of settlement, population and local history, and who at one or another time had received their training or inspiration from Mályusz and his Ethnohistory School. This is all the more so as — notwithstanding major ideological differences between ethnohistory and Marxist historiography — the latter also concentrates largely on social and economic developments and on the role of the masses (people) in the shaping of history.

Mályusz as an Historian

Contrary to Szekfű, the father of the Hungarian *Geistesgeschichte* School, Mályusz is not known primarily as a synthesizing historian, for outside of his brief German language interpretation of medieval Hungarian history *(Geschichte des ungarischen Volkstums,* 1940)(54) he did not author an overall synthesis of Hungarian historical evolution. But this was due almost exclusively to the embryonic state of ethnohistorical research in Hungary, and the need for basic source research and fundamental monographic studies before a major synthesis could be undertaken. Had the Hungarian Ethnohistory School been given the chance to develop further along the lines outlined during the 1930's and early 1940's, Mályusz would undoubtedly have authored the first significant ethnohistorical synthesis of the Hungarian past.

While Mályusz's chance to produce a definitive synthesis never presented itself, he did produce a number of partial syntheses on specific periods of Hungarian history; and these tell us a great deal about him as a synthesizing historian. The most interesting and worthwhile of his period-syntheses written before 1945 all deal either with the fifteenth and early sixteenth or with the early eighteenth century. The first of these periods, which has generally been known as the age of the Hungarian Renaissance, is covered by two of Mályusz's most brilliant essays. Entitled *The Hungarian Society in the Age of the Hunyadi's* (1939) and *The Hungarian State at the End of the Middle Ages* (1940), they were written respectively for the *King Matthias Corvinus Memorial Album* and for the second volume of the *History of Hungarian Civilization,* which Mályusz edited under the title *The Hungarian Renaissance.*(55) The significance of the first of these essays is also attested to by the fact that in 1941 Mályusz was awarded for it the coveted "Berzeviczy Prize" of the Hungarian Academy of Sciences.

In these two studies — going beyond the immediate period under consideration — Mályusz clarified the whole question of the development of Hungarian society between the thirteenth and the sixteenth centuries; and did so despite the long-standing contradictory historical views on that period that have crystallized in the course of the previous centuries. Contrary to the traditional views, which held that Hungarian society had never passed through the so-called "feudal stage" in the Western classical sense of that term, Mályusz proved conclusively that the Hungarian version of feudalism did in fact dominate much of the fourteenth and fifteenth centuries in Hungary, and that only at the end of this period did Hungarian social evolution turn from *feudalism* to *estatism.*

In proving his thesis, Málysz first clarified the concept of feudalism along the lines of Max Weber's conclusions, and then he examined its Hungarian counterpart, known as the *familiaris* system. He found these two systems basically identical, with the exception that — contrary to the Western feudal states — Hungary had never fallen apart into semi-independent feudal political entities, and that the Hungarian feudal lord had never gained full jurisdictional rights over the freemen in his province. But the relationship between the lord and the vassal (the *"familiaris")* in Hungary was basically identical with that of its Western counterpart.(56)

As Mályusz convincingly demonstrated, the power of the feudal lords, and therefore the whole feudal system in Hungary began to be undermined with the emergence of Matthias Corvinus to the Hungarian throne (1458-1490). By the mid-fifteenth century the lords have concentrated so much economic and political power in their hands that they were at the point of paralyzing royal power. To prevent this likelihood and the consequent disintegration of the unitary state, King Matthias allied himself with the disaffected lower nobility (who were the vassals of the lords) and encouraged their merging into a separate *estate,* with increasing greater and more significant roles in the national *diet* and the country's administrative system. The result was the birth of *estatism (rendiség),* wherein the two main estates, with the occasional presence of the burghers (the clergy did not constitute a separate estate in Hungary), counterbalanced each other and permitted the re-consolidation of royal power and centralization.

Mályusz recognized that with the death of Matthias Corvinus in 1490 and the coming of the ineffective Jagellonian kings (1490-1526), the lords again emerged into a position of pre-eminence over the lower nobility. But by that time the transformation from *feudalism* to *estatism* could not be reversed. Ultimately the lords were forced to yield; particularly when the lower nobility allied itself with the powerful Zápolya family whose members had secret aspirations for the Hungarian throne. And thus the concept of the co-equality of the two estates and the equality of all members of the nobility as a whole came to be accepted. It found expression in Werbőczy's famous *Tripartitum* (1514), which codified the principle of *"una et eadem nobilitas"* (one and the same nobility) and reshaped the structure of the Hungarian noble society from a vertical into a horizontal one.(57)

Mályusz viewed the confrontation between the proponents of feudalism (lords) and estatism (lower nobility) as inevitable, and the resulting social and political transformation as desirable. He realized that in light of the advancing Turkish danger this confrontation and the resulting social and political transformation came at a very inopportune moment. But while recognizing that the resulting lack of internal unity was largely responsible for Hungary's humiliation at Mohács (1526), Mályusz could not regard the internal "party struggles" *per se* as immoral and self-destructive. It was the conditions outside Hungary's frontiers that made them such, and that ultimately shaped them into one of the most significant causes for the country's fall and disintegration.

In addition to problems of Hungary's social and institutional transformation during the late medieval period, the problem that interested Mályusz the most was the question of the development of the freedom of conscience in Hungary, particularly as reflected in the freedom of religious convictions. He tackled this question in a number of his major works, most of which deal with the eighteenth century. One of the most brilliant of these is his synthesis, *The Society of the Rákoczi Age* (1935) on the turbulent first decade of that century (1703-1711), which he wrote for the *Rákoczi Memorial Album*.(58) In this work Mályusz for the first time pointed out the uniqueness and progressive nature of Prince Francis Rákóczi II's religious policies, at the time when the Habsburg controlled lands of Hungary were still ruled by the overzealeous religious fanaticism and intolerance that generally characterized the Age of the Baroque. Thus, in that age when the principle of *cuius regio, eius religio* was still the accepted solution for religious questions, Rákóczi's Hungary had already declared religious equality and freedom of conscience for all. But more importantly, these principles were not only declared; they were also implemented. Going from village to village, a head count was taken of all the inhabitants, and then the existing churches and schools were assigned to the religion of majority, while simultaneously permitting the minorities to build their own churches and schools, and to keep their own priests or preachers. The latter, that is the protection of the rights of the minorities in each village was particularly new and pathbreaking in that age of intolerance, and it certainly was more characteristic of the spirit of the Enlightenment than of the Age of Baroque. The victory of the Habsburgs in 1711 brought this whole noble experiment to an end for well over a half century. Ironically, it took another Habsburg, the "revolutionary emperor" Joseph II, to reverse this trend of renewed religious intolerance in Habsburg-controlled Hungary, and to proclaim again the principle of religious toleration.

Joseph II and his enlightened religious policies became the subject of another of Mályusz's major works, his monumental *The Toleration Edict: Joseph II and Hungarian Protestantism* (1939).(59) Based on the archives of the Austrian *Staatsrat* (which were unfortunately destroyed during the Second World War), Mályusz drew a thorough and balanced picture not only of Joseph's religious policies, but also of the whole religious question in eighteenth-century Hungary. This study of nearly 750 pages is accompanied by a volume of edited sources *(Documents on the History of the Toleration Edict,* 1940), which preserves for us many of the significant documents lost in the holocaust of the war.(60)

Among Mályusz's post-1945 works which most approximate a major synthetic work is his recent *Ecclesiastical Society in Medieval Hungary* (1971), which is impressive both as a work of pedantry and detail, as well as a synthetic social analysis of medieval Hungary.(61) This work gives the most detailed modern description of the development of Hungarian ecclesiastical society, including the various classes of secular and monastic clergy, their literary and intellectual life, as well as of the emergence of the lay intelligentsia in fifteenth-century Hungary. Although published only recently in an updated and revised form, Mályusz's *Ecclesiastical Society* was written prior to 1945, and thus it is basically the product of the pre-Marxist Ethnohistory School.

In addition to his role as the founder of a major school of Hungarian historiography and the author of a number of social syntheses on several epochs of Hungarian history, Mályusz's major contributions came in the area of source research, source analysis and source publication. His volume in the interwar *Fontes* series *(The Papers of Palatinate Archduke Alexander Leopold,* 1926) has already been mentioned, as have some of his contributions in the area of historical methodology.(62) His next major effort came in 1940 with the above-mentioned companion volume to his *The Toleration Edict.* This was followed in the post-World War II period by his three-volume *Sources on the Age of Sigismund* (1951-1958),(63) and by several major monographs on medieval Hungarian historical sources and institutions. The most noteworthy of these is his *The Thuróczy Chronicle and its Sources* (1967), prepared for the Soviet Academy of Sciences and containing perhaps the best summary and evaluation of all medieval Hungarian chronicle literature from the eleventh to the fifteenth century.(64) Some of the other works in this category include his *The Council of Constance and the Hungarian Ecclesiastical Patronage* (1958), *The Gesta of the Age of Stephen V* (1972),(65) and dozens of major studies of source criticism in a number of prominent collective works, yearbooks and journals.(66)

Like Szekfű's *Geistesgeschichte* School, Mályusz's Ethnohistory School also came to an end in 1945. This was a natural result of the emergence and triumph of historical materialism in Hungarian historiography, which new orientation could not co-ordinate its philosophy and socio-political goals with those of any of the earlier idealist schools of history. But as no viable school or philosophy of history passes without leaving its imprint upon its successor, both *Geistesgeschichte* and ethnohistory have left their imprint on post-1945 Hungarian historical scholarship: Szekfű's *Geistesgeschichte* more as a vibrant philosophical orientation to be rivalled and subdued; and Mályusz's ethnohistory more as a *Volk*-oriented sociological school to be imitated, but without its ethnic ideological content.

Chapter XIII

THE NATIONAL ROMANTIC SCHOOL

As we have seen earlier, by the 1930's the ideas-oriented *Geistesgeschichte* School appeared to be triumphant — not only in historiography, but also in most of the so-called "spiritual sciences" *(Geisteswissenschaften).* Its position was aided both by the dominant "spirit" of contemporary Germanic Central and East Central Europe, as well as by the conservative political atmosphere in interwar Hungary. The leading trend in the entire German-dominated cultural world of that period appeared to be toward idealism and spiritualism, with a strong intolerance for everything that leaned toward materialism.

The triumph of *Geistesgeschichte,* however, was not nearly as thorough as it appeared. Underneath its seemingly victorious flags numerous rival forces were actively working for its reorientation or waiting for its downfall. These included idealist and materialist, conservative and progressive, rational and irrational forces — not to speak of the various radical or socialist tendencies which were limited in their freedom of action. Thus, the Szekfű-inspired Hungarian *Geistesgeschichte* School was not the unchallenged victor it was thought to be. Rather, it resembled a besieged, if powerful fortress, whose present and future was far from placid and secure.

The National Romantics and their Concept of History

We have already seen some of the idealist manifestations of these rival tendencies, including Mályusz's Ethnohistory School, as well as the divergent orientations represented by the views of Váczy, Deér, Baráth, Istványi and their followers. While these views diverged, they were all idealist and forward looking. This cannot be said about the traditionalist National Romantic School whose adherents were motivated more by emotions than by ideology.(1) They were the most vocal opponents of *Geistesgeschichte,* and their views most pleasing to the tradition-bound reading public. Simultaneously, however, they were least up-to-date in their methodology. The national romantics were represented by such diverse historians as the Protestant I. Rugonfalvi-Kiss and J. Zoványi, and the Catholic J. Csuday. In addition to their common national romantic ideological orientation, the first two of these historians were also driven in their anti-*Geistesgeschichte* onslaught by Szekfű's and his followers' alleged desire for the "re-Catholization" of Hungarian historical studies.(2) It made little difference to them that from Szekfű's point of view this "re-Catholization" meant simply a broader and more universal perspective in the evaluation of historical questions, as opposed to the undoubtedly provincial outlook of the otherwise respectable Transylvanian-Protestant *(kuruc)* view of Hungarian history.

Rugonfalvi-Kiss, Zoványi, Csuday and numerous others in this category were basically positivist by methodological training and mid-nineteenth-century national romantic by conviction. Some of the vocal but lesser members of this group, however, even lacked the positivist methodological training and operated more on the methodological, though not the overall intellectual and conceptual level of the pre-positivist autodidacts. The outstanding members of this group represented the generally gifted and untiring nineteenth-century compiler-historian type who produced many huge volumes, but usually without any metaphysical conceptions. They very seldom ventured into the area of synthesizing works, and if they did, their idea of an historical synthesis amounted roughly to placing all of the collectable facts next to one another in a chronological order, but without any higher order or system in mind. Although idealists, they were afraid of ideas; and when confronted with them in the course of their historical synthesizing works, they did not know what to do with them, nor how to integrate them into their studies. Although comfortable only when dealing with small, often insignificant topics, some of them were able to produce respectable, if dry monographs on more comprehensive topics, and even a number of relatively good narrative texts which required nothing beyond simple categorizations and narration. The nature and essence of a true historical synthesis, in the *Geistesgeschichte* or *Kulturgeschichte* (Civilization History) sense of that term, however, was completely beyond their comprehension. In fact, when confronted with such a synthesis, they usually found it garbled, misleading and incomprehensible.

Rugonfalvi-Kiss, the Leader of the National Romantic School

The most typical and outstanding member of the National Romantic School of the interwar period, and in terms of his impact on the

Hungarian reading public, perhaps the most important among the adherents of that orientation, was the noted Calvinist historian, I. Rugonfalvi-Kiss (1881-1957).(3) His preeminent position cannot be denied even though his impact was limited largely to the conservative-nationalist Protestant circles and to his primarily Protestant students at the University of Debrecen.

Starting out as an archivist, Rugonfalvi-Kiss was appointed to the chair of Hungarian history at Debrecen at the very moment of the foundation of the university in 1914, and remained in that position throughout the interwar years. During this period he produced several generations of historians, as well as a number of large tomes of relatively solid semi-positivistic works.(4) All of them, however, display basically the features that are characteristic of the National Romantic School. These include the over-idealization of the Protestant-Transylvanian-*kuruc* traditions and the role of the provincial gentry in upholding the nation's integrity and a rather superficial application of the established historical methodology of source criticism and source analysis as practiced by the great positivists of the late-dualist period.

Disregarding his over-traditional ideological orientation and his sectionalist (provincial-centered) approach to the study of Hungarian history, Rugonfalvi-Kiss's deficiencies in historical methodology were perhaps the most lamentable features of his scholarship. This deficiency was all the more reprehensible as he was not only a former student of L. Fejérpataky, one of the two most important transplanters of the German critical-philological method of source criticism to Hungary, but also the incumbent of the only chair of Hungarian history at one of Hungary's four interwar universities.(5)

Rugonfalvi-Kiss's romantic nationalism and his idealization of the role of the nobility and of the Protestant-Transylvanian-*kuruc* tradition are portrayed in the very title of his major works.(6) Most of these deal either with aspects of this tradition and the "national ideology" that motivated the anti-Habsburg struggles of the sixteenth and seventeenth century, or directly with the Hungarian and Székely (Transylvanian Hungarian) nobility's role in these struggles. In a topical sense, however, Rugonfalvi-Kiss's research and publication activities were varied and many-sided. He was equally at home in genealogy, as well as social, constitutional and institutional history.

Although Rugonfalvi-Kiss researched, complied and published an enviable amount of archival material in various specialized areas of history, he was neither able to separate the important and relevant sources from the unimportant and irrelevant ones with sufficient discernment, nor to evaluate them with the desirable critical acumen.

Thus, even if we were to discount his too traditional methodological and ideological approach, many of his conclusions would still have to be regarded as erroneous and often irrelevant. To this must be added his general inability or unwillingness to follow and to utilize the current research and conclusions of his fellow contemporary historians with whom he disagreed. For this very reason, his own achievements and conclusions were also generally disregarded and downgraded, even beyond their merit or demerit.(7)

Possessing no synthesizing abilities and refusing to familiarize himself with the new *Geistesgeschichte* philosophy and methodology, Rugonfalvi-Kiss never produced anything comparable to a true synthesis. Perhaps for this reason, he never developed a true philosophical conception of historical evolution; and whatever he had was rather naive and simplicistic — at least in its application to Hungarian history. As an example, he apparently believed that "human evolution was the composite of waves of idealism and materialism," which "isms" alternated, displacing one another and producing a sequence of epochs based respectively on the sanctity of "God, country (and) family", on the one hand, and on "the dethronization of all of these (concepts and institutions) in the name of individual (material) interests," on the other.(8) Along these lines, Rugonfalvi-Kiss regarded the glorious periods of Hungarian history the results of idealism and the country's misfortunes (e.g. Muhi (1241), Mohács (1526) and Trianon(1920)) the products of materialism — without, however, being able to offer a pragmatic and rational explanation for these conclusions.

Rugonfalvi-Kiss's traditionalism did not mean that he was a reactionary from the point of view of social progress. As a matter of fact, he often spoke up against the existing polarized social system dominated by large estates *(latifundia)* and big business, and in theory at least he was in favor of ordered social progress. Yet, he was still too traditional-minded to establish links with any of the active social reform movements of the interwar period.(9)

As a typical, if comparatively eminent representative of the National Romantic School, Rugonfalvi-Kiss disliked intensely both Szekfű and the *Geistesgeschichte* orientation Szekfű championed; the former, because of his alleged pro-Habsburg and Catholic bias, and the latter, because he was unable to comprehend its complex philosophy and its refined methodology. Thus, whenever Szekfű or his followers produced a new work of synthesis or penetrating analysis, it would immediately meet with the disapproval or outright attack of Rugonfalvi-Kiss or one of his disciples. As an example, when on the occasion of the tricentennial of Gabriel (Gábor) Bethlen's death, Szekfű published a refreshing new biography of that great seventeenth-century ruling prince of the semi-independent state of Transylvania (then the most important bastion of Hungarian nationalism and independence movement), and prefaced his study by a complex *Geistesgeschichte* synthesis of the social, economic and political realities as well as of the intellectual and spiritual currents of that period,(10) Rugonfalvi-Kiss immediately labeled this introduction a simple "magician's trick". He claimed that it was written with the purpose of "deceiving" the uninitiated reading public and thus conditioning them for the "false reinterpretation" of Bethlen and his role in Hungarian history.(11)

In view of Rugonfalvi-Kiss's antiquated and simplicistic approach, and in light of his sectionalist view of Hungarian history, Szekfű correctly regarded him and his fellow national romantic historians as being behind times and unable to keep up with the intellectual developments and demands of their own age. As he put it, tactfully including the whole of Hungarian historiography in his characterization: "The problem with us (Hungarian historians) is that the preceding generations failed to make the great methodological achievements of the past decades their own. (Thus,) when the German (Karl) Lamprecht and (George) Below were producing their great works, instead of trying to borrow their approach, most of our scholars were simply publishing facts without being able to digest them. Consequently, when their (the preceding generation's) works finally reached the reading public in the form of popular biographies and orations, these were filled with liberal-patriotic phraseology characteristic of the forties of the past century (1840's). Thus, (after reading their works,) in the mind of the poor reader there remained nothing of the nation's history, except some patriotic clichés and the aetherial figures of the national heroes."(12) In light of the wide prevalence of this outmoded historical writing, Szekfű was not at all surprised to find that "unless one still harps on the strings of the 1880's," he is immediately declared to be a "national enemy."(13) And here Szekfű touched on the most basic problem that divided the highly complex synthesizing *Geistesgeschichte* School and its adherents, from the fact-gathering, somewhat simplicistic and naively patriotic National Romantic School, and made it difficult for the "new history" to be acceptable among the traditional-minded provincial nobility and country intelligentsia of Hungary: It was simply too new, too strange and too incomprehensible to them.

Other Representatives of National Romanticism

The available polemical literature of the late 1920's and the 1930's, therefore, reveal to us the existence of at least two different worlds in Hungarian historical studies. These worlds were divided from one another in their respective approaches and scholarship by perhaps two or three generations in time, and were fighting on two different intellectual and methodological levels. This is evident not only from the Szekfű—Rugonfalvi-Kiss controversy of that period, but also from the polemics connected with the names of J. Zoványi (1865-1958), an unusually prolific Protestant Church historian, and J. Csuday (1852-1938), a Catholic priest-historian and the author of several large compendiums of Hungarian and European history. To these must be added numerous other historians and pseudo-historians, representing several shades and levels of the somewhat dillettante national romantic orientation in interwar historiography.

While Zoványi himself was one of Hungary's most respected and by far most productive Protestant church historians and the first "modern" practitioner of that sub-discipline (his precise positivist methodology in this field is still unsurpassed today), he too remained completely incomprehensive to the new complex *Geistesgeschichte* approach.(14) He was very apprehensive about the real or alleged goals of this school, and he too represented the national romantic view of history.

To Zoványi, Hóman's and Szekfű's *Magyar History* was simply a "Catholic-oriented re-evaluation" of Hungarian history, with the ultimate aim of "contaminating and falsifying the scholarly truth in every possible way," and of serving various special Habsburg and Catholic goals, such as the interests of the Jesuits.(15) But in addition to seeing the *Magyar History* only as a purposeful distortion of the past, Zoványi too was unable to perceive and to appreciate the methodological and philosophical attainments of the new synthesizing school, whose "many-sided (and) complex approach . . . had served as an example even to the ideologically opposed generation of historians of the subsequent period (i.e. Marxist historiography)."(16) Coming from an historian who in his later years had switched from *Geistesgeschichte* to Marxism, the above assessment is a compliment. It certainly points to the high methodological and philosophical level of the *Geistesgeschichte* School.(17)

Unlike Rugonfalvi-Kiss and Zoványi, J. Csuday was a Catholic historian.(18) Yet, his anti-*Geistesgeschichte* and anti-Szekfű manifestations, as reflected in the series of critical essays he wrote on the occasion of the publication of the *Magyar History,* are even stronger than those of the first two.(19) Being a Catholic historian of some note (even if an ex-priest), and being the author of several large narrative compendiums (but strangely enough no noteworthy research monographs),(20) Csuday could not very well speak up against Hóman's and Szekfű's real or alleged pro-Catholic bias. But he was extremely vehement in denouncing the coauthors' alleged "denationalization" (really demythologization) of Hungarian history.

Csuday's own approach and goal in the study and writing of history was undoubtedly different from Hóman's and Szekfű's approach and goal. These are clearly stated in the preface to the first edition of his two-volume *History of the Magyars* (1892):(21) "My purpose in writing this work," he states, "was patriotic love and the desire to make the history of our country as widely known as possible . . . The reader will vainly seek ideology and cold argumentation in my book, for I did not wish to tire him with such things . . . But if through my work I have contributed to this generation's clinging love for our country . . . then I have attained my goal and I have also received my reward."(22) Motivated by such goals as an historian, it is perhaps fortunate that Csuday's nine-volume (8,000 manuscript pages) "History of the Hungarian Nation", finished in 1928, never appeared in print.(23)

As to Csuday's specific views on Hóman's and Szekfű's *Magyar History?* They were totally negative. He was convinced that the two authors' sole purpose with this work was "to corrupt our national values, to bereave our heroes of the respect of many centuries, (and) to deprive the nation of that strength which we possess by virtue of our millennial constitution, the need for which is so great amidst dismembered Hungary's generations."(24)

Driven primarily by nationalistic goals, unaware even of many aspects of the positivist method of source criticism,distrustful of "ideologies and cold argumentations,"(25) and assuming that the synthesizing work of an historian consists only of putting facts (preferably as many as possible) next to one another without any system outside chronology, Csuday perhaps represented the National Romantic School of the interwar years better than either Rugonfalvi-Kiss or Zoványi. As the realm of only a few historians with adequate scholarly preparation, but simultaneously the hunting ground of throngs of self-proclaimed patriots and pseudo-historians, this "school" was doomed as all relics of an earlier age.(26) Yet, while having little future in Hungarian historical studies and counting few trained professionals among its ranks, the views and approach of the romantic nationalist were very popular among the ''educated public'' — particularly among the provincial townsmen and the country gentry.(27) What was even worse, however, it was this ''school'' that set the level and tone of the history-consciousness and attitude of the semi-educated masses, and thus the attitude of much of the nation.(28)

Chapter XIV

THE POPULISTS AND THEIR CRITICISM OF *GEISTESGESCHICHTE*

Somewhat related to the general outlook of the National Romantic School (though on a higher intellectual, if lower professional level) were the views of the populist-oriented intellectuals of the 1930's. Like the national romantics, most of the populists also disagreed with Hóman's and Szekfű's interpretation of Hungarian history essentially along the same lines, though they did not necessarily disagree with the *Geistesgeschichte* orientation and methodology. The large majority of these populists, however, were not historians but literary men; consequently the methodological aspects of an historical school had no real meaning and importance to them.

The roots of Hungarian populism reach back to the turbulent and emotion-packed years of the post-Trianon (1920) period; and the movement was the result of the same desperate atmosphere that produced Szekfű's bitterly introspective and soul-searching *Three Generations*.(1) Convinced that they had been betrayed by the West, which they hitherto had idealized and tried to emulate, Hungarian intellectuals began to turn inward. This inward turn was both personal, producing Szekfű-type soul searching, as well as national, trying to find solace, salvation and eventual resurrection for their mutilated nation and country. They hoped to find this salvation primarily in the "ethnic and spiritual strength" of the peasant masses and in the special folk culture of Magyardom. This in turn produced a kind of idealization of the peasant as the only real and uncorrupted source of Magyar "ethnic strength" and spirituality.(2)

Soon the ranks of these folk-oriented intellectuals increased through the rise of a growing number of second-generation populists (the generation of the 1930's), many of whom were already from the ranks of the idealized peasant stock and in general represented the healthiest and most progressive non-revolutionary forces in the somewhat stifling atmosphere of interwar Hungary's pseudo-gentry world. This "generation of the thirties," even more than their predecessors, looked to the Magyar peasant masses as the only hope for the nation's future.

They were fully convinced that "it was the Magyar peasant — free from ethnic and cultural degeneration — who was called upon to renew the life-spring of the nation, to regenerate Hungarian society and to form a new intellectual elite, willing and able to give the stagnant society and mutilated nation an effective leadership."(3)

Whatever the motivation of the populists, their turning to the peasant and to peasant culture for the renewal of Hungarian society was basically a healthy phenomenon. When the Hungarian populist intellectuals turned to the Magyar folk culture for inspiration and strength for an eventual national resurrection, however, they found themselves suddenly confronted with a known, yet unexpected phenomenon. They found a sizable portion of the carriers of that culture, the landless Magyar peasant masses, in a state of economic and social privation. Thus, the first thing they had to undertake was the elevation of the nation's three million agrarian proletariat (commonly known as the "three million beggars") to a level of decent human existence, that in turn they may serve as a truly potential force for the nation's regeneration along lines best suited for the ethnic and national needs of Magyardom.(4) One of the results of their activities was the birth of the Hungarian "'Village Explorers" movement, the Hungarian version of the "Movement to the People" with aims somewhat similar to those of the *Narodniki* in late nineteenth-century Russia.(5)

Some of them went only so far as to depict the life and miserable existence of the peasantry, along with their sadly undervalued and misunderstood folk culture. Others, however, did not stop here, but drew up plans — both realistic and utopian — for the desired regeneration of their nation.

In the pursuit of their goals, the populists placed the greatest emphasis on the alleged regenerative power of Magyar folk spirit and folk culture. They regarded these as having played the primary role in the past achievements of their nation and believed that the Magyars would again have to turn to the power of the folk spirit for strength and inspiration. For this reason — like Szekfű and the *Geistesgeschichte* historians — the populist intellectuals also wanted a total reinterpretation of Hungarian history. But their reinterpretation was to be along completely different lines.

According to the populists' scheme, the unique Magyar enthnicity and spirituality (and consequently not the Szekfű-advocated universal spirit and alien influences) should be emphasized as having played the primary role in the shaping of Hungarian history. Thus, the populist intellectuals had little or no real quarrel with the spirituality of the

Geistesgeschichte approach, nor with its complex synthesizing methodology which they envied and hoped to emulate. They too believed in the preeminence of the spiritual over material forces. But, along with a number of respected professional historians of various schools (e.g. S. Domanovszky, F. Eckhart, E. Mályusz, I. Hajnal, etc.) most of them could not accept the Hóman-Szekfű type of reinterpretation which — rightly or wrongly — placed an almost exclusive emphasis on the role of alien (mostly Western) influences in Hungarian historical evolution, and thus in effect emasculated the Magyar mind of all originality. Through such a self-effacing method there could be no Magyar resurrection. Nor could there be a real Magyar national history — as expressed by E. Mályusz, the father of the populist-oriented, but highly professional Ethnohistory School.(6) This did not mean that the populists (let alone the ethnohistorians) subscribed to the sonorous views and claims of the more extreme national romantic historians. It simply meant that, along Herderian lines, they too believed in the uniqueness of the Magyar soul and ethnicity. They were convinced that only through the reliance upon Magyar ethnic strength and Magyar spiritual and cultural values can the nation hope to follow its "special Magyar road" to its "special Magyar goal," amidst the gigantic world struggles and ultimate showdown that is bound to come between the two opposing forces of capitalism and socialism.(7)

The "Father" of Hungarian Populism: Dezső Szabó

Among the earliest spokesmen of Hungarian populism, who simultaneously was perhaps the most vociferous critic of the Hóman-Szekfű type of reinterpretation of Hungarian history, was the great novelist and celebrated social ideologist of that period, D. Szabó (1879-1945),(8) not to be confused with an historian of the same name to be discussed below. Along with the poet E. Ady (1877-1919)(9) and the novelist Z. Móricz (1879-1942),(10) Szabó was one of the ideological fathers of Hungarian populism who was fully convinced that he knew both the cause, as well as the remedy of his nation's malady. He diagnosed the first as over-reliance on and imitation of alien (mostly urbanized and proletarized) cultural, intellectual and spiritual models; and identified the latter as the need to return to the values and way of life of the Hungarian village. "Let us shape our way of thinking (and) attitude to the village" said Szabó as paraphrased for him by one of his assessors. "He who returns to it (the way of life of the village) shall bloom again like a fruit tree replanted into the soil."(11)

D. Szabó undoubtedly over-idealized the virtues of Magyar ethnicity and culture, the purest form of which he found in the Magyar peasants of the Hungarian village. Thus, he came to equate the defense of the best aspects of Magyar ethnicity and culture with the protection and material elevation of the Hungarian peasantry. Consequently, he also believed that Hungarian historiography henceforth should "examine all (historical) phenomena, institutions and personalities of the Hungarian past (only) from the point of view of what biological needs of the Magyar race they served; how much they enhanced or hindered the great productive masses of Magyardom, (i.e.) their physical and spiritual progress; why were they useful or detrimental (to the nation); (and) what were the consequences (of their activities) upon the life of Magyardom?"(12)

The Ideologist of Second-Generation Populism: László Németh

While undoubtedly talented, Szabó was one of those intellectuals who had an absolute confidence in the correctness of his judgments, but seldom generous to the views of others. Thus, whatever the merits of his views and literary achievements, they were tainted by his truly unfair treatment of those with whom he disagreed; and the authors of the *Magyar History* were no exceptions to this rule. He was particularly vicious in his criticism of Szekfű, and of the latter's emphasis on the importance of the universal spirit, and in particular of Western intellectual and cultural elements on Hungarian history and civilization.(13) Szabó's anti-Szekfű tirades, however, had little impact outside the ranks of the petty bourgeois nationalist circles and perhaps some of the anti-*Geistesgeschichte* intellectuals.

Not so in the case of the more sophisticated and tacit L. Németh (1901-1975), another populist critic of Szekfű who never descended to the level of Szabó's sarcastic castigations of his opponents. Németh's writings, even if critical in intent, were characterized by a cultivated restraint and an intellectual brilliance that captivated the attention and the respect of even his staunchest ideological adversaries.(14)

Although basically of a different makeup, Németh started out as Szabó's disciple. Thus, he generally agreed with the master's criticism of Szekfű's pro-Western and pro-Habsburg orientation, and he too was apprehensive about the latter's constant search for the alleged influences of the Western spirit in Hungarian historical evolution. In his numerous essays and studies of the 1930's (collected and published in such volumes as his *Magyars and Europe* (1935), *In Minority* (1939), *The*

Revolution of Quality (1940-1943)(15) Németh was driven by three considerations: The desire to break down the walls of Hungarian provincialism so as to permit the influx of certain "suitable" elements of European culture and European ideas; the hope of rediscovering and re-evaluating the Hungarian past and in particular the role of those great Hungarians whose original contributions to Hungarian civilization have been lost in the constant search for Western influences; and finally the goal of outlining the future course of his nation along the lines of a synthesis between the dominant ideas of the age and the deeply rooted special Magyar cultural traditions.(16)

Németh's philosophical approach was basically that of a *Geistesgeschichte*-oriented intellectual. Like Szekfű, he too started from the Diltheyan conceptions. His views, however, were influenced even more by those of Spengler and Ortega y Gasset relative to the role of the masses and of the elites. Moreover, under Szabó's continued influence, Németh placed a much greater emphasis on the role of Magyar ethnicity than did the father of Hungarian *Geistesgeschichte* historiography. Whereas to Szekfű "the Magyar nation had no ethno-biological . . . only emotional-cultural-moral-historical identity," Németh's ideas — like those of Szabó — were filled with ethno-mythical conceptions.(17) Németh regarded the ethnically pure Magyars (whom he called the "deep Magyars") as the real upholders of the nation and as the carriers of the "eternal" Magyar values. Their counterparts were the mongrelized "diluted Magyars" who, in his estimation, had played a rather limited and negative role in the past and whose role was bound to be limited in the future.

In his social program, Németh rejected both capitalism and socialism and opted for a "third road" or "third alternative" solution. This "special Magyar road" to a "special Magyar goal" was basically an eclectic program. Its goal was a relatively egalitarian society, based on the notion of "quality" as opposed to "quantity;" its qualitative aspect represented by a growing new intellectual "middle class," rising out of the ethnically and spiritually uncorrupted peasantry, eventually destined to include much of the Magyar nation.(18) Given these views, naturally Németh was also oriented toward the Magyar peasants and toward their folk culture, and consequently rejected the heavily Western-oriented and European-based notions of Szekfű.(19)

Other Populist Ideologists

In addition to D. Szabó and L. Németh — who represented respectively the first and second generation of Hungarian populism — the movement gave birth to several other great intellectuals, who in turn represented several shades of the populist ideology of the 1930's. The most important among these, in terms of their contemporary impact were perhaps P. Veres (1897-1970), G. Féja (b. 1900), G. Illyés (b. 1902), F. Erdei (1910-1971), G. Ortutay (b. 1910) J. Darvas (1912-1973), Z. Szabó (b. 1912) and I. Kovács (b. 1913), none of whom, however, were historians. While they had their own differences (some of them moving toward socialism, others toward nationalism and parliamentary democracy), they all generally agreed with D. Szabó's and L. Németh's criticism of Szekfű's over-emphasis of Western influences in Hungarian civilization to the detriment of native elements.(20)

Szekfű and Hungarian Populism

Not being professional historians, the views of the populist intellectuals naturally had only a limited impact on professional historical writing in Hungary. Szekfű himself regarded their writings as representative of the "lyrical conception of history" and dismissed many of their notions as poetry, or at best wishful thinking by individuals who could afford to be poetic when allegedly writing history. In his view, the historical descriptions of some of the populists and national romantics often had no more relationships to historical reality than Dante's description of the Paradise to the real one (if there is such a thing).(21)

Szekfű also berated the "peasant myth" of the populists and their simultaneous demeaning of the Hungarian middle classes, who allegedly represented the biologically and culturally mongrelized "diluted Magyars". "It can only happen among us" said Szekfű, "that there are educated (and) cultured individuals who, like obstinate children, break their dolls just because these are not dressed in peasant costumes."(22)

If having only a limited and superficial impact on professional historiography, the populists gained droves of followers among the amateurs, self-proclaimed "historians" and various other opponents of the Szekfű-led *Geistesgeschichte* School — even though many of their own ranks accepted the *Geistesgeschichte* approach. The populist movement also produced many epigons and pseudo-populists who — in their disenchantment with the West and Western culture — began to turn toward the East and to various manifestations of Turanism.(23)

While the populists and the various pseudo-populist groups could not even agree among themselves on their ideological, political and cultural goals, for a while they were united by their common dislike of Hóman's and Szekfű's reinterpretation of Hungarian history, and by their common emphasis on the primacy of Magyar ethnic and cultural elements in Hungarian civilization.(24) The latter emphasis and goal undoubtedly had many positive results, among them Béla Bartók's and Zoltán Kodály's achievements in folk music, the social reform movements of the 1930's aimed at elevating the Magyar peasants to a level of decent human existence, and the birth of E. Mályusz's Ethnohistory School(25) with its systematic and scholarly treatment of the social, cultural and spiritual evolution of the Magyar masses. Moreover, not all populist-oriented intellectuals disagreed with Szekfű and his followers in every respect. A number of them, such as M. Babits (1882-1941) — while disliking certain aspects of the *Geistesgeschichte* approach and polemizing against it — recognized the positive features of that school, saw the brilliance of Szekfű's great synthesis of Hungarian history and were willing to acknowledge it. Thus, Babits gave credit to Szekfű both for his unusual ability to handle ideas through the complex comparative and synthesizing methods, as well as for his merciless demythologization of the national past and of its previously untouchable heroes.(26) Szekfű on his part was also influenced by the populists; and while reluctant to acknowledge it, much of his peasant sympathies of the 1930's had their roots in the populist movement of that period.

Chapter XV

INTERWAR HUNGARIAN POSITIVISM

The overall triumph of the *Geistesgeschichte* philosophy and methodology in interwar Hungarian historiography, and the violent onslaught against this triumphant school by the remnants of the national romantic orientation, as well as by the populist intellectuals, left the basically well-trained and professionally devoted positivist historians in a difficult position. On the one hand, they disliked and distrusted both the philosophically oriented *Geistesgeschichte* School (with its air of alleged intellectual superiority, but subjective methodology), as well as the sonorous and often dilettante members of the National Romantic School. On the other hand, being devotees of a philosophy and methodological approach that was regarded as *passé* in the interwar period and unwilling to defend their position though the loud and often unprofessional methods of the national romantics, they were soon pushed into the background, and were generally viewed as relics of the past. This was particularly true about some of the greatest old-time positivists whose long life obliged them to witness the constant berating, scoring and virtual dismantling of their lives' works (e.g. Marczali, Károlyi, Angyal and Szádeczky-Kardoss, or the slightly younger Hodinka, Erdélyi, Aldásy and Kováts).(1)

The scorn and neglect of the *Geistesgeschichte* historians however, was also directed at some of the best disciples of these positivist historians who — although of the same generation as Szekfű and Hóman — remained faithful to the philosophy and methodology of Hungarian positivism as practiced by the great masters of that school. (These young positivists included D. Szabó, J. Holub, G. Balanyi, A. Divéky, etc.)(2) Thus, even if they held academic positions beyond the first few years after the consolidation of the new orientation in Hungary, these were usually away from the center of Hungarian intellectual life, at one of the regional universities (i.e. Szeged, Pécs, Debrecen and after 1940, Kolozsvár). Or if they held these positions in Budapest, it was either because they had already been appointed to those posts before the triumph of the *Geistesgeschichte* School and remained non-controversial after it (e.g. Angyal and Aldásy until 1929 and 1932, respectively), or they worked in a field where they had no competitors (e.g. the financial and economic historian F. Kováts after 1934).(3) Others made great efforts to adjust to the new orientation as best as they could (e.g. I. Lukinich after 1925).(4) Still others, with their embedded positions and established prestige (and perhaps a partial and superficial adjustment to the new orientation) would have been beyond the reach of the prophets of the *Geistesgeschichte* School even if the latter would have wished to move against them (e.g. S. Domanovszky, I. Szentpétery, etc.).(5) Moreover, a number of them who held at least as much respect for positivism as for *Geistesgeschichte,* also created their own "schools," producing internal splits and even rivalries within the new idealist-oriented trend of the interwar period (e.g. Eckhart, Mályusz and Hajnal).(6)

The Fall of Marczali

The greatest loser in this confrontation between positivism and *Geistesgeschichte* was undoubtedly the already mentioned H. Marczali (1856-1940), the most outstanding synthesizer of the Positivist School and the Hungarian historian who is best known in the Anglo-Saxon world.(7) After producing some of the most respected monographs and syntheses of the Hungarian Positivist School (both on Hungarian and on general European topics),(8) serving as one of the most important transplanters and disseminators of the scientific method in Hungary, and after a quarter century of teaching at the University of Budapest, where he produced several generations of well-trained scholars (including the founders of the *Geistesgeschichte* School),(9) Marczali found himself suspended (1919) and eventually forcibly retired (1924) from his university chair. The official reason given was his alleged sympathies for the revolution of 1919. In all probability, these allegations had no basis of fact. Throughout his lifetime Marczali's philosophical outlook remained basically that of a mid-nineteenth-century liberal; and as such, he looked with equal dislike both at the tehnically-oriented philosophies of the Right, as well as at the revolution-oriented philosophies of the Left. What hurt him most, however, was not so much his lack of ideological flexibility, but rather his condescending and frigid personality. This personality trait left him isolated throughout his lifetime and also prevented him from establishing a "school" of his own — either in the form of a common philosophical trend, or simply as a group of supporters. Thus, standing alone and unsupported, while occupying a position coveted by the prospective heralds of the new idealist school, and lacking even the slightest humility to ask for the support of those who may still have helped him, Marczali was sacrificed in the name of "progress." From a personal point of view, however, his dismissal may have been less painful than the fact that he had to witness the systematic demeaning and dismantlement of the achievements of the school he had best represented — and then by the best students he himself had produced.(10)

In light of the above one can hardly be surprised that during the last two decades of his life Marczali became a thoroughly embittered man. He spent most of his time either producing small and innately valueless works in order to make a living,(11) or trying to get back at his detractors as best as his now curtailed abilities would permit. In doing the latter, however, Marczali did more disservice for Hungarian historiography as a whole than for his opponents. An example of such a disservice is his French language contribution to the volume published by the *Revue Historique* in 1927 on the historiographical achievements of the previous half century.(12) In his essay on Hungarian historiography, Marczali painted a rather desolate and unfair picture of the achievements of Hungarian historical studies. Thus, although one of the greatest historians Hungary had produced, Marczali could not keep himself from using a personal injury — however unfair — from inflicting a serious damage on the European name of the whole of Hungarian historiography.

Károlyi's Continued Influence

Although essentially in the same general category as Marczali, the situation was still basically different for both A. Károlyi and D. Angyal — the two other oldest and most respected members of the great positivist generation.

Contrary to Marczali, Károlyi (1853-1940) was primarily an archivist who spent most of his active scholarly life in Vienna, and who — along with the noted Hungarian Balkan specialist L. Thallóczy — served as the focal point of the famed "Viennese School" of Hungarian historiography stretching from the late nineteenth century into the 1930's.(13) Károlyi's scholarly contributions to Hungarian historical studies are very impressive. These appeared either as masterly positivistic monographs and essays on limited topics, or as examplary source publications in the *Monumenta* and the *Fontes* series. Yet, their value was at least matched by the additional training in source criticism he had provided to several generations of young Hungarian historians who, following their university education, went to the Viennese archives to practice their trade. In addition to Szekfű, who spent two decades in Vienna, these included such scholars as the older Hodinka and Takáts, and the younger Eckhart, Hajnal, Lukinich, Baranyai and Miskolczy.

Although among the truest representatives of positivist historical research and writing, and although showing little inclination to adjust to the new *Geistesgeschichte* orientation, contrary to the unfortunate Marczali, Károlyi retained his influence throughout the 1920's and 1930's. This paradoxical situation was due to a number of factors, not the least of which was his extremely close relationship to K. Klebelsberg (the minister of religion and public education of that period) and his continued leadership position at the important Viennese centers of Hungarian historical research (e.g. The Hungarian Institute for Historical Research of Vienna and the Collegium Hungaricum).(14) To these factors may be added the great respect that Károlyi commanded even among the prophets of the new *Geistesgeschichte* School. He had befriended and patronized most of these younger scholars in the past and the majority of them regarded him as the greatest practitioner of scientific source criticism. No less important was the fact that — contrary to the less fortunate Marczali — Károlyi was neither a teaching scholar, nor a synthesizer and thus he appeared to pose no challenge to the synthesizing *Geistesgeschichte* historians.

Although already a septegenarian and an octogenerian during the 1920's and 1930's, respectively, the unusually vigorous Károlyi still contributed five weighty volumes of well over three thousand pages to the important *Fontes* series of Hungarian source publications, of which over eleven hundred pages consisted of detailed monographical elaborations of the various topics covered by these volumes.(15) As usual, his source research, source criticism and historical analyses were so enviably thorough and precise that, in addition to serving as examples to other volumes in the series, they excited the continued attention and respect of even the greatest *Geistesgeschichte* historians who generally paid less attention to source criticism than their positivist predecessors.

Angyal, the Longest Surviving Member Of the Old Positivists

The third member of the great positivist generation who survived the fall of the dualist age and lived on to see the Second World War was D. Angyal (1857-1943), a partially autodidactic humanist-oriented scholar, who was equally at home in history, literary history, as well as literary criticism.(16) However, lacking the vigorous methodological training of Károlyi, and not having the unusual prolific writing ability of

Marczali, as a researcher and a writer Angyal did not quite measure up to these two masters. He was, however, more versatile than either Károlyi or Marczali. Moreover, in addition to his scholarly output, which was indeed still very impressive, Angyal was one of the most beloved professors at Budapest (1909-1929). Despite his relatively short tenure there, he had inspired several generations of young Hungarians in the love of history.

In looking at Angyal's scholarly output, we find that contrary to his own characteristically modest estimate of himself,(17) he was indeed a prolific scholar. He produced over thirty independent works, close to two hundred studies and articles, and over hundred-fifty reviews. Moreover, he edited the collected works of several Hungarian literary figures (e.g. F. Kölcsey, S. Kisfaludy, J. Péterfy, etc.), and also served as editor of the *Historical Review* (1912-1922), *Yearbook of the Hungarian Institute for Historical Research in Vienna* (1931-1935), as well as several other publications.(18) Angyal thus wrote and edited much more than most historians of his generation, and did so on innumerable topics and in various areas and disciplines. When we examine his publications more closely, however, we find that only a minority of his monographs are based on archival research. The majority of them are closer to semi-popular summaries than to research volumes. Some of the major exceptions to this rule are his volume in the Szilágyi-edited "Millennial History" on the seventeenth century, his biographies of Imre Thököly (1888-1889) and Gábor Bethlen (1900), respectively, and his contribution to the *Fontes* series on an aspect of post-1849 developments.(19)

In his historical methodology Angyal was basically a nineteenth-century Hungarian positivist, though less vigorous and pedantic than either Károlyi or Marczali. Ideologically he was a moderate conservative, strongly attached to traditions, but not opposed to ordered social progress. Moreover, like the great nineteenth-century romantic liberal historian M. Horváth, Angyal also assigned a notable role to the principle of "freedom" as a moving force in Hungarian history. During the interwar years his conservatism became more explicit, due undoubtedly to his increasing nostalgical longing for the slow-moving ordered society of the Francis Josephian age.

In addition to Károlyi, Marczali and Angyal, the three "old men" of the interwar Hungarian Positivist School, the various shades of persistent positivism in Hungary were represented by such diverse scholars, belonging to several generations, as the Transylvanian source-collector L. Szádeczky-Kardoss, the Slavic specialist A. Hodinka, the socio-cultural historian L. Erdélyi, the medievalist A. Áldásy, the economic historian F. Kováts, the East Europeanists I. Lukinich, A. Divéky and V. Biró, the legal-constitutional historians J. Király, Z. Kérészy, J. Illés, B. Iványi, B. Baranyai and J. Holub, and the political historian D. Szabó, as well as others.

The Transylvanianist Szádeczky-Kardoss

Of these positivist historians, the Transylvanian L. Szádeczky-Kardoss (1859-1935) — K. Szabó's successor to the Chair of Hungarian History at the University of Kolozsvar — was both the oldest and among the most prolific.(20) He produced over two dozen major volumes, including the first major summary of the history of Hungarian industry and guild system.(21) In line with his background and position at Kolozsvár, the large majority of his publications dealt with aspects of Transylvanian history. He edited a great deal, including several volumes in the *Monumenta* series.(22) His methodology, source criticism and the whole scholarly apparatus of his source editions reflected basically the late-nineteenth-century level of scholarship.

This holds also true for his monographic works, which are either biographies of some Transylvanian-Hungarian political figures, or the elaboration of some specific problems in Transylvanian-Hungarian history. Szádeczky-Kardoss's only longer work of synthesizing nature (outside the above-mentioned history of the guild system) in his rather late *History and Constitution of the Székely Nation* (1927) which, however, is also closer to a descriptive account than to a true synthesis.(23)

On the basis of his works, his methodology and outlook Szádeczky-Kardoss may have been almost as close to the national romantics as to the positivists. Contrary to the former, however, he would never get involved in heated debates against the *Geistesgeschichte* historians whose approach remained totally incomprehensible to him. For this reason, and also because of his age and retirement in 1930, Szádeczky-Kardoss was not a major factor in interwar Hungarian historiography. Rather, he stood there in the first half of the period like a relic of the distant past.

Hodinka, the ''Dean''
of Interwar Slavist Historians

The situation was somewhat different with A. Hodinka (1864-1946) who, for over two decades, was successfully professor of Hungarian history (1914-1923) and then of European history (1923-1935) at the University of Pozsony (transferred to Pécs in 1923).(24)

As a sometime fellow at Theodore Sickel's Institution for Austrian Historical Research (1889-1891) and as a member of the Károly-Thallóczy Circle in Vienna (1892-1906), Hodinka received a much better methodological training than the slightly older Szádeczky-Kardoss. Moreover, as an important pioneer of Slavic, particularly Ruthenian studies in Hungary, he had the advantage of working in an area where he had few competitors. Thus, contrary to Szádeczky-Kardoss, Hodinka enjoyed considerable recognition and had more than average influence in interwar Hungarian historiography — even though his relationship with the *Geistesgeschichte* historians was a limited and an uneasy one.

Hodinka was essentially a source gatherer and a source critic and did not produce synthetic works of major consequence and controversy. His greatest efforts were spent in making accessible Slavonic (Ruthenian, Russian and South Slavic) sources for the study of Hungarian history.

Hodinka's best and probably still most consulted work is his bilingual publication, *The Hungarian-Related Sections of the Russian Annals* (1916).(25) Based on the up to then twenty-three published volumes of the *Complete Collection of Russian Annals (1841-1911),* this pioneering work contains all of the known chronicle parts and references which have relevance to the history of Hungary and the Magyars. Its primary weakness is that it is not sufficiently annotated, and thus it may lead to some misinterpretations on the part of the non-specialist.

Being primarily a collector, analyzer and editor of sources, Hodinka left no major syntheses. His only important work of synthetic nature is his *History of the Greek Catholic Bishopric of Munkács* (1909), which is supplemented by a collection of relevant documents of which, however, only one volume appeared.(26) Hodinka also wrote several other monographs on the Carpatho-Ruthenians, on South Slavic developments, as well as on the history of his adopted city Pécs. His ultimate goal was to write a complete history of the Ruthenians of historic northeastern Hungary. But despite a commission from the Hungarian Academy for his work, he was never able to complete his intended *opus magnum*.(27)

Not being a synthesizer, nor a controversial historian, Hodinka had no open disagreement with the *Geistesgeschichte* historians. This was still remarkable, however, in view of the fact that during the 1920's and early 1930's the University of Pécs (through Thienemann and the *Minerva)* was one of the two important centers of *Geistesgeschichte* studies in Hungary. Hodinka's quiet personality and the general respect he enjoyed as a conscientious and able scholar protected him from all possible pressures from the direction of the new school. Yet, it was quite evident that he felt much more at home in the traditional world of Marczali, Károlyi and Angyal than in the complex and controversial world represented by Szekfű, Hóman and their followers.

Holub, the Greatest of Young Positivists

This was also true about Hodinka's fellow historian and successor in the chair of Hungarian history at Pécs, J. Holub (1885-1962).(28) Although two decades Hodinka's junior and the product of the same vigorous and *avant garde* system that produced Szekfű, Holub was still basically closer to the old positivists than to the flamboyant new *Geistesgeschichte* historians.

Although an incumbent of the chair of Hungarian history for a decade and a half (1923-1938), Holub was basically a constitutional historian, with some additional interest in genealogy, diplomatics and heraldry. For this very reason, when the opportunity presented itself in 1938, he moved over to the chair of legal and constitutional history at Pécs (1938-1952).

Of the ten to twelve historians who at various times had occupied the chairs of legal and constitutional history at interwar Hungary's four (after 1940, five) universities, Holub was both among the youngest and also among the best-trained scholars.(29) Moreover — discounting two of the old positivists (A. Timon and J. Illés) whose teaching activities reached from the prewar into the interwar period, and who had published their textbooks before the war — of all interwar constitutional historians only Holub managed to complete and to publish this virtually obligatory task before the end of the period in 1944.(30) Not even F. Eckhart, Holub's celebrated and highly regarded, if controversial and somewhat *Geistesgeschichte*-oriented rival at the University of Budapest managed to do so until after the war in 1946; although this delay may have been due to political reasons to be discussed in another chapter. Holub's achievement was all the more meaningful as his synthesis of Hungarian constitutional developments was the first to break with the traditional approach of interpreting these developments purely on the basis of published laws and decrees. Contrary to Timon, Illés and several of the older constitutional scholars, Holub for the first time examined legal and constitutional developments as reflections of contemporary society and of the needs and values of that society. This may be due to a large degree to the fact that, contrary to most Hungarian constitutional historians, Holub was trained primarily as an historian and not as a legal scholar.

As opposed to the older positivists discussed above, Holub was not a very prolific writer. Whatever he wrote, however, was generally of better quality than the works of many of his fellow constitutional historians, save perhaps those of Eckhart. Although of good quality, his writings tended to lack the flair that characterized the writings of some of the *Geistesgechichte*-oriented historians, including Eckhart.

Besides his two-volume *Outline of Hungarian Constitutional History* (1944-1947) — which reveal him to have been an historian of excellent methodological preparation in the best traditions of positivist historiography — Holub's major publications include his *History of Zala County* (1929), with a special emphasis on the evolution of its medieval system of civil and church administration,(31) several studies on the historical evolution of the Hungarian Diet, and a number of studies on medieval Hungarian property rights, administrative offices and problems of genealogy and heraldry.(32)

All in all, Holub was an excellent scholar, representing the best traditions of positivist Hungarian historiography in an age when positivism was not in vogue. For this reason, and also because of his confinement to one of Hungary's regional universities, his influence in interwar historiography was perhaps less than warranted by the quality of his scholarship. Yet, perhaps for this very reason, and because of his lack of involvement with idealist philosophies and ideologies, he was one of the two constitutional historians (the other one being Eckhart) who managed to retain his university chair into the 1950's even after the total triumph of Marxist ideology in Hungarian historical studies.

Szabó, an Early Positivist Rival of Szekfű

If J. Holub was one of the two outstanding representatives of Szekfű's and Hóman's generation of the lingering positivism of the interwar period, than the other was undoubtedly D. Szabó (1882-1966), not to be confused with the populist writer of the same name discussed above.(33) He was incumbent of the chair of world or universal history at the University of Debrecen (1924-1959), parallel with the national romantic Rugonfalvi-Kiss, who held the chair of Hungarian history at that institution.

Like Szekfű, Holub, Eckhart and several other outstanding members of the interwar generation (including the much younger Mályusz and Szabó's namesake, the populist writer) D. Szabó too was educated at the

University of Budapest and also received additional training at the Hungarian Historical Research Institute in Vienna. But contrary to the others, he had developed a personal admiration and fondness for the great, albeit somewhat morose positivist scholar-professor H. Marczali. Thus, after Marczali's forced retirement and elimination from all positions of influence in the profession, it was D. Szabó who best represented (along with Holub) the Marczali-type positivist research. He did so, however, with considerably less synthesizing ability than his former professor.

Szabó's primary interest was research and source criticism. He wrote a number of solid and detailed monographs based on his wide research, all of which centered on political and administrative problems of either the sixteenth or the eighteenth century. Thus, his first major work, *The History of Hungarian Diets During the Age of Louis II* (1909),(34) dealt with the period just before the catastrophe of Mohács in 1526. Although a solid and well-documented study, it was immediately and severely criticized by the more philosophically-oriented Szekfű for failing to provide a synthetic view of contemporary society (e.g. social classes, institutions, administrative organs of the state, etc.) and thus presenting the material contained therein in a kind of vacuum. While from a theoretical point of view Szekfű was undoubtedly right, it is rather questionable whether — given the state of contemporary Hungarian historical studies and the nature of Szabó's work — he had the right to expect all that from a monograph of that type published in 1909.(35)

Whatever the merits of this encounter between Szabó and Szekfű, it certainly showed the divergent orientation of these two young historians (27 and 26 years old, respectively). Despite their common intellectual roots, they were obviously moving in two different directions: Szabó along the paths outlined by their masters Marczali, Fejérpataky and perhaps Mika; and Szekfű in the direction of new frontiers represented by such contemporary pioneer historians and thinkers as K. Lamprecht, E. Troeltsch, H. Rickert, Ortega y Gasset and most of all that lonely genius W. Dilthey.(36)

Following this encounter, Szabó's and Szekfű's paths moved progressively further apart. Szabó did make some adjustments in his subsequent works in the direction pointed out by Szekfű, as is evidenced by his *Struggles for Our National Monarchy 1505-1526* (1917),(37) but in general he remained distrustful of the *Geistesgeschichte* School. At the same time, however, he would never engage in any such debates with Szekfű and his disciples as did the national romantics, led by Rugonfalvi-Kiss, his colleague at Debrecen.

In his later works Szabó moved from the sixteenth to the eighteenth century, and devoted most of his attention to the question of serfdom and serf-landowner relationship under Maria Theresa and her successors. His massive *The History of the Systematization of Feudal Obligations in Hungary in the Age of Maria Theresa* (1933), which deals with the administrative aspects of serf reforms, appeared in the *Fontes* series.(38) Szabó also prepared a second follow-up volume, but the corrected proofs of that work were destroyed during the Second World War. His subsequently re-constituted and expanded second version was never published due to lack of funds. It is, however, available in a manuscript form, and there are plans for its publication in Hungary as soon as financial conditions permit.(39)

Chapter XVI

EAST EUROPEAN STUDIES IN INTERWAR HUNGARY

In light of the important positions and continued scholarly activities of historians like Károlyi, Angyal, Hodinka and the much younger Holub and Szabó throughout the interwar period, it is rather evident that the triumph of *Geistesgeschichte* historiography was not nearly as complete as superficial observations would indicate. This lack of real defeat of positivism — which undoubtedly was pushed into a defensive position — is even more evident when we examine the ranks of scholars who worked in such diverse fields as social, cultural, legal and constitutional history, as well as East European studies.

The continued prevalence of positivism does not mean of course that these fields were free from *Geistesgeschichte* influences that seemed to permeate the whole atmosphere of interwar historical studies. It simply means that, while trying to adjust to some of the intellectually acceptable aspects of this idealist and philosophically oriented school, some of the more traditional scholars refused to be taken in by the rush to the *Geistesgeschichte* bandwagon — as did some of the opportunists or honest Szekfű epigons. A number of these scholars were sufficiently independent intellectually to liberate themselves from Szekfű's tutelage and even to establish their own schools (e.g. Domanovszky, Eckhart, Mályusz and Hajnal). Others, however, simply paid lip service to the *Geistesgeschichte* ideology, and then went ahead to write their basically positivistic works.

Probably the most typical member of this basically positivist group, whose members tried to adjust superficially to the new orientation, was I. Lukinich (1880-1950), the "dean" of the younger generation of Hungarian East Europeanists, who was the first incumbent of the chair of East European history at the University of Budapest (1929-1950). Lukinich was also one of the few graduates of the University of Kolozsvár to rise to the upper ranks among Hungarian historians.(1)

The Origins of East European Studies

Although none of Hungary's institutions of higher learning had chairs of East European history until the late 1920's, the roots of serious research in this area reach back to the mid-nineteenth century. They are connected partially with the establishment of the first Hungarian university chair in Slavistics at the University of Budapest in 1849 — to which later similar chairs were added in Roumanian (1862), Croatian (1895) and Ruthenian (1919)(2) — and partially with the scholarly activities of the statesman-historian B. Kállay (1839-1903).(3)

Kállay was a politician and a diplomat, a governor of occupied Bosnia-Herzegovina (1882-1903), who supported Count Julius Andrássy's expansive Balkan policy to counterbalance Russian penetration into the Balkans. But as an historian he was sufficiently detached to merit the attention and respect of most contemporary scholars. Thus, his *The History of Serbians, 1780-1815* (1877) and his posthumously published *The History of the Serbian Uprising, 1807-1810* (1909), both of which appeared also in German, are still among the most reliable works on that period, and make Kállay into one of the great pioneers of Serbian historiography.(4)

Kállay was among the first Hungarian scholars to study South Slavic and Turkish consciously so as to be able to use these languages for scholarly and diplomatic purposes. His work was continued by the younger L. Thallóczy (1858-1916), who already appeared strong at the epoch-making Hungarian Historical Congress of 1885, and who subsequently became one of the founders of the so-called "Károlyi-Thallóczy Circle" in Vienna. This Circle eventually served as the nucleus of the "Viennese School" of Hungarian historiography, that contributed much to the qualitative improvement of Hungarian historical sciences. It was the Viennese School that polished many of Hungary's future great historians into some of the best trained research scholars in the area. For a while the Károlyi-Thallóczy Circle also counted among its members the noted Czech Balkan specialist, Josef Konstantin Jireček (1854-1918).(5)

While Kállay limited his scholarly activities to writing monographs largely on the basis of unpublished sources, Thallóczy initiated a large-scale source publication activity, particularly on South Slavic history. With the help of a number of younger scholars (including A. Hodinka, A. Áldásy, S. Horváth, S. Barabás, J. Gelchich, J. Krcsmarik and G. Szekfű) he published about a dozen volumes on Hungary's relationship with such South Slavic lands and provinces as Croatia, Serbia, Ragusa,

(Dubrovnik), the Banate of Jajcza, as well as several other protectorates of medieval Hungary. He also dealth with other aspects of Balkan history, both in the form of source publications (many of which appeared in the *Monumenta Hungariae Historica* series), as well as in monographic elaborations.(6) Thallóczy was also among the first Hungarian historians who recognized the economic aspects and forces of history. Along with I. Ácsády and K. Tagányi, he displayed a clearly recognizable economic orientation in his works.(7)

Imre Lukinich and the Emergence of a New Generation

From among the scholars who were connected with Thallóczy's source publishing activities in Vienna, the already discussed A. Hodinka was perhaps the historian who inherited most of the master's interest in Slavic and East European history.(8) Hodinka retained this interest throughout his lifetime, even though he had never held a chair of East European history. But this was due to the simple fact that not until 1929, when he was already sixty-five years old, was the first chair of East European history finally established at the University of Budapest.

The honor of occupying Hungary's first university chair in East European history went to the crypto-positivist Lukinich, who — along with A. Divéky, V. Bíró and G.J. Miskolczy — was the official representative of East European historiography in interwar Hungary.(9)

Although not a philosophically oriented historian, nor a real synthesizer, Lukinich was among the most prolific of interwar historians. He wrote or edited close to fifty independent volumes. Granted that some of these were memorial albums or other collective works that required little critical editing, but over thirty of them were either independent monographs or critically edited source publications, with extensive annotations and introductory studies. Lukinich, however, did not have the critical acumen, nor the prestige of such great interwar historians as Hóman, Szekfű, Eckhart, Hajnal or Mályusz.

When we examine the topics of Lukinich's dozens of publications, we find that he was first of all a specialist of Transylvanian-Hungarian history, and only secondarily was he an East Europeanist in the conventional sense of that term. In fact outside of Polish-Hungarian-Transylvanian connections, there was nothing beyond Hungary's (and therein Transylvania's) history that caught his attention. In this sense he was almost a replica of his former professor at Kolozsvár, L. Szádeczky-Kardoss, and hardly different from one of the other East Europeanists, V. Bíró.

While some of Lukinich's close to twenty monographs are significant, particularly those that deal with the internal and external developments of Transylvania during the Turkish period, he made his most important contributions in source publications. There he proved to be an excellent positivist master. His most significant critical source publications include *The Diary of János Ferdinand Auer* (1923) and *The History and Sources of the Peace Treaty of Szatmár* (1925) in the *Fontes* series, *The History and Sources of the High Treason Trial of Francis Rákóczi II* (1935) in the *Archivum Rákóczianum* series, and the multi-volumed *Archives of the Podmaniczky Family* (1937-1943).(10) The first three of these deal with the Turkish and immediate post-Turkish periods of Hungarian history, while the last series contains sources on the history of the northern highlands of medieval Hungary (Slovakia).

Next to these source publications and next to some of his excellent monographs on the political, military, social and institutional history of Transylvania,(11) Lukinich's synthesizing attempts are relatively unimportant. An example is his *A History of Hungary in Biographical Sketches* (1930),(12) which also appeared in English, and which is a rather simplicistic account. His institutional histories and his biographical works are much better, although they too tend to give less than either his topical monographs or his source publications.

Vencel Bíró and East European Studies at Kolozsvár

Among the remaining three interwar professors of East European history at Hungarian universities, the Transylvanian V. Bíró (1885-1962) was in many ways simply a less accomplished Lukinich, with perhaps an even greater concentration on Transylvanian history.(13) At the time of his appointment to the new chair of East European history at the University of Kolozsvár (Cluj), following the return of Northern Transylvania to Hungary in 1940, Bíró was already somewhat advanced in age. He was also an accomplished historian of the Piarist Order in Transylvania, although not in the same class as Lukinich. Nor was he given much of a chance to produce his own disciples. His tenure at the university was simply too short and too chaotic, and the return of Northern Transylvania to Roumania in 1945 soon led to his forced retirement.

Bíró's only synthetic work is his *History of Transylvania* (1944), which grew out of his university lectures.(14) But he authored a number of good positivistic topical monographs and biographies, as well as a few less significant institutional histories. All of them, however, are strictly limited to Transylvanian history.(15) His only work which contains elements of non-Transylvanian history in his *The Translyvanian Ambassadors at the Porte* (1921), in which he tried to evaluate the significance of the Turkish impact on the development of his more immediate homeland.(16)

Adorján Divéky and East European Studies at Debrecen

The situation was somewhat different with the other two incumbents of chairs of East European history, Divéky and Miskolczy, in that both of them had some interests outside the frontiers of historic Hungary. This was particularly true about A. Divéky (1880-1965) who, prior to his appointment to the University of Debrecen, had spent some two decades in Poland. During much of this period he was lecturer of Hungarian language and literature and later director of the Hungarian Institute at the University of Warsawa.(17)

Like Lukinich and Bíró, Divéky was also basically a positivist historian. But unlike the former of the two, he made no real effort to conform to the requirements of *Geistesgeschichte* historiography. Nor was Divéky a productive scholar, and he never attempted to produce a synthetic work. Even so, however, he authored at least a half dozen major studies, virtually all of which deal with aspects of Polish-Hungarian historical relations and are available in both of these languages. Only a minority of these studies cover relatively longer periods of history, such as those that deal with sixteenth and seventeenth-century economic, and nineteenth-century political relations.(18)

Divéky's significance as an East Europeanist lies primarily in having made the study of Polish-Hungarian relations a legitimate topic of Hungarian historical research. This is all the more significant, as Polish-Hungarian relations were among the most durable and most important in the history of Hungary's millennial foreign relations.

Gyula (Julius) Miskolczy and Geistesgeschichte Influences in Hungarian East European Studies

While Divéky's interest centered primarily on Poland and on Polish-Hungarian relations. G.(J.) Miskolczy (1862-1961) wrote most of his notable works on Hungarian-Croatian and Hungarian-Habsburg relations.(19) His most important work is undoubtedly the two-volume *History and Documents of the Croatian Question During the Age of the Feudal State* (1927-1928), which appeared in the *Fontes* series and which immediately established Miskolczy as one of the top authorities of the Croatian question.(20) It was primarily on the basis of this work that he was named the first actual incumbent of the chair of Southeast European history at the University of Budapest in 1935, following Milan Šufflay's inability to occupy that chair.

Šufflay (1879-1931) was a noted Croatian historian who earlier had co-edited with Thallóczy and Jireček the *Acta et Diplomata Albaniae* (1913-1918), a significant collection of Albanian historical sources. He had been named to the newly created chair at the University of Budapest in 1928. The Yugoslav government, however, refused to grant him an exit visa. Subsequently, Šufflay was assassinated in Yugoslavia (1931), which then permitted the University of Budapest to name his successor.(21)

Šufflay's successor, and in effect the first actual incumbent of the chair of Southeast European history at Budapest was Miskolczy, who had already spent some two decades in Vienna and Rome in various scholarly positions. Miskolczy differed considerably from all of the above East Europeanists in that he was a dedicated disciple of *Geistesgeschichte* historiography. This dedication is most evident in his synthesis of modern Hungarian history since 1526.(22) Published in 1956, this work is in many ways a distilled version of Szekfű's great *Magyar History,* but with certain differences. The most significant of these is Miskolczy's even greater desire to liberate himself from a Hungarocentric view of history. In his estimation, however righteous they may be, those views were still "representative of provincialism."(23)

Miskolczy's effort to free himself from a Hungarocentric view of Danubian history is also evident in his last major work, *Hungary in the Habsburg Monarchy* (1959), in which he tried to examine the role of Habsburg-Hungarian relations from the vantage point of the Habsburg imperial court.(24) His general approach to the study of Hungarian history is best expressed in this sentence: "Overheated nationalism cannot be a healthy fermenting element in Hungarian history; nor the adoration of the state; only the elevation of the people to the level of humanitarian morality."(25) Like many of the true *Geistesgeschichte* historians of interwar Hungary who followed Szekfű's lead, Miskolczy too was a Hungarian populist and a European cosmopolitan simultaneously. They idealized the liberating European spirit and culture, but they saw Hungary's future largely in the regenerated ethnic, spiritual and cultural strength of Magyardom. This was particularly true after the 1930's, when the Hungarian Ethnohistory

School and the Hungarian populist movement have both begun to influence the thinking of the more cosmopolitan *Geistesgeschichte* historians.

Non-Teaching East Europeanists: Thim, Steier and Veress

With the establishment of various chairs of East European history, the center of gravity of Hungarian East European studies naturally shifted to the universities and brought about a relative decline in the influence of non-university scholars. The decline of the latter's influence, however, did not mean that they ceased to function. On the contrary, some of the most significant interwar publications still came from the pens of such non-teaching scholars as J. Thim, L. Steier and E. Veress. All three of them wrote extensively, although their main contributions to East European studies in Hungary came in the form of critically edited source publications.

The oldest of these scholars was J. Thim (1864-1959), who was able to combine his official calling (medicine) with his love of history; and what is more, he excelled in both fields.(26) Having been born in South Hungary, and having acquired fluency in several South Slavic languages and dialects, he turned his attention very early to the study of Serbian history and literature. In 1892 he published his first major work, *The History of the Serbians from the Most Ancient Times to 1848,* which is still the only major Magyar language synthesis of ancient and medieval Serbian history.(27)

Between 1921 and 1936 Thim served as the official physician at the newly founded Collegium Hungaricum in Vienna and during this period he established a close relationship with the professional historians who were in residence at the Collegium. Under their influence he began a systematic collection of historical sources relative to the Serbian national renaissance in Southern Hungary. The result was his monumental *The History of the Serbian Uprising of 1848-49 in Hungary* (1930-1940), which contains a 500 page synthetic elaboration of this question, along with nearly 1600 pages of appended documents.(28) While the synthetic part of this work does not have the flare of similar works by *Geistesgeschichte* historians, it is among the most objective and reliable source publications in the *Fontes* series. Moreover, due to the vastness of the collection on this topic, it will remain an indispensible work for a long time to come. It is to be lamented that the rest of his collection, running into several additional volumes, remained unpublished because of the World War.

Thim has authored altogether about ninety-seven different historical studies. The most significant of these all deal with Serbian developments in Southern Hungary. The foundations he had laid in this are not only significant, but they are altogether indispensible for historians of the Serbian national revival movement.

Notwithstanding his significant achievements, Thim was not a professional historian. This also holds true for another important member of interwar East Europeanists, L. Steier (1885-1938).(29) While Thim was a physician, Steier started out as an engineer. Subsequently, however, he opted for journalism, and then gradually he moved over to history.

As in the case of Thim, Steier's place of birth in Northern Hungary (Slovakia) has influenced his interest within history. His very first major work deals with the problems of his immediate homeland *(The Slovak Question,* 1912).(30) And even when he switched his attention to the Revolution of 1848, he produced his most significant works on the same problem area. These include his editing of the memoires of L. Beniczky on the Slovak movement of 1848, and his great source publication *The Slovak Nationality Question in 1848-49* (1937) — both for the *Fontes* series.(31) These source publications, with their monograph size introductory studies, will undoubtedly remain Steier's most significant scholarly works. However, such other monographic elaborations of the problems of 1848 as his *Görgely and Kossuth* (1924) and *Haynau and Paskievich* (1925) are also standard works on the momentous events of the mid-nineteeth century.(32)

Being the advocate of a Hungarian-Slovak compromise within the context of a reconstituted greater Hungary, Steier also authored a number of political studies. The most extensive of these is his German language study entitled *The Rape of Hungary* (c. 1930).(33) Such revisionist works, however, tell us more about Steier as a publicist than an historian. His last significant work was a major history of the whole Slovak question. Due to Steier's untimely death, however, this work never appeared in print.

———

The third member of the three great non-teaching Hungarian East Europeanists of interwar Hungary was E. Veress (1868-1953), whose interest centered on Transylvania and on Hungarian-Roumanian historical relations.(34) Contrary to Thim and Steier, however, Veress was a professional historian and archivist. He was also a very prolific scholar who authored well over a dozen major monographs and edited over two dozen volumes of sources.

The most significant of Veress's source publications (which undoubtedly have more lasting value than his monographs) include a five-volume collection of sources on sixteenth and seventeenth-century Transylvania *(Fontes Rerum Transylvanicarum,* 1911-1921) and an eleven-volume collection on Transylvania, Moldavia and Wallachia *(Private Documents on the History of Transylvania, Moldavia and Wallachia,* 1921-1939).(35) Also significant are his source publications on late sixteenth and early seventeenth-century Transylvanian political figures, including Prince Stephen Báthori (1533-1586), General George Basta (1544-1607) and the Jesuit diplomat Alfonso Carrillo (1553-1618) — all of which appeared in the *Monumenta Hungariae Historica* series.(36) His equally important *Roumanian-Hungarian Bibliography, 1473-1838* (1931) appeared with the support of the Roumanian Academy of Sciences, as did his above-mentioned eleven-volume source collection.(37)

Veress worked very rapidly. This haste perhaps explains why the critical level of his source publications is generally below the standard of Hungarian source publishing in the interwar period. Another explanation may be that, having been educated during the early 1890's at the University of Kolozsvár (Cluj), he simply failed to update his methodology in accordance with the general improvement of the critical method in twentieth-century Hungarian historiography.

One of the most significant aspects of Veress's publications is that his belief in the necessity of coexistence among the peoples of the Danubian Basin is reflected in them. And this belief is also reflected in his various other professional activities, including his long service as the professional Roumanian interpreter of the Budapest Circuit Court.

In terms of their publications, the non-teaching historians Thim, Steier and Veress have all contributed as much to the furthering of Hungarian historical studies on Eastern Europe as any of their teaching colleagues; although — with the exception of Steier — they were perhaps less willing to synthesize. Moreover, outside of Veress, their use of the critical method of source criticism was also up to the general standard of that period. Veress, on the other hand, published more and was a vocal spokesman of Danubian cooperation.

Linguistic and Literary Scholars in Interwar East European Studies

Although — in light of the earlier foundation of the Budapest chairs of Slavistics (1849), Roumanian (1862), Croatian (1895) and Ruthenian (1919) — East European languages gained earlier recognition in Hungarian higher education than East European history, the study of the region's history came to be more emphasized during the interwar period. Simultaneously, however, the quality of East European linguistic and literary scholarship also improved — due largely to the rise of a new generation of better trained scholars.

In the area of general Slavistics, the work of J. Melich (1872-1963), who taught at the University of Budapest for three decades (1911-1941), was particularly significant. His pioneering studies on Slavic loan words in the Magyar language, and his related works on Hungary's ethnic-linguistic composition at the time of the Magyar conquest were rightfully acclaimed for their precision and accuracy.(38) This also holds true for the scholarly achievements of Melich's student and successor I. Kniezsa (1898-1965), who held the same chair right up to his death. A number of Kniezsa's major studies deal with the ethnic-linguistic frontiers of medieval Hungary, based on the linguistic analysis of geographical names, while others deal with Hungarian orthography. Kniezsa also continued Melich's work on Slavic loan words. All of his works are of the highest quality, and have been assessed so by a number of internationally known scholars.(39)

Next to the scholarly accomplishments of Melich and Kniezsa, the works of the incumbents of the chairs of Ruthenian, Croatian and Roumanian languages and literatures during the interwar period are more modest. This is particularly true for the scholarship of S. Bonkáló (1880-1959), who held the chair of Ruthenian (1919-1924) and later Ukrainian (1945-1948) languages and literatures. Most of them are introductory summaries on the literature and culture of the Carpatho-Ruthenians. In light of their pioneering nature, however, they are still significant.(40)

To a lesser degree, this also holds true for the works of J. Bajza (1885-1938), the incumbent of the chair of Croatian language and literature at Budapest (1923-1938).(41) Although Bajza was a prolific writer, many of his works have the flavor and quality of publicistic studies. Discounting some of his earlier literary essays, the majority of his works deal with the question of the Hungarian-Croatian union of some eight hundred years. Like Veress in the case of the Roumanians, Bajza was a strong supporter of a new compromise and collaboration between the Magyars and the Croatians. This idea is a constant theme in all of his writings.

Although the first to be established among the various chairs of East European languages at the University of Budapest, none of the incumbents of the Roumanian chair were productive scholars until the late 1920's. Not until the appointment of the Italian Carlo Tagliavini (1928-

1935) did Hungarian Roumanian studies emerge from their obscurantism. For the first time, significant scholarly works appeared, especially in philology. It was upon the foundations laid by Tagliavini that the Hungarian linguist L. Tamás (b. 1904) built the Budapest chair of Roumanian language and literature into a respectable center for Roumanian studies. That, however, came about only during the 1940's.(42)

A parallel chair of Roumanian studies at the University of Kolozsvár (Cluj) was much more fortunate in having as its first significant incumbent G. Moldován (1845-1930), a noted scholar of Roumanian folklore and ethnology. Moldován's tenure, however, ended with the loss of Transylvania (1886-1919), and not until 1940 was there another similar chair established under Hungarian control. But the tenure of the new incumbent, S. Siluca (b. 1884) was simply too short and chaotic (1940-1944) to have had a significant impact on Hungarian scholarship in that area.(43)

Interestingly and significantly, Hungary had no chair for Russian language and literature until 1945, when Russian studies were initiated on a mass scale, with the participation of numerous Russian guest professors.(44) Whatever occurred in Russian studies prior to 1945, did so primarily at the Budapest chair of general Slavistics. As an example, O. Asbóth (1852-1920), one of the earlier incumbents of that chair, produced a number of aids for Russian linguistic studies.(45) Similarly, S. Bonkáló, the above-mentioned incumbent of the chair of Ruthenian studies, authored a history of Russian literature.(46) But these were generally modest works, and the most significant studies on Russian history, literature and linguistics were translated works, usually from one of the Western languages.

The Achievements and Shortcomings of Interwar East European Studies

In assessing interwar Hungarian European studies as represented by the works of the incumbents of Hungary's four university chairs of East European history and by the achievements of their non-teaching colleagues, we find that in general these scholars were less interested in East European studies *per se* than in Hungary's relations with its immediate neighbors. Moreover, a number of them worked on the history and culture of areas which prior to 1918 were part of historic Hungary (e.g. Transylvania, Ruthenia, Slovakia, the Serbian inhabited regions of Southern Hungary, and to a lesser degree even Croatia), and as such their history was really part of Hungary's millennial history.

The situation was basically identical with the literary and linguistic works of the incumbents of the chairs of East European languages and literatures. Next to a few summarizing works and language study aids, most of their scholarly publications centered on Hungarian-Slavic and Hungarian-Roumanian linguistic, literary and cultural relations — and these largely within the borders of historic Hungary. Moreover, until the rise of Melich, Kniezsa, Tamás, Bajza and a few other interwar scholars, many of these works were of modest quality.

Besides the limited geographical interests of Hungarian East and Southeast European studies (discounting Turkology, Byzantinology and Finno-Ugric studies, all of which occupy a special place in Hungarian scholarship),(47) the second factor that characterized this collective discipline was its relative late start. It is indeed strange that it took the Magyars so long to realize the need for the study of the history and culture of their immediate neighbors. This can only be attributed to an overdose of Hungarocentrism in pre-1918 Hungarian scholarship. But the simultaneous over-accentuated Western orientation may also have been a cause. It obliged Hungarian scholars to place the study of Classical and Western Civilization above the study of the civilization of their immediate neighbors. This phenomenon, though lamentable, was common throughout East Central Europe, and it remained a recognizable feature even of interwar historical and literary scholarship in Hungary. This is evident, among others, from the multivolumed *Geistesgeschichte* synthesis of world history published during the mid-1930's. Although entitled *Universal History* (1935-1936), it is basically the history of Western Civilization. Moreover, in its volumes of 600 to 700 pages each, the history of East and Southeast Europe (including the Byzantine and the Ottoman Empires) is dismissed in scant thirty to thirty-five pages.(48)

While the neglect of East European studies, which was so evident during the dualist period, lingered on to a degree even during the interwar years, the latter period also saw the rise of an awareness of the need of improving research in that area. This new awareness was the byproduct of the Treaty of Trianon (1920) and of the general belief that Hungary's mutilation may have been averted had the Magyars been more familiar with the history, culture and thinking of the nationalities most vital to their interests. Moreover, it was also motivated by the desire to probe into the possibility of reconstituting historic Hungary by demonstrating the alleged cultural and intellectual pre-eminence of the Magyars among the nations of the Carpathian Basin and its immediate vicinity.

Such broadening of the awareness of the Magyars about the surrounding lands, nations and cultures was the very essence of the cultural and educational policy of Count Kunó Klébelsberg and of his successor in the ministry of religion and public education, the noted medievalist Bálint Hóman.(49) The establishment of the four chairs of East European history was only one of the numerous manifestations of this cultural policy. We have already seen some of the others in the form of the foundation of several Collegium Hungaricums, research institutes, university chairs and lectureships at dozens of major European universities. Another result was the establishment in 1941 of the first domestic Hungarian historical research institute — within the so-called Teleki Institute — for the purposes of studying the historical, ethnic, social, economic cultural and political developments of East Central and Southeastern Europe, with a special attention to the nationality question. (The other components of the Teleki Institute were the Political Science Institute and the Transylvanian Scientific Institute).(50)

From the vantage point of Hungarian East European studies, the most significant of these institutional developments was undoubtedly the establishment of the Hungarian Historical Research Institute which, since 1949, functions as the Institute of History of the Hungarian Academy of Sciences. In addition to producing a flood of excellent basic studies on the area, this institute also drew together numerous gifted young scholars. Born during the decade of the First World War, their ranks included such subsequently noted historians, linguists and literary scholars as K. Benda, J. Berlász, Cs. Csapodi, L. Elekes, L. Gáldi (1910-1974), M. Gyóni (1913-1955), G. Győrffy, L. Hadrovics, L. Makkai, Z.I. Tóth (1911-1956) and many others. Even today, the surviving members of this generation and their students populate most of the related university departments and research institutes of the Hungarian Academy and make up the core of the best East Europeanists in Hungary. But as they rose to prominence primarily after 1945 under the aegis of Marxism, the evaluation of their scholarly achievements belongs to a later chapter of Hungarian historiography.

Finally, mention must also be made of the primary advocate of East Central European interdependence and cooperation, the literary historian István Gál (b. 1912), and of his journal, the *Apollo* (1934-1939). Convinced that Hungary's only realistic course was the acceptance of her position as one of the small nations of the Danubian Basin, Gál became a champion of "new humanism," to be based on mutual respect and understanding among the nationalities of the area.

To advance this goal, Gál and his followers wrote extensively on the history of East Central European interaction and interdependence, and — in addition to the *Apollo* — they published several collective works on this topic. In doing so, they promoted the cause of "new humanism." Simultaneously, however, they also aided the spread of East European studies in Hungary.(51)

Chapter XVII

DOMANOVSZKY AND THE HUNGARIAN CIVILIZATION OR *KULTURGESCHICHTE* SCHOOL

We have observed that outside the lonely G. Miskolczy, all of interwar Hungary's prominent East Europeanists (including all chair holders, as well as such prominent non-teaching historians as J. Thim, L. Steier and E. Veress) were basically solid positivists. They represented various shades of the *fin de siècle* generation (Károlyi, Marczali, Fejérpataky, Angyal, Mida, etc.). Major exceptions to this rule can be found only among the young upcoming generation of East Europeanists, who were products of Szekfű himself, or of such other idealist-oriented historians of the University of Budapest as Eckhart, Mályusz, Hajnal or Miskolczy. This young generation began to emerge during the late 1930's and the early 1940's, and congregated largely in the Teleki Institute, or around such national-political scholarly journals as Szekfű's *Hungarian Review (Magyar Szemle)* and G. Ortutay's *Hungarology (Magyarságtudomány)*.(1)

Thus, the lingering positivism dominated Hungarian East European studies right up to the late 1930's or early 1940's, just as much as it ruled interwar Hungarian historical studies at all three regional universities (Szeged, Pécs, Debrecen). Only at the University of Budapest did *Geistesgeschichte* gain a clear ascendancy, where it began to dislodge positivism ever since the mid-1920's. This gain at Budapest, however, was ominous, both because of the prestige, as well as the size of Hungary's main university. (By the mid-1930's Budapest had more chairs of history than all of the other universities combinted.)(2)

To a lesser degree than at Budapest, this move toward *Geistesgeschichte* history was also true for Szeged, where by the early 1930's the chair of Hungarian history also fell under idealist and *Geistesgeschichte* influences. This came with the appointment of E. Mályusz (1930-1932) and subsequently J. Deér (1932-1940) as Szádeczky-Kardoss's successors. The chairs of Hungarian cultural history, European history and legal-constitutional history, however, continued to remain under the sway of positivism, as did the various chairs of history at Debrecen and Pécs.(3)

Naturally, very few, if any of these positivist teaching historians remained totally free of *Geistesgeschichte* influences. Sensing the trend of the times, a number of them made some noteworthy attempts to try to adjust to the requirements of this seemingly triumphant school. These attempts, however, were usually unsuccessful, for it would have required a total philosophical re-education of these "old school" historians. Not having regarded philosophy as an essential part of the training of an historian, many of these positivists lacked the essential foundations for such readjustment.

This lack of success in readjustment was rather evident — as we have seen — in the case of the prolific East Europeanist scholar I. Lukinich.(4) But this was equally true for the most celebrated exponent of Hungarian *Kulturgeschichte,* the influential and highly regarded S. Domanovszky who, during his three and a half decades of professorship at the University of Budapest, came to serve as the symbol and very essence of the Hungarian Civilization School.

The Beginnings of the Hungarian Civilization or Kulturgeschichte School

The roots of Hungarian Civilization or *Kulturgeschichte* School(5) reach back to the second half of the nineteenth century, and more specifically, to the Budapest professorship of A. Kerékgyártó (1866-1898).(6) The relatively modest achievements of Kerékgyártó in this area were radically expanded and improved upon during the 1890's and early 1900's by the emergence of three separate yet related schools of history: The Economic History School, connected with the *Hungarian Economic History Review* and the scholarly activities of such historians as K. Tagányi, I. Acsády, S. Takáts and F. Kováts; the Organic Sociological School, which centered on the journal *Twentieth Century* and found expression in the writings of such bourgeois liberals or pseudo-Marxists as O. Jászi, G. Pikler, E. Szabó, P. Ágoston and P. Szende; and finally R. Békefi's Hungarian *Kulturgeschichte* School, connected with the latter's newly founded chair at the University of Budapest (1898).(7) Although not the first of its kind in Hungary, the establishment of this chair resulted in the first organized research and training in the study of the various aspects of Hungarian cultural and socio-economic history.(8) It also led to the writing of sixty published doctoral dissertations in the Békefi-edited series, *Studies in Kulturgeschichte* (1902-1911).(9)

While the economic and sociological schools soon faded away with the demise of their respective journals in 1906 and 1918 respectively, and while Békefi's own interest and activities centered primarily on educational history and the history of religious orders,(10) these collective efforts and achievements were not in vain. Subsequently they were synthesized into several interwar schools, and in particular into the *Kulturgeschichte* Schools of Domanovszky at Budapest and of Erdélyi at Szeged, and to a lesser degree into Mályusz's Ethnohistory School.

Others profited too, including the triumphant *Geistesgeschichte* synthesizers, whose syntheses contained a much fuller and more integrated treatment of human life and culture than any of the earlier compendiums written by positivist historians. Naturally, some of this indebtedness to the late-dualist historical schools was more readily acknowledged than others. Thus, the politically discredited organic sociologists — whether of bourgeois radical or Marxist variety — were given less credit than they deserved. And this was true even for Acsády of the Economic History School, whose pioneering *History of Hungarian Serfdom* was thought to be too "materialist in taste" to be fully acceptable to most interwar historians.(11)

László Erdélyi

Of the two incumbents of Hungary's two interwar *Kulturgeschichte* chairs, L. Erdélyi (1868-1947), the holder of the Kolozsvár-Szeged chair between 1911 and 1938, was simply too eccentric for his own good.(12) As the author of close to forty independent works, of which at least half (including several attempts at a definitive synthesis of Hungarian social, cultural, economic and institutional history) are of fundamental value,(13) Erdélyi was indeed a gifted and in many ways original historian. His monomaniac personality, his over-confidence in his own perceptive abilities, his tendency to get involved in violent and mostly unnecessary scholarly debates and finally his inability to accept the fact that he too may have been subject to error, eventually led to his gradual excommunication from most active scholarly circles. What was even worse, however, these factors also led to the partial disregard of his own worthy and noncontroversial contributions to Hungarian historical scholarship.(14) Nonetheless, Erdélyi did produce a number of excellent scholar-historians at Szeged. Once out of reach of their master's direct influence, the best of these historians generally declined to follow Erdélyi on his erratic paths.(15)

In spite of Erdélyi's basically valid claim of being Hungary's first trained and interwar Hungary's only synthesizing historian of the *Kulturgeschichte* School, and notwithstanding the originality of his scheme for Hungarian social, economic and cultural evolution, due to the factors described above, Erdélyi fell progressively out of the main stream of interwar Hungarian historical studies. This falling out, however, was also enhanced by the fact that — while an adherent of an idealist philosophy of history — in his methodology and approach Erdélyi was basically a positivist historian. Furthermore, he was also known for paying little attention to the claims and achievements of other historians and historical schools of interwar Hungary, who then reciprocated in kind. Thus, the center of contemporary Hungarian *Kulturgeschichte* studies soon stabilized in Budapest and came to be centered primarily, though not exclusively, on Domanovszky's chair at Hungary's main university.

Sándor Domanovszky

Known to the reading public primarily through the large five-volume *History of Hungarian Civilization* or *Hungarian Kulturgeschichte* (1939-1942), for which he served as the editor-in-chief, S. Domanovszky (1877-1955) was one of interwar Hungary's most important, though generally least controversial and therefore less-heralded historians.(16) As one of the earliest products of the rigorous Marczali and Fejérpataky seminars and of Békefi's pioneering courses in cultural history at the University of Budapest, Domanovszky was and remained a positivist both in his methodology and in his historical philosophy. In his ideological and philosophical outlook, however, he had also been influenced by the Tagányi-led Economic History School, as well as by the Organic Sociological School of the bourgeois radicals. But much of these influences were gradually displaced during the interwar years by a progressive, if superficial adherence to the Szekfű-introduced *Geistesgeschichte* orientation. This was particularly true for the 1930's and early 1940's, when it became fashionable for all historians with claim to prominence to pay at least lip service to the new philosophical and synthetic approach.(17)

While making some adjustments himself in the direction of *Geistesgeschichte,* Domanovszky never felt at home in the new trend. Through its emphasis on the pre-eminence of spiritual and intellectual forces the new school was more suitable to a philosophically oriented historian than to one interested largely in social and economic history. Thus, Domanovszky never became a *Geistesgeschichte* historian. Nor did he ever become a true synthesizer, even though retaining his interest in the broader social, economic and cultural trends. He stuck to his source criticism and monographic elaborations and to his important organizing and administrative activities in Hungarian historical studies.

From the vantage point of historical scholarship, Domanovszky's most valuable work is undoubtedly his great five-volume *Life and Papers of Palatinate Joseph* in the *Fontes* series on Hungary's greatest viceroy and palatinate of the Habsburg family, who governed the country for over half a century (1795-1847).(18) This work constitutes an indispensible documentary collection, source criticism, as well as a synthetic evaluation of late eighteenth and early nineteenth-century Hungarian and Habsburg developments — surpassed in the pedantry of its scholarship only by some of Károlyi's and Mályusz's contributions to the same *Fontes* series.

Domanovszky's remaining works may be divided roughly into four categories: Critical analyses of medieval chronicles and evaluation of their meaning for Hungarian history (e.g. the chronicles of Dubnic, Buda, Pozsony, Esztergom, Simon de Kéza, Heinrich Mügeln, the Hunnic chronicle, etc.); studies in medieval and early modern Hungarian economic, social and constitutional history (e.g. on various tariff systems, Hungary's economic connections and trade routes, urban market privileges, succession to the throne, the question of "junior kingship", etc.); school texts for Hungarian and world history courses on the secondary level (of which he authored at least a dozen); and finally, a number of short synthesis-attempts in the area of social, economic and commercial history.(19) The most important among the latter are his German language *The Historical Evolution of Hungary with Emphasis on its Economic Developments* (1913) and *The Foundation of Social Sciences and Economic History* (1922).(20) Neither of these, however, grew into the expected definitive socio-economic-cultural synthesis of the Hungarian past.

Domanovszky's only larger synthetic summary of the whole of Hungarian historical evolution is his German language *History of Hungary* (1923), written for the *Bibliothek der Weltgeschichte* (Library of World History) series.(21) Born under the immediate impact of Trianon and Hungary's territorial mutilation, this work naturally has some revisionist flavor. Otherwise it is a solid positivistic descriptive history, with more than the customary attention to economic and social developments. Yet, however commendable, this work could not take the place of the needed definitive *Kulturgeschichte* synthesis of Hungarian history which Domanovszky should have written, and which none of Erdélyi's several and rather peculiar syntheses could supply.

Domanovszky as an Organizer of Scholarship

Domanovszky's importance as a publishing historian(22) was at least equalled by his role as a calm leader and balancing factor in the turbulent waters of interwar Hungarian historical studies, as well as by his role as a teaching professor at the University of Budapest. In the latter capacity he produced several generations of well-trained historians, whom he indoctrinated with an appreciation of the hitherto underprivileged fields of economic, social and in particular agricultural history. Moreover, he also prevented them from falling unchallenged under the one-sided influence of *Geistesgeschichte.*

Following his inheriting of Békefi's chair of Hungarian *Kulturgeschichte* at the University of Budapest in 1912, which he held for thirty-six years right up to 1948, Domanovszky soon emerged as one of the most important personalities in the Hungarian Historical Association. This was all the more meaningful as — contrary to the dualist period, when the Academy's Historical Commission was preeminent — the Historical Association ruled Hungarian historical studies almost unchallenged during the whole interwar period. Thus, he served as the Association's second and later first vice president for over two decades (1923-1944), while also editing the Association's journal, the *Századok* (Centuries) for three decades (1913-1943). Moreover, he had a rather close and confidential relationship with Klebelsberg, Hungary's all-important minister of culture during the 1920's. As such, Domanovszky's influence over the Hungarian historical profession was considerable. True to his unassuming personality, however, he exercised this influence rather carefully and tacitly.

Domanovszky's influence was also considerable as a teaching historian, even though in the long run he was unable to generate a comprehensive *Kulturgeschichte* School in the strict sense of that term, just as he was unable to produce a comprehensive social-economic-cultural synthesis of Hungarian history. During his most active years as a teaching historian (i.e. from the late 1920's to the early 1940's), when he produced most of his students, Domanovszky's interest turned progressively toward agricultural history. Thus, most of the dissertations written under him during this period dealt with the development of Hungarian agriculture, which then were published in the series *Studies in the History of Hungarian Agriculture* that he edited between 1930 and 1943.(23) While these studies show considerable divergence in their philosophical orientation, as well as historical methodology — due no doubt to the injection of ill-digested *Geistesgeschichte* into positivism, which combination tended to confuse Domanovszky and his students — they did in fact bring forth much new information and produce needed new interpretations on limited topics. Whatever its shortcomings, therefore, Domanovszky and his Agricultural History School (as it is also called at times)(24) represented the most viable socio-economic orientation in interwar Hungarian historiography. Moreover, due to Domanovszky's great influence in the profession, he also represented a kind of check on the sprawling power of the *Geistesgeschichte* historians — even though he himself tended to fall progressively under their influence.

The History of Hungarian Civilization

As mentioned earlier, Domanovszky is known to the reading public primarily in connection with the five-volume *History of Hungarian Civilization* or *Hungarian Kulturgeschichte,* which is often simply, and quite incorrectly, attributed to him alone.(25) This is all the more paradoxical as his role in bringing together this undertaking — intended to be a kind of counter-balancing companion to Hóman's and Szekfű's *Magyar History* — was not nearly as great as it is presumed. Thus, contrary to the general belief, Domanovszky was only one of five general editors of this project; the other four including the equally important historians E. Mályusz and I. Szentpétery, as well as the less prominent G. Balanyi and E. Varjú. Moreover, the actual editing of the individual volumes was also the work of other historians, such as P. Váczy (vol. I), E. Mályusz (vol. II), I. Lukinich (vol. III), I. Wellman (vol. IV), and G. Miskolczy (vol. V). Finally, the whole idea and initiative for this project came from the dedicated, though not very celebrated cultural historian E. Varjú (1873-1944). Varjú also served as the project's most important moving spirit and did all the work connected with the illustrations of the five magnificent volumes. In fact, Domanovszky himself was gained for the project by the enthusiastic Varjú.(26) The former then lent his enormous prestige to secure the necessary funds for the undertaking. In this manner Domanovszky's name became associated with the *History of Hungarian Civilization,* linking him at least as closely to this work as S. Szilágyi's name was linked to the ten-volume "Millennial History" during the 1890's.

If the *History of Hungarian Civilization* started out as a project to counterbalance the *Magyar History's* (Hóman-Szekfű's) all-out *Geistesgeschichte* interpretation of Hungarian history,(27) then it did so rather half-heartedly, and certainly with less than the desired success. A closer examination of the content of the individual volumes (whether the introductory essays, the individual topical studies, or Domanovszky's preface to the whole project)(28) reveals that despite the editor-in-chief's voiced or unvoiced opposition to the Szekfű-type historical writing, the work as a whole is at least as much a proof for the all-pervasive influence of the *Geistesgeschichte* orientation, as it is an anti-*Geistesgeschichte* compendium. Thus, although the *History of Hungarian Civilization* started out as a project of the powerful anti-*Geistesgeschichte* group within the Hungarian Historical Association, it fast turned into a hybrid work, incorporating several shades of positivist, as well as idealist philosophies of history. While the two major figures of the *Geistesgeschichte* School, Szekfű and Hóman, were excluded from the ranks of its editors and contributors, historians of various philosophical orientations were freely intermixed. They included among their ranks even many of Szekfű's and Hóman's students, not to speak of a number of other lesser lights of the *Geistesgeschichte* School.

In addition to the unavoidable ideological kaleidoscope and quality differences that characterized the work of the sixty-nine scholars who participated in the project, there were major ideological differences even among the editors of the individual volumes, who also authored the major introductory studies on the periods covered by each of the five volumes. Thus, in these tone-setting essays virtually all important orientations were represented: From the basically positivist Lukinich (vol. III),(29) through the father of the Ethnohistory School E. Mályusz (vol. II)(30) and the young Domanovszky-disciple I. Wellman (vol. IV),(31) to such *Geistesgeschichte* synthesizers as the East Europeanist G. Miskolczy (vol. V.),(32), the medievalist P. Váczy (vol. I),(33) and the exponent of state symbolism and charismatic kingship J. Deér (also Vol. I).(34) This was also true about the component studies of each of the five volumes, many of which lacked ideological harmony with the lead-essay of that particular volume.

The hybrid nature of this first major synthesis-attempt of the history of Hungarian civilization is evident already from Domanovszky's introductory essay to the whole project, where he struggled valiantly but not quite successfully to synthesize his own basically positivistic philosophical outlook with that of the fashionable *Geistesgeschichte* orientation. Thus, notwithstanding his antipathy to *Geistesgeschichte,* Domanovszky also followed the basic Diltheyan concept of dividing knowledge into natural-physical sciences *(Naturwissenschaften)* versus spiritual-intellectual sciences *(Geisteswissenschaften).*(35) Moreover, he also rejected the contention of all system-building schools to the effect that there are laws which allegedly govern the progress and the pattern of history. As he said: "In nature, everything evolves according to strict laws . . ., but historical processes are not governed by such laws. There nothing repeats itself . . ., (and) all those attempts which, under the impact of the positivist philosophy of history, tried to establish regular patterns in historical evolution (e.g. P. Barth, K. Breysig, etc.), had advanced only so far as to establish certain analogies."(36) In other words, while trying to dethrone or at least lessen the influence of the *Geistesgeschichte* School, Domanovszky himself attacked the philosophical foundations of the positivist system he represented. Thus, while generally opposing idealism and irrationalism, at this time Domanovszky appeared to speak up for an idealist and irrational interpretation of history, placing himself dangerously close to the position of the *Geistesgeschichte* historians.

This ideological and methodological uncertainty displayed by Domanovszky is also evident in most of the component essays of this work, except perhaps in those of Deér, Váczy and Mályusz, each of whom represented a definite orientation of history. Consequently, the *History of Hungarian Civilization* symbolizes equally the attempt of the anti-*Geistesgeschichte* forces to have their views expressed, as well as their ultimate inability to escape the pervasive influence of the triumphant school.

Despite the tremendous scholarly and financial effort that went into the *History of Hungarian Civilization,* this work never became a true rival of Hóman's and Szekfű's *Magyar History.* This was due at least partially to the above discussed ideological and methodological uncertainties. At the same time, however, its relative lack of success (as compared to the *Magyar History)* also stemmed from the basic fact that the *Hungarian Civilization* was not really a true synthesis, but rather a collection of scores of specialized, if popular essays. Moreover, it also suffered from the absence of all scholarly apparatus (footnotes, source citations, bibliography, etc.). As such, it gave the appearance of being simply a bulky and expensive popular work, rather than a major scholarly summary of Hungarian culture and civilization. Thus, the editors' primary aim to produce a definitive scholarly, yet popular compendium of Hungarian social and cultural developments failed. The *Hungarian Civilization* was simply too large, too bulky and too expensive for popular consumption. It also appeared too late to have a pervasive influence on interwar historical studies. Moreover, because of its popularizing aim, it proved to be much less useful to the scholars and scholarly-oriented readers than if published with the full scholarly apparatus.(37)

Structurally, the individual volumes of the *Hungarian Civilization* are uniform. Each contains fourteen to eighteen topical essays, preceded by a lengthy introductory study (a synthesis of the period it covers) by the editor of the specific volume. The only exception to this rule is the first volume, which contains two major introductory studies. The editor of the volume, P. Váczy, apparently did not feel competent to discuss the history, culture and society of the conquering Magyars prior to their conquest of the Carpathian Basin, and thus he delegated this task to the champion of state symbolism J. Deér.

Although there are slight variations — depending on the social, economic and cultural conditions of the period covered — the topical essays of each of the five volumes deal basically with such fundamental areas as (1) race, people, nation and nationality, (2) settlement patterns, (3) social structure, (4) agriculture, (5) industry and commerce, (6) military technology and systems of defense, (7) life styles of the royal court, aristocracy, nobility, bourgeoisie and peasantry, (8) home, home life and clothing, (9) health and medical knowledge, (10) religion and ideology, (11) education, (12) literature, books, the reader and the writer, (13) the spiritual-intellectual ''sciences'', (14) manufacturing, technology and the natural sciences, (15) various types of arts (graphic, plastic and performing arts), (16) and finally music.

The periodization used in the *Hungarian Civilization,* like the whole work itself, is also of a hybrid variety, containing both old and new elements. In general, the periodization pattern established by the authors of the *Magyar History* appears to have triumphed, despite the efforts of the editors toward an independent course. This is particularly evident from the second and the fourth volumes, covering the fifteenth (c. 1380-1526) and the eighteenth (c. 1685-1790) centuries and entitled respectively the ''Hungarian Renaissance'' and the ''Hungarian Baroque and Enlightenment.'' As in Szekfű's synthesis, the inbetween two centuries covered by the third volume are characterized in this work by the Turkish conquest of Hungary, and as such this characterization has no relationship to the alleged life styles of that period as required by a full-fledged *Geistesgeschichte* approach. This in turn produced a good century and a half of vacuum between the Renaissance and the Baroque life styles, even though according to the Western European pattern and the *Geistesgeschichte* approach these two life styles should have followed one another. As mentioned above and discussed in an earlier chapter,(38) the separation of these two life styles (and thus the violation of the *Geistesgeschichte* approach) was first committed by Szekfű, the father of the Hungarian *Geistesgeschichte* School himself. It was immediately condemned by many historians, including E. Mályusz, one of Szekfű's most severe and able critics, who regarded it as a distortion of the idealist pattern of historical evolution. Mályusz was undoubtedly right from the vantage point of European intellectual and artistic developments, which determine or at least reflect contemporary life styles. Within the peculiar Hungarian context, however, Szekfű too had sufficient reasons and arguments to back up his own periodization scheme. Now with the appearance of *Hungarian Civilization* and its rather similar periodization scheme, Szekfű appears to have been vindicated by his very critics and opponents. And willingly or otherwise, this appears to include even Mályusz, the editor of the second volume dealing with the Hungarian Renaissance.(39) One cannot help feeling, however, that Mályusz and a number of idealist but basically anti-*Geistesgeschichte* historians were simply compelled by circumstances to work within a periodization scheme to which they did not really subscribe.

Kováts and the Continuation of the Economic History School

The five volumes of the *History of Hungarian Civilization,* which appeared during 1939 to 1941, represented in some ways the apogee of the Domanovszky-led Hungarian *Kulturgeschichte* School. These volumes also gave an added luster to Domanovszky as an historian. Not that Domanovszky was in great need for such an addition to his fame. He had long been recognized as the most important of the interwar socio-economic historians. Yet, however important, he was not alone in the field. That he had at least one serious rival is best demonstrated by the absence of his name from the Hóman-edited *New Paths of Hungarian Historiography* (1931), where the relevant chapter on economic and social history was written by I. Dékány, a noted sociologist and social philosopher, who appeared to fit better into the philosophically oriented *Geistesgeschichte* scene. Moreover, there was also the older F. Kováts whose earlier association with the Tagányi-founded Economic History School and the *Hungarian Economic History Review* (1894-1906) made him into a kind of pioneer of Hungarian social and economic history.(40) Yet, for various reasons Kováts never came to rival Domanovszky; and the latter retained his preeminence over both Dékány and Kováts throughout the interwar period. The reasons for this, however, must be sought more in the personality and scholarly orientation of the latter two scholars than in Domanovszky himself.

Ferenc Kováts (1873-1956) started very young as a brilliant and promising economic historian. At twenty-seven he became Tagányi's successor as the editor of the *Hungarian Economic History Review* (1901), and at thirty a professor at the Pozsony Law Academy (later to become the University of Pozsony). His early publications were also noteworthy, and before his thirtieth year he had already published five major studies on various aspects of medieval Hungarian social and economic developments. These included such topics as medieval urban taxation, urban welfare system, shipping on the Danube, Western Hungary's commercial activities during the Middle Ages, as well as a synthesis-attempt on Hungarian monetary history.(41) Moreover, he contributed extensively both to the *Review* under his editorship, as well as to the first major Hungarian *Encyclopedia of Economics (Közgazdasági Lexikon)* published between 1898 and 1901.(42) With such a start, one could well presume that Kováts would soon emerge as Hungary's number one economic and social historian. This expectation, however, was not fulfilled. While Kováts continued to advance in rank at the universities of Pozsony (1914-1921) and Szeged (1921-1934), and the School of Economic Sciences at the Technical University of Budapest (1934-1943), and while he remained number one in the somewhat narrow field of medieval Hungarian urban history, his total impact on interwar Hungarian historical studies was rather limited.

Kováts continued his research throughout the interwar period and he published a number of worthy studies and source collections in his area of specialization, but he remained basically a source collecting historian and monographer of narrow topics. Philosophies and social theories were alien to him, as was the art of historical synthesizing. For this reason he was never able to complete a single compendium on Hungarian economic and social evolution, even though he had a commission from the Historical Association for a synthesis of Hungarian monetary history.(43)

In addition to lacking synthesizing ability, Kováts also had a quiet and unassuming personality. Consequently, he was never able to make his presence felt in the ideologically saturated, turbulent world of interwar Hungarian historical studies. He was respected; both his earlier and later works were utilized by others; but it was the synthesizers of his research efforts who reaped the fruits of much of his work, and enjoyed the sunshine of popularity. It seems that — even though relatively still young in 1918 — with the collapse of the old order and the world of positivist historiography, Kováts's world also collapsed. Certainly, in the new world of interwar *Geistesgeschichte* historiography he was no less alien and forlorn than were the much older relics of the positivist age: Marczali, Angyal and Károlyi.

Dékány and His Sociological Orientation

The situation was quite different with the younger I. Dékány (1886-1965) who — given the conditions — could undoubtedly have become a much more serious rival to Domanovszky. That this was a distinct if distant possibility is evidenced by the fact that — as mentioned before — it was not Domanovszky but Dékány who was called upon by Hóman to contribute the chapter on economic and social history to his *New Paths of Hungarian Historiography*.(44) It is also made more likely by Dékány's theoretical and synthetic mind and approach which fitted well into the *Geistesgeschichte* orientation. That ultimately Domanovszky prevailed and remained throughout the interwar years the undisputed head of the Hungarian *Kulturgeschichte* School was due both to his entrenched position and general influence among Hungarian historians, as well as to the fact that Dékány was not really an historian, but rather a social theorist and a philosopher of history.

After serving for many years as an important figure in the leadership of the Hungarian Philosophical Association (as its executive secretary and later its vice president), as well as in the hierarchy of the Hungarian Sociological Association (as its president), and after editing for many years the Hungarian Academy's *Philosophical Library*, the Philosophical Association's yearbook the *Athenaeum*, and the series *Pedagogical Library*, in 1942 Dékány became the first incumbent of the Chair of Social Philosophy at the University of Budapest. Thus, while holding important positions for two decades, not until the early 1940's was Dékány given a chance to start his own school of social theory within Hungarian historical studies. This obviously worked against him in his possible challenge to Domanovszky.

Even though relatively advanced in age (56), Dékány's appointment held momentous possibilities for Hungarian historical studies, and more specifically for the basically positivist oriented and largely anti-theoretical Hungarian *Kulturgeschichte* School represented by Domanovszky and his followers. The rapid collapse of the old order (1944-1945) and Dékány's subsequent ejection from his university chair (1946) only four years after his appointment, however, changed the picture completely and prevented the development of his theoretically oriented school of social history.

Dékány was basically an eclectic thinker who tried to create a new historical school by merging the views of classical sociology with the conceptions and approach of *Geistesgeschichte* historiography. Thus, in his study in the *New Paths of Hungarian Historiography,* he stressed the all-importance of social and economic theories in the writing of history, as well as the need to create models and systems based on "speculative social philosophical categories." He claimed that fact gathering was the obligation of clerks, statisticians and archivists. The duty of historians is to use these facts by building them into a complex system of social and economic evolution. Moreover, the system for the study of Hungarian history, in his view, had to be shaped to the special conditions of Hungarian historical developments. The historians who were willing to undertake such system-building had an obligation to utilize the relevant historical facts through a process that he called "selective synthetization."(45)

Although interesting in itself, Dékány's study was so theoretically oriented that it had little meaning and very little impact on the development of Hungarian social and economic history studies in the 1930's and 1940's. This also holds true for most of his other works on various aspects of social structure, social philosophy and social psychology, all of which had more impact on the nascent Hungarian sociological studies than on the discipline of history. And this may even hold true for his basic historical handbook, *The Methodology of Hungarian Historiography* (1925)(46) written for the Hóman-edited *Handbook of Hungarian Historical Sciences.*

All in all, one might conclude that, while interwar Hungarian historiography was basically *Geistesgeschichte* oriented, and while there were some attempts to make even Hungarian social, economic and cultural history fall in line with this dominant orientation, the Domanovszky-led Hungarian *Kulturgeschichte* School remained basically a positivist phenomenon. And this was true even though neither Domanovszky, nor his followers were able to escape the pervasive philosophical and methodological influences of the dominant *Geistesgeschichte* School.

Chapter XVIII

LEGAL AND CONSTITUTIONAL HISTORY AND THE "DOCTRINE OF THE HOLY CROWN"

Ferenc Eckhart

If Szekfű represented the new *Geistesgeschichte* School, Mályusz the Ethnohistory School, and Domanovszky the *Kulturgeschichte* or Civilization School of interwar Hungarian historical studies, then F. Eckhart (1885-1957)(1) appeared on the scene as the representative of a new school of legal and constitutional history — freed from much of the image-distortions and phantom-conclusions that plagued the Hungarocentric *Weltanschauung* (world view) of its predecessors. Eckhart's appearance on the scene of Hungarian legal and constitutional history around 1930 was so momentous that his rise serves as a dividing line between two distinct phases of interwar Hungarian constitutional history: The first of these still linked to the spirit and approach of the dualist age, characterized among others by an interpretation of legal and constitutional developments purely in light of published laws; and the second, by the influx of the complex synthesizing method of the *Geistesgeschichte* School, as well as by an attempt to lift legal and constitutional historical studies out of their sterility, and to examine constitutional developments in light of the social and economic trends and the dominant spirit of a particular age.

Eckhart's name appeared suddely and forcefully on the Hungarian historical scene in 1931, and did so in connection with a major and bitter controversy about the nature of the "Doctrine of the Holy Crown," that erupted immediately after the appearance of his essay "Legal and Constitutional History" in the Hóman-edited *New Paths of Hungarian Historiography*.(2)

Interestingly enough, Eckhart's essay was not written with the intention of attacking the outdated Doctrine of the Holy Crown. He merely touched on this question, along with numerous other questions of dubious foundations in Hungarian legal and constitutional history. His single most important purpose (as was the case with the authors of the other essays in this volume) was to prepare a program for the modernization and updating of the methodological and interpretative aspects of his discipline in the general direction of the new *Geistesgeschichte* orientation.

Although Eckhart himself was not an all-out disciple of the *Geistesgeschichte* School (about which he had considerable reservations), he still regarded that orientation as a major step forward as compared to the national romantic orientation that had dominated twentieth-century legal and constitutional history far more than it did the other sub-disciplines of Clio's art. Thus he hoped to move his discipline into the stream of contemporary Western scholarly developments by joining the triumphant *Geistesgeschichte* School — at least superficially. This was all the easier to do, as he too was basically a believer in the important (if not dominant) role of the human spirit in history. Thus, Eckhart was convinced that "law is always the product of the spiritual life of certain communities," the most important among which is the nation itself.(3) It is the nation which produces the "national spirit," which in turn determines the nature of its institutions, including those of its legal and constitutional system. Contrary to the pure *Geistesgeschichte* historians, however, Eckhart attributed no exclusiveness to the spiritual forces in the development of a nation's legal and constitutional system. To him social and economic forces were equally important.(4) And it was precisely the absence of consideration for these socio-economic forces that he missed in the works of the older generations of legal and constitutional historians, and that he hoped to remedy through the total reorientation and reinterpretation of his discipline.

When launching his critical reinterpretative program in 1931, Eckhart had hardly settled into his professorial chair of legal and constitutional history at the School of Law of the University of Budapest. Having been appointed in 1929, he received the same chair that had been held before him both by the relatively colorless traditionalist J. Király, as well as by the universally respected great nineteenth-century positivist I. Hajnik.(5) At various times, parallel chairs were held by the somewhat Király-like, though more productive, but also more romantically inclined J. Illés (1917-1944),(6) who managed to retain his chair and his somewhat outmoded views throughout the interwar years; and up to 1925 by the highly idealized, if relatively gifted myth-creator A. Timon (1891-1925),(7) the most powerful formulator and exponent of the so-called "Hungarocentric view" of Hungarian constitutional developments. The latter had monopolized the ideological orientation of Hungarian legal and constitutional history from the early 1890's through the mid-1920's, and his Hungarocentric views became thoroughly imbedded into the mentality of the Hungarian learned classes. Thus, even though not mentioned by name, much of Eckhart's brilliant plea for realism and modernity in the study of Hungarian legal and constitutional history was in fact directed against these basically politically motivated, generally unscholarly, but highly popular and almost sacrosanct views of Timon — his former professor, and in a way his predecessor at the University of Budapest.

The Beginnings of Hungarian Legal and Constitutional History

In looking at the past of Hungarian legal and constitutional history, it appears that its period of highest emotional pitch, but lowest scholarly attainment (from the point of view of objective historical scholarship) was reached during the three decades preceding Eckhart's appointment in 1929; a period that also coincided with the virtually unrivalled dominance of Timon's constitutional theories. Preceding the age of Timon, there were at least two relatively great periods in the history of this discipline.(8) The first of these was connected with the names of the two Kovachich's (father Márton György, and son József Miklós), and it lasted through the last quarter of the eighteenth and the first quarter of the nineteenth century. The second period encompassed the second half of the nineteenth century, and was represented largely by the Budapest professorship of G. Wenzel (1850-1889) and I. Hajnik (1872-1901).

As already seen in an earlier part of this work, the two Kovachich's were the last prominent members of the great eighteenth-century Hungarian Source Collecting Schools, which established the foundations upon which various nineteenth-century synthesizing schools could build and develop.(9) The Kovachich's merit relative to legal and constitutional history lies in the fact that much of what they have collected and edited was in the area of Hungary's constitutional developments. Thus, for the first time Hungarian legal-constitutional historians could stand on firm foundations. Moreover, the Kovachich's work was of a critical and precise nature, far superior to the editorial work of their immediate successor, G. Fejér.(10)

Gusztav Wenzel

As opposed to the basically source-collecting Kovachich's, both Wenzel and Hajnik were diversified scholars who, in addition to some source publications, also produced a number of excellent monographs and synthetic compendiums. Thus, G. Wenzel (1812-1891)(11) was one of the outstanding members of the great pre-positivist generation of nineteenth-century Hungarian historians, who included among their ranks such outstanding practitioners of Hungarian historical sciences as M. Horváth, L. Szalay, F. Rómer, as well as the literary historian F. Toldy. Although — like most members of his generation — Wenzel was basically an autodidact historian, he became both the first major synthesizing scholar in his field, as well as the first professor to teach legal and constitutional history at the University of Budapest. He was also the first to produce a scholarly compendium of European constitutional developments in Hungarian.

Wenzel was both a prolific and a versatile scholar. His prolificness is attested to by at least three dozen authored and edited volumes (including the twelve-volume *New Archives of the Árpádian Age* in the *Monumenta* series); (12) while his versatility is evidenced by numerous monographs and synthetic works on such diverse topics as Hungarian civil, urban and mining law, the relationship between national, provincial and local law systems, the history of Hungarian cities, mines and agriculture, as well as compendiums of Hungarian and European constitutional developments.(13)

Although still somewhat weak in the area of source criticism, Wenzel was perhaps the first historian of Hungarian legal and constitutional developments in the modern scholarly sense of those terms. An Austrian by birth, he became thoroughly Magyarized, and his works also display some of the nationalist flavor that was virtually unavoidable in that age of nationalism, and that colored the words of all Central and East European historians of that period.

Imre Hajnik

Wenzel's pioneering efforts in the area of legal-constitutional history were continued and further developed by his student and subsequent colleague at the University of Budapest, I. Hajnik (1840-1902), who became the greatest of the positivist legal and constitutional historians of Hungary.(14) Although somewhat less prolific than Wenzel, Hajnik's dozen or so major works (which include two excellent but incomplete syntheses of both Hungarian and European constitutional developments)(15) were on the highest level of contemporary Hungarian positivist scholarship, comparable in exactness and precision to the works of G. Pauler, the "father" of Hungarian positivism.

In addition to his historical syntheses (which, however, cover only the medieval developments), we find among Hajnik's major works monographic studies on such diverse topics as the evolution of the entailed estates, representation in the Hungarian feudal diet, the system and operation of medieval Hungarian courts of law, the right of law suit, the evolution of the office of the high sheriff *(főispán)* in the Hungarian county system, etc.(16) — all of which were pace-setting in their time and subject matter.

During the three decades of his incumbency in one of the Budapest chairs of legal and constitutional history, Hajnik produced several generations of legal-constitutional historians. None of these, however, were able to come up to the level and scholarly achievements of their master. Thus, while less successful than the older Salamon or the younger Marczali, Angyal or Békefi in producing great students in their respective fields, Hajnik's own scholarly achievements are no less imposing in his own field;(17) and his name is also connected with the formulation of the first modern version of the so-called "Doctrine of the Holy Crown".

The Doctrine of the Holy Crown

The origins of this doctrine — the critical handling of which by Eckhart produced such a furor during the 1930's — goes back to the Hungarian Middle Ages.(18) In all probability it was a byproduct of the constitutional development whereby St. Stephen's crown emerged as the symbol of the power and essence of the Hungarian state. This process was completed by the fifteenth century. In the first part of sixteenth century, however, the doctrine was further complicated by Werbőczi's *Tripartitum* (1515),(19) which merged the state and the Hungarian nobility *("Natio Hungarica")* into a kind of mystical union, in analogy of the "Mystical Body of Christ" as used in reference to the Catholic Church and its faithful. This process continued in the eighteenth century, however, the doctrine was further complicated by Werbőczy's and religious elements (e.g. the concept of the "Regnum Marian-num").(20) Finally, in the period following the Austro-Hungarian Compromise of 1967, in light of the difficulties with the national minorities, the doctrine ultimately emerged as the symbol of unity of the lands and peoples of the Crownlands of St. Stephen (Historic Hungary).

Hajnik, who was the first to give a modern formulation to this theory during the 1870's, traced its origins back to the fourteenth century, and connected it with the new landowning system that developed under the Anjou dynasty. According to this system, all freely owned lands were declared to have been derived from, and dependent upon the power of the Holy Crown. This system, in turn was the byproduct of the new land distribution that came into being during the previous two centuries through the division of much of the royal lands among the rising nobility, and the consequent growing dependence of the monarch upon the material and military support of this class. This dependence then resulted in a new and closer relationship between these two sources of power (the monarch and the nobility) and found expression in the Doctrine of the Holy Crown, according to which the crown of St. Stephen "came to symbolize the public power shared by the king and the nation (nobility)."(21) Thus — as summed up for Hajnik by a recent scholar — "the territory of the state became the territory of the Holy Crown; the royal income and possessions (became) the possessions of the Holy Crown; all ownership rights found their roots in it (the Holy Crown); and all owners of free estates . . . (came) to share in its power (and thereby became) members of the Holy Crown."(22)

Subsequently, this doctrine was further refined, stretched and augmented both by such basically positivist scholars as G. Concha (1846-1933). K. Kmety (1863-1929) and A. Balogh (1866-1951),(23) as well as by such national romantics as Timon and his followers. And this also holds true for the idea-oriented and partially politically motivated *Geistesgeschichte* historians, such as those connected with the large folios of the *St. Stephen Memorial Album,* published on the occasion of the ninth centennial of St. Stephen's death (1938).(24) It was in this work where this doctrine reached the apogee of its refinement and sublimation.

Timon's Refining of the Doctrine of the Holy Crown

While all of these schools and individuals have added something to this doctrine, the most extreme, least realistic, yet most popular version of the Doctrine of the Holy Crown was formulated by the twentieth-century national romantic A. Timon.(25) His two most important contributions to Hajnik's formula of this doctrine consisted of his further refinement of the close relationship that allegedly existed between this doctrine and the indivisible unity of the lands and the peoples of the Crownlands of St. Stephen, and his claim to the effect that this doctrine was unique in Europe, and thus the product of the Magyar genius.(26)

According to the first of these claims, the "mystical union" which previously (prior to the emergence of the bourgeois-democratic order of 1848) had bound only the state and the nobility into an indivisible union with the Holy Crown — was now extended to all of the citizens of Historic Hungary, irrespective of their class or national origins. In line with this theory, Timon pointed to the alleged "unparalleled earliness and singular purity" of Hungarian statehood and constitutionalism, all of which he attributed to the unusual "state-forming capacities of the Magyars."

As to the second of his claims, Timon was convinced that "the Doctrine of the Holy Crown is the visible manifestation of that constitutional mentality which had existed in the soul of the Magyar people from times immemorial, (and) which became manifest during the feudal age, as a reaction against the feudal concepts which tried to penetrate (into Hungary) from the West."(27) In other words, in Timon's views this doctrine was simply a part of medieval Hungarian constitutionalism that managed to withstand and overcome the Western forces of feudalism, and bound "the whole Magyar nation, along with the king who wore the Holy Crown, into . . . a living organism, which in medieval sources is referred to as the Body of the Holy Crown . . ."(28) Timon appeared to be convinced of the validity and historicity of this myth-filled doctrine, just as much as he was convinced that "the sovereign national existence and national independence of the Magyar nation stands or falls with the Holy Crown."(29)

Thus, the Doctrine of the Holy Crown came to its full mystical bloom with Timon's rise and lengthy dominance of Hungarian legal and historical thinking. Once his theories had been accepted and popularized on a mass scale, there was no escape from them, unless one wished to risk the wrath of the powerful and the condemnation of the nation. And this applied equally to the members of the historical profession, as well as to the public in general. The latter naturally possessed little critical sense in this area. But the professional historians and constitutional scholars also accepted Timon's theories without much opposition. They did so either out of conviction (it certainly appealed to their national pride), or because they saw no way out without considerable risk to themselves. This was true even for such excellent critical scholars as H. Marczali — as reflected in his two German language works in the area of legal and constitutional history.(30) But Marczali was not a specialist in this area, as were such other members of his generation as K. Óvári (1844-1925) and S. Kolosvári (1840-1922), constitutional historians at the University of Kolozsvár (1872-1916 and 1972-1910 respectively),(31) or the already mentioned J. Király (1858-1929), Timon's colleague at the University of Budapest (1896 1902-1928).(32) Notwithstanding their legal training (or perhaps precisely because of it) all of these scholars regarded the Doctrine of the Holy Crown as one of the basic and untouchable foundations of Hungarian constitutionalism and statehood.

This was also true for most of their students (with the exception of Eckhart and his followers) who held the six or seven chairs of legal and constitutional history at Hungary's four interwar universities. These included such traditionalist oriented scholars as Z. Kérészy (1868-1952) of Pozsony and Pécs, J. Illés (1871-1944) of Budapest, I. Ereky (1876-1943) of Pozsony and Szeged, M. Bochkor (1877-1920) of Kolozsvár, and B. Iványi (1878-1964) of Debrecen and Szeged; as well as such younger and more modernistic scholars as B. Baranyai (1882-1945) of Debrecen and the already treated neo-positivist J. Holub of Pécs.(33)

The Doctrine of the Holy Crown During the Interwar Period

Although basically unchanged, Timon's theories about the meaning of the Doctrine of the Holy Crown acquired additional political significance after the collapse of the Dual Monarchy and the consequent dismemberment of Hungary. Henceforth it had to serve also as a sacred symbol and promise of the eventual reunification of historic Hungary, as well as of the "constitutional continuity" of the interwar social and political system. In this way it gave a semblance of legitimacy to the new "kingdom without a king" that was Hungary of the interwar period.

The political implications and goals of the Timon version of this doctrine were of course readily apparent even prior to 1918 — as these were admitted by G. Ferdinándy (1864-1924), a noted constitutional scholar at the University of Budapest. In a study published in 1917, Ferdinándy openly alluded to the Doctrine of the Holy Crown as a "legal fiction" which must be utilized fully to preserve Hungary's integrity and "independence" within the Habsburg Empire. But more than this, Ferdinándy also regarded this doctrine as a powerful weapon with which to counterbalance the centrifugal tendencies of the non-Magyar nationalities of the Hungarian State.(34)

Following the establishment and consolidation of dismembered Hungary's "neo-Baroque system" in 1920, this doctrine became a rallying point and instrument of political struggle for several political groups. These included the various legitimists and other usually conservative patriotic groups, all of which were angling for power within the much reduced possibilities of the dismembered Hungarian State and society. The ideologists of these groups added nothing to the Timon version of this doctrine, but simply twisted it back and forth to suit their immediate political needs and goals. Thus, the revered Doctrine of the Holy Crown became a political instrument in the struggle among the pro-Habsburg forces, the advocates of various "national dynasties," as well as the forces of Regent Nicholas Horthy, who also had his views and goals relative to the vacant throne of Hungary.(35)

As opposed to the clearly politically motivated nationalist power groups within the country (all of which accepted the doctrine as a symbol of unity and reunification of the lands and peoples of historic Hungary) the situation was rather different with the much more sophisticated ideologists of the emerging *Geistesgeschichte* School. The *Geistesgeschichte* historians also accepted the essence of the doctrine, and they too ascribed an important role to the "power" of the Holy Crown in the reunification of Hungary. But while subscribing to this doctrine — true to their polished taste and philosophical refinement — they were further reworking it into an even more sophisticated doctrine, approximating in every sense the mystical and symbolic characteristics of the "Mystical Body of Christ" concept as advocated by the Catholic Church.

The Saint Stephen Memorial Album

The climax to the *Geistesgeschichte* elaboration of this doctrine came in 1938 on the ninth centennial of the death of St. Stephen, Hungary's first Christian king, from whom both the Holy Crown and the basic concepts of this doctrine were ultimately derived. The *Geistesgeschichte* views of this doctrine received the fullest possible orchestration in the three large folio volumes of the *Saint Stephen Memorial Album,* edited for this occasion by Hungary's learned prince primate, Justinian Serédi.(36)

In his introduction to this grandiose work, Serédi re-emphasized the belief that "St. Stephen's crown . . . unites symbolically the king and the nation, (and) contains, personifies and represents all constitutional privileges, the original source of which is God, as symbolized by the icons on the Holy Crown."(37) Serédi's editorship of these volumes, and his tone-setting essay underlined even further the closeness of the relationship that had evolved between religion, as represented by the Catholic Church, and the mist-shrouded Doctrine of the Holy Crown.

Among the numerous contributions to the *Saint Stephen Memorial Album,* the study which most expressed the *Geistesgeschichte* conception of the Holy Crown Doctrine is the one by B. Hóman. This great, but hardly philosophically oriented historian exerted himself in this study beyond his capacities to try to synthesize the great king and the doctrine connected with his name into a sublime irreality. Thus, to Hóman, St. Stephen's soul or spirit personified "the indissoluble synthesis of the consciousness, Christlike faith (and) Occidental spirit of the Magyars, (whose) culture is the traditional Hungarian Catholic faith, (that is) the Christian Hungarian Civilization that binds the elements of European culture into a harmonious unity." Hóman saw St. Stephen as the "first European Magyar," who, responsible for producing "the European Magyar race and people of today," who, while truly European, still "retain their ancient ethnic characteristics (virtues)," and who have ruled the Carpathian Basin for a whole millennium with wisdom and prudence.(38)

Totally different was Szekfű's contribution to this volume. Although much more philosophical than Hóman, Szekfű was less inclined to mythologize history. Thus, his picture of Hungary's first Christian king was not that of an aetherized demigod, but rather that of a medieval *Realpolitiker* and a conservative reformer, whose spirit re-emerged once more during the nineteenth century in the person of Count István Széchenyi (1791-1860).(39) To Szekfű, Széchenyi represented the ideal "European Christian universalism," combined with an element of realism and self-criticism, that was also advocated by his younger contemporary, the great thinker and statesman Baron József Eötvös (1813-1871).(40) And in searching for an early Magyar advocate of this nineteenth-century realism, self-criticism and Christian universalism, he found it in Hungary's first Christian king. This approach was all the more acceptable to Szekfű in 1938, as by that time he had begun to turn away from his earlier emphasis on Hungary's obligatory membership in the "German Christian Cultural World," and St. Stephen's anti-German stand (his struggle against the Saxon emperors) made him into an ideal prototype of an anti-German European Magyar.

Szekfű's conceptions about the Doctrine of the Holy Crown were also more terrestrial than those of Hóman and most of the other contributors to the *Saint Stephen Memorial Album.* These approximated essentially the demythologized views of Eckhart. At the same time, however — while refusing to go along with the trend that transformed St. Stephen and his Crown into a mystified spirituality — Szekfű also spoke up against the "new paganism" represented by various pan-Turanian groups in Hungary. The latter, driven by misdirected national emotions, tried to deprive Hungary's first king of all of his undeniable achievements and glory, and worked to turn the gaze of the Magyars from Europe back to the land of their alleged origins, Asia. In Szekfű's view, this ethnic-based Hungarian Turanism was simply another version of "the new paganism (Nazism) supported by the official forces of the Great German Empire (Third Reich)."(41)

While virtually all of the nearly fifty essays in the memorial album had something to say about the Doctrine of the Holy Crown, it was also treated in a separte study by M. Nagy, a noted scholar of Hungarian public law.(42) Nagy's essay, however, had little new or interesting to offer. It was basically a dry summary of the nature and evolution of the doctrine, based largely on Timon's views, with only a slight effort to add some *Geistesgeschichte* coloring to it. As such, it was considerably less significant than either Hóman's or Szekfű's essay, and subsequently Eckhart was fully justified in claiming that "it contributed nothing new to the solution of this question."(43)

Although Nagy's essay was neither original, nor very inspiring, the spirit of this doctrine did in fact permeate the whole grand project. Thus, the *Saint Stephen Memorial Album* was largely a kind of orchestrated climax to the triumphant march of the Doctrine of the Holy Crown, just before its total dethronement from the Hungarian constitutional scene in 1945.(44) During the 1930's, however, no one could as yet foresee its imminent demise, and thus it ruled unchallenged in the neo-Baroque world of interwar Hungary. This was due both to political expediency, as well as to the fact that under Timon's unchallenged rule of Hungarian constitutional history, it had penetrated and saturated the thinking of Hungary's leading classes, and thus it became a kind of sacrosanct cornerstone of the very foundations of Hungarian constitutionalism, society and national policy. It was this sacrosanct cornerstone then which came under Eckhart's attack in 1931.

Eckhart's Attack Against the Timonian System

When Eckhart initiated his onslaught against Timon and his archaic teachings, he was convinced that the time for the scholarly reexamination of Hungary's constitutional developments had finally arrived. He also believed that Hungarian society had reached the point where it can tolerate the critical treatment of questions "which yesterday were still in the center of political controversy."(45) Thus, certain about the timeliness of his undertaking, and believing that he could best do it under the triumphant flags of the *Geistesgeschichte*

School, Eckhart launched an attack against the whole Timonian system (based on "patriotic watchwords" and not on "sources which can withstand scholarly criticism")(46) in the intended handbook of Hungarian *Geistesgeschichte* historiography, the Hóman-edited *New Paths.*

In outlining the ideal new paths of Hungarian legal and constitutional historical research, Eckhart pointed to two important considerations to be taken into account. The first of these was the need to study the socio-economic developments of Hungarian society at a given time, before accepting that contemporary legal paragraphs are reflective of those developments. As he pointed out, "if a charter (contemporary document) contradicts the law, the latter can always be dismissed. The customary law (that evolved out of society) has unconditional primacy over the (enacted) law . . . (Thus), under no circumstances could (enacted) law alter privileges which grew out of society itself."(47)

The second consideration stressed by Eckhart was the need to rely extensively on the comparative method, through the examination of social and institutional analogies among contemporary nations at any given time of their history.

In Eckhart's view, the first of these considerations would prevent legal historians from arguing over the meaning of a given term in a legal paragraph, for if the law (or any of its paragraphs) was not reflective of contemporary socio-economic conditions, than it may as well be disregarded. The second consideration would protect constitutional scholars from mistakes such as — for example — devoting heavy tomes to the examination of the alleged similarity between English and Hungarian constitutional developments. (This was only one of many popular fallacies held by them prior to Eckhart's emergence.) "If we know," said Eckhart "that English economic conditions and the English social evolution are substantially different from those of their Hungarian counterpart, than we may as well presume that the constitutional developments of these two peoples cannot possibly be similar."(48)

Eckhart's natural conclusion from the above was that if Hungarian scholars are to work with analogies, than these anaolgies of Hungarian constitutional and other institutional developments must be drawn from countries whose social and economic developments were roughly similar to those of Hungary. And here he clearly pointed to Poland and especially to Bohemia whose developments approximated those of Hungary. Eckhart found that the social and economic developments of these three countries were clearly similar, as were their spiritual and intellectual traditions, which stemmed largely from Frankish-German roots.

It was in this connection that Eckhart pointed to the similarity between the Hungarian and the Czech versions of the crown doctrine, according to both of which the personified crown (and not the king) became the source of all legal and constitutional powers in the "Lands of the Hungarian Holy Crown" and the "Lands of the Czech Crown."(49) With this assertion Eckhart unwittingly made two major tactical mistakes: First, he attacked the universal Magyar belief in the uniqueness and unparalleled superiority of Hungarian constitutional developments; and second, he compared and equated these developments with those of the intensely disliked Czechs — who allegedly had a major role in the dismemberment of the "Lands of the Hungarian Holy Crown" or the "Crownlands of St. Stephen." This was more than the provincial-oriented Hungarian public opinion could take. Eckhart's attack on Timon and on the latter's questionable scholarship were now interpreted as an attack against the honor and integrity of the Magyar nation itself. And thus the bitter campaign against Eckhart and his demand for a sound legal-historical scholarship began.

Campaign against Eckhart and his Reinterpretation of Hungarian Legal and Constitutional History

The campaign against Eckhart was organized not so much by historians (many of whom had never fully accepted Timon's theories), but by scholars of public law who had been educated in the belief of the uniqueness and superiority of Hungarian constitutional developments. Now with Eckhart's desire to put the study of Hungarian constitutional developments on a sound footing, they saw their whole archaic dreamworld shaken, and they felt puzzled and frightened.

The constitutional experts were joined in this attack by two other groups as well: The highly "patriotic," but superficial journalists in search of cheap sensation and public attention; and the sonorous parliamentarians in search of political laurels and votes. These two groups apparently were convinced — or so they claimed — that Eckhart's attack against the "illusion of the Holy Crown" was also an attack against the "illusion of the unity of the country," and thus against the "holiest of (Hungary's) national goals (irredentism)."(50) Moreover, they felt that by undermining the belief in the uniqueness of the Doctrine of the Holy Crown through reference to the Czech analogy, Eckhart made himself virtually into an unpaid servant of Hungary's most vicious national enemies.

The true scholars — even if disagreeing with Eckhart — were of course less vicious in their attacks; but they too felt their world shaken. Moreover, they viewed his attempts at this reinterpretation to be both over-anxious and untimely. Thus, even such eminently qualified and relatively detached critics as the older legal-constitutional historian Kérészy — who held this chair at the University of Pozsony and Pécs between 1914-1938 — expressed his doubts about the correctness of the analogy of the Czech and Hungarian crown doctrines — regarding it unlikely that this doctrine had played such a significant role in Czech constitutional developments as in its Hungarian counterpart.(51) But going beyond pure scholarly considerations, Kérészy too expressed the belief that Eckhart's views may have considerable adverse effects on Hungary's revisionist goals. For, by equating Hungary's constitutional developments with those of some of the surrounding peoples — so he believed — the Magyars in fact have relinquished their claim to cultural pre-eminence in the Carpathian Basin, and consequently also their claim to political leadership in the area.

The controversy soon reached the parliament itself, where several Timon-educated "patriots" demanded Eckhart's dismissal from his university chair. That they did not succeed was due only to the all-out support of Count Kunó Klebelsberg(52) — the broad-minded minister of religion and public education of that time — and to the solidarity of his most noted colleagues in the historical profession. Among the latter, particularly important was Domanovszky's and Mályusz's support, both of whom were scholars of influence, and both of whom believed in a scholar's right to free expression.(53) Furthermore, they also liked Eckhart's refusal to become totally enslaved by the new *Geistesgeschichte* philosophy. Both of them objected to the demand on the part of *Geistesgeschichte* historians for exclusiveness, and appreciated Eckhart's unwillingness to capitulate to them by denouncing the achievements of the Positivist School. Domanovszky also agreed with Eckhart in his most important theses. These included his emphasis on social and economic factors in the study of constitutional developments; his attempt to lift Hungarian constitutional scholarship out of its Hungarocentric world; and his insistence upon studying the history of Hungarian legal and constitutional system within the context of the broader East Central European social, economic and constitutional developments.

While the influential Domanovszky's defense was more important, the young Mályusz went even further in his defense of Eckhart. After pointing out one of the major positive features of Eckhart's study — namely his attempt to coordinate and to synthesize the best elements and achievements of the positivist and the *Geistesgeschichte* schools — Mályusz bluntly asserted that "the Doctrine of the Holy Crown is nothing but another version of the organic state concept which became dominant everywhere (in Europe) during the Middle Ages . . . This doctrine, along with many similar concepts — as for example the medieval version of the social contract theory — was part of contemporary *Weltanschauung* (world view) . . . The feudal type of evolution that also took roots on Hungarian soil and these elements of thought proceeded in a parallel line, only to meet occasionally, until finally — under the impact of (certain) political conditions — (István) Werbőczy (1458-1591) molded them together consciously."(54) In effect what Mályusz did in this study was to defend Eckhart by agreeing with him about the lack of uniqueness of the Doctrine of the Holy Crown and of the whole Hungarian constitutional development. But more than this, Mályusz also prepared a program for Eckhart in the latter's endeavor (in wake of this controversy) to trace the evolution of the crown doctrine, and thus clear himself before the nation.

In his major work on *The History of the Doctrine of the Holy Crown,* published ten years later (1941),(55) Eckhart followed through Mályusz's basic recommendations and discussed the evolution of this doctrine within the context of the organic state concept. In this work, however, he injected more *Geistesgeschichte* ideas than in his earlier study — perhaps to accommodate somewhat the prophets of that dominant school.

Eckhart's Major Works and His Impact

As clearly evident from the above, Eckhart's impact on Hungarian legal and constitutional historical studies was immense, and his role was essentially similar to those of Szekfű, Domanovszky and Mályusz in their own respective sub-disciplines. In addition to the influence of his basically objective, critical and synthetic approach, this impact was most significant in the area of social and economic developments; that is in his attempts to view legal and constitutional questions in light of the contemporary social system. It is not surprising, therefore, that — in spite of his official position of being Hungary's foremost legal and constitutional historian — Eckhart wrote more in the area of social and economic history than in his official field.

As an example, his very first major work, *The Economic Policy of the Viennese Court in Hungary in the Age of Maria Theresa* (1922) was in the area of socio-economic history. So were his last major works, including his posthumous sequence to the above study, *The Economic*

Policy of the Viennese Court in Hungary 1780-1815 (1958). The others included his *The Serf Policies of the Viennese Court 1761-1790* (1956), and his *Manorial Jurisdiction in the 16th-17th Centuries* (1954). All of these works were pioneering studies, and all of them made a major imprint on Hungarian historical studies.(56)

Eckhart also authored the first scholarly, and partially *Geistesgeschichte* synthesis of modern Hungarian economic history, entitled *Hundred Years of Hungarian Economic Life* (1941).(57) This work was an undertaking that neither the economic historian F. Kováts, nor the socio-cultural historian Domanovszky was able to complete, and which remained the only and unchallenged compendium of Hungarian economic developments until the recent synthesis by I. Berend and G. Ránki *(Hundred Years of Hungarian Economy,* 1972).(58)

In his official field of Hungarian legal and constitutional history, Eckhart's contributions were less numerous, but — in their impact — hardly less significant. Outside his tone-setting essay of 1931 in the *New Paths of Hungarian Historiography,* his most important contribution was undoubtedly his *Hungarian Constitutional and Legal History* (1946), which was the first one-volume modern synthesis that covered the history of constitutional developments right up to 1944.(59) Although finished some years earlier as a basic textbook for his course at the University of Budapest, this work remained unpublished until 1946 — perhaps for fear of another concentrated attack against him by the self-appointed champions of Timon's archaic world.

Like Szekfű and Domanovszky at Budapest, and Holub at Pécs, Eckhart was also among those few historians who — contrary to Mályusz and others — were able to retain their university chairs even after 1945. In fact, as we have seen, he produced some of this most important works on social and economic history during the post-1945 period — at the same time while trying to synthesize his semi-positivist, semi-*Geistesgeschichte* views with the teachings of the newly triumphant historical materialism. While one can hardly question the great merit of his post-1945 works, Eckhart's attempts to blend these three distinct and basically contradictory philosophies of history was less than successful.

Positivist Interwar Legal and Constitutional History: József Illés at Budapest

Parallel with Eckhart's activities at the University of Budapest, post-Timonian legal and constitutional historiography was also represented by a number of excellent traditional scholars of the Positivist School. But with Illés's exception, they were all located at Hungary's three regional universities. They included the older Kérészy (Pécs) and Iványi (Debrecen and Szeged), and the younger Baranyai (Debrecen) and Holub (Pécs).

As summed up recently, J. Illés (1871-1944), Eckhart's older colleague at the University of Budapest (1917-1944), was "one of the last representatives of the conservative, ideologically strongly feudalistic school of Werbőczy eulogists,"(60) who wrote virtually nothing during the interwar years, but devoted his efforts primarily to politics and to Greek Catholic religious affairs. Illés's primary area of scholarly interest was the legal and constitutional system of the Hungarian Middle Ages. But he pursued active scholarly research only prior to his appointment to the University of Budapest in 1917. His most significant monographs (all written during the two decades prior to his appointment) dealt with such diverse topics as taxation, inheritance, marriage contracts, etc. during the age of the Árpáds and the Anjous in Hungary.(61)

Illés's only summarizing work is his *Introduction to the History of Hungarian Law,* first published in 1910, but used throughout the interwar years as a university textbook along with Timon's older and even more traditional work.(62) (Not until the end of World War II did Holub (1944) and Eckhart (1946) appear with their own compendiums of Hungarian constitutional history, when the coming of historical materialism made these texts outdated almost from the start.)

Although a rather typical representative of the old school, Illés was more reliable and less myth-seeking than Timon and his followers. Moreover, he was also responsible for organizing the first research seminar on legal and constitutional history at the University of Budapest, and consequently produced a number of noteworthy students (e.g. A. Degré).(63)

Zoltán Kérészy at Pozsony and Pécs

Not very unlike in outlook was Z. Kérészy (1868-1953), a member of the same generation as Illés, and a professor of legal and constitutional history at the University of Pozsony (soon transferred to Pécs) for two and a half decades (1914-1938).(64) Like Illés, Kérészy too was an historian with a conservative mentality, and had a legal rather than an historical training. But he worked more in the traditions of the highly respected positivist scholar I. Hajnik (his former professor at Budapest) than in those of the flamboyant and largely uncritical Timon. Moreover, unlike Illés at Budapest, Kérészy did not cease writing after his appointment to his university chair. On the contrary, he produced at least half of his major works during the interwar years. On the whole, Kérészy was a more prolific writer than Illés, and he appears to have been less rigid in his conservative ideological orientation.

While Illés dealt primarily with the civil institutions of the Middle Ages in Hungary, Kérészy was first of all a specialist of canon law. It was in this area where he produced his *opus magnum,* his four-volume compendium on *Catholic Canon Law* (1927-1929).(65) Kérészy also authored a large, if unfinished *Textbook of Canon Law* (1903),(66) as well as numerous monographs on such topics as the Hungarian monarch's veto power over papal elections *(ius exclusivae),* Catholic Autonomy in Hungary, mixed marriages, and on the legal privileges of the clergy *(privilegium fori).*(67) He also devoted at least a half a dozen studies to the question of the evolution and functioning of the Hungarian dietary system.(68)

As mentioned earlier, Kérészy too joined Eckhart's critics after the appearance of the latter's plea for the reorientation of Hungarian constitutional history. His *Feudal Concepts and Hungarian Constitutional Developments* (1931),(69) however, was a rather moderate criticism. It certainly had nothing in common with the violent and subjective attacks of the publicists, politicians and various other prophets of the Timonian ideas.

During the two and a half decades of his professorial tenure, Kérészy had made the University of Pécs into one of the important centers of Hungarian constitutional historical research. Moreover, although possessing less material and scholarly resources than his colleagues at Budapest, he produced some outstanding students (e.g. the constitutional and cultural historian F. Somogyi).(70) Kérészy, of course, was aided in his work by his colleague and successor J. Holub, who until Kérészy's retirement held the chair of Hungarian history at Pécs (1923-1938). No less important was the presence of J. Vinkler (b. 1886), a professor of trial law at Pécs, who was the author of the largest interwar compendium on a specific aspect and period of Hungarian legal history, the two-volume *Hungarian Juridical System and Civil Legal Proceedings from the Battle of Mohács (1526) till 1848* (1921-1927).(71)

Béla Iványi at Debrecen and at Szeged

Another prominent member of the traditionalist school of interwar legal and constitutional historians was B. Iványi (1878-1964), Illés's and Kérészy's counterpart at Debrecen (1914-1926) and later at Szeged

(1926-1937).(72) Like Kérészy and Illés, Iványi too was basically an empiricist in his source research and criticism, and a mixture of positivist and romantic nationalist in his ideological outlook. But unlike the former two, he was almost exclusively a source publisher. His emphasis was on genealogy and on urban legal history. Thus he published large documentary collections on the history and legal system of a number of free royal cities (e.g. Bártfa, Eperjes, Göncz and Körmend), as well as on the genealogy of several prominent historic families (e.g. Bánffy, Teleki, Zrínyi, Batthyány, Festetich, Pázmány).(73)

Although Iványi wrote with almost equal ease on such diverse topics as legal, church, cultural, economic and military history, most of his summarizing works are only short studies. The two exceptions are his monograph on *The Origins of Urban Citizenship Rights* (1936) and his mimeographed *Notes on Hungarian Constitutional and Legal History* (1926), which contained his traditional university lectures at the Universities of Debrecen and Szeged.(74)

Although the incumbent of two consecutive chairs of legal and constitutional history, Iványi was closer to a nineteenth-century source publisher than to a twentieth-century synthesizer. Moreover, his interest was more in genealogy and urban developments than in legal and constitutional history in the strict sense of these terms. As such, Iványi's achievements in his official field cannot really be compared to those of Kérészy, Illés or Holub.

Béla Baranyai at Debrecen and József Holub at Pécs

Contrary to Illés, Kérészy and Iványi, and similarly to Eckhart, both Baranyai and Holub were modernistic scholars and had better training in historical methodology. Baranyai had received some of his post-university training at the Hungarian Historical Research Institute at Vienna under A. Károlyi's leadership; while Holub was trained first of all as an historian at Eötvös College, and only secondarily as a legal scholar — a phenomenon that was unusual among Hungarian constitutional historians.

B. Baranyai (1882-1945) was Iványi's successor at the University of Debrecen (1927-1945). He was a well-trained and careful scholar, but very unproductive.(75) In the course of his scholarly career he never managed to complete more than half a dozen major articles. Although he also finished his intended *opus magnum* about Cardinal Kollonich's *Einrichtungswerk dér Königreichs Ungarn* (1689) (76) on how to break the anti-Habsburg opposition of the Hungarian Estates, but it never appeared in print. Thus, despite his two decades of professorial work and his carefully prepared published essays, Baranyai has no major place in Hungarian constitutional historical studies.(77)

The situation is rather different with J. Holub (1885-1962), discussed in conjunction with interwar positivist historiography.(78) Although perhaps less productive than his colleague and predecessor Kérészy, as holder of the chairs of Hungarian (1923-1938) and later Hungarian legal and constitional history (1938-1952) at the University of Pécs, Holub did produce a number of major monographs, as well as a highly regarded critical synthesis of Hungarian constitutional developments. As the best trained interwar constitutional historian outside Eckhart, most of Holub's studies were excellent and pioneering. Yet, he too wrote more than he published.(79)

Perhaps partially for the above reason, Holub's influence in contemporary historical circles was less pervasive than warranted by the quality of his works. Probably even more important reasons, however, were his attachment to positivism and his absence from Budapest. This is particularly evident in comparison with Eckhart, whose interwar scholarly publications did not really exceed those of Holub, but who wielded considerably more influence.

The Rise of a New Generation

At the time of the fall of the old order (1918-1920), among the major sub-disciplines of history, Hungarian legal and constitutional historical studies were undoubtedly in the most archaic stages of development. And this was so both from the ideological, as well as from the methodological point of view. As we have seen, university level training was still primarily in the hands of scholars with legal training, who lacked the critical methodological outlook of historians, and who consequently were more prone to myth-creating than their trained colleagues in history.

With the appearance of Eckhart, and to a lesser degree Holub, on the scene of Hungarian historical studies, however, the education of legal and constitutional historians underwent a major reorientation. For the first time, prospective scholars of constitutional developments began to go through the same rigorous training previously reserved only for prospective historians. As their number increased, so did their influence. And this was true, notwithstanding the fact that traditional legists remained in majority among interwar chairholders of constitutional history.

In light of the above, during the 1930's there began a systematic dismantling of the archaic ideological and methodological structure of Hungarian constitutional historical studies. And this process continued, even though contemporary Hungary's official leadership was prone to the perpetuation of the traditional views as developed in Timon's works. Ultimately, while some myths remained, and others were transformed to suit the ethereal views of the *Geistesgeschichte* historians, the newly initiated critical scholarship was reaping its rewards. For the first time demythologized scholarly works began to appear on a large scale on many aspects of Hungarian constitutional developments, and a new generation of young legal historians arose, whose views and approaches differed radically from those of their teachers and predecessors.

The most noted and promising among these young scholars included F. Somogyi (b. 1906),(80) a student and later colleague of Kérészy and Holub at Pécs; A. Degré (b. 1909),(81) a student of Illés and Eckhart at Budapest, and subsequently a professor of legal history at Pécs (1951-1957); and the even younger G. Bonis (b. 1914) who, as Eckhart's favorite and perhaps most gifted student, became the first and youngest incumbent of the chair of legal and constitutional history at the reconstituted University of Kolozsvár (1940-1947), and then at the University of Szeged (1948-1957).(82) This brilliant and promising young generation, however, was doomed to partial if temporary scholarly demise. With the switch to Marxist legality between 1945 and 1948, they suddenly found themselves confronted with a totally different and unexpected situation at a very critical point in their career. As a result, Somogyi left Hungary, and subsequently switched his attention from legal to socio-cultural history; while Degré and Bonis tried to readjust themselves to the new conditions as best as they could, and ultimately emerged as prominent Marxist legal and constitutional historians. For a while they participated in the education of a new generation of Marxist legal historians, but ultimately they both ended up as archivists (1957), having been displaced by the new generation they had helped to produce.

Some of the other members of the young interwar generation of legal and constitutional historians included I. Meznerics (b. 1907), L. Torday (b. 1910), A. Murárik (1914-1939), K. Szoika (c. 1918-c. 1944), and A. Csizmadia (b. 1910).(83) Of these youngest members of the interwar generation, however, only Csizmadia remained faithful to legal history and reached a university professorship in his field, ultimately becoming the director of the Institute of Legal History at the University of Pécs. Csizmadia is also the primary author of the first major and definitive Marxist legal history synthesis, entitled *Hungarian State and Legal History* (1972).(84)

Chapter XIX

EUROPEAN AND WORLD (''UNIVERSAL'') HISTORY STUDIES

The Heritage of the Dualist Period

Late nineteenth and early twentieth-century Hungarian positivist scholarship has done much to bring the level of Hungarian historiography up to the level of its Western counterparts. In general these efforts were successful. There were, of course, exceptions, the most important being the area of European and world history studies. Due to financial, manpower and various other limitations, Hungarian scholarship in that area simply could not measure up to Western standards.

As mentioned in an earlier section of this study, outside of certain selected fields necessary for the study of Magyar origins and Hungarian history (e.g. Byzantinology, Turkology, Finno-Ugric Studies), Hungarian historical scholarship had done very little in the area of non-Hungarian history.(1)

There were, nonetheless, some positive developments during the dualist period. Thus, in 1866 a separate chair for world history (the first of its kind in Hungary) was established at the University of Budapest,(2) followed in 1872 by the establishment of a second chair at the University of Kolozsvár.(3) This in turn was followed in 1879 by increasing the number of chairs in world history at Budapest to three (ancient, medieval and modern);(4) and in 1914, by the creation of two additional chairs at the newly established universities of Pozsony and Debrecen.(5) Moreover, the same period also saw the appearance of several major compendiums of world history, including F. Somhegyi's three-volume *General World History* (1851-1856),(6) F. Ribáry's eight-volume *Illustrated World History* (1878-1886),(7) S. Márki's four-volume *World History* (1910-1911)(8) and H. Marczali's twelve-volume *Great Illustrated World History* (1898-1904).(9) The latter is still the most extensive Hungarian-written synthesis of the history of mankind. (The more recent ten volume *World History* published during the 1960's, while roughly of the same size as Marczali's work, is not a product of Hungarian historiography, but simply a translation of a Soviet work.)(10)

Despite these achievements, however, Hungarian scholarship of the dualist period was unable to produce anything basic and original in the field of European and world history. Thus, none of the above compendiums contained much original, and even many of the important monographic works were basically summaries of Western works, rather than results of original research.

The General State of World History Studies During the Interwar Period

If the situation in the area of world and European history studies was far from ideal during the dualist period, it showed little improvement during much of the interwar period. This was so at least until the 1930's, when several representatives of a "new course" appeared on the scene, either under the *Geistesgeschichte* flags, or under Hajnal's Sociological School.

Although by the beginning of the interwar period the number of university chairs for world history has increased to six (not counting the chairs in classical philology, a number of whose occupants also dealt with ancient history), the scholarly makeup of the incumbents remained essentially similar to that of the dualist period. Most of them were good historians, but with a few exceptions they were basically scholars of Hungarian history.

At Budapest, for example the chair of modern history was held by the flamboyant A. Ballagi (1880-1924), and then by the elderly D. Angyal (1925-1929), who transferred briefly from his chair of Hungarian history — the area where he produced virtually all of his scholarly works. Simultaneously, the chair of medieval history was held by A. Áldásy, a reliable positivist scholar of medieval historiography and genealogy, who at least produced some respectable works on church history and the crusades. He held his chair for two decades until his death (1912-1932). Thereafter his chair remained vacant until the appointment of P. Váczy (b. 1904) in 1942, a brilliant young scholar of the *Geistesgeschichte* School. The chair of ancient history, on the other hand, continued to be occupied by classical scholars (e.g. I. Heinlein (1915-1941) and A. Förster (1942-1947)) who added only modestly to Hungarian scholarship in ancient history.(11)

The situation was hardly different at Szeged (Kolozsvár's successor), where the prolific S. Márki (1898-1925) was followed by the not very productive J. Fógel (1926-1941), whose standard studies all dealt with Hungarian or Hungarian-related topics,(12) and all of them appeared before his appointment to the Szeged professorship. The appointment of his successor, L. Tóth (1895-1958) did not change matters either. Even though Tóth had previously held chairs of world history at three separate universities in rapid succession (Pécs, 1935-1940, reconstituted Kolozsvár, 1940-1942, and Szeged, 1942-1950), his modest scholarly output consisted only of some short studies on the age of the Hungarian Renaissance, and a number of similar brief studies on the papal court of the same period.(13)

Tóth's two predecessors at the University of Pécs, the Transylvanianist I. Lukinich (1918-1923) and the Slavist A. Hodinka (1923-1935), were both excellent scholars of the Positivist School, but their interests lay basically in Hungarian and in East Central European history. They were particularly interested in historic Hungary and its attached provinces, but had virtually no interest in any other part of the European continent, let alone the world.(14)

If anything, the situation at Debrecen was even worse. The first incumbent in the chair of world history was J. Pokoly (1866-1933), a Protestant church historian, who produced a number of major monographs on the history of Protestantism in Hungary, but wrote virtually nothing in European and world history. It was hardly surprising, therefore, that he took the first chance that came along to move over to the chair of church history at Debrecen after less than a decade (1914-1923) as a mismatched incumbent in the chair of world history.(15)

Pokoly's successor, the Marczali-trained D. Szabó (1882-1966) was certainly an able interwar historian of the declining Positivist School. But like most of his colleagues and counterparts, he was not a European, nor a world historian. As discussed in an earlier chapter, all of his major works dealt with sixteenth to eighteenth-century Hungarian developments.(16) Moreover, during his long tenure (1924-1959) in the Debrecen chair of world history, Szabó apparently did not even make an effort to produce something in the non-Hungarian field.

There were, of course, exceptions to this rule even among traditional historians. But there were generally men of limited immediate influence on the development of Hungarian historiography. Thus, there was the prolific J. Horváth, who never managed to get a permanent university chair; G. Balanyi, who secured his chair too late; and the internationally respected A. Alföldi, who worked in a field that was too limited in its scope.

Of these three historians, J. Horváth (1881-1950) appears to have been the most prolific, but also the least careful scholar.(17) Not counting his profuse outpouring of articles, he has authored well over fifty independent volumes. This may perhaps explain the uneven quality of his work. Another explanation may be that he worked in late modern and recent history and he wrote a number of his works under the influence of existing political conditions. This was particularly true for his works that deal with the developments leading to the Treaty of Trianon (1920) and its consequences, a number of which also appeared in Western languages.(18)

Despite these shortcomings, Horváth authored numerous studies of good scholarly quality. His monographs and syntheses on Hungarian diplomatic history are particularly significant. But some of his major syntheses on general European political and diplomatic history were also useful in their time. He used a number of them as university textbooks while lecturing as adjunct professor at the University of Budapest (1924-1944).(19)

Although not quite as prolific as Horváth, G. Balanyi (1886-1963) was also a prolific historian.(20) He resembled Horváth both in his interest in modern and recent history, as well as in his willingness to publish on the causes and consequences of the collapse of Austria-Hungary. Where they differed was in Balanyi's interest in medieval church history, which undoubtedly stemmed from his being a Catholic priest. Balanyi was particularly interested in the history of religious orders, and in this area he authored a number of significant works.(21)

Having been appointed to the chair of world (European) history at the re-established Hungarian University of Kolozsvár (Cluj) only in 1943, and having been dismissed from the re-Roumanianized university already in 1948, Balanyi's tenure was too short and plagued by too many adverse circumstances to have produced a significant impact on Hungarian historical studies.

————

The situation was different with A. Alföldi (b. 1895) who, after professorships at the universities of Debrecen (1923-1930), Budapest (1930-1947) Bern (1948-1952) and Basel (1952-1956), ultimately ended up as professor of Roman history at the Institute of Advanced Studies of Princeton (1956).(22) During his career in Hungary, Alföldi concentrated on early Roman history and on the history of the Carpathian Basin under Roman rule. He published his most significant works in the form of articles — many of them in Western languages. Most of them were critical analyses of sources, which gained him considerable recognition in international scholarly circles. Simultaneously, however, the nature of this work prevented him from gaining significant influence over the development of Hungarian historical studies.

In addition to the innate value of his publications, Alföldi's greatest contribution to Hungarian historiography was the production of a number of noted students of Roman history and "Hungarian archeology," many of whom are still the best Hungarian scholars in the area.(23)

———

Thus, while there were achievements in certain limited areas, in light of the above, it is rather evident that the situation in European and world history in interwar Hungarian historical studies was far from satisfactory. In a number of ways it approximated the situation of the dualist period. Virtually all chairholders were scholars of Hungarian history, who had only peripheral interest in general European or world developments, and some of them (e.g. D. Szabó) did not even make an effort to produce anything in their official fields. Moreover, with the exception of Horváth (who was only an adjunct professor at Budapest), none of the chairholders managed to produce a substantial synthesis of European or world history. To these factors we may also add the general conservative philosophical and methodological approach of these historians. This not only placed them into the traditional spectrum of the existing historical schools, but also prevented them from accepting and applying the new methodological tools of synthesis developed in contemporary Western Europe and North America.

István Hajnal and the "New Course" of World History Studies

Although the basic content and approach of interwar Hungarian scholarship and university level teaching in the area of European and world history remained basically unchanged, a "new course" did in fact emerge during the 1930's. This new course was connected primarily with the rise of I. Hajnal (1892-1956) and his "Sociological School," which school disliked almost equally the ethereal idealism of the *Geistesgeschichte* School, as well as the exclusive materialism of Marxism. Simultaneously, however, this reorientation was also due to the influx of *Geistesgeschichte* ideas into the study of European and world history in interwar Hungary. This is particularly evident from the works of such young scholars as P. Váczy, B. Iványi-Grünwald and others who became associated with the multivolumed *Universal History* during the 1930's.

———

The most significant among the historians of the new course was undoubtedly I. Hajnal, who was appointed to the Budapest chair of modern universal history (as European and world history came to be called during the interwar period) in 1930.(24) Like Szekfű, Mályusz and Eckhart in their respective fields, Hajnal too brought a totally new orientation into Hungarian historical studies. Hajnal's orientation, however, did not fit into the dominant *Geistesgeschichte* School. If anything, Hajnal's philosophy of history was more materialistic than idealistic. Yet, it had no relationship to historical materialism. The Marxist view of history remained unacceptable to Hajnal to the very end.

As one of the most noted students of L. Fejérpataky, the father of Hungarian scientific diplomatics, Hajnal also started out in that field. His doctoral dissertation, for example, dealt with the chancery of king Béla IV of the thirteenth century.(25) Later, however, he became interested in comparative paleography and in the history of work and technology. More specifically, he began to examine the impact of the rise of literacy and technical progress upon historical evolution.(26)

Although Hajnal had never authored a major work on the philosophy of history, he had elaborated his own view of history in a number of shorter studies.(27) One of these is his bibliographical essay that he appended to his snythesis of the early modern age, a major volume that appeared in the yet to be discussed multivolumed *Universal History* (1935-1937).(28)

In this essay Hajnal acknowledged that "modern thought holds that (historical) progress is the product of a purposeful and logical spirit."(29) Yet, he made no secret of his own scepticism about this philosophy. To him this reference to an undefinable and abstract "spirit" was too subjective an explanation to be acceptable. Nor did he believe that the "alleged goals or logical aspirations" of humanity determine human progress. In his view, " 'causality' and 'rationality' in themselves have no creative powers. They are simply functional, valueless conceptions . . . Rationality can just as much hinder, as it can advance (historical progress)."(30)

In contrast to the alleged history-shaping role of a rational or irrational spirit, or in contrast to the similar role of the logical goals and aspirations of humanity, Hajnal believed that "social evolution depends on the mode of coexistence of human beings;" or to put it in other terms, "upon the type of life-stuff (the quality of human species) that human society is able to come up with, as well as on the tools at its disposal (i.e. intellectual and technical achievements)."(31)

In studying the mechanism and functioning of human social progress, Hajnal appeared to place considerable emphasis on the notions of "customariness" and "institutionality." The former in effect meant in his terminology the process whereby "society regulates itself without any specific goals, (simply) on the basis of the intimate cohabitation (of its members)."(32) Up to a certain stage of social evolution, this cohabitation or coexistence is regulated by customs or customary laws. In a traditional society, "there is no possibility for anyone to rise at the expense of others . . . (except) through the inner development of one's individual potentialities." These potentialities produce "methods (of social progress) which evolve and move toward perfection . . . through objective 'expertise'." These expertise or skills, in turn, become institutionalized in society. Hence the importance of "institutionality" or institutions in historical progress.

The development of these methods or skills in society is being carried on — according to Hajnal — "by the ever newly emerging classes of secure existence." These classes develop a kind of addiction to productivity *(üzemiség),* which manifests itself both in the pure intellectual, as well as in the technical spheres.

In Hajnal's view, this process (i.e. the development of these methods or skills) begins simultaneously with the rise of verbalism in society, and grows proportionately with the switch to literacy. (Hence Hajnal's emphasis on the significance of literacy in human social progress.) The result is the growth of "intellectualism," which displaces "customariness" and rises to an unrivalled leadership role in social evolution. Soon thereafter this "intellectualism" itself becomes institutionalized by assuming the character and function of an "administrative social organization." Its ultimate base is still constituted by the rank and file (the masses), who are not really part of this institutionalized intellectualism, but without whose participation and well-being "no cultural technology can hope to succeed." Thus, the rank and file contribute the element of "personal production" or "work without the exploitation of others" to social progress, which — after all — is still "the basis of all progress."

Hajnal also believed that the rank and file are usually connected with "cooperative type organizations," which have their special interests and goals. These mass-dominated cooperative organizations generally oppose the "administrative social organizations," which represent "intellectualism in society" and control most of the "tools" and "methods" of social progress.

As an example, Hajnal pointed to the institution of feudalism (or "estatism" as he called it), which in his estimation was basically the result of "more refined methods of social organization" whose formation could not be explained simply in terms of "political, economic or any other one-sided point of view." Thus, in its West European form, Hajnal believed feudalism or "estatism" to have been basically an administrative type of social organization, and therefore an institution that represented the leadership ("intellectualism") as opposed to the rank and file in society.(33)

Hajnal applied his philosophy of history in several of his basic monographs on the role of literacy and technological progress in history, as well as in a number of synthetic works. The latter included his penetrating study on nineteenth-century class society in the Domanovszky-edited *History of Hungarian Civilization*,(34) as well as his volume on the early modern age in the multi-volumed *Universal History.*

Universal History

Sponsored by the Szekfű-led "Hungarian Review Society," the *Universal History* (1935-1937)(35) was intended to be a kind of *opus magnum* of interwar Hungarian scholarship in world history, and thus a companion to Hóman's and Szekfű's *Magyar History.* This aim, however, was only half fulfilled. Despite the editorship of this major project by Hóman, Szekfű and Kerényi (all of whom were apostles of the *Geistesgeschichte* philosophy of history), only two of the four large volumes could pass as unqualified products of the *Geistesgeschichte* School. Neither Hajnal's volume on the early modern period,(36) nor the Kerényi-edited volume on ancient history(37) turned out to be an all-out product of that philosophy. Whereas Hajnal carried his own special philosophy of history into synthesis of sixteenth through eighteenth-century developments, the volume on ancient history under Kerényi's editorship was the cooperative effort of eight Hungarian, German and American scholars who represented perhaps eight different orientations.(38) Consequently, like the ambitious *History of Hungarian Civilization* (1939-1942), the *Universal History* also represented more than one orientation and thus failed to live up to the expectations of the *Geistesgeschichte* School. The two volumes that met these expectations to the fullest extent were those on medieval and modern history, written respectively by P. Váczy and B. Iványi-Grünwald.(39)

Of these two scholars, the still functioning Váczy was particularly significant and promising. As discussed in an earlier chapter of this work, it was Váczy who became the ablest young exponent of the

Hungarian *Geistesgeschichte* School in the field of European and world history, and who ultimately succeeded to Áldasy's chair of medieval history at the University of Budapest (1942-1961).(40) In wake of a number of brilliant monographs — all of which displayed the spirit of *Geistesgeschichte* and the doctrines of "charismatic kingship" and "state symbolism" best developed by the young medievalist J. Deér(41) — Váczy produced his major synthesis on the European Middle Ages. This volume conformed fully to the demands and expectations of the *Geistesgeschichte* School, as did his shorter studies and syntheses on the Hungarian Middle Ages.

Váczy's counterpart for the modern period was B. Iványi-Grünwald, who was similarly a disciple of *Geistesgeschichte,* but who was also active as a publicist.(42) As befitting a true *Geistesgeschichte* historian, Iványi-Grünwald placed the role of the "intellectual-spiritual elite" into the mainstream of historical evolution. He did so because — contrary to Hajnal — he was convinced that the direction and pace of social evolution is dictated by the influence of this intellectual elite whose members serve as "the educators, directors, leaders and myth-creators" of society. For the most recent period, Iványi-Grünwald perceived a kind of "mechanization" of the "guiding spirit" that possessed the intellectual elite; a mechanization that came about under the impact of "modern economic forces." Notwithstanding the forceful presence of these mechanized forces, however, Iványi-Grünwald had no doubts about the ultimate triumph of spirituality.(43)

———

As we have seen, interwar Hungarian historiography was generally weakest in the field of European and world history, and most of the university chairs were held by traditional scholars who had little or no interest in European history beyond the limits of the political and cultural influences of medieval Hungary. The appearance of Hajnal and such young *Geistesgeschichte* historians as Váczy and Iványi-Grünwald, however, produced major philosophical and methodological reorientations in European and world history studies in interwar Hungary. Although neither of these orientations was able to develop fully, the scholarly activities and publications of these scholars brought a new and refreshing air into Hungarian historiography. Moreover, Hajnal's philosophy and scholarship has left an imprint even upon the emerging Marxist School, notwithstanding his own inability to accept the ideology of historical materialism.

Chapter XX

AUXILIARY AND ALLIED SCIENCES OF HISTORY

Although limited to such traditional fields as archeology, numismatics, diplomatics, heraldry and sfragistics — the origins of the study of the auxiliary and allied sciences of history on the university level in Hungary reaches back to the late eighteenth century.(1)

After a period of decline during the first half of the nineteenth century (connected with the Age of Romanticism and the period of national revival), the age of dualism — which witnessed a general rise in the quality and scope of historical studies — also saw a progressive improvement in the area of auxiliary and allied sciences. This improvement was connected partially with the activities of the basically autodidact, but able A. Horvát at the University of Budapest (1846 1857-1894),(2) and partially with the emergence of the Positivist School in Hungarian historical studies in the period after 1870. Particularly important was the latter development, which brought about the introduction of the critical philological method of source criticism, developed and perfected during this period in Germany. On the one hand, this gave birth to a new breed of scientific historical scholarship in Hungary, represented by such scholars as G. Pauler, V. Fraknói, S. Márki, A. Károlyi, H. Marczali, L. Fejérpataky, J. Karácsonyi and others.(3) On the other hand, it resulted in the introduction of this scientific method into Hungarian university training through the professorial activities of S. Mika, S. Márki, and above all H. Marczali and L. Fejérpataky.(4) Furthermore, it also resulted in the expansion of some of the traditional auxiliary fields of history under the activities of the Hungarian Heraldic and Genealogical Association,(5) as well as in the writing of a number of badly needed methodological and critical handbooks on several areas and aspects of the auxiliary and allied sciences.(6)

But however impressive its achievements in a number of areas, the period of positivist historiography had a number of weak spots in the field of auxiliary sciences. The most evident of these weaknesses was its over-emphasis on heraldry and genealogy, as well as on a number of other traditional sub-disciplines, such as diplomatics, numismatics and sfragistics.(7) This traditionalism, however, was a natural byproduct of the needs of contemporary society and of the general orientation of contemporary historical studies. Thus, the semi-feudal society of the dualist age still held the study of family origins and dynastic connections in unduly high regard. Moreover, contemporary Hungarian historiography — as all historiographies of Central and Eastern Europe — was still basically medieval oriented. Consequently, it refused to give serious consideration to the study of the modern period, and none of the major official source publications reached even into the eighteenth century.(8)

Another weakness of Hungarian historiography of the dualist period was in the area of methodological handbooks, where even many of the traditional fields were under-represented.(9) The big breakthrough in this area came during the interwar period, in the form of the Hóman-edited *Handbook of Hungarian Historical Sciences* series, discussed in conjunction with the major publication projects of that period.(10) Although one of the largest, most needed and most commendable undertakings of interwar Hungarian historiography, this project too fell far short of its goals. Thus — as we have seen — of the originally planned forty-nine volumes only thirteen appeared in print; and even these were largely in the traditional fields. As an example, of the strictly methodological-philosophical volumes only G. Kornis' *Philosophy of History* (1924) and I. Dékány's *Methodology of Historical Sciences* (1925) could be regarded as being up-to-date at the time of their publication.(11) None of the "modern" auxiliary sciences, such as historical geography, historical statistics, ethnography, cultural anthropology, etc. were represented — not to speak of the then basically unknown or unused psychoanalysis, plant geography, chemical date analysis, and other similar new sub-disciplines.

History of Hungarian Historical Sciences

While there were problems and deficiencies in all the auxiliary, allied or sub-disciplines of history, the one area where the practitioners of Hungarian auxiliary sciences failed most was in the area of the history of Hungarian historical studies.

To start with, a definitive history of Hungarian historical studies has never been attempted by an Hungarian historian.(12) Of the two compendiums that predate my own, the first and still the largest work is that of the Swiss-German scholar, Alexander Flegler (1803-1892), who wrote his *History of Hungarian Historical Writing* in the middle of the nineteenth century. (It appeared only in Hungarian in 1877.)(13) The second and slighter work, *A Short History of Hungarian Bourgeois Historiography* appeared in 1969,(14) and it came from the pen of Emma Lederer (b. 1898), the first Marxist incumbent of the Budapest chair of historical auxiliary sciences (1950-1969). Although products of two different ages and two different schools of history, in terms of their chronological coverage these two works complement one another. Yet, they cannot take the place of a needed scholarly compendium. Moreover, neither of them is the product of Hungarian historiography of the pre-Marxist age, which is the subject of our own summary.

Although published in 1877, Flegler's *History of Hungarian Historical Writing* was written largely during the 1850's under the influence of the great nineteenth-century national liberal historian L. Szalay, and consequently it reflects Szalay's basically liberal and realism-oriented philosophy of history.(15) Starting with the medieval chronicles reflecting Hungary's Hunnic traditions (of which he was sceptical like Szalay), and working himself through the great humanist histories, the Baroque memoires, the eighteenth-century source collections and the large synthesizing works of his own or immediately preceding age, and ending with Szalay's great synthesis of the 1850's, Flegler handled the history of the development of Hungarian historical studies with an unusual skill an enviable perceptiveness. His ideological guideline was classical liberalism, but his source of inspiration was Szalay. It is rather evident from his work that Flegler regarded Szalay's historical works as the best that Hungarian historiography has produced. Thus, Flegler's second related work, *Reflections on Ladislaus Szalay and on his History of the Hungarian Empire* (1866)(16) can be regarded both as a sequel to his *History of Hungarian Historical Writing,* as well as a profession of faith in the ideals and scholarship of Szalay.

Flegler's accomplishment in his time was so great that it still has to be equalled by Hungarian historiographers. The recent sequel to his work by E. Lederer, *A Short History of Hungarian Bourgeois Historiography,* is a much slighter work and deals largely with the post-Flegler period. As a product of Hungarian Marxist historiography, its discussion and analysis lies outside the scope of the present study. Yet, due to the scarcity of works in this area, a brief comment about it may still be in oder.

About one-fifth of the one hundred and fifty pages of Lederer's work is devoted to a brief summary of contemporary Western developments in historical studies, while four-fifths is devoted to Hungarian historiography, with an emphasis on important historians, significant historical syntheses, and on the latter's ideological orientations. This approach has its usefulness, but it seems that the author has made no attempt to integrate European and Hungarian developments into a synthetic whole.(17) Lederer's summary is nonetheless a very useful work — particularly in light of the total absence of more extensive and more synthetic histories of Hungarian historiography.

Outside of these two summaries, there exist only detailed monographs and shorter studies on the subject. These include critical discussions and analyses of sources, of historical syntheses and of historians, and brief summaries on specific periods of Hungarian historical studies. The best and most readily available of these studies are from the pens of Marczali, Angyal, Hóman and Mályusz, and from a number of currently active Marxist scholars, including A. Csizmadia, A. Degré, L. Elekes, G. Ember, F. Glatz, P. Gunst, P. Hanák, M. Mann, L. Makkai, E. Niederhauser, Z.P. Pach, E. Pamlényi, G. Ránki, A. Várkonyi and I. Wellmann.(18) The scholarly activities and achievements of these historians, however, are beyond the chronological limits of this summary.

Marczali's and Angyal's most readily available related essays appeared in the appropriate sections of the representative summary of Hungarian literary history by the positivist scholars of the dualist period, the two-volume *History of Hungarian Literature,* edited by Z. Beőthy (1848-1922), the dean of contemporary literary historians.(19) While Marczali's and Angyal's essays are good summaries of the development of historical studies of a particular age, from our own vantage point they are somewhat superficial descriptive essays. They certainly make no attempt to deal with the main historical and ideological currents of the age, nor with the economic, social and spiritual forces that may have guided the hands of the practitioners of Clio's art at a specific time of historical scholarship in Hungary.

As products of a totally different milieu, Hóman's and Mályusz's studies in historiography are of a much higher quality. This judgement applies equally to their critical source analyses, as well as to their summaries of specific periods or sub-disciplines of Hungarian historical studies. Hóman's related essays and studies were all collected and published in the second volume of his collected works, entitled *Historiography and Source Criticism* (1938).(20) As evidenced by this work, Hóman was an impeccable source critic, whose achievements in this area were equalled only by a few contemporary historians, such as Szentpétery and Mályusz. (It should perhaps be mentioned here that while Szekfű was also a good source critic, his published works in this area are negligible as compared to his syntheses.)

The most significant of Hóman's studies about the history of Hungarian historical studies include *The First Period of Hungarian Historiography* (1923), *The Foundation of Our Scientific Historiography in the Eighteenth Century* (1920), and *The History of Source Research and Source Criticism in Hungary* (1925).(21) The last of these appeared as one of the volumes of the *Handbook of Hungarian Historical Sciences.* Its primary shortcoming is that it has little to offer on the more recent period. This, however, is a shortcoming that is shared by most of the volumes in the series and reflects the traditionalist tendencies of contemporary Hungarian historical studies.(22)

As for Mályusz, while the majority of his historiographical works appeared after 1945, he also did considerable work in this area in the interwar period. The most significant of his earlier historiographical works include his critical study on *The Chronicle of Johannes Thuróczy* (1944), and his assessment of the state of interwar Hungarian historical studies in his *The Hungarian Historical Sciences.* (1942).(23) The latter work is particularly useful for the history of Hungarian historiography, for in addition to giving a rather thorough analysis of two of the most important schools of history (i.e. Szekfű's *Geistesgeschichte* School and his own Ethnohistory School), Mályusz also discussed and evaluated the role of the most significant institutions of scholarly research. These include the Hungarian Academy of Sciences, the four universities, the museums and the archives (particularly the Hungarian National Archives), as well as a number of existing and proposed historical research institutes. Among Mályusz's post-1945 works of historiography, the most important is his *The Thuróczy Chronicle and its Sources* (1967).(24) In addition to a thorough analysis of this significant medieval chronicle, this study also contains the best summary of the development of medieval Hungarian historical studies. Most of Mályusz's other post-1945 historiographical studies are by-products of the above work.

C. A. Macartney

While not strictly part of Hungarian historiography, when dealing with Hungarian historical studies one cannot afford to bypass the related works of the noted British scholar C.A. Macartney (b. 1985). This is all the more so as most of his studies contain original research and many of them appeared only in Hungary. Within the context of Hungarian historiography Macartney is undoubtedly the twentieth-century Flegler. His seven-part *Studies in the Early Hungarian Historical Sources*

(1938-1951),(25) his summarizing volume *The Medieval Hungarian Historians* (1955),(26) and his oft-cited *The Magyars in the Ninth Century* (1930),(27) are not only unique in any language other than Magyar, but they are also enviable within the context of similar Magyar language studies. In point of fact, outside of Hóman's briefer study, not until the appearance of Mályusz's more recent summary of medieval Hungarian historiography have Hungarian historians produced anything comparable to Macartney's critical survey of medieval Hungarian historical studies. It is to be lamented that Macartney's works are used and cited by Hungarian historians far less than their scholarly worth would merit. This may be due partially to linguistic, and partially to ideological considerations. (28)

History of the Auxiliary Sciences of History

If the History of Hungarian historical studies has been a stepchild of Hungarian historical research, this was not equally true for all of the sub-diciplines. As an example one might mention the case of the auxiliary sciences of history which – due to Hóman's efforts on behalf of the *Handbook of Hungarian Historical Sciences* — did find an author. Written by a noted Budapest archivist A. Gárdonyi (1874-1946), *The History of the Auxiliary Sciences of History* appeared in 1926 as one of the volumes of the *Handbook*.(29) Gárdonyi's works turned out to be a good traditional summary, with excellent notes and a good bibliography. Due to its almost exclusive emphasis on the traditional auxiliary sciences, however, it became partially outdated even during the interwar period. With the rapid growth of the non-traditional fields, and the partial obsolescence of a number of the formerly highly regarded fields, however, this is even more true today. The need for a more up-to-date summary is great indeed.

Szentpétery: The ''Dean'' of Interwar Auxiliary Sciences of History

Although there were several prominent scholars active in the area of the auxiliary and allied sciences of history who have contributed to the *Handbook of Hungarian Historical Sciences* (e.g. A. Áldásy, E. Bartoniek, I. Dékány, L. Dézsi, A. Gárdonyi, B. Hóman, G. Kornis and G. Moravcsik) and to the appropriate sections of the *New Paths of Hungarian Historiography* (e.g. F. Eckhart, T. Gerevich, E. Mályusz, G. Németh, T. Thienemann, F. Tompa and others), the official representative and exponent of the auxiliary sciences in interwar

Hungarian historical studies was I. Szentpétery (1878-1950),(30) the author of the still unsurpassed Hungarian methodological handbook of source criticism, *Hungarian Diplomatics* (1930).(31)

As perhaps the most gifted of Fejérpataky's students in the area of auxiliary sciences, Szentpétery inherited and held his master's Budapest Chair in Heraldry and Genealogy for almost three decades (1923-1950). Even prior to his appointment to Budapest, Szentpétery had made a name for himself through his publications — having produced some six independent volumes (mostly source criticisms), forty major studies, and numerous lesser works. Subsequently he added another half a dozen volumes and two dozen major studies while also serving as editor-in-chief of a new critical edition of medieval Hungarian chronicles in Latin *(Scriptores rerum Hungaricarum tempore ducum regumque stirpis Arapadianae gestarum)*.(32) Of his major post-1923 works two were specifically methodological handbooks *(Chronology* and *Hungarian Diplomatics)*,(33) both of which were written for the Hóman-edited *Handbook of Hungarian Historical Studies.* Most of the others were source criticisms, critical source editions or critical regestas of medieval Hungarian royal diplomas.(34)

Szentpétery's works were impeccable in their scholarly execution, matching those of Fejérpataky. If anything, he tried to improve upon his master's critical methodology, although there was not much he could do in that area. As to his ideological orientation? Szentpétery was basically an apolitical individual, but sufficiently traditionalist to feel comfortable in the neo-Baroque atmosphere of interwar Hungary. Although a positivist both by training and by the very nature of his sub-discipline, like most of his colleagues, he too tried to go along with the dominant *Geistesgeschichte* orientation. Thus, he made an effort to point out some of the "spiritual" aspects of his discipline, such as the importance of the style, form and composition of medieval documents in reflecting the spiritual and intellectual world of the medieval mind.(35) Most of his efforts in this direction, however, proved to be futile, for the majority of the traditional auxiliary sciences simply did not lend themselves well to *Geistesgeschichte* treatment.

Before succeeding to his master's (Fejérpataky's) chair at Budapest, Szentpétery spent some five years at the University of Debrecen (1918-1923), at interwar Hungary's only chair of auxiliary sciences outside that of Budapest.(36) With his transfer to Budapest, however, the Debrecen chair was terminated and the University of Budapest again became the sole possessor of a special chair for the auxiliary sciences and historical methodology.

In addition to his own scholarly contributions to his field, Szentpétery's greatest contribution to Hungarian historical studies came in the form of the production of a number of excellently trained research scholars. These included the promising, but untimely deceased G. Istványi, as well as such other functioning historians as I. Borsa, L.B. Kumorovitz and L. Szilágyi. Moreover, Szentpétery's influence was also significant in the development of his two successors in the chair of auxiliary and allied sciences of history at the University of Budapest, E. Lederer (1950-1969) and I. Sinkovics (1969-).

Although neither a controversial, nor a highly heralded historian, Szentpétery was one of the greatest and among the most influential historical scholars of interwar Hungary. He represented the objective and scientific aspects of historical studies in that great age of historical subjectivism. He was in every way a true disciple of the greatest master of source criticism, Fejérpataky — an historian who, while generally unheralded in his lifetime, is remembered and appreciated by many generations of successive historians.

Chapter XXI

CONCLUSIONS AND THE BEGINNINGS OF MARXIST HISTORIOGRAPHY

Having examined the evolution of Hungarian historiography in the course of its millennial development, we have found that it had passed through the same basic stages that had characterized its West European counterparts. Starting with the heroic legends and national oral traditions, between the eleventh and the fifteenth century it gave birth to various annals, hagiographies and the increasingly more complex gestas and chronicles — the majority of them written in Latin. This was followed by the birth of the more critical and synthetic humanist historiography — still primarily in Latin; the Magyar language historiography of the Reformation of the same period; the political memoire literature of the Baroque Age of the mid-seventeenth to the early eighteenth century, which flowered mostly in Transylvania; and the great source collecting schools of the Jesuit and Protestant scholars of the eighteenth century. In that century of enlightenment, the efforts of Hungarian historians resulted for the first time in major systematic, although as yet mostly uncritical source collections; and at the turn of the eighteenth to the nineteenth century, in the first relatively critical multivolumed syntheses of Hungarian historical development.

As has been shown, the first half (and in particular, the second quarter) of the nineteenth century — which coincided both with the Age of Romanticism, as well as with the period of Hungarian national revival — brought about a significant decline in the qualitative level of Hungarian historical studies; a decline that was represented especially by the over-romanticized works of I. Horvát and his followers. After the fall of the Revolution of 1848-1849 and the consequent end to the overheated atmosphere of the national revival period, however, the development of Hungarian historiography again resumed its normal course. The post-revolutionary period of the 1850's and 1860's saw the birth of the synthesizing National Liberal School, represented primarily by the great histories of L. Szalay and M. Horváth. Simultaneously, however, it also witnessed the growing involvement of the Hungarian

Academy's Historical Commission (1854), as well as of the newly founded Hungarian Historical Association (1867) in the promotion of systematic historical research and in the initiation of a number of major source, serial and periodical publications. These developments, in turn, were followed during the 1870's by the birth and development of the great Hungarian Positivist School that came to dominate Hungarian historical studies through much of the dualist age (1867-1918) and retained considerable influence even during the interwar period (1918-1945).

A most important achievement of Hungarian positivism (which in its Hungarian context was less of a philosophy of history than a critical scientific methodology) was that it raised the scholarly level of Hungarian historical research to its West European counterparts. No less important, however, was the fact that it produced hundreds of excellent research monographs and an equal number of critically selected and edited source publications on many aspects of Hungarian history. Its weakest area was synthesizing — a weakness that also characterized many of the West European positivist schools.

During the last two decades of dualism (c. 1896-1918), the hold of positivism on Hungarian historiography began to decline. And even though the core of the school and its scientific methodology remained unimpaired, this same period also saw the emergence of several competing schools of history. These included such basically traditional orientations as the Economic History School connected with the *Hungarian Economic History Review* (1894-1906); Bekefi's Hungarian Civilization or *Kulturgeschichte* School; as well as the overly nationalistic National Romantic School, reborn under the leadership of K. Thaly. But they also included the *avant garde* Organic Sociological School of the "bourgeois radicals," centered on the journal *Huszadik Század* (Twentieth Century), which drew its inspiration from the ideas of Darwin, Spencer and even Karl Marx. Moreover, during the last years of dualism, there also appeared the extremely subjective and idealist *Geistesgeschichte* School, based largely on the irrational philosophy of W. Dilthey — the school that became the dominant orientation in the historiography of interwar Hungary.

With the collapse of the Austro-Hungarian Empire and therein of historic Hungary, the whole dualist social, political and psychological order came to an abrupt end. The optimism of the dualist age was suddenly displaced by the pessimism of the post-Trianon period; and the monumental, exact and too factographic positivist historiography by the largely meditative, subjective and synthesizing *Geistesgeschichte* orientation. It was this Dilthey-inspired irrational, yet enviably intellectual and philosophical school that characterized the historiography of the interwar period, and produced the greatest and as yet unsurpassed synthesis of Hungarian historical developments (Hóman's and Szekfű's *Magyar History);* and did so, while at the same time perfecting further the critical aspects of historical source research.

The impact of the Hungarian *Geistesgeschichte* School — represented primarily by G. Szekfű and by his writings — was so overpowering that for a considerable time this school was thought to have imposed a monolithic rule on interwar Hungarian historical studies. As has been shown, however, the "*Geistesgeschichte* period" in Hungarian historiography was far less homogeneous than had been assumed both during and after that period. And while this idealist philosophical orientation, with its "irrational" and subjective history-reconstructing methodology, was undoubtedly the most significant trend in interwar Hungarian historical studies, its influence was tempered by the continued presence of several traditional, and a number of new schools of history. Thus, positivism continued to survive among the professional university and research scholars who retained control over the majority of the university chairs; the less scholarly national romanticism still exercised the widest influence over the uninitiated reading public; and there even arose a number of largely idealist rival schools, which began to undermine the position of the *Geistesgeschichte* School almost from the moment of its foundation. The most significant of these rival schools was undoubtedly E. Mályusz's Ethnohistory School, which emphasized the role of the "people" *(Volk)* as opposed to the state, and sought to enhance the history-shaping role of the "Magyar Spirit" as opposed to the "Universal Spirit" of the *Geistesgeschichte* historians. But they also included F. Eckhart's realism-oriented Legal History School that hoped to demythologize Hungarian constitutional history; as well as I. Hajnal's slightly anti-idealist Universal History School that emphasized the primary role of "work" and "technological progress" as history-shaping forces. In point of fact, notwithstanding the powerful anti-communist stance of the interwar Hungarian political regime, by the 1930's even some Marxist influences were beginning to appear in Hungarian historical studies.

As pointed out earlier, the first appreciable influence of historical materialism in Hungary appeared during the last two decades of the dualist period and manifested itself largely in the Organic Sociological

School(1) — especially in the writings of Ervin Szabó (1877-1918).(2) In point of fact, Szabó's posthumous *opus magnum, Social and Party Struggles in the Hungarian Revolution of 1848-1849* (1921) is rightfully regarded as the most significant pioneering work of the budding Marxist historiography in Hungary.(3)

Although, following the collapse of the socialist and communist experiences in Hungary in 1918-1919, most of the Marxist oriented *literati* and social scientists have left the country, some of the late-dualist Marxist traditions have survived. Furthermore, after a decade of slumber, they surfaced again during the 1930's and early 1940's, and did so largely in the writings of Erik Molnár (1894-1966), a jurist and self-trained historian, who consequently is justly regarded as the "father" of the thriving Marxist historiography in Hungary.(4) Although Molnár's contributions to Marxist historical studies in Hungary came largely after 1945, he had examined and clarified from the Marxist point of view numerous aspects of Hungarian social and economic developments already before 1945. Writing under various pseudonyms (e.g. Erik Jeszenszky, István Pálfai and Lajos Szentmiklósy), he dealt especially extensively with the social history of medieval Hungary *(The Society of the Árpádian Age,* 2 vols., 1943) and with Hungarian proto-history *(The Ancient History of the Magyars,* 1942).(5)

In his efforts to establish the foundations of Marxist historical scholarship in Hungary, Molnár was aided by a number of younger scholars and intellectuals, including the brilliant but irreconcilable ideologist József Révai (1898-1959),(6) the still younger sociologically oriented historian Aladár Mód (1908-1973),(7) and later even by some of the left-leaning populist social scientists, who eventually joined hands with the communists.(8) Whereas Révai dealt largely with Marxist aesthetics and literary criticism and the populists were interested primarily in sociological studies and sociographies, Mód authored the first Marxist synthesis of Hungarian historical developments of the past four hundred years. His *Four Centuries of Struggle for Independent Hungary* (1943, republished in seven different editions in the course of the next decade) became the basic guide and handbook of Hungarian historians in the period between 1945 and 1956.(9)

All in all, it is perhaps correct to say that while the interwar Hungarian political regime had pushed the Marxist orientation to the underground, and the visible influence of that school could in no way compare to that of any of the other interwar schools, the foundations of Hungarian Marxist historiography were laid during the 1930's and early 1940's. Moreover, while the triumphant march of the *Geistesgeschichte* School made it difficult for all other schools to thrive, interwar Hungarian historiography was nonetheless multicolored. And this also holds true for the intellectual heritage of the upcoming young historians of the early 1940's, a generation born largely during the decade of the First World War (e.g. É. Balázs, I. Barta, I. Bakács, K. Benda, J. Berlász, C. Csapodi, A. Csizmadia, L. Elekes, G. Ember, K. Eperjessy, S. Gallus, G. Györffy, Z. Jakó, D. Kosáry, E. Kovács, L. Makkai, F. Maksay, Z.P. Pach, E. Pamlényi, J. Perényi, G. Perjes, I. Sinkovics, L. Szilágyi, Z.I. Tóth, I. Wellman and others).(10) While heavily saturated with *Geistesgeschichte* influences, they had also been subjected to the influences of many other contemporary historiographical orientations. Ultimately, the majority of them ended up in the ranks of the Marxist historians, although some of them did so undoubtedly due to the force of circumstances. With the collapse of the old order and the rise of a new one in 1944-1945, based on its interwar foundations, Marxist historiography also emerged in full force. Then, with official support, historical materialism displaced all other ideological and philosophical orientations and opened a totally new chapter in the history of Hungarian historical studies — a chapter that is still too close in time for an objective evaluation.(11)

NOTES

PREFACE

1.) Paul Coles, *The Ottoman Impact on Europe,* New York, 1968, 205.
2.) *Ibid.,* 202.

Chapter I
THE DEVELOPMENT OF MEDIEVAL HISTORIOGRAPHY

1.) Hungarian historiography had been rather negligent in the area of the history of Hungarian historical studies. Up to now only two summaries have appeared: The first from the pen of the German-Swiss Alexander Flegler *(Történetírás),* which covered Hungarian historiography up to the middle of the 19th century; and the second from the pen of Emma Lederer, the former incumbent of the chair of historical auxiliary sciences at the University of Budapest *(Történetírás),* which covered the period between the mid-19th century and 1945. The situation is considerably better for specific periods and certain specialized areas of Hungarian historiography. Thus, in addition to a number of significant studies in Hungarian, medieval Hungarian historiography has also been treated in English by the noted British historian, C.A. Macartney *(Studies, Historians,* etc.). Next to the specialized studies and chronicle-analyses, the best summaries of medieval and early modern Hungarian historiography can be found in a number of large multivolumed Hungarian literary histories, such as those of Beőthy *(MIT),* Pintér (*MIT, MI),* and especially the most recent work prepared by the Institute of Literary History of the Hungarian Academy of Sciences under the editorship of István Sőtér *(MIT).* For brief summaries of Hungarian historiography see Molnár, "Historical Sciences," Borsody, "Historiography;" Vardy, *Historiography;* and *idem,* "Történetírás."

2.) One of the best scholarly collections of the Hungarian heroic legends is the old, but reliable work by Gyula Sebestyén, *A magyar honfoglalás mondái* (The Legends of the Hungarian Conquest), 2 vols., Bp. 1904-1905. Dénes Lengyel's *Régi magyar mondák* (Old Hungarian Legends), Bp. 1972, is a recent popular collection. For some critical treatment of Hungarian legends see Sándor Sólymossy, "Monda" (Legend), in *Magyarság néprajza,* III, 183-255; and Lajos Vargyas, "Kutatások a népballada középkori történetéhez" (Research on the Medieval History of Volk Ballads), *Et,* 71 (1960), 479-523.

3.) In addition to Sólymossy's study above, see also Sőtér, *MIT,* I, 24-28; Beőthy, *MIT,* I, 118-128; Mályusz, *Thuróczy-krónika,* 9-21; Marcartney, *Historians,* 1-57; Csóka, *Történeti irodalom,* 99-330; Horváth, *Kezdetei;* and Kardos, *Középkori kultúra.*

4.) Henrik Marczali, ''A krónikák'' (Chronicles), in Beöthy, *MIT,* I, 142-148; Pintér, *MIT,* I, 133-138; Sőtér, *MIT,* I, 55-59. The best collection of Hungarian and non-Hungarian sources for the Magyar conquest period are to be found in *A magyar honfoglalás kútfői* (The Sources of Magyar Conquest), ed. Gyula Pauler and Sándor Szilágyi, Bp. 1900. For a more recent annotated collection of medieval Hungarian chronicles see Emericus Szentpétery, ed., *Scriptores rerum.* See also Csóka, *Történeti irodalom,* 341-427; Mályusz, *Thuróczy-krónika,* 21-46; Macartney, *Historians,* 59-84; Hóman's numerous related studies in his *Történetírás,* 45-291; Györffy, *Krónikáink;* and József Gerics, *Legkorábbi gesztaszerkesztéseink keletkezésrendjének problémái* (The Problems of the Origin-Sequences of Our Earliest Chronicles), Bp. 1961.

5.) Sőtér, *MIT,* I, 59-62; Csóka, *Történeti irodalom,* 99-330, 364-369, 399-427. See also the Western language studies by ifj. János Horváth, ''La Légende majeure de l'évêque Gerald et les débuts de notre historiographie médiévale,'' *AUSB, Sectio Philologica,* 3 (1961), 3-22; *idem,* ''Quellenzusammenhänge der beiden Gerhard-Legenden,'' *AA,* 8 (1960), 439-454; and *idem,* ''Die Entstehungszeit der grossen Legende des Bischofs Gerhard,'' *AA,* 8 (1960), 185-219.

6. In addition to Sőtér, *MIT,* I, 78-79; Pintér, *MIT,* I, 138-140; and Macartney, *Historians,* 85-88; see also Tihamér Turchányi, ''Rogerius mester Siralmas Éneke a tatárjárásról'' (Master Rogerius's Carmen Miserable about the Mongol Conquest), *Sz,* 37(1903), 412-430; and László Bendeffy, *Az ismeretlen Juliánusz* (The Unknown Julian), Bp., 1936, 161-166.

7.) Macartney, *Historians,* 89-109; Mályusz, *Thuróczy-krónika,* 42-57; Hóman, *Történetírás,* 274-291; Sőtér, *MIT,* I, 80-88; Elemér Mályusz, *Az V. István-kori gesta* (The Geste of the Age of Stephen V), Bp. 1971; *idem,* ''Krónika-problémák'' (Chronicle Problems), *Sz,* 100 (1966), 713-762; and József Gerics, ''Gesztáink'' (Our Gestes), *ÉT,* 19(1964), 675-680.

8.) The reference here is to the now generally accepted hypothesis of Gyula László, which holds that the late Avars of the 7th century were really Magyars. See particularly László's ''Les problèmes soulevés par le groupe à la ceinture ornée de griffon et de rinceaux de l'époque avare finissante,'' *AAr,* 17 (1965), 73-75; *idem, Hunor és magyar nyomában* (In Search of Hunor and Magyar), Bp. 1967; and *idem, A honfoglalásról* (About the Conquest), Bp. 1973. In the latter work László also discusses the history of the development of his hypothesis (pp. 66-76). For his most recent brief, but excellent summary of his hypothesis see his ''A 'kettős honfoglalás'-ról,'' (On the Double Conquest), in *NyKu,* 15 (1974), 18-23.

9.) For a discussion on the difference between a gesta and a chronicle in its Hungarian context see Hóman-Szekfű, I, 292-300.

10.) On the chronicles of the Anjou Age in general see Macartney, *Historians,* 133-142; Mályusz, *Thuróczy-krónika,* 57-77; and Sőtér, *MIT,* I, 88-93. See also Ágnes Kurucz, ''Anjou-kori történetíróink kérdéséhez'' (On the Question of Our Historians of the Anjou Age), *ITK,* 68 (1964), 358-368; Géza Karsai, ''Névtelenség, névrejtés és szerzőnév középkori krónikáinkban'' (Anonymity, Hidden Names and Authors in our Medieval Chronicles), *Sz,* 97 (1963), 666-676; and Ágnes Szigethi, ''A propos de quelques sources des compositions de la Chronique Enluminée'' *AHA,* 14 (1968), 177-214. For the most recent scholarly bilingual facsimile edition of the Illustrated Chronicle see, *Képes Krónika — Chronica Pictum,* 2 vols., ed. László Mezey, introduced by

Dezső Dercsényi and Klára Gárdonyi (Csapodiné), Bp. 1964.

11.) On this "secular Latin culture" of fifteenth-century Hungary see Rábán Gerézdi, *A magyar világi líra kezdetei* (The Beginnings of Hungarian Secular Lyrics), Bp. 1962; Tibor Kardos, "Deák-műveltség és a magyar renaissance" (Latin Culture and Hungarian Renaissance), *Sz,* 73 (1939), 295-338, 449-491; Sőtér, *MIT,* I, 170-179; and the relevant sections of Horváth, *Kezdetei.*

12.) See Mályusz, *Thuróczy-krónika,* 72.

13.) *Ibid.,* 73.

14.) For a facsimile edition with a good historical introduction see Vilmos Fraknói, *Chronica Hungarorum impressa Budae 1473,* Bp. 1900. See also Sándor Domanovszky, "Budai Krónika," *Sz,* 36 (1902), 615-630, 729-756 and 810-831, which is also available as an independent publication.

15.) On Kara and Hess see Vilmos Fraknói, *Kara László budai prépost, a könyvnyomtatás meghonosítója Magyarországon* (L. Kara, Provost of Buda, the Pioneer of Book Printing in Hungary), Bp. 1898; Jenő Fitz, *Hess András a budai ősnyomdász* (A. Hess, the Pioneer Printer of Buda), Bp. 1932; and *idem, A magyar nyomdászat, könyvkiadás és könyvkereskedelem története* (The History of Hungarian Printing, Book Publishing and Book Trade), Bp. 1959, 96ff.

16.) Mályusz, *Thuróczy-krónika,* 74.

17.) Sándor Domanovszky, "A Dubnici Krónika," *Sz,* 33 (1899), 226-256, 342-355 and 411-451, which is also available as an independent publication.

18.) The anonymous compiler of the *Dubnic Chronicle* criticized king Matthias Corvinus for his foreign policy which was directed toward the conquest of Austria, Moravia and Bohemia, rather than toward defending Southern Hungary from the Turks.

19.) On Thuróczy's *Chronica Hungarorum* see Mályusz, *Thuróczy-krónika,* 81-199; *idem, Thuróczy János krónikája* (The Chronicle of Johannes Thuróczy), Bp. 1944; and *idem,* "Thuróczy János krónikája és a Corvina" (The Chronicle of Johannes Thuróczy and the Corvina), *FK,* 12 (1966), 282-302. For a recent Hungarian edition of Thuróczy's chronicle see *Thuróczy János, Magyar krónika — Chronica Hungarorum,* tr. and ed. by László Geréb, intr. by Tibor Kardos, Bp. 1957. Due to problems of translation, however, this work cannot take the place of older Latin editions.

20.) Mályusz, *Thuróczy-krónika,* 105-141.

21.) *Ibid.,* 185-199.

22.) The reference here is to the works of Engel, Fessler, Virág and Budai. Cf. Ch. V.

Chapter II

HUMANIST HISTORIOGRAPHY

1.) On Hungarian humanism in general see Sőtér, *MIT,* I, 247-259; Horváth, *Megoszlása;* Kardos, *Humanizmus;* Klaniczay, *Reneszánsz és barokk,* 7-38; Sándor V. Kovács, "Humanista levelek, levélíró humanisták" (Humanist Letters, Letter-Writing Humanists), in *Magyar humanisták,* 5-50; and *Renaissance et Réformation.*

2.) On medieval Hungarian universities and scholarly life see, Astrik L. Gabriel, *The Medieval Universities of Pécs and Pozsony,* Frankfurt am Main, 1969; L.S. Domonkos, "The History of the Sigismundean Foundation of the University of Óbuda (Hungary)," *Studium Generale,* 3-33; Andor Csizmadia, "The Origins of University Education in Hungary," *AJ,* 9 (1967), 127-160; *idem, A pécsi egyetem a középkorban* (The University of Pécs in the Middle Ages), Bp. 1965; and, *A pécsi egyetem történetéből* (From the History of the University of Pécs), Pécs, 1967 (vol. I of *JT).*

3.) For excellent social, cultural and political analyses on the age of Matthias Corvinus see the two representative works on that period, the *Mátyás-Emlékkönyv,* and Mályusz, *Magyar renaissance.* See also the more recent essays by L. Elekes, "Essai de centralisation de l'Etat hongrois dans la second moitie du XVe siècle," *Études,* I, 437-467; and T. Kardos, "Zentralisation und Humanismus in Ungarn des 15. und 16. Jahrhunderts," *Renaissance et Réformation,* 397-414.

4.) On the important Italian-Hungarian connections during the humanist period see T. Kardos, "Le relazioni umanistiche italo-ungheresi e il loro carattere," *AUSB Sectio Philologica,* 4 (1962), 27-49; *idem, Studi e ricerche umanistiche italo-ungheresi,* Debrecen, 1967; Jolán Balogh, "I mecenati ungheresi del primo Rinascimento," *AHA,* 13 (1967), 205-212; and Dénes Huszti, *Olasz-magyar kereskedelmi kapcsolatok a középkorban* (Italian-Hungarian Commercial Relations in the Middle Ages), Bp. 1941; Italian resumé on pp. 110-120.

5.) On Bonfini and on his *Rerum Ungaricarum Decades* see Tibor Kardos's introductory study to the recent incomplete Hungarian edition of Bonfini's work, *Mátyás király* (King Matthias), Bp. 1959, 7-64. Earlier studies on Bonfini include Mihály Zsilinszky, "Bonfini Antal történetírói jellemzése" (Antonio Bonfini's Characterization as an Historian), *Sz,* 11 (1877), 510-527; and Horváth, *Megoszlása,* 147-161. The most recent critical edition of Bonfini's history is the *Rerum Ungaricarum Decades,* ed. J. Fogel, B. Iványi and L. Juhász, 4 vols., Lipsae-Bp. 1936-1941.

6.) The 1543 edition, published in Basel by Márton Brenner, contained only the first thirty of Bonfini's forty-five books. The first complete edition was published by Johannes Zsámboki (Sambucus, Sambuci) in 1568 in Basel. Péter Kulcsár's *Bonfini Magyar történetének forrásai és keletkezése* (The Sources and Origins of Bonfini's Hungarian History), Bp 1973, is the most recent analysis of Bonfini's history.

7.) For a general description of the post-Mohács period and of Hungarian political, economic, social and cultural developments into the twentieth century see Szekfű's classic, if somewhat pessimistic and controversial analysis in Hóman-Szekfű, III-V; the appropriate volumes of the *MMT,* III-V; Julius Miskolczy, *Ungarn in der Habsburger Monarchie,* Vienna, 1959; and Molnár, *Magyarország.* For briefer English language summaries see Sinor, *History,* 151-297; Macartney, *History,* 65-243; Kosáry, *History,* 92-438; and Kosáry-Várdy, *History,* 61-381. On the literary, cultural and scholarly aspects of the sixteenth and seventeenth centuries see Horváth, *Reformáció;* Klaniczay, *Reneszánsz és barokk;* Nemeskürty, *Széppróza;* István Sinkovics, "Európai műveltség a magyar végvárak mögött" (European Culture Behind Hungarian Frontier Fortifications), *Sz,* 77 (1943), 154-172; and Sőtér, *MIT,* I, 267-542 and II, 5-325. On the historiography of the sixteenth century see Beöthy, *MIT,*

I, 187-195; Pintér, *MIT*, II, 145-163; and Sőtér, *MIT*, I, 279-294, 332-339, 362-372, 388-405, 425-437; Molnár, "Historical Sciences," 162-163; Vardy, *Historiography*, 16-17, 59-60; and *idem*, "Történetírás," 155-156.

8.) On these three great humanist scholars see Pongrácz Sörös, *Brodarics István*, Bp. 1907; Pál Schleicher, *Oláh Miklós és Erasmus* (Miklós Oláh and Erasmus), Bp. 1941; Ignácz Acsády, "Verancsics Antal és Szerémi György" (Antal Verancsics and György Szerémi), *ITK*, 4 (1894), 1-59; and Pongrácz Sörös, *Verancsics Antal élete* (The Life of Antal Verancsics), Esztergom, 1898.

9.) On Zsámboki and some of the lesser memoire writers see György Székely's introduction to György Szerémi, *Magyarország romlásáról — De Perditione Hungarorum*, tr. L. Erdélyi and L. Juhász, ed. Gy. Székely, Bp. 1961, 7-22; Lajos Thallóczy, *Csömöri Záy Ferenc* (Ferenc Záy of Csömör), Bp. 1885; János Illésy, "Sámboki János történetíróról" (On Historian Johannes Zsámboki), *Sz*, 33 (1899), 524-532; Endre Bach, *Un humaniste hongrois en France* (Zsámboki), Szeged, 1932; and Nemeskürty, *Széppróza*, 276-281.

10). On "Magyar Reformation" see Horváth, *Reformáció*; Klaniczay, *Reneszánsz és barokk*, 64-150; Imre Révész, *Magyar református egyháztörténet. I.* (Hungarian Reformed Church History), Debrecen, 1938; Tamás Esze, "The Beginnings of the Hungarian Reformed Church," *NHQ*, 9 (1968), 127-135; and L. Makkai, "The Hungarian Puritans and the English Revolution," *AH*, 5 (1958), 13-45.

11.) On some of the wandering Protestant preachers of the sixteenth century see Imre Révész, *Dévay Bíró Mátyás első magyar reformátor életrajza és irodalmi működése* (The Biography and Literary Works of Mátyás Dévai Bíró, the First Hungarian Reformer), Bp. 1863; Jenő Sólyom, "Dévai Mátyás tiszántúli működése" (The Trans-Tisza Activities of Mátyás Dévai), *EbT*, 2 (1959), 193-217; Gyula Czakó, *Méliusz Juhász Péter*, Debrecen, 1904; Sándor Szent-Iványi, *A magyar vallásszabadság* (Hungarian Religious Freedom), NY-Lancaster, Mass., 1964; László Makkai, "Dávid Ferenc és a népi reformáció Magyarországon" (Ferenc Dávid and the Popular Reformation in Hungary), *TeTa*, 114 (1955), 484-488; Antal Pirnát, *Die Ideologie der Siebenbürger Antitrinitarien in den 1570-er Jahren*, Bp. 1961; Imre Révész, "Krisztus és Antikrisztus Ozorai Imre műveiben" (Christ and Anti-Christ in the Works of Imre Ozorai), *ThSz*, 4(1928), 167-199; and János Balázs, *Sylvester János és kora* (János Sylvester and his Age), Bp. 1958.

12.) On Benczédi-Székely and his age see Mihály Zsilinszky, "A magyar nemzeti történetírás kezdete" (The Beginnings of Hungarian National Historiography), *Sz*, 12 (1878), 769-789; and Josef (Turóczi-) Trostler, "Die Anfänge der ungarischen Geschichtsprosa," *UJ*, 14 (1934), 114-134.

13.) On Gáspár Heltai see Varjas's introduction to the most recent critical edition of his chronicle, *Magyar krónika*, ed. Béla Varjas, Bp. 1943. See also Waldapfel, *Tanulmányok*, 43-71; Németh, *Katedrám*, 78-83; Antal Pirnát and Ferenc Végh, "Uj adatok Heltai Gáspárról" (New Data on Gáspár Heltai), *ITK*, 66 (1956), 66-74.

14.) For a recent facsimile edition of this work see Gáspár Heltai, *Cancionale*, ed. and intro. Béla Varjas, Bp. 1962.

15.) The Hungarian historical ballads are discussed by Pál Erdélyi, "A XVI. és XVII. századi magyar históriás énekek" (Hungarian Historical Ballads of the 16th and 17th Centuries), *MK*, 11 (1868), 119-179; and Szabolcsi, *Magyar zene*, I, 101-156. On Tinódi and his followers see, Ignácz Acsády, "Tinódi Sebestyén," *BpSz*, 47 (1899), 1-24 and 181-213; Szabolcsi, *Magyar zene*, I, 39-61; Klaniczay, *Reneszánsz és barokk*, 39-53; Horváth, *Reformácio*, 183-214 and 457-479; Lajos György, *Valkai András*, Kolozsvár 1947; and *Tanulmányok Tinódiról és szemelvények műveiből* (Studies about Tinódi and Selections from his Works), ed. I.K. Horváth and I. Nagyszabados, Sárvár, 1956.

16.) In addition to studies mentioned above (notes 1, 3 and 7), see also Tibor Kardos, "Adatok a magyar irodalmi barokk keletkezéshez" (Data on the Beginnings of Hungarian Literary Baroque), *MsT* (1942), 63-93.

17.) On Forgách see Pongrácz Sörös, "Forgách Ferenc kortörténete" (Ferenc Forgach's Contemporary History), *Sz*, 31 (1897), 97-106 and 201-209; Vencel Bíró, *Forgach Ferenc mint történetíró* (Ferenc Forgách as an Historian), Kolozsvár, 1908; and Antal Pirnát, "Forgách Ferenc," *IT* (1955), no. 1, 17-32. Forgách's *Commentary* was published by Ferenc Toldy in the *MHHS* series, XVI, Pest, 1866.

18.) On some of Forgách's contemporaries see Lajos Szádeczky, *Kovacsóczy Farkas*, Bp. 1891; Albert Gárdonyi, "Abafai Gyulai Pál" (Pál Gyulai of Abafa), *Sz*, 40 (1906), 894-910; Endre Veress, *Berzeviczy Márton*, Bp. 1911; *idem*, "A történetíró Báthory István király" (King Stephan Báthory the Historian), *EM* (1933), 377-412; and Márton Papp, *Brutus J. Mihály és Báthory István magyar humanistái* (Michael J. Brutus and the Hungarian Humanists of Stephan Báthory), Bp. 1940.

19.) On Szamosközy see Árpád Károlyi, "Szamosközy István történeti maradványai" (The Historical Fragments of István Szamosközy), *BpSz*, 17 (1878), 246-274; Gyula Szekfű, *Adatok Szamosközy István történeti munkáinak kritikájához* (Data on the Critiques of István Szamosközy's Historical Works), Bp. 1904; and István Sinkovics's introduction to a recent incomplete edition of Szamosközy's history, *Erdély története* (History of Transylvania), tr. István Borzsák, ed. István Sinkovics, Bp. 1963, 7-29.

20.) *A magyarok történetéből* (From the History of the Magyars), tr. László Juhász, ed. György Székely, Bp. 1962, is the most recent incomplete edition of Székely's introduction to the above work (pp. 7-34); József Holub, *Istvánffy Miklós históriája hadtörténeti szempontból* (Miklós Istvánffy's History from the Viewpoint of Military History), Szekszárd 1909; Károly Bóta, *Istvánffy Miklós*, Bp. 1938; and Jenő Berlász, "Istvánffy Miklós könvtáráról" (On Miklós Istvánffy's Library), *OSZKÉ 1959*, Bp. 1961, 202-240.

21.) On Gáspár Bojti-Veres, János Bethlen, Farkas Bethlen and János Szalárdi see Sőtér, *MIT*, II, 85, 208-210; Sándor Makoldy, *Bojthi Veres Gáspár élete és történetírói munkássága* (The Life and Historical Activities of Gáspár Bojthi-Veres), Nagykároly, 1904; Gyula Bodnár, *Bethlen János erdélyi kancellár és történetíró* (János Bethlen, Chancellor of Transylvania and Historian), Nagyvárad, 1922; Pál Svéda, *Bethlen Farkas históriája* (Farkas Bethlen's History), Pecs, 1938; and Detre Horváth, "Szalárdi János és Siralmas krónikája" (János Szalárdi and His Sorrowful Chronicle), *Sz*, 57-58 (1923-1924), 94-122.

Chapter III

BAROQUE HISTORIOGRAPHY: POLITICAL MEMOIRES

1.) For general historical background on the seventeenth and early eighteenth centuries see the appropriate sections of the Hóman-Szekfű; *MMT:* Molnár, *Magyarország;* Sinor, *History;* Macartney, *History;* Kosáry, *History;* and Kosáry-Várdy, *History.* On the Age of Baroque and Baroque spirituality see Werner Weisbach, *Der Barock als Kunst der Gegenreformation,* Berlin, 1921; René Wellek, "The Concept of Baroque in Literary Scholarship," *JAAC,* 5 (1946), 77-109; Helmut Hatzfeld, "The Baroque from the Viewpoint of the Literary Historian," *JAAC,* 14 (1955), 156-164; Victor Tapié, *Baroque et Classicisme,* Paris, 1957; and Imre Bán, *A barokk,* Bp. 1962. For the Hungarian Baroque specifically see Szekfű's excellent, if controversial chapter in Hóman-Szekfű, IV, 366-416, and Elemér Mályusz's critique of the same, "Magyar reneszánsz, magyar barokk," *BpSz,* 241 (1936), 159-179, 293-318, and 242 (1936), 86-104, 154-174. See also Turóczi-Trostler, *Magyar-Világ,* I, 308-317; Andreas Angyal, "Barockforschung und ungarische Literaturgeschichte," *AL,* 1 (1957), 243-249; Klaniczay, *Reneszánsz és barokk,* 303-339, 361-436; and Sőtér, *MIT,* II, 5-9, 113-126, 150-153, 326-331, 500-504. For a view of the world of Baroque aristocracy, where much of Hungarian Baroque literature was born, see Gábor Tolnai, *Régi Magyar főurak* (Hungarian Lords of Old), Bp. (1939), 82-160.

2.) On Transylvania and on its special development during the sixteenth and seventeenth centuries see László Makkai, *Histoire de Transylvanie,* Paris, 1946; Kálmán Benda, "Les bases sociales du puvoir des princes de Transylvanie," in *Renaissance et Réformation,* 439-447; Tibor Wittman, "Quelques problèmes des luttes d'indépendance de Transylvanie contre les Habsbourg et de leur idéologie," *AUSAH,* 10 (1962), 9-18; and *idem,* "L'idéologie de la centralisation de la principauté de Transylvanie et ses rapports européens," *Renaissance et Réformation,* 431-438. See also Gyula Szekfű, *Bethlen Gábor,* Bp. 1929, which gives a vivid picture of the European framework of seventeenth-century Transylvanian developments. For the social developments of that period consult László Makkai, *A kuruc nemzeti összefogás előzményei* (The Antecedents of the "Kuruc" National Unification Movement), Bp. 1956.

3.) *Veresmarti Mihály megtérése historiája* (The Story of Mihály Veresmarti's Conversion), ed. Arnold Ipolyi, Bp. 1875. See also Ipolyi's biography of Veresmarti, *Veresmarti Mihály XVII, századi író élete és munkái* (The Life and Works of Mihály Veresmarti, a 17th Century Writer), Bp. 1875.

4.) On Hungarian Baroque political memoires in general see Károly Máté, "A magyar önéletírás kezdetei" (The Beginnings of Hungarian Autobiographical Literature), *M,* 5 (1926), 120-166; Sőtér, *MIT,* II, 208-215; Pintér, *MIT,* II, 344-361; and Beöthy, *MIT,* I, 334-346, 466-474. For the most recent edition of Kemény's autobiography, see *Kemény János önéletírása és válogatott levelei* (János Kemény's Autobiography and selected Letters), ed. and intro. Éva V. Windisch, Bp. 1959.

5.) In addition to Máté's study above, see Sándor Szilágyi, "Kornis Gáspár feljegyzései" (Memoire Fragments of Gáspár Kornis), *UMM,* 2 (1860), 333-351; Dávid Angyal, *Késmárki Thököly Imre* (Imre Thököly of Késmark), 2 vols., Bp. 1888-1889; and Gábor Tolnai, "Szegény együgyű fejedelem" (Poor Simple Prince), in his *Évek-Századok* (Years-Centuries), Bp. 1958, 132-145. Thököly's memoires and diaries were published in the *MHHS* series, vols. 15, 18, 23 and 24. For Apafi's memories see, *I. és II. Apafi Mihály naplója* (The Diaries of Mihály Apafi I and II), ed. Ernő Tóth, Kolozsvár, 1900; and *Apafi Mihály naplója (The Diary of Mihály Apafi), ed.* Istvan Bias, *Marosvásárhely,* 1910.

6.) For a recent edition of Bethlen's autobiography see *Bethlen Miklós önéletírása* (Miklós Bethlen's Autobiography), 2 vols., ed. Éva V. Windisch, intr. Gábor Tolnai, Bp. 1955. See also Elemér Gyárfás, *Bethlen Miklós kancellár* (Chancellor Miklós Bethlen), Dicsőszentmárton, 1924; László Németh, "Bethlen Miklós," in his *Katedrám,* 125-135; and Gábor Tolnai, "Bethlen Miklós," in his *Vázlatok,* 42-67.

7.) On Zrinyi see Tibor Klaniczay, *Zrinyi Miklós,* Bp. 1954; 2nd ed., 1964. Géza Perjés, *Zrinyi Miklós és kora* (Miklós Zrinyi and his Age), Bp. 1965; and *Zrinyi Miklós összes müvei* (Miklós Zrinyi's Complete Works), 2 vols., ed. Csaba Csapodi and Tibor Klaniczay, Bp. 1958.

8.) *Memoires du Prince Francois Rákóczy sur la Guerre de Hongrie depuis l'année 1703 jusqu'à sa fin* appeared as vols. 5 and 6 of (Domokos Brenner), *Histoire des Revolutions de Hongrie,* 6 vols., The Hague, 1739. His political testament also appeared in French a few years later, *Testament politique et morale du Prince Rákóczi,* The Hague, 1751. Rákóczi's confessiones, however, were published only a century and a half after his death in Latin, *Principis Francisci II, Rákóczi. Confessiones et Aspirationes Principis Christiani,* Bp. 1878. Most of his letters appeared in the *Archivum Rákóczianum,* vols. 1-10 ed. Kálmán Thaly, Bp. 1873-1889; vols. 11-12, ed. Imre Lukinich, Bp. 1935. Rákóczi's most recent biography is by Béla Köpeczi and Ágnes R. Várkonyi, *II. Rákóczi Ferenc,* Bp. 1955. See also Gábor Tolnai, "Rákóczi az író" (Rákóczi as a Writer), in his *Vázlatok,* 68-87; and Sőtér, *MIT,* II, 371-387.

9.) Sőtér, *MIT,* II, 387-396; Lajos Szádezky-Kardoss, "Gr. Bethlen Kata élete és végrendeletei" (The Life and Testaments of Countess Kata Bethlen), *Sz,* 29 (1895), 523-545; and Németh, *Katedrám,* 136-168. For a recent edition of Kata Bethlen's memoires see, *Bethlen Kata oneletirasa* (Data Bethlen's Autobiography), ed. and intr. Mihály Sükösd, Bp. 1963.

Chapter IV

THE SOURCE COLLECTING HISTORIOGRAPHY OF THE EIGHTEENTH CENTURY

1.) On the question of Catholic-Protestant controversy see the three studies by Imre Révész, *Esquisse de l'histoire de la politique religieuse hongroise entre 1705 et 1860,* Bp. 1960; *idem, Bécs Debrecen ellen* (Vienna versus Debrecen), Bp. 1966; and *idem, Sinai Miklós.*

2.) An example of an early sixteenth-century source collector was Gergely Gyöngyösi (15th-16th c.), for a while the General of the Paulist Order (1528-1530), whose source collecting activities preceded those of the Dutch Bollandists and the Hungarian Jesuits. On the evolution of European critical historical scholarship see Barnes, *Historical Writing,* 99-276.

3.) In addition to Barnes's work see Emil Menke-Glückert, *Die Geschichtsschreibung der Reformation und Gegenreformation*, Leipzig, 1912.

4.) On the Hungarian source collecting schools of the eighteenth century and on the evolution of scientific historiography in Hungary see Hóman, *Tudományos történetírásunk; idem, Forráskutatás;* and Kosáry, *Bevezetés*, II, 136-139, 213-216, 589-597. For Hevenesi see Sőtér, *MIT*, II, 409-411; and Hóman, *Történetírás*, 337-351, 395, 397-398.

5.) On the beginnings of the Protestant Source Collecting School and on Debreceni-Ember see Sőtér, *MIT*, II, 458-461; Gyula Ferenczy, *Debreczeni Pál életrajza* (A Biography of Pál Debreczeni), Debrecen, 1882; Kálmán Révész, "Debreceni Ember Pál egyháztörténelme" (The Church History of Pál Debreceni-Ember), *PEIL*, 22 (1884), 1375-1381; and István Harsányi, "Debreczeni Ember Pál eddig ismeretlen kéziratai" (The Hitherto Unknown Manuscripts of Pál Debreczeni-Ember), *PSz*, 27 (1915), 412-416.

6.) On Czvittinger and Rotarides see Sőtér, *MIT*, II, 462-464; Hóman, *Történetírás*, 397-398; Turóczi-Trostler, *Magyar-Világ*, II, 64-75; Mihály Verő, "Czvittinger és az Allgemeines Gelehrten-Lexikon" (Czvittinger and the Allgemeines Gelehrten-Lexikon), *EPhK*, 21 (1907), 412-416; and Robert Gragger, "Egy magyar tudós sorsa. Rotarides Mihály" (The Fate of a Hungarian Scholar. Mihály Rotarides), in *Klebelsberg-Emlékkönyv*, 437-452.

7.) On Péter Bod see Hóman, *Történetírás*, 398; Sőtér, *MIT*, II, 562-565; Imre Mikó, "Bod Péter élete és munkái" (The Life and Works of Péter Bod), *BpSz*, 15 (1862), 233-255 and 16 (1862), 3-87; Imre Révész, *Bod Péter mint történetíró* (Péter Bod as an Historian), Kolozsvár, 1916; and János Herepai, "Adalékok Bod Péter életrajzához" (Data for Péter Bod's Biography), *ITK*, 66 (1962), 341-343.

8.) On the *Staatenkunde* School and Bél see Hóman, *Történetírás*, 401-405; Sőtér, *MIT*, II, 465-471; Flegler, *Történetírás*, 144-150; Antal Bodor, *Bél Mátyás emlékezete* (Remembering Mátyás Bél), Bp. 1936; Zoltán Losonczi, *Bél és a magyar tudomány* (Bél and Hungarian Scholarship), Bp. 1927; Rezső Szalatnai, "Bél Mátyás," *ÉT*, 9 (1954), 1187-1189; and Imre Wellmann, "Bél Mátyás és a Magyar Tudós Társaság terve 1735-ben" (Mátyás Bél and his Plan for a Hungarian Academy in 1735), *MT*, 10 (1965), 738-741.

9.) For a previously unpublished section of Bél's *Notatia* on Transdanubia see Edit B. Thomas and Gyula Prokop, "Bél Mátyás: Hungariae Novae Notatia. Membrum 3. De Sabaria," *VSz*, II, (1959), 37-57.

10.) On Sinai see the thorough biography by Imre Révész, *Sinai Miklós*. On Cornides and Wallaszky see Sőtér, *MIT*, II, 560, 566-567; Hóman, *Történetírás*, 409-410; and Mihály Zsilinszky, *Wallaszky Pál élete* (The Life of Pál Wallaszky), Bp. 1910.

11.) On Timon see Flegler, *Történetírás*, 140-141; Hóman, *Történetírás*, 399; and Sőtér, *MIT*, II, 411-412.

12.) On Kaprinay see Hóman, *Történetírás*, 400; and Sőtér, *MIT*, II, 560.

13.) Kollár has been treated in a number of recent studies, including Andor Csizmadia, "Egy 200 év előtti országgyűlés évfordulójára" (On the Anniversary of a Diet 200 Years Ago), *JKö*, 19 (1965), 214-227; Dezső Dümmerth, "Történetkutatás és nyelvkérdés a magyar-Habsburg viszony tükrében. Kollár Ádám működése" (Historical Research and the Linguistic Question in Light of Hungarian-Habsburg Relations. The Activities of Ádám Kollár), *FK*, 12 (1966), 391-413. See also Sőtér, *MIT*, II, 556, 566; and

Hóman, *Történetírás*, 406-407.

14.) Here I am referring primarily to the works of Gyula László and Jenő M. Fehér. For László's related works see Ch. I, n. 8. See also Fehér's projected multivolumed work: *A nyugati avarok birodalma* (The Empire of the Western Avars), of which two volumes have already appeared under the title, *Az avar kincsek nyomában* (On the Track of the Avar Treasures), Buenos Aires, 1972, and *Korai avar kágánok* (Early Avar Kagans), Buenos Aires, 1973.

15. On Pray see Hóman, *Történetírás*, 407-409; Sőtér, *MIT*, II, 561-562; and Flegler, *Történetírás*, 150-156. See also the standard biographies by Gáspár Lischerong, *Pray György élete és munkái* (The Life and Works of György Pray), Bp. 1937; and Mihály Paintner, *Pray György életrajza* (The Biography of György Pray), Győr, 1937.

16.) On the fate of the "Hevenesi-to-Kaprinay Collection" see András Tóth, " 'Holt' kéziratgyüjtemények élete" (The Life of 'Dead' Manuscript Collections), *MK*, 74 (1958), 49-50.

17.) On Katona see Flegler, *Történetírás*, 151-161; Hóman, *Történetírás*, 140; and Georgius Fejér, *Memoria Stephani Katona*, Buda, 1835.

18.) On the two Kovachich's see the three studies by Éva V. Windisch, *Kovachich Márton György élete és munkássága* (The Life and Works of Márton György Kovachich), Bp. 1947; *idem*, "Kovachich Márton György és a magyarországi levéltari anyag feltárása a XIX. század elején" (M. G. Kovachich and the Beginnings of Hungarian Archival Research at the Start of the 19th Century), *LK*, 37 (1966), 63-112; and *idem*, "Kovachich Márton György és a magyar tudományszervezés első kisérletei" (M.G. Kovachich and the Initial Attempts at Organizing Hungarian Scholarship), *Sz*, 102 (1968), 90-144.

19.) For Hungarian historiography of the turn of the 18th to 19th century see Beöthy, *MIT*, I, 807-819; Lékai, *Történetírás; idem*, "Historiography"; and Géza Ballagi, *A politikai irodalom Magyarországon 1825-ig* (Political Literature in Hungary till 1825), Bp. 1888.

20.) On Fessler see Flegler, *Történetírás*, 181-188; János Koszó, *Fessler Ignácz Aurél élete és szépirodalmi működése* (The Life and Literary Activities of I.A. Fessler), Bp. 1915; *idem, Fessler Ignácz Aurél a regény és történetíró* (I.A. Fessler, Novelist and Historian), Bp. 1923; István Fenyő, "Fessler Oroszországban" (Fessler in Russia), *ITK*, 67 (1963), 720-722; and Peter F. Barton, *Ignatius Aurelius Fessler. Vom Barockkatholicizmus zur Erweckungsbewegung*, Wien-Köln-Gratz, 1969.

21.) For Engel, Budai and Virág cf. Flegler, *Történetírás*, 173-181, 189-196; Lajos Thallóczy, "Johann Christian von Engel und seine Korrespondenze," *UR*, 4 (1915), 247-385; István Borzsák, *Budai Ézsiás és Klasszika-filológiánk kezdetei* (E. Budai and the Beginnings of Our Classical Philology), Bp. 1955; Mátyás Bajkó, "Budai Ézsiás, 1766-1841," *MP*, 6 (1966), 434-436; Mihály Zsilinszky, "Virág Benedek mint történetíró" (B. Virág as an Historian), *Sz*, 14 (1880), 207-222; Waldapfel, *Tanulmányok, 225-233; and* Sőtér, *MIT*, III, 98-100, 203.

22.) In addition to Lékai's *Történetírás* and "Historiography", see Pamlényi, *Horváth*, 13-20; Mihály Zsilinszky, *Horvát István*, Bp. 1884; Éva V. Windisch, "Könyvtári munka a reformkorban az Országos Széchenyi Könyvtárban" (Librarianship in the National Széchenyi Library during the Reform Period), *OSZKÉ 1957*, 249-282; and Dezső Dümmerth, "Horvát

István ifjúsága" (I. Horvát's Youth), *EKE*, I (1962), 179-199. Horvát's diary has recently appeared in print under the title, *Mindennapi: Horvát István pest-budai naplója, 1805-1809* (Diary: I. Horvát's Diary of Pest-Buda, 1805-1809), ed. Alfréd Temesi and Józsefné Szauder, Bp. 1967.

23.) On Fejér as an historian and archivist see András Tóth, "Az egyetemi könyvtár Fejér György igazgatósága alatt, 1824-1843" (The University Library Under the Directorship of G. Fejér, 1824-1843), *MK*, 75 (1959), 265-279; János Zsidi, *Fejér György*, Bp. 1936; and Hóman, *Történetírás*, 421-422.

Chapter V

THE DEVELOPMENT OF "SCIENTIFIC" HISTORIOGRAPHY IN THE NINETEENTH CENTURY

1.) Lékai, *Történetírás*; *idem*, "Historiography;" and Pamlényi, *Horváth*, 13-20. See also Biró, *Történelemtanításunk*. For an evaluation of Budai's and Spanyik's textbooks see *ibid.*, 61-64, 84-90, 111-128, 178-181, 187-188.

2.) See Ch. IV.

3.) On the Hungarian Academy and on its relationship to historiography see Károly Szász, *Gróf Széchenyi István és az Akadémia megalapítása* (Count I. Szechényi and the Foundation of the Academy), Bp. 1880; and Lukinich, "Történettudomány," 127-142.

4.) On Mailáth, Péczely, Teleki, Gévay, Bajza, young Horváth and their generation see Flegler, *Történetírás*, 215-242; Sőtér, *MIT*, III, 200-205, 523-535, 585-589; István Kolos, *Mailáth János gróf 1786-1855* (Count J. Mailáth 1786-1855), Bp. 1838; Bálint Csűry, *Teleki József gróf mint nyelvész* (Count J. Teleki as a Linguist), Bp. 1909; József Bajza (Jr.), "Bajza József mint történetíró" (J. Bajza as an Historian), *Sz*, 42 (1908), 289-300; and Biró, *Történelemtanításunk*, 65-81, 181-188, 270-271.

5.) For a general historical introduction to the half century preceding the Revolution of 1848 see the relevant sections of the standard surveys mentioned in Ch. II, n. 7. On the cultural and social background of that period consult Gyula Kornis, *A magyar művelődés eszményei 1777-1848* (The Ideals of Hungarian Culture 1777-1848), 2 vols., Bp. 1927; Béla Zolnai, *A magyar Biedermeier* (Hungarian Biedermeier), Bp. ca.1940; and József Zoltán, *A barokk Pest-Buda élete* (The Life of Baroque Buda-Pest), Bp. 1963.

6.) The relationship between the absolutism of the post-revolutionary period and the revival of Hungarian historical scholarship was first noted by Lukinich in his *Történelmi Társulat*, 15-16. See also the observations of Hóman, *Történetírás*, 422-423.

7.) The two works in question are: József Eötvös, *A XIX. század uralkodó eszméinek befolyása az álladalomra*, 2 vols., Vienna-Pest, 1851-1854; and László Szalay, *Magyarország története*, 6 vols., Leipzig, 1852-1854 and Pest, 1857-1859. On these two great nineteenth-century thinkers see Paul Bődy, "Baron Joseph Eötvös and his Critique of Nationalism in the Habsburg Monarchy, 1848-1854," *Hi*, 28 (1966), 19-47; *idem*, *Joseph Eötvös and the Modernization of Hungary 1840-1870*, Philadelphia, 1972; Steven Bela Vardy, *Baron Joseph Eötvös: The Political Profile of a Liberal Hungarian Thinker and Statesman*, Ph.D. Diss., Indiana University, Bloomington, Ind.,

1967; *idem,* "Baron Joseph Eötvös: Satesman, Thinker, Reformer," *DR,* 12 (1968), 107-119; *idem,* "Baron Joseph Eötvös on Liberalism and Nationalism," *SNCE,* Ser. 2, no. 1 (1967-1968), 65-73; Gábor Szalay, "Szalay Lászlóról" (About L. Szalay), *BpSz,* 153 (1913), 75-99, 228-258; and Dávid Angyal, "Szalay László," *BpSz,* 157 (1914), 1-22, 187-228.

8.) The syntheses in question are Szalay's above-mentioned six-volume *Magyorország története* and Mihály Horváth's even more extensive *Magyarország történelme* (History of Hungary), 6 vols., Pest, 1860-1863, 2nd ed., 8 vols., Pest, 1871-1873. On these two great historians see Flegler, *Történetirás,* 220-224, 242-257. On Szalay see also Ervin Pamlényi, "Szalay László: Magyarország története" (L. Szalay's History of Hungary), *Sz,* 98 (1964), 1370-1379; and Hatvany, *Emberek,* I, 600-606. On Horváth see Pamlényi, *Horváth;* Sándor Márki, *Horváth Mihály 1809-1878,* Bp. 1917; and Hatvany, *Öt évtized,* 325-323.

9.) On the foundation of the Hungarian Historical Association and on its impact on Hungarian historical studies, see Ágnes R. Várkonyi, "A Történelmi Társulat megalakulásának előzményeihez" (On the Antecedents of the Foundation of the Historical Association), *Sz,* 101 (1967), 1185-1190; Ferenc Glatz, "A Magyar Történelmi Társulat megalakulásának története" (The History of the Foundation of the Hungarian Historical Association), *ibid.,* 233-267; Győző Ember, "A Magyar Történelmi Társulat száz éve" (One Hundred Years of the Hungarian Historical Association), *ibid.,* 1140-1169; Éva H. Balázs. "A Történelmi Társulat könyvkiadásánk 100 éve" (One Hundred Years of Book Publishing of the Historical Association), *ibid.,* 1169-1173; Miklós Incze, "A száz esztendős Századok" (One Hundred Years of the *Századok), ibid.,* 1174-1176; Domokos Kosáry, "A Társulat társadalmi bázisa és annak hatása a történetszemléletre" (The Social Basis of the Society and its Impact on the Philosophy of History), *ibid.,* 1177-1180; and István Sinkovics, "A történettudomány és a népszerűsités" (Historical Scholarship and Popularization), *ibid.,* 1180-1185.

10.) On the establishment of the Academy's Historical Commission and its activities see Lukinich, *Történelmi Társulat,* 16-18; *idem,* "Történettudomány," 133-134; and Jánosné Fráter, *A Magyar Tudomdnyos Akadémia Történettudományi Bizottságának működése 1854-1949* (The Functioning of the Historical Commission of the Hungarian Academy of Sciences), Bp. 1966 (mimeographed).

11.) For the source publishing activities of the Academy's Historical Commission see Lukinich, "Történettudomány," 134-136; Hóman, *Történetirás,* 424-426; Kosáry, *Bevezetés Magyarország,* I, 223-232; and Emeric Lukinich, *Les editions des sources de l'histoire Hongroise 1854-1930,* Bp. 1931, 5-85. The latter two works also contain a rather complete list of the Academy's source publications.

12.) On some of these prominent historians see Antal Pór, *Ipolyi Arnold váradi püspök élete és munkái vázlata* (The Life of A. Ipolyi, the Bishop of Várad, and the Outline of his Works), Pozsony, 1886; Antal Hekler, "Ipolyi Arnold emlékezete" (Remembering A. Ipolyi), *Sz,* 57-58 (1923-1924), 235-246; Ortutay, *Irók,* 202-210; Ernő Marosi, "Das romantische Zeitalter der ungarischen Kunstgeschichtsschreibung," *AUSB, Sec. Hist.,* 7 (1965), 43-78; Tivadar Ortvay, *Pesty Frigyes emlékezete* (Remembering F. Pesty), Bp. 1891; Sándor Szilágyi, *Szabó Károly emlékezete* (Remembring K. Szabó), Bp.

1896; Dezső Csánki, "Szabó Károly emlékezete" (Remembering K. Szabó), *Sz,* 57-58 (1923-1924), 689-694; Sándor Szilágyi, *Salamon Ferenc emlékezete* (Remembering F. Salamon), Bp. 1895; Vilmos Fraknói, *Szilágyi Sándor emlékezete* (Remembering S. Szilágyi), Bp. 1902; Dezső Csánki, "Szilágyi Sándor emlékezete" (Remembering S. Szilágyi), *Sz,* 61-62 (1927-1928), 337-343; Miklós Mann, "Adatok a Századok történetéhez Szilágyi Sándor szerkesztői korszakából, 1975-1899" (Data on the History of the *Századok* during the Period of Sándor Szilágyi's Editorship, 1875-1899), *Sz,* 102 (1968), 205-239; *idem,* "Ráth Károly élete és munkássága" (The Life and Works of K. Ráth), *Sz,* 99, (1965), 836-860; Alfréd Lengyel, "Megemlékezés a Dunántúli Történetkedvelők példamutatásáról" (Remembering the Examples of the Trans-Danubian Friends of History), *Ar,* 10 (1968), 163-176; and Ferenc Kollányi, *Knauz Nándor emlékezete* (Remembering N. Knauz), Bp. 1911.

13.) For the political, social and cultural developments in Hungary during the dualist period see Gusztáv Gratz, *A dualizmus kora. Magyarország története 1867-1918* (The Age of Dualism. History of Hungary 1867-1918), 2 vols., Bp. 1934; Sándor Pethő, *Világostól Trianonig* (From Világos to Trianon), Bp. 1926; Gyula Mérei, *Magyar politikai pártprogrammok 1867-1914* (Hungarian Political Party Platforms 1867-1914), Bp. 1934; Viktória M. Kondor, *Az 1875-ös pártfúzió* (The Party Fusion of 1875), Bp. 1959; *Studien zur Geschichte der Österreichisch-Ungarischen Monarchie,* ed. V. Sándor and P. Hanák, Bp. 1961; and Adalbert Toth, *Parteien und Reichstagswahlen in Ungarn 1848-1892,* München, 1973.

14.) On the Historiographical developments of the dualist period and on the role of Kálmán Thaly see Várkonyi, "Historiográfiai törekvések"; *idem,* "Scientific Thinking"; *idem, Thaly,* and Lederer, *Történetírás,* 29-91. On Thaly and the National Romantic School see also Ch. VI.

15.) On the enumerated historians see József Illés, *Hajnik Imre és a magyar jogtörténet* (I. Hajnik and Hungarian Legal History), Bp. 1928; Degré, "Magyar jogtörténetírás;" Remig Békefi, *Pauler Gyula emlékezete* (Remembering G. Pauler), Bp. 1913; Antal Áldásy, "Fraknói Vilmos, 1843-1924," *Sz,* 57-58 (1923-1924), 837-841; Albert Berzeviczy, *Fraknói Vilmos emlékezete* (Remembering V. Fraknói), Bp. 1927; Ferenc Rottler, "Fraknói Vilmos történetírói pályakezdése 1861-1871" (V. Fraknói's Early Career as an Historian, 1861-1871), *Sz,* 103 (1969), 1046-1076; and Gunst, *Acsády.*

16.) On Márki see *Márki-Emlékkönyv,* which contains a short biography by Vencel Bíró; Imre Lukinich, "Márki Sándor, 1853-1925," *Sz,* 59-60 (1925-1926), 329-333; and János Banner, *Márki Sándor emlékezete* (Remembering S. Márki), Gyula, 1961. On Károlyi, Marczali, Angyal, Szádeczky-Kardoss and Hodinka see Ch. XV; on Thallóczy Ch. XVI; on Fejérpataky Ch. XX; on Tagányi and Takáts n. 26, this chapter; on Békefi n. 29, this chapter and Ch. XVII; on Erdélyi Ch. XVII; and on Áldásy Ch. XIX.

17.) On Thaly and on the ideology of the National Romantic School see Várkonyi, *Thaly;* Dezső Veszprémy, *Dr. Thaly Kálmán életrajza* (The Biography of Dr. K. Thaly), 2 vols., Bp. 1928-1931; Pál Horváth, "Adalékok a nemzeti ideológia multjának elemzéséhez a magyar jogi historizmus történetéből" (Data for the Analysis of the Past of the Nationalist Ideology in Light of Legal Historicism), *JK,* 21 (1966), 164-173; Károly Pikéthy, *Beksics Gusztáv, a szabadelvű magyar gondolat publicistája* (G. Beksics, the Publicist of the Hungarian Liberal Thought), Ph.D. Diss., University of Kolozsvár, 1944; Zsuzsa L. Nagy, "A 'nemzeti állam' eszméje Beksics Gusztávnál" (G. Beksics's Idea of a 'National State'), *Sz*, 97 (1963), 1242-1278; and Ágnes R. Várkonyi, "Kuruc költészet és pozitivizmus" (*Kuruc* Poetry and Positivism), *Sz*, 95 (1961), 729-737. On Timon and Ballagi see Degré, "Jogtörténetírás a dualizmus korában," 303-312; "Jogtörténetírás," 77-79; and György Balanyi, "Ballagi Aladár, 1853-1928," *Sz*, 61-62 (1927-1928), 845-847.

18.) For the view that positivism had penetrated Hungary already during the 1830's and 1840's see Várkonyi, *Pozitivista történetszemlélet*, II. On positivism in general see W.M. Simon, *European Positivism in the Nineteenth Century*, Ithaca, N.Y., 1963; Ágnes R. Várkonyi, *A pozitivista történetszemlélet*, Bp. 1970; and Tivadar Thienemann, "A positivizmus és a magyar történetírás" (Positivism and Hungarian Historiography), *M*, 1 (1922), 1-28. See also Pauler's two pace-setting essays, "A positivizmus hatásáról a történetírásra" (On the Influence of Positivism upon Historiography), *Sz*, 5 (1871), 527-545, 624-641; and *idem*, "Comte Ágost és a történelem" (August Comte and History), *Sz*, 7 (1873), 225-241, 391-406, 462-481.

19.) See particularly Tibor Baráth, "Comte pozitivizmusa és a magyar pozitivizmus" (Comte's Positivism and Hungarian Positivism), in *Szentpétery-Emlékkönyv*, 5-30, which basically denies that Hungarian positivism was positivism from a philosophical point of view. See also Ch. XI.

20.) On the role of the "Viennese School", Sándor Mika at Eötvös College, and the great positivists Marczali and Fejérpataky, see Glatz, "Eötvös Kollégium." On Fejérpataky and Mika see also Antal Áldásy, *Fejérpataky László emlékezete* (Remembering L. Fejérpataky), Bp. 1924; Dezső Csánki, "Fejérpataky László 1857-1923," *Sz*, 55-56 (1921-1922 (sic)), 706-708; Hóman, *Történetírás*, 483-501, 525-526; and Anonymous, "Mika Sándor, 1859-1912," *Sz*, 46 (1912), 398-400. On Marczali, Károlyi and Thallóczy see Chs. XIII and XIV; on Fejérpataky Ch. XIX.

21.) *A magyar nemzet története*, ed. Sándor Szilágyi, 10 vols., Bp. 1895-1898. Its most noted authors included Henrik Marczali (I 2, II, VIII), Antal Pór (III 1), Gyula Schönherr (III 2), Vilmos Fraknói (IV), Ignác Acsády (V, VII), Dávid Angyal (VI), Géza Ballagi (IX), Sándor Márki (X 1) and Gusztáv Beksics (X 2). On this major synthesis see the recent study by Miklós Mann, "A milleneumi 'Magyar Nemzet Története' szerkesztési munkálatairól" (On the Editorial Work of the Millennial 'History of the Hungarian Nation'), *Sz*, 102 (1968), 1117-1148; and the reminiscences of one of its authors, Angyal, *Emlékezések*, 99-100.

22.) *A nagy képes világtörténet*, ed. Henrik Marczali, 12 vols., Bp. 1898-1904. Its authors included Marczali himself (VI-XII), Gaston Maspero and Albert Fogarassy (I), Gyula Gyomlay (II), József Geréb (III), Samu Borovszky (IV/1), Ignác Goldziher (IV/2), Sándor Mika (V), Jenő Csuday (VI/1) and Gyula Schönherr (VI/2).

23.) The works in question are: József Szalay, *A magyar nemzet története*, rev. and exp. by Lajos Baróti, 4 vols., Bp. 1896-1898; Ignác Acsády, *A magyar birodalom története*, 2 vols., Bp. 1903-1904; Ákos Beöthy, *A magyar államiság fejlődése, küzdelmei*, 3 vols., Bp. 1900-1906; Gyula Andrássy (Jr.),

A magyar államiság fönnmaradásának és alkotmányos szabadságának okai,3 vols., Bp. 1901-1911 (its first vol. appeared in English under the title, *The Development of Hungarian constitutional Liberty,* tr. C. Arthur and I. Ginever, London, 1908); and Henrik Marczali, *Magyarország története,* Bp. 1911. The most interesting and original of these works was Acsády's history. For a violent contemporary reaction see János Dudek, *Kritikai tanulmányok Acsády Ignácnak A magyar birodalom története cimű művéről* (Critical Studies on I. Acsády's History of the Hungarian Nation), Nyitra, 1904.

24.) The reference here is to Mihály Horváth's studies on the history of industry, commerce and agriculture in Hungary. Cf. Horváth, *Kisebb munkái.*

25.) On the Hungarian Economic History School and on the roles of Tagányi, Takáts and Kováts see Steven Bela Vardy, "The Hungarian Economic History School: Its Birth and Development," *JEEH,* 4 (1975), 121-136; and Edit Izsépy, "A Magyar Gazdaságtörténelmi Szemle történetéhez" (On the History of the Hungarian Economic History Review), *Sz,* 103 (1969), 1077-1103. On Tagányi and Takáts see also József Holub, "Tagányi Károly, 1858-1924," *Sz,* 57-58 (1923-1924), 833-837; Hóman, *Történetirás,* 528-530; Erik Molnár's introduction to Károly Tagányi's *A földközösség története Magyarországon* (The History of Communal Landownership in Hungary), ed. Erik Molnár, Bp. 1950, 3-12; Miklós Nagy, *Takáts Sándor élete és munkássága* (The Life and Works of S. Takáts), Bp. 1937; *idem, Takáts Sándor emlékezete* (Remembering S. Takáts), Bp. 1937; Kálmán Benda's introduction to Sándor Takáts's *Művelődéstörténeti tanulmányok a XVI-XVII. századból* .(Socio-Cultural Studies from the 16th-17th Centures), ed. Kálmán Benda, Bp. 1961, v-xiv; and Steven Bela Vardy, "The Ottoman Empire in European Historiography: A Reevaluation by Sándor Takáts," *TR,* II, 9 (1972), 1-16.

26.) *A magyar jobbágyság története,* Bp. 1906; 3rd ed., Bp. 1948. On Acsády's work consult Gunst, *Acsády,* 209-235; and Pál Sándor, "A magyar agrár- és paraszttörténet polgári irodalmának kritikájához" (On the Critique of Bourgeois Hungarian Historiography on Agricultural and Peasant History), *Sz,* 88 (1954), 373-419.

27.) Among his thirty odd volumes, Takáts's most significant work is his *Rajzok a török világból* (Sketches from the Turkish World), 3 vols., Bp. 1915-1917. The Fourth volume of this work appeared under the title, *A török hódoltság korából* (From the Age of Turkish Conquest), Bp. 1928.

28.) On the origins of *Kulturgeschichte* see Barnes, *Historical Writing,* 310-329. Its Hungarian counterpart is treated by Vardy, "*Kulturgeschichte.*" On Békefi see Dezső Csánki, "Békefi Remig, 1858-1924," *Sz,* 57-58 (1923-1924), 830-833; Sándor Domanovszky, *Békefi Remig emlékezete* (Remembering R. Békefi), Bp. 1924; and *Békefi-Emlékkönyv,* which contains a list of Békefi's published works, as well as a study on the doctoral dissertations written under his direction.

29.) On Domanovszky and on the further development of the Hungarian *Kulturgeschichte* or Civilization School, see Ch. XV.

30.) The Bourgeois Radicals, who congregated around the *Huszadik Század,* and who basically made up the Organic Sociological School, have received ample treatment in recent years. The most significant of the major studies include: György Fukász, *A magyar polgári radikalizmus történetéhez, 1900-1918. Jászi Oszkár ideológiájának bírálata* (On the History of Hungarian Bourgeois Radicalism, 1900-1918. A Critiques of Oscar Jászi's Ideology), Bp. 1960;

Zoltán Horváth, *Magyar századforduló. A második reformnemzedék története, 1896-1914* (The Hungarian *Fin de Siecle*. The History of the Second Reform Generation, 1896-1914), Bp. 1961; and László Márkus, *A szociáldemokrata történetfelfogás jellemzéséhez. A kezdetektől 1918-ig* (On the Characterization of the Social Democratic View of History. From the Beginnings to 1918), Bp. 1963. See also József Révai, *Etudes Historiques*, Bp. 1955, which discusses the role of Endre Ady and Ervin Szabó in the bourgeois radical movement; and László Mihalik, "Ervin Szabó als Historiker," *AUSB, Sec. Hist.*, 9 (1967), 281-288.

Chapter VI

THE END OF THE OLD ORDER AND THE SEARCH FOR THE NEW

1.) On Kálmán Thaly and the National Romantic School see the works listed in Ch. V. n. 14 and 17.

2.) Aladár Schöpflin, "Thaly Kálmán revisiója" (The Revision of K. Thaly), *Ny.* Feb. 1, 1914.

3.) Gyula Szekfű, *A száműzött Rákóczi*, Bp. 1913. Interestingly enough, Szekfű dedicated this volume to Sándor Mika, his former professor at Eötvös College. For an extensive and detailed contemporary review of this work see Franz (Ferenc) Eckhart's essay in the *MIÖG*, 36, n. 2 (1914). Reprint 15 pp.

4.) Rákóczi's most recent biography by Béla Kőpeczi and Ágnes R. Várkonyi (*II. Rákóczi Ferenc*, Bp. 1955) tries to find a midpoint between the extreme versions of this controversy. On the other hand, Viktor Padányi's essay (*Rákóczi*, Melbourne, 1961), again presents an over-idealized view of Rákóczi.

5.) The best short summary of this controversy can be found in Várkonyi, *Thaly*, 309-336. The bibliography of the early and most intense phase of the "Rákóczi Controversy" was collected and published by Árpád Hellebrant in the 1914-1917 issues of the *Századok*. For short bibliographical essays see Kőpeczi-Várkonyi, *Rákoczi*, 397-307; and Várkonyi, *Thaly*, 412-418.

6.) On Ballagi see Balanyi's study cited in Ch. V. n. 17; and Béla Zolnai, "Thaly, Ballagi, Riedl," *IT*, 43, n. 3 (1961), 318-319. See also two of Szekfű's contemporary polemical studies listed in n. 16, this chapter.

7.) Várkonyi, *Thaly*, 311.

8.) Szekfű to Aladár Schöpflin. Vienna, Feb. 7, 1914. Cited in *ibid.*, 312.

9.) Szekfű to Aladár Schöpflin. Vienna, Feb. 22, 1914. Cited in *ibid.*, 312.

10.) Szekfű, *A száműzött Rákóczi*, 335.

11.) For Szekfű's general assessment of Thaly as an historian see *ibid.*, 369-375.

12.) Várkonyi, *Thaly*, 314.

13.) Domokos Kosáry, "A történetíró" (The Historian), in *Szekfű-Emlékkönyv*, 17-39.

14.) On this defense of Szekfű see 'Akadémikusok megnyilatkozása Szekfűről" (The View of Academicians about Szekfű), *Est.* Mar. 29, 1914; "A művelt nagyközönséghez" (To the Learned Public), *Vi*, Apr. 29, 1914; and the views of the Bourgeois Radicals expressed in *PN.* Mar. 26, 1914. For Andrássy's views see his pamphlet, *A száműzött Rákóczi* (The Exiled

Rákóczi), Bp. 1914. Some of the related views of Andrássy, Angyal, Békefi, Károlyi, Tagányi and Takáts were collected and reprinted by Szekfű in a leaflet entitled "A legilletékesebb szaktudósok egész sora nyilatkozott Szekfű könyvéről" (A Whole Series of the Most Qualified Scholars Have Expressed Their Opinions About Szekfű's Book) (Bp. 1914). For a good summary of Szekfű's defense see Várkonyi, *Thaly*, 320-324.

15.) Béla Grünwald (1839-1891) was a gifted politician, legal scholar and historian, who wrote the penetrating if controversial history of Hungarian social and political developments in the eighteenth and early nineteenth centuries. His *A régi Magyarország, 1711-1825* (Hungary of Old, 1711-1825), Bp. 1889, was a scathing criticism of the reactionary role of the Hungarian nobility; while his *Az új Magyarország. Gr. Széchenyi István* (New Hungary. Count Stephen Széchenyi), Bp. 1890, touched also upon the alleged emotional instability of the "great reformer." The publication of these works initiated such violent attacks against Grünwald that he ultimately committed suicide in Paris on May 4, 1891.

16.) Szekfű's polemical studies include his *Felelet a Száműzött Rákóczi dolgában* (Reply in Connection with the Exiled Rákóczi), Bp. 1914; "Megjegyzések Márki Nyilatkozatára" (Reflections on Márk's Open Letter), *TöSz*, 3 (1914), 635-637; *Ujabb válasz bírálóimnak* (A New Reply to my Critics), Bp. 1914; and *Mit vétettem én? Ki gyalázta Rákóczit?* (What Have I Sinned? Who Slandered Rákóczi?) Bp. 1916. See also Ballagi's reply, *Az igazi Rákóczi* (The True Rákóczi), Bp. 1916.

17.) *Geistesgeschichte* will be treated in Chs. VII-X.

18.) *A magyar állam életrajza*, Bp. 1918. The first edition appeared in German under the title, *Der Staat Ungarn*, Stuttgart-Berlin, 1917. The other work is his *Három nemzedék. Egy hanyatló kor története*, Bp. 1920.

19.) Sándor Pethő, *Szekfű Gyula történetírása* (G. Szekfű's Historical Writings), Bp. 1933, 10.

20.) For a contemporary critique of Szekfű's *Three Generations* see Elemér Mályusz, "A reformkor nemzedéke" (The Generation of the Reform Period), *Sz*, 57-58 (1923-1924), 17-15.

21.) In addition to the standard histories listed in Ch. II, n. 7, for the interwar period see also Oscar Jászi, *Revolution and Counterrevolution in Hungary*, London, 1924; C.A. Macartney, *Hungary and her Successors*, Oxford, 1937; *idem, October Fifteenth: A History of Modern Hungary, 1929-1945*, 2 vols., Edinburgh, 1956-1957; Iván T. Berend and György Ránki, *Magyarország gazdasága az első világháború után* (Hungary's Economy after the First World War), Bp. 1966; Elek Karsai, *A budai Sándor-palotában történt, 1919-1941* (It Happened in the Sándor Palace of Buda, 1919-1941), Bp. 1967; and István Deák, "Hungary," in *The European Right: A Historical Profile*, ed. by Hans Rogger and Eugen Weber, Berkeley and Los Angeles, 1966, 365-407.

22.) See Chs. VII and X.

23.) See Ch. XVIII.

24.) See Ch. XII.

25.) See Ch. XIX.

Chapter VII

THE REORIENTATION AND REORGANIZATION OF INTERWAR HUNGARIAN HISTORICAL SCIENCES

1.) On interwar Hungarian cultural and educational policy see Magyary, *Tudománypolitika,* 3-17, 603-618; and István Király, "A reakció iskolapolitikája" (The Educational Policies of Reaction), *TáSz,* 1 (1946), 280-286.

2.) On Klebelsberg and on his cultural-educational policy see József Huszti, *Gróf Klebelsberg Kunó életműve* (The Lifework of Count K. Klebelsberg), Bp. 1942; Glatz, "Klebelsberg,"1176-1200; and *idem,* "Historiography," 273-293.

3.) On Klebelsberg's "neo-nationalism" consult his own work entitled *Neonacionalizmus,* Bp. 1928. See also the following works: Sándor Balogh, "Klebelsberg és a magyar neonacionalizmus" (Klebelsberg and Hungarian Neo-Nationalism), *Va,* 2 (1959), 22-30; *idem,* "A bethleni konszolidáció és a magyar 'neonacionalizmus' " (The Bethlen Consolidation and Hungarian 'Neo-Nationalism'), *Tsz,* 5 (1962), 426-448; and Mihály Mák, "A neonacionalizmus terjesztésének főbb módszerei az ellenforradalmi rendszer idején" (The Chief Methods of the Propagaion of Neo-Nationalism in the Age of the Counterrevolutionary Regime), *PeSz,* 13 (1963), 441-451.

4.) On these two goals of the Hungarian Historical Association see "A Magyar Történelmi Társulat Alapszabályai" (The Bylaws of the Hungarian Historical Association), *Sz* 101 (1967), 1143-1152.

5.) Glatz, "Klebelsberg," 1177.

6.) On the relative roles of the Academy's Historical Commission and the Historical Association prior to 1918 see Lukinich, *Történelmi Társulat;* and *idem,* "Történettudomány".

7.) Glatz, "Klebelsberg," 1178-1179.

8.) Magyary, *Tudománypolitika,* 115-116.

9.) Glatz, "Klebelsberg," 1179, n. 14.

10.) Quotations from Klebelsberg's speeches at the annual meetings of the Historical Association in 1917 and 1918, as quoted by Ember, "MTT," 1155-1156. See also Klebelsberg, *Beszédei, cikkei és törvényjavaslatai* (Speeches, Studies and Parliamentary Bills), Bp. 1927, 16.

11.) See Glatz, "Klebelsberg," 1188-1191; and *idem,* "Historiography," 284-285.

12.) For Klebelsberg's and Hóman's institutional foundations see Magyary, *Tudománypolitika,* 454-472; and "A külföldi magyar intézetek" (Hungarian Institutions Abroad), in *Tiszti Névtár,* 377-378.

13.) On the Hungarian Historical Research Institute, which was one of the three component institutes of the Teleki Institute, see Ch. XVI.

14.) Ember, "MIT," 1157.

15.) *Fontes Historiea Hungaricae Aevi Turcici* (Sources for the History of Hungary during the Turkish Age), Bp. 1923- ; and *Fontes Historiae Hungaricae Aevi Recentoris* (Sources for the History of Hungary during the Modern Age), Bp. 1921-. For a complete list see Appendix.

16.) *Auer János Ferdinánd pozsonyi nemes polgárnak héttoronyi fogságában írt naplója, 1664*(The Diary of J. F. Auer, a Noble Citizen of Pozsony, Written during his Captivity in the Seven Towers, 1664), Bp. 1923.

17.) These plans were later published as a supplement to the *Századok* under the title *A Magyar Történelmi Társulat forráskiadási szabályzata* (Regulations of the Hungarian Historical Association Concerning the Publication of Sources), Bp. 1920.

18.) See Klebelsberg's presidential address, *Sz,* 52 (1918), 225-230.

19.) Section 3 of the above-cited *Regulations.*

20.) For a complete list of the published volumes of the *Fontes* series see Appendix.

21.) On this misuse of Széchenyi's ideas see Szekfű's preface to his *A mai Széchenyi*(Today's Széchenyi), ed. Gyula Szekfű, Bp. 1935, 1-3.

22.) The question of the scarcity of funds and the role of aristocratic Maecenases is discussed by Glatz, "Klebelsberg," 1194-1199. On the Baranyai affair see Baranyai's letter to Klebelsberg. Vienna, Dec. 9, 1922. Cited in *ibid.,* 1197.

23.) See Elemér Mályusz's relevant observations in his *Történettudomány,* 77.

24.) Sections 1, 2 and 4 of the above-cited *Regulations.*

25.) *A magyar történettudomány kézikönyve,* ed. Bálint Hóman, Bp. 1924-1934.

26.) Quotations from the statement of the Hungarian Historical Association, Oct. 7, 1920, as reproduced on the inside front cover of the initial volumes of the series.

27.) For a complete plan of the *Handbook* see Appendix.

28.) The *Handbook*'s published volumes are listed in the Appendix.

29.) On Hóman see Ch. X.

30.) On the "Hungarian National Collection University" see Magyary, *Tudománypolitika,* 605-618; and *idem, A magyar tudományos nagyüzem megszervezése* (The Organization of Centralized Scholarly Research in Hungary), Bp. 1931.

31.) Glatz, "Historiography," 293. For some additional assessments on Klebelsberg see: Sándor Domanovszky, "Gróf Klebelsberg Kunó," *Sz,* 66 (1932), 257-260; Bálint Hóman, "Emlékbeszéd Gróf Klebelsberg Kunó felett" (Memorial Address Over Count K. Klebesberg), *Sz,* 67 (1933), 241-249; Lipót Baranyay, "Emlékezés Klebelsberg Kunó grófra" (Remembering Count K. Klebelsberg), *Sz,* 76 (1942), 259-271; and Sándor Domanovszky, "Emlékezés gróf Klebelsberg Kunó elnökségére" (Remembering Count K. Klebelsberg's Presidency), *Sz,* 76 (1942), 384-406. For critical treatment of Klebelsberg's cultural policies see, István Király, "A magyar reakció iskolapolitikája" (The Educational Policies of Hungarian Reactionarism), *TáSz,* 1 (1946), 280-286; Magda Jóború, *A középiskola szerepe a Horthy-korszak művelődéspolitikájában* (The Role of the Secondary Schools in the Cultural Policies of the Horthy Regime), Bp. 1963; *idem,* "A nevelés szelleme a Horthy-korszak középiskolájában" (The Spirit of Education in the Secondary Schools of the Horthy Period), *PeSz,* 12 (1962), 308-320; Ottó Szabolcs, "A Klebelsberg-féle iskola-politika osztály jellegének kérdéséhez" (On the Class Nature of Klebelsberg's Educational Policies), *PeSz,* 12 (1962), 51-58; and Károly Tar, "Klebelsberg Kunó nacionalista neveléspolitikája" (K. Klebelsberg's Nationalist Educational Policies), *AUD, Ser. Ped.,* 9/1 (1963), 33-52.

Chapter VIII

THE EMERGENCE OF SZEKFŰ AND THE GEISTESGESCHICHTE SCHOOL

1.) On the politicization of historiography as reflected in textbooks, see Miklós Mann, "Politikai propaganda az ellenforradalmi rendszer történelemkönyveiben" (Political Propaganda in the Textbooks of the Counterrevolutionary Regime), *Sz,* 100 (1966), 962-968; and Béla Beller, "A Horthy-rendszer 'hazafias' nevelésének forrásainál" (At the Sources of the 'Patriotic' Education of the Horthy Regime), in Ravasz, *Tanulmányok,* 221-279.

2.) On Dilthey and on *Geistesgeschichte* in general see Wilhelm Dilthey, *Pattern and Meaning of History,* ed. and intr. by H.P. Rickman, New York, 1962; G. Simmel, *Die Probleme der Geschichtsphilosophie,* 4th ed., München-Leipzig, 1922; Collingwood, *Idea of History;* Béla Fogarasi, "Az interpretáció problémaja a szellemtörténetben" (The Problem of Interpretation in *Geistesgeschichte), At,* 5 (1919), 20-31; Ákos Pauler, "A szellemtörténet kategóriái" (Categories of *Geistesgeschichte), M,* 2 (1923), 1-10; János Barta, "Szellem, szellemtudomány, szellemtörténet" (Spirit, Spiritual Sciences, *Geistesgeschichte), At,* 17 (1931), 184-193; and Joó, *Bevezetés.* For its Hungarian version see especially Mérei, "Szekfű," 180-256; Szigeti, *Szellemtörténet;* and Lederer, *Történetírás,* 92-162. For a brief English language summary see Vardy, *Historiography,* 67-68.

3.) Mérei, "Szekfű," 187.

4.) *Ibid.*

5.) Vardy, *Historiography,* 26-27, 63-64; and Lukács, *Szellemtörténet,* 7-51.

6.) See particularly Szigeti, *Szellemtörténet,* 82-132.

7.) Hóman-Szekfű, I, 10-11.

8.) Mályusz, *Történettudomány,* 38.

9.) *Ibid.,* 46.

10.) Mérei, "Szekfű," 188.

11.) For a discussion of Hóman's and Szekfű's *Magyar History* see Ch. X.

12.) See Ch. IX.

13.) See Sándor, *Magyar filozófia,* I, 83-95, 233-259, 427-442; *EKL,* 24, 521; József Halasi-Nagy, "Pauler Ákos," *M,* 12 (1934), 149-177; Anna Zsigmond (Madarászné), "Pauler Ákos, a Horthy-korszak hivatalos filozófusa" (A. Pauler, the Official Philosopher of the Horthy Regime), *Va,* 2 (1959), 31-40; József Galántai, *Egyház és politika, 1890-1918* (Church and Politics, 1890-1918), Bp. 1960; József Huszti, *Hornyánszky Gyula emlékezete* (Remembering G. Hornyánszky), Bp. 1933; Károly Maròt, *Hornyánszky Gyula,* Bp. 1934; Pál Sándor, *Két magyar filozófus: Böhm Károly és Brandenstein Béla* (Two Hungarian Philosophers: K. Böhm and B. Brandenstein), Bp. 1944. For English language summaries of these early twentieth-century developments cf. Szendrey, *Historiography,* 289-299; and Vardy, *Historiography,* 28-29, 64.

14.) *Der Staat Ungarn.* Stuttgart-Berlin, 1917. Its Hungarian version: *A magyar állam életrajza,* Bp. 1918; 2nd ed., Bp. 1923.

15.) See Szekfű's preface to the first Hungarian edition of *A magyar állam életrajza,* 3-15.
16.) See Szekfű's introduction to *ibid.,* 17-21.
17.) *Ibid.,* 190-191.
18.) Scattered in several of his works to be discussed below. See also Mérei, "Szekfű," 194; and Szigeti, *Szellemtörténet,* 186-187.
19.) *Három nemzedék. Egy hanyatló kor története* (Three Generations. The History of a Declining Age), Bp. 1920. Expanded version: *Három nemzedék és ami utána következik* (Three Generations and What Follows), Bp. 1934. For a contemporary review of the first version see György Balanyi, *Sz,* 55-56 (1921-1922), 255-259. See also E. Mályusz' critical study cited in Ch. VI, n. 20.
20.) *Három nemzedék,* 4; and *Három nemzedék II,* 6-7.
21.) Lederer, *Történetirás,* 110.
22.) *Három nemzedék,* 32.
23.) *Ibid.,* 83.
24.) Széchenyi and the First Generation are treated on pp. 9-146.
25.) *Ibid.,* 149-231.
26.) *Ibid.,* 174.
27.) *Ibid.,* 228.
28.) The Third Generation is treated on pp. 235-325.
29.) For Szekfű's views on the question of "race" see particularly his two studies, "A faji kérdés és a magyarság" (The Racial Question and Magyardom), and "Fajbiológia vagy történeti egység" (Racial Biology or Historical Unity), in *Történetpolitikai tanulmányok,* 53-92, 93-109.
30.) For a brief English language summary of this problem see Kosáry-Várdy, *History,* 275-278. For additional related studies see Zsigmond Pál Pach, "Az ellenforradalomi történetszemlélet kialakulása Szekfű Gyula Három nemzedékében" (The Development of the Counterrevolutionary View of History in G. Szekfű's *Three Generations),* *TSz,* 5 (1962), 387-425; János Varga, "Magyar szellemtörténet — Magyar nacionalizmus" (Hungarian *Geistesgeschichte* — Hungarian Nationalism), *Kr,* 4 (1966), 6-13; and Jenő Szűcs, "A magyar szellemtörténet nemzet-koncepciójának tipológiájához" (On the Typology of the National Conception of Hungarian *Geistesgeschichte),* *TSz,* 9 (1966), 245-269. On Dezső Szabó and on the Right Radicals see Ch. XIV.

Chapter IX

THE "MINERVA CIRCLE" AND OTHER PROPHETS OF GEISTESGESCHICHTE

1.) On the literary developments of this period see Sőtér, *MIT,* VI, 11-36. Thienemann and the Minerva Circle are discussed in *ibid.,* 68-69; Németh, *Két nemzedék,* 439-448; and Lukács, *Szellemtörténet,* 52-134. See also *MIL,* II, 251-252.
2.) This goal of the Minerva Society is usually quoted on the inside front cover of its publications.
3.) Lukács, *Szellemtörténet,* 52.

4.) On the University of Pécs and on its scholarly activities see Szabó, *Erzsébet Tudományegyetem.*

5.) Lukács, *Szellemtörténet,* 52-54.

6.) *Ibid.,* 53-54.

7.) Between 1924 and 1944 about 159 "Minerva Books" appeared in print. Cf. *MIL,* II, 252.

8.) On the *Hungarian Review (Magyar Szemle)* consult Ch. X.

9.) Lukács, *Szellemtörténet,* 54-55. See also the list of reprints on the rear cover of the "Minerva Books".

10.) Lukács, *Szellemtörténet,* 55.

11.) *Ibid.,* 56.

12.) Lajos Prohászka, *A vándor és a bujdosó,* Bp. 1934. On Prohászka see Sándor, *Magyar filozófia,* I, 225-233.

13.) Gyula Szekfű, "Nem vagyunk bujdosók" (We Are Not Fugitives), *MSz,* 32 (1938), 391-396; and *idem,* "Lírai történetszemlélet" (Lyrical View of History), *MSz,* 36 (1939), 297-306.

14.) Károly Pap, *Zsidó sebek és bűnök,* Bp. 1935. Cf. Miklós Lackó, "Az uj szellemfront történetéhez" (On the History of the New Spiritual Front), *Sz,* 106 (1972), 919-985, especially 952-954; Németh, *Két nemzedék,* 337-342; and Károlyné Pap, *Bűnbánat. Regényes visszaemlékezések* (Penitence. Romantic Reminiscences), Bp. 1962.

15.) Lukács, *Szellemtörténet,* 56.

16.) Quoted on the inside front cover of the *Minerva,* starting with the 1931 issues.

17.) Lukács, *Szellemtörténet,* 59-60.

18.) *Ibid.,* 63.

19.) Tivadar Thienemann, *Irodalomtörténeti alapfogalmak,* Bp. 1930; and *idem,* "Irodalomtörténet," in Hóman, *New Paths,* 53-86. For contemporary reviews of Thienemann's *Basic Concepts* see Aladár Schöpflin's in *Ny,* 23 (1930), 212-213; László Németh's in *Tanu,* 1 (1932-1933), 106-126; and István Hajnal's in *Sz,* 67 (1934), 73-75. For a more recent assessment see Lukács, *Szellemtörténet,* 87-116.

20.) On Horváth as a literary synthesizer of the *Geistesgeschichte* School see Sőtér, *MIT,* IV, 44-54; *MIL,* I, 474-475; Klaniczay, *Marxizmus,* 9-35; Keresztúry, *Örökség,* 345-367; Dezső Tóth, "Horváth János irodalomszemléletéről" (On J. Horváth's Literary Views), *ITK,* 69 (1959), 1-18; János Barta, "A mester nyomában" (In the Master's Path), *IT,* 47 (1958), 193-207; and Szabolcsi, *Változó világ,* 235-238.

21.) Dezső Keresztúry, "A magyar önismeret utján" (On the Path of Hungarian Self-Recognition), in Szekfű, *Mi a magyar?,* 137-168, quotation from p. 164.

22.) Lukács, *Magyar irodalom,* 494.

23.) Dezső Kerecsényi, "Két évtized" (Two Decades), *PSz,* 41 (1932), 112-125. Strangely enough, although Horváth preferred the synthetic recreation of the past in his works, his great populist contemporary, Dezső Szabó, had constantly accused him of being too factographic and devoid of conceptions. See for example Szabó's "Szellemi életünk tragédiája I: Horváth János könyve Petőfiről" (The Tragedy of Our Intellectual Life I: J. Horváth's Book on Petőfi), in Szabó's *Panasz* (Complaint), Bp. 1923, 39-55; and *idem,* "Szellemi életünk tragédiája II: A magyar irodalomtörténetírás" (The Tragedy of Our

Intellectual Life II: Hungarian Literary Scholarship), in *ibid.*, 56-80. Horváth's most significant works include his unfinished three-volume synthesis of Hungarian literary history: *A magyar irodalmi műveltség kezdetei* (The Beginnings of Hungarian Literary Culture), Bp. 1931; *Az irodalmi műveltség megoszlása* (The Diffusion of Literary Culture), Bp. 1935; and *A reformáció jegyében* (In the Sign of the Reformation), Bp. 1953. A collection of his significant literary essays appeared under the title *Tanulmányok* (Studies), Bp. 1956.

24.) On Kornis see Sándor Balogh, "Kornis Gyula 'Nemzeti megújhódás' cimű tanulmányának margójára" (On the Margin of G. Kornis's Study 'National Revival'), *Va,* 2 (1959), 47-50; Károly Tar, *Kornis Gyula neveléstfilozófiájának főbb sajátossagai* (The Chief Characteristics of G. Kornis's Educational Philosophy), Bp. 1964; and Sándor, *Magyar filozófia,* I, 167-182. Kornis's most significant works include: *A lelki élet* (Spiritual Life), 3 vols., Bp. 1917-1919; *Bevezetés a tudományos gondolkodásba* (Introduction to Scholarly Thinking), Bp. 1922; *Történetfilozófia* (Philosophy of History), Bp. 1924; *A magyar művelődés eszményei, 1777-1848* (The Ideals of Hungarian Culture, 1777-1848), 2 vols., Bp. 1927; *Kultúra és nemzet* (Culture and Nation), Bp. 1928; *Magyar filozófusok* (Hungarian Philosophers), Bp. 1930; *Az államférfi* (The Statesman), 2 vols., Bp. 1933; *Szellemi élet* (Intellectual Life), Bp. 1938; *Századunk tudományának szelleme* (The Spirit of the Science of Our Century), Bp. 1942; *A tudományos gondolkodás* (Scientific Thinking), 2 vols., Bp. 1943; and *Tudomány és Társadalom* (Science and Society), 2 vols., Bp. 1944.

25.) Kornis, *A tudományos gondolkodás,* I, 14-15.

26.) On Dékány see *MÉL,* I, 362.

27.) The works in question are: *A társadalomfilozófia alapfogalmai,* Bp. 1933; *A mai társadalom,* Bp. 1943; and *A történettudomány módszertana,* Bp. 1925. Some of Dékány's other significant works include: *Bevezetés az interpszichikai megismerés elméletébe* (Introduction to the Theory of Inter-Psychological Knowledge), Kolozsvár, 1919; *Bevezetés a társadalom lélektanába* (Introduction to Social Psychology), Pécs, 1923; *Tudományelméleti alapok a társadalomtudományban* (Foundations of Scientific Theory in Social Sciences), Bp. 1926; *A történelmi kultúra útja* (The Path of Historical Culture), Bp. 1930; and *A magyarság lelki arca* (The Spiritual Complexion of Magyardom), Bp. 1942.

Chapter X

TRIUMPH OF THE GEISTESGESCHICHTE SCHOOL

1.) Gyula Bisztray, "A 'Magyar Szemle' " (The 'Hungarian Review'), in *Szekfű-Emlékkönyv,* 86-108; and *MIL,* I, 156.

2.) Gyula Szekfű, "A magyar folyóirat problémája" (The Problems of a Hungarian Periodical), *MSz,* 1 (1927), 1-4; quotation from p. 4.

3.) Bisztray, "A 'Magyar Szemle'," 90-92.

4.) Quotations from Szekfű, "A magyar folyóirat problémája," 4.

5.) The list of contributors include such names as Mihály Babits, Lajos Bartucz, István Bethlen, Gyula Bisztray, Sándor Eckhardt, Gyula Farkas,

Tibor Gerevich, Gusztáv Gratz, Ferenc Herczeg, Bálint Hóman, János Horváth, Benedek Jancsó, Dezső Keresztúry, Zoltán Kodály, Gyula Kornis, Imre Kovács, Antal Leopold, László Ravasz, Károly Viski, Béla Zolnai, Miklós Zsirai and Szekfű himself.

6.) The *Vigilia* first appeared in 1935, and it is still being published, Cf. *MIL*, III, 529; and Pál Peöcz, "A politikai katolicizmus 'reformnemzedéke' " (The 'Reform Generation' of Political Catholicism), *TSz*, 7 (1964), 112-151.

7.) Bisztray, "A 'Magyar Szemle'," 97, 101. On Sándor Eckhardt see *MIL*, I, 274.

8.) "Magyar Szemle Könyvei," "Kincsestár," and "Magyar Szemle Klasszikusai."

9.) See below, this chapter.

10.) The books in question are: János Horváth, *A magyar irodalmi műveltség kezdetei*, Bp. 1931; *idem, Az irodalmi műveltség megoszlása*, Bp. 1935; Gyula Farkas, *A "Fiatal Magyarország" kora*, Bp. 1932; Gusztáv Gratz, *A dualizmus kora, 1867-1918*, 2 vols., Bp. 1934; Gyula Szekfű, ed., *Mi a magyar?*, Bp. 1939; and *idem, Állam és nemzet. Tanulmányok a nemzetiségi kérdésről*, Bp. 1942. Some of the others in the series include works by Gyula Szekfű, István Weis, Mihály Babits, Ferenc Julier, István Genthon, Virgil Bierbauer, Sándor Eckhardt and Gyula Németh. For a list see the dust jackets of the later volumes.

11.) Quotations from the inside rear cover of the published volumes of the series. The rear covers also contain a list of the published volumes.

12.) Sándor Eckhardt, *Az ismeretlen Balassi Bálint*, Bp. 1943. Other volumes in the series include works by János Horváth, Árpád Markó, Gyula Bisztray and Dezső Kerecsényi. Cf. *MIL*, II, 156.

13.) Bálint Hóman and Gyula Szekfű, *Magyar történet* (Magyar History), 8 vols., Bp. 1927-1934.

14.) See Hóman's preface, *ibid.*, I, 5-8.

15.) *Ibid.*, 6.

16.) All quotations from *ibid.*, 7-8.

17.) Although a great and prominent historian, due to his rightist political involvements during the 1930's and early 1940's and his subsequent conviction as a war criminal in 1946, Hóman has not been treated fairly by post-World War II historiography. One of his crticis had even called him *tehetségtelen* (meaning "untalented" or perhaps "ignorant"). This is an unfair judgement about Hóman as an historian who — before his unfortunate involvement in rightist politics — was an excellent medievalist. On the above view on Hóman see Szigeti, *Szellemtörténet*, 142. Adequate studies on Hóman are nonexistent. For additional information see Lederer, *Történetírás*, 118-125, 172-173; *idem, Bevezetés*, 137-138; and István Király, "A magyar reakció iskolapolitikája" (The Educational Policies of Hungarian Reactionarism), *TáSz*, 1 (1946), 280-286. For a list of Hóman's scholarly works see *BMTIÉ*, IV (1934), 434-443; and Hóman, *Művelődéspolitika*, 655-674. On Hóman's fate after 1945 see Ödön Málnási, "Dr. Hóman Bálint," in his *Magyar mártyrok* (Hungarian Martyrs), London, 1958, 24-26; and Zoltán Szitnyai, "Hóman utolsó útja" (Hóman's Last Sojourn), in his *Szellemi tájakon* (In Spiritual Lands), Chicago, 1971, 136-143. For an early assessment of Hóman as an historian see László Tóth, *Hóman Bálint a történetíró* (B. Hóman, the Historian), Pécs, 1939.

18.) Hóman's over-exertion is particularly evident from some of his interpretative essays reprinted in his *Történetírás*, 9-44, 439-456, 457-466, 467-472. On the difference between Hóman and Szekfű as *Geistesgeschichte* synthesizers see Németh, *Két nemzedék*, 428-439.

19.) On Szekfű's periodization problems see Elemér Mályusz's remarks in Varga, *Vita*, 125-127.

20.) Hóman-Szekfű, III and VI.

21.) Mályusz in Varga, *Vita*, 127-128; quotations from p. 128.

22.) *Ibid.*, 126.

23.) Based on a personal conversation with Mályusz, Spring 1970. On the Szekfű-Mályusz controversy regarding the Hungarian Renaissance and Baroque see Elemér Mályusz, "Magyar reneszánsz, magyar barokk," *BpSz*, 241 (1936), 159-179, 293-318, and 242 (1936), 86-104, 154-174; and Szekfű's reply, "Válaszom a Magyar történet dolgában" (My Answer Relative to the Magyar History), *BpSz*, 242 (1936), 371-384.

24.) See Vardy, *Historiography*, 30-31, 66-67.

25.) Gyula Szekfű, "A politikai történetírás" (Political Historiography), in Hóman, *New Paths*, 397-444.

26.) Quotations from *ibid.*, 438.

27.) *Ibid.*, 439.

28.) *Ibid.*, 440.

29.) Cf. Ch. VIII. See also Hóman-Szekfű, VIII; Szekfű, *Három nemzedék*; *idem*, *Széchenyi igéi*; *idem*, *Mai Széchenyi*; and Andor Tarnai, "Szekfű és a 'nemzetietlen kor' irodalomtörténete" (Szekfű and the Literature of the 'Anti-National Age'), *ITK*, 64 (1960), 189-198.

30.) This shift is also implied in Hóman's cited introduction to the *Magyar history*. For additional scholarly criticism of this work see the contemporary reviews on vols. I, IV, V and VI by Sándor Domanovszky in *Sz*, 63-64 (1929-1930), 423-429, 881-903, and *Sz*, 67 (1933), 308-315; on vols. II and III by Józesef Holub in *Sz*, 69 (1935), 192-205; and on vol. VII by György Balanyi in *Sz*, 71 (1937), 356-360.

31.) For more recent Marxist assessments of the "Hóman-Szekfű," see Lederer, *Történetírás*, 122-136, Mérei, "Szekfű," and the studies by Pach, Szűcs and Varga cited in Ch. VIII, n. 30.

32.) *A magyar történetírás új útjai*, ed. Bálint Hóman, Bp. 1931, has already been cited earlier as *New Paths*.

33.) Bálint Hóman, "A történelem útjai" (The Paths of History), in *New Paths*, 7-52.

34.) Quotations from *ibid.*, 42-44.

35.) *Ibid.*, 50-51.

36.) Cf. n. 25, above. Quotation from *ibid.*, 444.

37.) Tivadar Thienemann, "Irodalomtörténet" (Literary History), *ibid.*, 53-86. See also Ch. IX.

38.) Tibor Gerevich, "Művészettörténet" (Art History), *ibid.*, 87-140.

39.) *Ibid.*, 128.

40.) *Ibid.*

41.) István Dékány, "Gazdaság- és társadalomtörténet" (Economic and Social History), *ibid.*, 183-236.

42.) Imre Révész, "Egyháztörténelem" (Church History), *ibid.*, 141-182.

43.) Elemér Mályusz, "A népiség története" (The History of Ethnicism), *ibid.*, 237-268; and Ferenc Eckhart, "Jog- és alkotmánytörténet" (Legal and Constitutional History), *ibid.*, 269-320. See below Chs. XII and XVIII.

44.) Imre Szentpétery, "Történelmi segédtudományok" (Historical Auxiliary Sciences), *ibid.*, 321-352.

45.) *Ibid.*, 321.

46.) *Ibid.*, 326. See also Ch. XX.

47.) Ferenc Tompa, "Régészet" (Archeology), *ibid.*, 353-364; and Gyula Németh, "Nyelvtudományunk és a történetírás" (Our Linguistic Scholarship and Historiography), *ibid.*, 365-396.

48.) Lederer, *Történetírás,* 118-122; quotations from p. 121. For a contemporary view of the *New Paths* see Sándor Domanovszky's review in *Sz,* 65 (1931), 273-279.

Chapter XI

THE DIFFUSION AND DIFFERENTIATION OF GEISTESGESCHICHTE HISTORIOGRAPHY: THE RISE OF A YOUNG GENERATION

1.) The best known of these short syntheses include: Miklós Asztalos and Sándor Pethő, *A magyar nemzet története* (The History of the Hungarian Nation), Bp. 1933; D.G. Kosáry, *A History of Hungary,* Cleveland-New York, 1941; Pál Török, *Magyarország története* (The History of Hungary), Bp. 1942; and Antal Balla, *Magyarország története,* Bp. 1942. While also influenced by Hóman's and Szekfű's *Magyar History,* Ferenc Eckhart's *A Short History of the Hungarian People,* London, 1931, displays much originality in its interpretation.

2.) On the *Universal History* see Ch. XIX.

3.) *Emlékkönyv Szent István király halálának kilencszázadik évfordulójára* (Memorial Album on the Occasion of the Nine-Hundreth Anniversary of King Saint Stephen's Death), 3 vols., ed. Jusztinián György Serédi, Bp. 1938.

4.) Antal Szerb, *Magyar irodalomtörténet,* Kolozsvár, 1934, and over a dozen editions since. For Szerb's excellent introductory essay on the nature and application of the *Geistesgeschichte* philosophy and methodology to the history of literature see one of the earlier editions of this work. For some penetrating studies on Szerb see István Sőtér's postscript to Szerb's *Világirodalomtörténet* (The History of World Literature), Bp. 1958. See also Sőtér, *MIT,* VI, 724-726; and Németh, *Kiadatlan tanulmányok,* I, 321-327.

5.) On Joó see E(ndre) F(ischer), "Joó Tibor, 1901-1945", *Sz,* 79-80 (1945-1946), 312; Lederer, *Történetírás,* 145-147; and Szendrey, *Historiography,* 345-350.

6.) Joó, *Bevezetés a szellemtörténetbe,* Bp. 1935.

7.) *Ibid.*, 8.

8.) Joó, *Mátyás és birodalma,* Bp. 1940.

9.) Joó, *A magyar nemzeteszme,* Bp. (1939); *idem, Magyar nacionalizmus,* Bp. 1941; and *idem, Vallomások a magyarságról,* Bp. 1943.

10.) On Váczy see *MIL*, III, 456; *ELTE története*, *526-542;* and *Erdély Magyar Egyeteme*, 402.

11.) On Iványi-Grünwald see *MIL*, I, 516; and Lóránt Czigány, *Hungaria. The Béla Iványi-Grünwald Collection*, London, 1967.

12.) On Kosáry see *Prominent Hungarians*, 225; and Glatz, "Eötvös Kollégium," 804-805.

13.) Dominic G. Kosáry, *A History of Hungary*, Cleveland-New York, 1941. Szekfű's introduction on pp. vii-ix. Hungarian version: Domokos Kosáry, *Magyarország története*, Bp. 1943. A much expanded English version, with a new second part added by Steven Béla Várdy, *History of the Hungarian Nation*, Astor Park, Flo., 1969.

14.) See Ch. XIX.

15.) *Gr. Széchenyi István, Hitel*(Count Stephen Széchenyi's "Credit"), ed. and intro. by Béla Iványi-Grünwald, Bp. 1930. Iványi-Grünwald's study is on pp. 5-268.

16.) Iványi-Grünwald's most significant related publication is his *Széchenyi magánhitelügyi koncepciójának szellemi és gazdasági előzményei és következményei a rendi Magyarországon, 1790-1848* (The Spiritual and Economic Precedents and Consequences of Széchenyi's Conception on Private Credit in Feudal Hungary, 1790-1848), Pecs, 1927.

17.) See Ch. XIX.

18.) Váczy, *A hűbériség szerepe Szent István királyságában*, Bp. 1932; *idem*, *Die erste Epoche des ungarischen Königtums*, Bp. 1935; and *idem*, *A magyarság a román és gót stílus korában*, Bp. 1939, which first appeared in *Magyar művelődéstörténet*, I, 91-161. See Ch. XVII.

19.) Váczy, *A szimbolikus államszemlélet kora*, Bp. 1922.

20.) On Deér see *Sz*, 79-80 (1945-1946), 313; Lederer, *Történetírás*, 143-145; *ELTE története*, 528; *Prominent Hungarians*, 84; and Elemér Homonnay, "Dr. Deér József történész, 1905-1974" (Dr. J. Deér, historian, 1905-1974), *Szittyakürt* (Cleveland), 14/3 (March 1975), 5.

21.) Deér, *Pogány magyarság-Keresztény magyarság* (Pagan Magyardom — Christian Magyardom), Bp. 1938, 22.

22.) *Ibid.*

23.) Deér, *Heidnisches und Christliches in der altungarischen Monarchie*, Szeged, 1934; and the work listed under n. 21.

24.) Deér, *Pogány magyarság — Keresztény magyarság*, 25.

25.) *Ibid.*, 24, 26.

26.) *Ibid.*, 189. See also such other related works by Deér as *A magyar törzsszövetség és patrimóniális királyság külpolitikája* (The Foreign Policy of the Hungarian Tribal Federation and Patrimonial Monarchy), Kaposvár, 1928; *idem*, *Die Anfänge der ungarisch-kroatischen Staatsgemeinschaft*, Bp. 1936; *idem*, "A magyarság a nomád kultúrközösségben" (The Magyars within the Nomadic Cultural Community), in *Magyar művelődéstörténet*, I, 21-90; and *idem*, *Die Entstehung des ungarischen Königtums*, Bp. 1942. Deér's last major work is his *Die Heilige Krone Ungarns*, Vienna, 1966. Cf. Gyula László's review in *Sz*, 106 (1972), 459-470.

27.) On Istványi see István Hajnal, "Istványi Géza, 1913-1943," *Sz*, 77 (1943), 266; and Várkonyi, *Pozitivista történetszemlélet*, I, 266-267.

28.) Istványi, "Szellemtörténet, neopozitivizmus, új történelmi realizmus," *PSz*, 47 (1938), 118-124.

29.) See *ibid.*, 122. This close relationship between Istványi's program and Hajnal's philosophy of history was first suggested to me by Professor Mályusz in a letter dated March 30, 1975.

30.) See Joó, "Tudomány és nemzedék. Szellem és társadalom" (Scholarship and Generation. Spirit and Society), *PSz,* 47 (1938), 196-200. See also Istványi's reply in *ibid.*, 264-267.

31.) Várkonyi, *Pozitivista történetszemlélet,* I, 267. Istványi's most significant works include: *A magyarnyelvű írásbeliség kialakulása* (The Development of Magyar Language Literacy), Bp. 1934; "A középlatin filológia külföldön és Magyarországon" (Medieval Latin Philology Abroad and in Hungary), in *Szentpétery-Emlékkönyv,* 183-206; "A generális congregátio" (The General Congregation (of the Nobility)), *LK,* 17 (1939), 50-83 and 18-19 (1940-1941), 179-207; and "A három országrész társadalma" (The Society of the Trisected Country), in *Magyar művelődéstörténet,* III, 99-128.

32.) On Lederer see *MIL,* II, 26. Her most significant works include: *Az iparososztály kialakulása* (The Development of the Artisan Class), Bp. 1928; *A középkori pénzüzletek kialakulása Magyarországon, 1000-1458* (The Rise of Medieval Money Economy in Hungary, 1000-1458), Bp. 1932; *Egyetemes művelődés történet* (Universal History of Civilization), Bp. 1935; *Az ipari kapitalizmus kezdetei Magyarországon* (The Beginnings of Industrial Capitalism in Hungary), Bp. 1952; *A feudalizmus kialakulása Magyarországon* (The Rise of Feudalism in Hungary), Bp. 1959; and the oft-cited *A magyar polgári történetírás rövid története* (A Short History of Hungarian Bourgeois Historiography), Bp. 1969.

33.) On Málnási see József Süli's introduction to Málnási's *A magyar nemzet őszinte története* (The Candid History of the Hungarian Nation), 2nd ed., München, 1959, 7-13. This work also contains a complete list of Málnási's interwar publications on pp. 285-286.

34.) On Asztalos see *MIL,* I, 64-65. His significant works include: *Kossuth Lajos kora és az erdélyi kérdés* (The Age of Louis Kossuth and the Transylvanian Question), Bp. 1928; *A magyar nemzet története* (The History of the Hungarian Nation), with Sándor Pethő, Bp. 1933; *II. Rákóczi Ferenc és kora* (F. Rákóczi II and his Age), Bp. 1934; *A nemzetiségek története Magyarországon* (The History of the Nationalities in Hungary), Bp. 1934; and *A történeti Erdély* (Historical Transylvania), Bp. 1936.

35.) On Baráth see *Erdély Magyar Egyeteme,* 402; *Hungarians in America,* 2nd ed., 28, 3rd ed., 16; and *Prominent Hungarians,* 30.

36.) Baráth, *Az új Magyarország történetírása,* Kolozsvár, 1942, reprinted with a different title in his *A külföldi magyarság ideológiája* (The Ideology of Hungarians Abroad), Montreal, 1975, 223-235. This program was very severely criticized by István Hajnal in the *Sz,* 76 (1942), 453-459. See also Tibor Joó's critique, "Irányított tudomány" (Directed Scholarship), *Magyar Csillag,* 1 (Oct. 1941), 62-64; and György Komoróczy's review of Baráth's *Magyar történet* (Magyar History), 2nd ed., Kolozsvár, 1941, in *Sz,* 76 (1942), 329-331. During the 1930's Baráth has authored a number of studies on historiography, which are often cited. These include: *L'histoire en Hongrie, 1867-1936,* Paris 1936, reprinted from the *Revue Historique* (1936); "Kelet-Európa fogalma a modern történetírásban" (The Concept of Eastern Europe in Modern Historiography), in *Domanovszky-Emlékkönyv,* 23-43; and "Comte pozitivizmusa és a magyar pozitivizmus" (Comte's Positivism and Hungarian

Positivism), in *Szentpétery-Emlékkönyv*, 5-30. Since 1945 Baráth has turned to the study of Hungarian proto-history and produced a controversial three-volume work entitled *A magyar népek őstörténete* (The Proto-History of the Magyar-like Peoples), Montreal, 1968-1974, wherein he takes the origins of the Magyars back to the ancient Near East.

37.) Hajnal, "Istványi Géza," 266.

Chapter XII

MÁLYUSZ AND THE HUNGARIAN ETHNOHISTORY SCHOOL

1.) On Mályusz see *MTAA1* (1933), 189-193; *MTAT* (1941), 25-26; *MIL*, II, 182; *Sz*, 102 (1968), 1282-1283; Lederer, *Történetírás*, 152-154; Szigeti, *Szellemtörténet, passim;* and Vardy, *Historiography*, 39-44, 72-75. I have also relied on personal conversations, as well as on my correspondence with Professor Mályusz.

2.) Quoted from Mályusz's letter to me, dated March 30, 1975.

3.) As Mályusz writes: "I did not turn against *Geistesgeschichte*, only against Szekfű's and Hóman's interpretation and use of the same — being as they were guided by ulterior motives, the desire for success (and) in search of cheap glories." *Ibid.*

4.) On ethnohistory see János Weidlein, "A dűlőnévkutatás történeti vonatkozásai" (The Historical Implications of Research into Place Names), *Sz*, 69 (1935), 665-672; Antal Fekete-Nagy, "Településtörténet és egyháztörténet" (Settlement History and Ecclesiastical History), *Sz*, 71 (1937), 417-431; Csaba Csapodi, "Megjegyzések a településtörténet módszeréhez" (Comments on the Methodology of Settlement History), *Sz*, 78 (1944), 272-274; Imre Wellmann, "Néprajz és gazdaságtörténet" (Ethnography and Agricultural History), *Et*, 58 (1947), 8-18; Ferenc Maksay, "Néprajz és település történet" (Ethnography and Settlement History), *Et*, 59 (1948), 49-54; and Pál Sándor, "A magyar agrár-és paraszttörténet polgári irodalmának kritikájához" (Contributions to the Critique of Bourgeois Historical Literature on Hungarian Agriculture and Peasant History), *Sz*, 88 (1954), 373-419.

5.) Mályusz, "A népiség története" (The History of Ethnicity), in Hóman, *New Paths*, 237-268; quotations from p. 240.

6.) On Imre Madzsar see *Sz*, 79-80 (1945-1946), 306.

7.) Angyal, *Emlékezések*, 118.

8.) Glatz, "Eötvös Kollégium," 804.

9.) Mályusz, *Turóc megye kialakulása*, Bp. 1922. For a contemporary assessment of this work see Hóman's review in *Sz*, 55-56 (1921-1922), 556-563.

10.) *Sándor Lipót főherceg nádor iratai, 1790-1795*, Bp. 1926. See also the contemporary review by Oszkár Paulinyi in *Sz*, 61-62 (1927-1928), 889-897.

11.) On Szádeczky-Kardoss see Ch. XIII.

12.) Although Mályusz had transferred from Szeged to Budapest in 1932, not until 1934 was he officially named to the chair of medieval Hungarian history.

13.) Lederer, *Történetírás*, 153.

14.) Mályusz, *Magyar történettudomány*, Bp. (1942). See also a similar earlier study by Mályusz, *A történettudomány mai kérdései* (The Current Problems of Historical Sciences), Kecskemét, 1931.

15.) Mályusz, "A népiség története," 244-252.

16.) Mályusz, *A magyar történettudomány*, 63.

17.) Otto Boelitz, *Das Grenz- und Auslanddeutschtum, Seine Geschichte und seine Bedeutung*, Berlin, 1926. See also Mályusz, "A népiség története," 244.

18.) On this clash between German and Hungarian ethnohistorical studies see Lederer, *Történetírás*, 154; and Mályusz's subsequent remarks in *Sz*, 92 (1958), 740-741.

19.) Mályusz, *A magyar történettudomány*, 55.

20.) *Ibid.*, 56-57.

21.) *Ibid.*, 59.

22.) Mályusz had actually published an even earlier study on this question, "Turóc megye vámhelyei és forgalma a középkorban" (Turóc County's Custom Stations and their Turnover in the Middle Ages), *Sz*, 53-54 (1919-1920), 34-56.

23.) Mályusz, "A helytörténeti kutatás feladatai" (The Goals of Local Historical Research), *Sz*, 57-58 (1923-1924), 538-566.

24.) This 1928 memorandum called specifically for the study of the changes that had occurred in the Hungarian-Slovak ethnic frontier in the course of the past centuries. Cf. Mályusz, *A magyar történettudomány*, 63.

25.) Mályusz, "A népiség története," 237-268.

26.) *Ibid.*, 239.

27.) Mályusz, *A magyar történettudomány*, 62.

28.) *Ibid.*

29.) For Mályusz's 1931 program see his "A népiség története," 250-268.

30.) Lederer, *Történetírás*, 154. See also Hóman's presidential address at the 1943 meeting of the Hungarian Historical Association where he made some unflattering remarks about Mályusz's ethnohistorical orientation, although without reference to Mályusz himself. Cf. *Sz*, 77 (1943), 137-153, especially p. 140.

31.) Lederer, *Történetírás*, 154.

32.) Mályusz, "Három folyóirat: Karpathenland, Deutsch-ungarische Heimatsblätter, Győri Szemle" (Three Periodicals: *Karpathenland, Deutsch-ungarische Heimatsblätter, Győri Szemle*), *Sz*, 68 (1934), 45-65

33.) Mályusz, *A magyar történettudomány*, 64.

34.) *Település- és Népiségtörténeti Értekezések*, ed. Elemér Mályusz, Bp. 1938-1943.

35.) The volumes published in this series include: Erik Fügedi, *Nyitra megye betelepülése* (The Settlement of Nyitra County), Bp. 1938; Emma Iczkovits (Iványi), *Az erdélyi Fehér megye a középkorban* (The Transylvanian Fehér County in the Middle Ages), Bp. 1939; Éva Balázs, *Kolozs megye kialakulása*, (The Development of Kolozs County), Bp. 1939; Ferenc Maksay, *A középkori Szatmár megye* (Szatmár County in the Middle Ages), Bp. 1940; Zsigmond Jakó, *Bihar megye a török pusztítás előtt* (Bihar County Before the Turkish Conquest), Bp. 1940; Márton Kovács, *A felsőőri magyar népsziget* (The Hungarian Ethnic Island of Felsőőr), Bp. 1942; Vilmos Koch, *Máramaros megye társadalma és nemzetiségei. A megye betelepülésétől a XVIII. sdzdadig* (Society and Nationalities of Máramaros County. From the Time of their

Settlement till the 18th Century), Bp. 1943; and Balázs Nagy-Kálózi, *Jászkunsági reformátusok beköltözése Bácskába II. József korában* (The Settlement of the Calvinists of Jászkunság in Báchka in the Age of Joseph II) Bp. 1943.

36.) For some of the significant publications of these students of Mályusz see *A magyar történettudomány válogatott bibliográfiája, 1945-1968* (The Selected Bibliography of Hungarian Historical Sciences, 1945-1968), ed. Institute of History, Hungarian Academy of Sciences, Bp. 1971.

37.) *Magyarság és Nemzetiség. Tanulmányok a magyar népiségtörténet köréből,* ed. Elemér Mályusz, with the collaboration of Bálint Hóman and Sándor Domanovszky, Bp. 1937-1946.

38.) Szabó, *Ugocsa megye,* Bp. 1937.

39.) On Szabó see György Szabad, "Szabó István, 1898-1969," *Sz,* 104 (1970), 516-518; Tamás Hoffmann, "Szabó István, 1898-1969," *AtSz,* 12 (1970), 520-521; and Varga, *Debreceni Tudományegyetem,* 204-205.

40.) Szabó's books in question are: *Ugocsa megye,* Bp. 1937; *A magyar parasztság története,* Bp. 1940; *A magyarság életrajza,* Bp. 1941; and *A nemzetiségek térnyerése és a magyarság,* Bp. (1942).

41.) Szabó, *A falurendszer kialakulása Magyarországon (X-XV. század),* Bp. 1966; and *idem, A középkori magyar falu,* Bp. 1969.

42.) Szabó's other significant works include: *Jobbágybirtoklás az örökös jobbágyság korában* (The Ownership Rights of Serfs in the Age of Hereditary Serfdom), Bp. 1947; *Tanulmányok a magyar parasztság történetéből* (Studies in the History of Hungarian Peasantry), Bp. 1948; *Ungarns Landwirtschaft von der Mitte des XIV. Jahrhunderts bis zu den 1530er Jahren.* Supplement to *AtSz* 2 (1960). Szabó also edited two of the major collective works on the history of the Hungarian peasantry: *Agrártörténeti tanulmányok* (Studies in Agricultural History), Bp. 1960; and *A parasztság Magyarországon a kapitalizmus korában, 1848-1914* (The Peasantry in Hungary in the Age of Capitalism, 1848-1914), 2 vols., Bp. 1965. His posthumous work, *Magyarország mezőgazdaságának története, 1350-1550* (The History of Hungarian Agriculture, 1350-1550), finished in 1968, should soon appear in print.

43.) Bálint Ila, *Gömör megye,* 3 vols., (vols. II-IV), Bp. 1944-1969.

44.) Maksay, *A magyar falu középkori településrendje,* Bp. 1971.

45.) Mályusz's and Domanovszky's preface to Szabó, *Ugocsa megye,* vii-ix.

46.) On the Szekfű-Mályusz controversy see their relevant polemical essays, including Szekfű's "A magyarság és kisebbségei a középkorban" (The Hungarians and their Minorities in the Middle Ages), *MSz,* 25 (1935), 5-13; *idem,* "Még egyszer középkori kisebbségeinkről" (Once More About Our Medieval Minorities), *MSz,* 39 (1940), 169-177; and *idem,* "Népek egymás közt a középkorban" (Nationalities Among Each Other in the Middle Ages), *MSz,* 41 (1941), 225-233. All three of Szekfű's studies are reprinted in his *Állam és nemzet,* 39-84. Mályusz's relevant studies include: "A középkori magyar nemzetségi politika" (Medieval Hungarian Nationality Policy), *Sz,* 73 (1939), 257-294, 384-448; and "Az egynyelvű ország" (The Monolingual State), *Sz,* 75 (1941), 113-139.

47.) On the anti-Mályusz attacks by various Szekfű epigons see Mályusz, *Történettudomány,* 5-15, which admittedly represents Mályusz's own summary of this question. To counterbalance it see also Szekfű's remarks about Mályusz as an historian in his *Állam és nemzet,* 83-84.

48.) See Hóman's preface to Szabó, *Ugocsa megye*, v.

49.) *Mi a Magyar?*, ed. Gyula Szekfű, Bp. 1939. The contributors to this volume included such noted scholars, artists and literary men as M. Babits, L. Bartucz, S. Eckhardt, G. Farkas, T. Gerevich, D. Kerecsényi, D. Keresztúry, Z. Kodály, L. Ravasz, K. Viski, B. Zolnai, M. Zsirai and Szekfű himself.

50.) On Mikecs see *MIL*, II, 228-229. I have also relied on Professor Mályusz's letter to me, dated April 24, 1975.

51.) Mikecs, *Csángók. A moldvai magyarság története*, Bp. 1941.

52.) On the relationship between ethnohistory and the populist movement see "Történészvita a népi írókról" (Historical Debate about the Populist Writers), *Sz*, 92 (1958), 732-757; and Lederer, *Történetírás*, 154.

53.) See Ch. XIV.

54.) Mályusz, *Geschichte des ungarischen Volkstums von der Landnahme bis zum Ausgang des Mittelalters*, Bp. 1940.

55.) Mályusz, "A magyar társadalom a Hunyadiak korában," *Mátyás-Emlékkönyv*, I, 309-433; and *idem*, "A magyar állam a középkor végén," *Magyar művelődestörténet*, II, 5-104.

56.) The *familiaris* system was first discovered and discussed by Gyula Szekfű in his *Serviensek és familiárisok* (Serviens's and familiaris's), Bp. 1912.

57.) The *Tripartitum* not only codified the principle of "*una et eadem nobilitas*," but also transformed the Hungarian peasants into serfs bound to the soil. On the *Tripartitum* see notes of Ch. XVIII.

58.) Mályusz, "Rákóczi-kor társadalma," *Rákóczi-Emlékkönyv*, II, 23-68.

59.) Mályusz, *A türelmi rendelet. II. József és a magyar protestantizmus*, Bp. 1939.

60.) Mályusz, *Iratok a türelmi rendelet történetéhez*, Bp. 1940. For an assessment of the above two volumes see Zoltán Varga's review in *Sz*, 75 (1941), 82-85. Information on the destruction of these documents during the war comes from Professor Mályusz's letter, dated March 30, 1975.

61.) Mályusz, *Egyházi társadalom a középkori Magyarországon*, Bp. 1971.

62.) See Ch. VII.

63.) *Zsigmondkori oklevéltár*, ed. Elemér Mályusz, 3 vols. (vols. I, II 1-2), Bp. 1951-1958.

64.) Mályusz, *A Thuróczy-krónika és forrásai*, Bp. 1967.

65.) Mályusz, *A konstanzi zsinat és a magyar főkegyúri jog*, Bp. 1958; and *idem*, *Az V. István-kori gesta*, Bp. 1971.

66.) In addition to the publications mentioned in this chapter, Mályusz's significant works include: *Thuróczy János krónikája* (J. Thuróczy's Chronicle), Bp. 1944; *Királyi kancellária és a krónikaírás a középkori Magyarországon* (Royal Chancery and the Writing of Chronicles in Medieval Hungary), Bp. 1974, which first appeared in *Le Moyen Age*, 75 (1969), 51-86, 219-254; and dozens of major studies on the pages of the *TSz*, *Sz*, *LK*, *PSz*, *Études*, *Nouvelles études* and several other periodicals and collective works.

Chapter XIII

THE NATIONAL ROMANTIC SCHOOL

1.) No study exists on the National Romantic School of the interwar period. For the background of this school during the dualist period see Várkonyi, *Thaly*. Scattered information can also be found in Várkonyi, *Pozitivista történetszemlélet*, I, 197-284. For a brief summary see Vardy, *Historiography*, 33-34, 68.

2.) On the alleged "re-Catholization" of Hungarian history see Bálint Hóman, "Történelem és katolicizmus" (History and Catholicism), in his *Történetírás*, 457-466; and Gyula Szekfű, "Magyar katólikus történetfelfogás" (Hungarian Catholic View of History), in *Katólikus írók*, 296-418. See also István Rugonfalvi-Kiss's review of Szekfű's *Bethlen Gábor, PSz*, 41 (1929), Szekfű's reply, *Kritika és terror* (Criticism and Terror), Bp. 1929 (reprint from *MK*); and Rugonfalvi-Kiss's book-size answer, *Az átértékelt Bethlen Gábor. Válaszul Szekfű Gyulának* (The Re-evaluated Gábor Bethlen. In Response to G. Szekfű), Debrecen, 1929. For an assessment of both Szekfű's and Rugonfalvi-Kiss's views see Pál Török, "Ujabb könyvek Bethlen Gáborról" (Recent Books on G. Bethlen), *BpSz*, 218 (1930), 465-478.

3.) On Rugonfalvi-Kiss see Ferenc Balogh, *A debreceni református kollégium története* (The History of the Reformed College of Debrecen), Debrecen, 1904, 83-84; Varga, *Debreceni Tudományegyetem*, 198-202, 301-302; and Szekfű's above-cited *Kritika és terror*.

4.) Some of Rugonfalvi-Kiss's major works include: *II. Rákóczi Ferenc erdélyi fejedelemmé választása* (The Election of F. Rákóczi II as the Prince of Transylvania), Bp. 1906; *A magyar helytartótanács története II. Ferdinand korában* (The History of the Hungarian Viceroyalty Council in the Age of Ferdinand II), Bp. 1907; *Az utolsó nemesi felkelés* (The Last Nobles' Insurrection), 2 vols., Győr, 1909-1911; *Bethlen Gábor életrajza* (The Biography of G. Bethlen), vol. I, Bp. 1922; *Trónbetöltés és dukátus az Árpád-korban* (Ascension to the Throne and the Ducal Office in the Age of the Árpáds), Bp. 1928; and *A nemes székely nemzet képe* (The Portrait of the Noble Székely Nation), 3 vols., Debrecen, 1939-1940.

5.) Rugonfalvi-Kiss was professor of Hungarian History at the University of Debrecen (1914-1943). Cr. Varga, *Debreceni Tudományegyetem*, 198.

6.) See works listed in n. 4, and such other lesser studies as *Az erdélyi fejedelmek nemzeti politikája* (The National Politics of the Transylvanian Princes), Bp. 1927; and *Az egységes magyar nemesi rend kifejlődése* (The Development of the Unitary Hungarian Noble Estate), Debrecen, 1932.

7.) See Varga, *Debreceni Tudományegyetem*, 198. This "downgrading" is evident even today from the comments by members of the older generation.

8.) Varga, *Debreceni Tudományegyetem*, 201.

9.) *ibid.*, 201-202.

10.) Gyula Szekfű, *Bethlen Gábor*, 7-26.

11.) See Szekfű, *Kritika és terror*, 5, which quotes Rugonfalvi-Kiss's review.

12.) *Ibid.*, 12-13.

13.) *Ibid.*, 13.

14.) On Zoványi see Géza Kathona, "Zoványi Jenő, 1865-1958," *EhT*, Új Folyam, 1 (1958), 258-262; and Imre Révész, "Zoványi Jenő centenáriuma"

(J. Zoványi's Centennial), *Sz,* 99 (1965), 1393-1403.

15.) Zoványi, *Szekfű és társai történetírása* (The Historiography of Szekfű and his Friends), Bp. 1938, 21.

16.) Révész, "Zoványi," 1399.

17.) A complete list of Zoványi's published works can be found in *EbT,* Új Folyam, 2 (1959), 118-131. His most significant works include: *Tanulmányok a magyar protestáns egyház és irodalom történetéből* (Studies in the History of the Hungarian Protestant Church and Literature), Sárospatak, 1887; *Theológiai Ismeretek Tára* (Repository of Theological Knowledge), 3 vols., Mezőtúr, 1894-1901; *Puritánus mozgalmak a magyar református egyházban* (Puritan Movements Within the Hungarian Reformed Church), Bp. 1911; *A reformáció Magyarországon 1565-ig* (Reformation in Hungary until 1565), Bp. 1922; and *A felvilágosodás története* (The History of Enlightenment), Bp. 1922.

18.) On Csuday see *MÉL,* I, 325.

19.) Jenő Csuday, *Nemzeti történetírásunk téves útjai* (The False Paths of Our National Historiography), Bp. 1932.

20.) Outside of his oft-republished Hungarian history to be mentioned below, Csuday's major works include: *A honfoglalás éve* (The Year of the Conquest), Szombathely, 1891; *Történelmi helynevek szótára* (The Dictionary of Historical Place Names), Bp. 1901; *A középkori intézmények bomlása és a renaissance* (The Disintegration of Medieval Institutions and the Renaissance), Bp. 1904 (vol. VI. of Marczali's *Great Illustrated World History).* See Chs. V and XIX.

21.) *A magyarok történelme,* 2 vols., Szombathely, 1891; 2nd ed. Vienna, 1897. German edition: *Die Geschichte der Ungarn,* 2 vols. Pressburg, 1900. Several other Hungarian editions followed.

22.) Csuday, *A magyarok történelme* (1897), I, 3.

23.) On this unpublished eight-volume work, *A Magyar nemzet története, 884-1922,* see Csuday's preface to his *Nemzeti történetírásunk téves útjai,* 3.

24.) *Ibid.,* 16.

25.) Csuday, *A magyarok történelme,* I, 3.

26.) As examples for the works of these pseudo-historians see the various pamphlets in the so-called "Rákóczi-Könyvek" (Rákóczi Books) series, published by the Országos Rákóczi-Szövetség (National Rákóczi Alliance), including Aladár Király's *Harc Rákóczi becsületéért* (Struggle for Rákóczi's Honor), Bp. 1931; and Pál Koróda's *Rákóczi élő tábora és az ellentábor* (Rákóczi's Living Supporters and their Adversaries), Bp. 1933. Another similar publication project was initiated by the publicist-historian Géza Kacziány under the title, "Tanulmányok a Hamisitatlan Magyar Történetírás Mezejéről" (Studies from the Field of Unfalsified Hungarian Historiography), 1933.

27.) On the intellectual level of the country gentry and the urban middle classes see Szekfű, *Három nemzedék II,* 407-421, 480-492; István Weis, *A mai magyar társadalom* (Hungarian Society of Today), Bp. 1930; János Makkai, *Urambátyam országa* (The Land of Mylord), Bp. (1942); György Ránki, "Gondolatok az ellen forradalmi rendszer társadalmi bázisának kérdéséhez az 1920-as évek elején" (Thoughts on the Social Basis of the Ruling Elite of the Counterrevolutionary Regime in the Period of the Early 1920's), *TSz,* 5 (1962), 353-369; and László Márkus, "A Horthy-rendszer uralkodó elitjének jellegéről'' (On the Characteristics of the Ruling Elite of the Horthy Regime), *TSz,* 8 (1965), 449-468.

28.) In addition to the post-Trianon section of Szekfű's *Három nemzedék II,* see János Szilágyi, *Munkásosztályunk általános műveltségi helyzete 1919-1945 között* (The General Cultural Level of Our Working Classes Between 1919 and 1945), Bp. 1964.

Chapter XIV

THE POPULISTS AND THEIR CRITICISM OF GEISTESGESCHICHTE

1.) For brief English language summaries of Hungarian populism see Kosáry-Várdy, *History,* 272-278; and Ignotus, *Hungary,* 168-173. See also Juhász, *Népi írók;* Sőtér, *MIT,* VI, 290-311; *MIL,* II, 356-361; Mihály Bimbó, ''Pszichologizálás és nacionalizmus'' (Psychologization and Nationalism), *AUD, Ser. M-L,* 13 (1967), 3-19; *idem, ''Történelmi szempontok a 'népi írók' mozgalmának megitélésébez'' (Historical Perspectives in the Evaluation of the Movement of the 'Populist Writers' ''), Al,* 18 (1967), 59-65; and *idem,* ''Révai József és a 'népi írók' történetszemléletének értékelése'' (J. Révai and the Assessment of the Historical Philosophy of the 'Populist Writers' ''), *SSS,* 2 (1967), 116-124. See also ''Történészvita a 'népi' írókról'' (Historians' Debate on the 'Populist' Writers), *Sz,* 92 (1958), 732-757; and József Révai's related studies in his *Válogatott írások,* II, 7-319. For an English language work on Hungarian populism see Charles G. Gáti, *The Populist Current in Hungarian Politics, 1935-1944.* Ph.D. Diss., Indiana University, Bloomington, Ind., 1965.

2.) Kosáry-Várdy, *History,* 272.

3.) *Ibid.*

4.) See the contemporary analyses by Szekfű, *Három nemzedék II,* 423-433; Zoltán Bodrogközy, *A magyar agrármozgalmak története* (The History of the Hungarian Agrarian Movements), Bp. 1929, 259-271; and Mihály Kerék's several related studies in the 1933 issues of the *MGSz* and *MSz.*

5.) As a result of the activities of the ''village explorers,'' a new literary genre, the so-called ''sociography'' was born, which was a semi-scholarly, but extremely realistic portrayal of the Hungarian countryside and peasant life. Perhaps the most dramatic among contemporary sociographies was Imre Kovács's *A néma forradalom* (The Mute Revolution), Bp. 1937. Some of the others included: Gyula Illyés, *A puszták népe* (The People of the Pusztas), Bp. 1936; Péter Veres, *Az Alföld parasztsága* (The Peasantry of the *Alföld),* Bp. 1936; Ferenc Erdei, *Futóhomok* (Drifting Sands), Bp. 1936; Géza Féja, *A viharsarok* (The Stormy Corner), Bp. 1937; József Darvas, *A legnagyobb magyar falu* (The Largest Hungarian Village), Bp. 1937; and Zoltán Szabó, *A tardi helyzet* (The Situation at Tard), Bp. 1936. On the Hungarian *narodniki* question see László Újvári, ''Narodnikok a magyar irodalomban'' *(Narodniks* in Hungarian Literature), *Kor* (1934), 905-909; and Ferenc Fejtő, ''Magyar narodnikok'' (Hungarian *Narodniks), Szo* (1935), 10-14.

6.) See Ch. XII. For the connection between populism and ethnohistory see *Sz,* 92 (1958), 740-741.

7.) Kosáry-Várdy, *History,* 272. The "Special Magyar road" or "third alternative" idea was best expressed by László Németh.

8.) Much has been written about Dezső Szabó. He has two standard biographies by Péter Nagy *(Szabó Dezső,* Bp. 1964) and Gyula Gombos *(Szabó Dezső,* München, 1969). His most important political essays appeared in the 100 odd volumes of the *Ludas Mátyás füzetek* (Ludas Mátyás Pamphlets), Bp. 1934-1942; and in his collected essays, *Az egész látóhatár* (The Whole Horizon), 3 vols., Bp. 1939. Sections of his unfinished autobiography were published under the title *Életeim* (My Lives), 2 vols., Bp. 1965. In addition to Nagy's and Gombos's biographies, see also János Samu, *Szabó Dezső,* Bp. 1935; the Dezső Szabó issues of the *Magyar Élet* (1935); and Sőtér, *MIT,* VI, 190-199.

9.) On Ady see Nyerges's introduction to *Poems of Endre Ady,* tr. and intr. by Anton N. Nyerges, ed. Joseph M. Értavy-Baráth, Buffalo, N.Y., 1969, 13-56; and József Révai, *Études Historiques,* Bp. 1955.

10.) On Móricz's role as an inspirer of the populist movement see Mihály Czine, "Móricz Zsigmond szülőföldje és népköltési útja" (Z. Móricz's Birthplace and his Collection of Folk Poetry), *ITK,* 62 (1958), 294-329; and Juhász, *Népi írók,* 11-12.

11.) Juhász, *Népi írók,* 13.

12.) Szabó, *Az egész látóhatár,* III, 14.

13.) The most vicious of Szabó's anti-Szekfű tirades was his *Ede megevé ebédem* (Edward Ate My Dinner), Bp. 1937 (Nos. 31-32 of his "Ludas Mátyás füzetek" series).

14.) On Németh see Sőtér, *MIT,* VI, 494-525; *MIL,* II, 346-349; Aladár Mód, "A harmadik út és Németh László útja" (The Third Alternative and L. Németh's Path), in Mód, *Sors,* 18-53; and Mód's three other related essays in *ibid.,* 54-128. For an earlier non-Marxist assessment of Németh see Gyula Szekfű, "Németh László és az ifjúság vezetése" (L. Németh and the Leadership of the Youth), *MSz,* 28 (1936), 161-167; and Juhász, *Népi írók,* 69-77.

15.) Németh's most significant essays on the fate of the Magyars appeared in his *Magyarság és Európa* (The Magyars and Europe), Bp. 1935; *Kisebbségben* (In Minority), Bp. 1939, 2nd ed., 1943; and *A minőség forradalma* (The Revolution of Quality), 4 vols., Bp. 1940-1943. Other related studies appeared recently in his *Kiadatlan tanulmányok.*

16.) *MIL,* II, 384.

17.) Kosáry-Várdy, *History,* 276.

18.) See particularly some of Németh's essays in his *A minőség forradalma.* For an English language work on Németh see Marian A. Low, *László Németh: A Study in Hungarian Populism,* Ph.D. Diss., Harvard University, Cambridge, Mass., 1966.

19.) See Németh, *Szekfű Gyula,* Bp. 1940; and Szekfű, "Lírai történetszemlélet," *MSz,* 36 (1939), 297-306. On the Szekfű-Németh debate see also Lederer, *Történetírás,* 147-148.

20.) On the enumerated populists see the studies listed in n.1. Some of the significant works of Veres, Féja, Illyés, Erdei, Darvas, Kovács and Z. Szabó are listed in n. 5. Ortutay's related works include *Parasztságunk élete* (The Lives of Our Peasantry), Bp. 1937; and *Kis magyar néprajz* (A Short Hungarian Ethnography), Bp. 1940.

21.) Szekfű, "Lírai történetszemlélet," 302.

22.) *Ibid.*

23.) On the question of Turanism in interwar Hungary see Szekfű, *Három nemzedék II,* 480-492; Gyula Németh, "A magyar turanizmus" (Hungarian Turanism), *MSz,* 11 (1931), 132-139; László Gál, "Műkedvelők az őstörténeti kutatásban" (Amateurs in the Research of Ancient History), *MSz,* 12 (1931), 262-272; and Béla Szépvizi-Balás, *Megjósolt történelmünk* (Our Foretold History), Gödöllő, c. 1930. See also the recent studies by László Zrinszky, "A turáni fajvallásról" (On the Turanian Racial Religion), *Vil,* 2 (1961), 38-41; and Joseph A. Kessler, *Turanism and Pan-Turanism in Hungary, 1890-1945.* Ph.D. Diss., University of California, Berkeley, Cal., 1967.

24.) See particularly Ferenc Vámos, *Hagyományok a máglyán. A magyar történetírás válsága* (Traditions on the Pyre. Crisis in Hungarian Historiography), Kecskemét, c. 1939. The work was a direct outgrowth of the Szekfű-Németh controversy, as displayed in Németh's *Kisebbségben* and Szekfű's "Lírai történetszemlélet."

25.) See Ch. XII.

26.) Mihály Babits, *Írók a két világháború közt* (Writers Between the Two World Wars), Bp. 1942, 145-158.

Chapter XV

INTERWAR HUNGARIAN POSITIVISM

1.) On the interwar positivists see Vardy, *Historiography,* 34-35, 68-69.

2.) See below this chapter and Chs. XVI and XIX.

3.) See below this chapter and Chs. XVII, XIX and XX.

4.) See Ch. XVI.

5.) See Chs. XVII and XX.

6.) See Chs. XII, XVIII and XIX.

7.) On Marczali see István Hajnal, "Marczali Henrik, 1856-1940," *Sz,* 74 (1940), 359-360; Bálint Hóman, "Hazai történetírásunk csődje" (The Bankruptcy of Our Historiography), in his *Történetírás,* 537-542; Emma Lederer, "Marczali Henrik helye a magyar polgári történettudományban" (H. Marczali's Place in Hungarian Bourgeois Historiography), *Sz,* 96 (1962), 440-469; Zoltán Tóth, *Marczali Henrik emlékezete* (Remembering H. Marczali), Bp. 1947; Neville Masterman, "Henrik Marczali, Historian," *NHQ,* 14 (1973), 150-157; and Lederer, *Történetírás,* 45-53.

8.) Some of Marczali's most significant monographs and source publications include: *A földrajzi viszonyok befolyása Magyarország történetére* (The Influence of Geography on Hungary's History), Bp. 1874; *A magyar történet kútfői az Árpádok korában* (The Sources of Hungarian History in the Age of the Árpáds), Bp. 1880; *Magyarország története II. József korában* (Hungary's History in the Age of Joseph II), 3 vols., Bp. 1882-1888; *Mária Terézia* (Maria Theresa), Bp. 1891; *A magyar történet kútfőinek kézikönyve* (Handbook of Hungarian Historical Sources), with D. Angyal and S. Mika, Bp. 1902; *Az 1790-91. országgyűlés* (The Diet of 1790-91), 2 vols., Bp. 1907; *Hungary in the Eighteenth Century,* Cambridge, 1910; *Ungarische Ver-*

fassungsgeschichte, Tübingen, 1910; and *Ungarisches Verfassungsrecht,* Tübingen, 1911. His major synthetic works are: *Ujkor története* (History of the Modern Age), 3 vols., Bp. 1883-1886 (part of the eight-volume *Ribáry's Illustrated World History);* the last six volumes of the *Nagy Képes Világtörténet*(Great Illustrated World History), 12 vols., ed. H. Marczali, 1898-1904; three volumes (I, II and VII) of the ten-volume *A magyar nemzet története* (History of the Hungarian Nation), ed. S. Szilágyi, Bp. 1895-1898; and his large one-volume synthesis of Hungarian history, *Magyarország története* (History of Hungary), Bp. 1911.

9.) See Ch. V.

10.) On this degrading of the old positivists, including Marczali, see Mályusz, *Történettudomány,* 36-38; and Angyal, *Emlékezések,* 100. On Marczali's dismissal from his university chair see Lederer, "Marczali," 467-468.

11.) Some of these later works which — as Lederer correctly expressed — "contain only some morsels of his knowledge," include: *A béke könyve* (The Book of Peace), Bp. 1920; *Hogy készült a nagy háború? (How Was the Great War Prepared?), Bp. 1923; and Erdély története* (History of Transylvania), Bp. 1935.

12.) Henrik Marczali, "Hongrie," in *Histoire et historiens,* I, 209-218. See also Hóman, *Történetírás,* 537-542; and Pál Arday's review of *Histoire et historiens* in *Sz,* 61-62 (1927-1928), 934-938. Both Hóman and Arday point out the unfairness and incompleteness of Marczali's essay.

13.) On Károlyi see Gyula Szekfű, "Károlyi Árpád a történetíró" (A. Károly, the Historian), in *Károlyi-Emlékkönyv,* 5-27; Sándor Domanovszky, "Károlyi Árpád, 1853-1940," *Sz,* 74 (1940), 357-359; Dávid Angyal, *Károlyi Árpad emlékezete* (Remembering A. Károlyi), Bp. 1943; and *idem, Emlékezések,* 149-153.

14.) On Károlyi's relationship to Klebelsberg see Glatz, "Klebelsberg," 1192-1194. Károlyi's activities in Vienna are discussed by Angyal, *Emlékezések,* 149-153; Szekfű, "Károlyi," 5-8, 22-23; and Glatz, "Historiography," 289-292. The Hungarian Institute for Historical Research in Vienna *(Bécsi Magyar Történetkutató Intézet — Institut für Ungarische Geschichtsforschung in Wien)* functioned between 1920 and 1947 in the palace of the Collegium Hungaricum (formerly the palace of the Hungarian Royal Guard, Museum Strasse 7, Wien VII). Cf. Antal Lábán, *A bécsi Collegium Hungaricum* (The Viennese Collegium Hungaricum) Bp. 1928; and G.C. Paikert, "Hungarian Foreign Policy in Intercultural Relations, 1919-1944," *ASEER,* 11 (1952), 42-65. The Historical Institute published annual Yearbooks *(Évkönyvek)* between 1931 and 1940, edited by directors Angyal (1928-1935) and Gyula Miskolczy (1935-1947). On Miskolczy see Ch. XVI.

15.) In addition to numerous other source publications, Károlyi published five volumes in the *Fontes* series and at least six in the *Monumenta* series. On these see the Appendix. His significant monographs include: *Adalékok a nagyváradi béke s az 1536-38-diki évek történetéhez* (On the History of the Peace of Nagyvárad and of the Years 1536-38), Bp. 1879; *A Dobó-Balassa-féle összeesküvés történetéhez,* 1569-72 (On the History of the Dobó-Balassa Conspiracy of 1569-72), Bp. 1879; *Illésházy István hűtlenségi pere* (The High Treason Trial of I. Illésházy), Bp. 1883; *A magyar alkotmány felfüggesztése 1673-ban* (The Suspension of the Hungarian Constitution in 1673), Bp. 1883;

Buda és Pest visszavívása 1686-ban (The Reconquest of Buda and Pest in 1686), Bp. 1886; and *A korponai országgyűlés 1605* (The Diet of Korpona in 1605), Bp. 1896. A number of Károlyi's excellent historical essays appeared in a volume entitled *Néhány történelmi tanulmány* (A Few Studies in History), Bp. 1930.

16.) On Angyal see Árpád Károlyi, "Angyal Dávid a történetíró" (D. Angyal, the Historian), *BMTIE*, 7 (1937), 1-12. Bálint Hóman, "Angyal Dávid," in his *Történetírás*, 534-537; György Balanyi, "Angyal Dávid, 1857-1943," *Sz*, 78 (1944), 155-157; László Péter, "Angyal Dávid a történész" (Dávid Angyal, the Historian), in Angyal, *Emlékezések*, 7-29.

17.) Angyal, *Emlékezések*, 153.

18.) For a list of Angyal's scholarly works see *BMTIE*, 7 (1937), 324-350.

19.) The books in question are: *Magyarország története II. Mátyástól III. Ferdinánd haláláig* (The History of Hungary from Matthias II to the Death of Ferdinand III), Bp. 1898; *Késmárki Thököly Imre életrajza, 1657-1705* (The Biography of I. Thököly of Késmárk, 1657-1705), 2 vols., Bp. 1888-1889; and *Falk Miksa és Kecskeméthy Aurél elkobzott levelezése* (The Confiscated Correspondences of M. Falk and A. Kecskeméthy), Bp. 1925. Some of Angyal's other significant works include the biographies of Dániel Berzsenyi (1899), Gábor Bethlen (1900), Pál Gyulai (1912), László Szalay (1913), Ferenc Kölcsey (1927), Count István Széchenyi (1928), the first part of a projected biography of Emperor Francis Joseph (1932), and Count Gyula Andrássy Sr. (1941). Angyal had also edited the complete literary works of Ferenc Kölcsey (10 vols., Bp. 1886-1887), Sándor Kisfaludy (8 vols., 1892-1893), Jenő Péterfy (3 vols., Bp. 1901-1903) and Béla Lederer (3 vols., Bp. 1906).

20.) On Szádeczky-Kardoss see Imre Lukinich, "Szádeczky-Kardoss Lajos, 1859-1935," *Sz*, 70 (1936), 125-126. On his predecessor at Kolozsvár see Dezső Csánki, "Szabó Károly emlékezete" (Remembering K. Szabó), *Sz*, 57-58 (1923-1924), 689-694.

21.) *Iparfejlődés és a czéhek története Magyarországon. Okirattárral, 1307-1848* (Industrial Developments and the History of Guilds in Hungary. With Documents, 1307-1848), 2 vols., Bp. 1913.

22.) Some of Szádeczky-Kardoss's monographic publications include: *Mihály havasalföldi vajda Erdélyben, 1599-1601* (Michael, Voyevod of Wallachia in Transylvania, 1599-1601), Bp. 1882; *A gróf Haller család története* (The History of the Count Haller Family), Bp. 1886; *Báthory István lengyel királlyá választása, 1574-1576* (The Election of I. Báthory as King of Poland, 1574-1576), Bp. 1887; *Komjáti Békés Gáspár, 1520-1579* (G. Békés of Komját, 1520-1579), Bp. 1887; *Izabella és János Zsigmond Lengyelországban, 1552-1557* (Isabella and John Sigismund in Poland, 1552-1557), Bp. 1888; *Kovacsóczy Farkas, 1576-1594* (F. Kovacsóczy, 1576-1594), Bp. 1903; *Konstantinápoly és magyar emlékei* (Constantinople and its Hungarian Memorials), Bp. 1903; *II. Rákóczi Ferenc Erdélyben* (Ferenc Rákóczi II in Transylvania), Bp. 1907; and *A székely határőrség szervezése, 1762-64-ben* (The Organization of the Székely Frontier Guards in 1762-64), Bp. 1908. Among his important source publications we find vols. V-VII of the eight-volume *Székely Oklevéltár* (Székely Archives), Kolozsvár, 1872-1899, 1934; and several volumes in the *Monumenta* series. On these see Appendix.

23.) *A székely nemzet története és alkotmánya*, Bp. 1927.

24.) On Hodinka see András Babics, "Hodinka Antal," *Je*, 7 (1964), 1147-1149; József Perényi, "Emlékezés Hodinka Antalról, 1864-1946" (Remembering A. Hodinka, 1864-1946), *Sz*, 99 (1965), 1403-1405; Steven Bela Vardy, "Antal Hodinka," *HHR*, 3 (1972), 266-274; József Pusztai's two remembrances in *DN*(July. 11, 1971), 7, and *DN*(Jan. 12, 1974), 5; and Hodinka's brief biography and list of publications up to 1940 in Szabó, *Erzsébet Tudományegyetem*, Pt. II, 382-387.

25.) *Az orosz évkönyvek magyar vonatkozásai*, Bp. 1916.

26.) *A munkácsi görög katholikus püspökség története*, Bp. 1909; and *A munkácsi görög szertartású püspökség okmánytara* (The Archives of the Greek Liturgical Bishopric of Munkács), vol. I, Ungvár, 1911.

27.) Hodinka's works on the Carpatho-Ruthenians include: *Adalékok az ungvári vár és tartomány és Ungvár város történetéhez* (Contributions to the History of the Castle, City and Province of Ungvár), Bp. 1918; *A kárpátaljai ruthének lakóhelyei, gazdaságuk és multjuk*(The Place of Settlement, Economy and Past of the Ruthenians of Sub-Carpathia), Bp. 1923 (and its briefer French version, "L'habitat, l'economie et le passé du peuple ruthene," *REHFO*, 2 (1924), 244-275; *II. Rákóczi Ferenc és a "gens fidelissima"*(Ferenc Rákóczi II and the "Gens Fidelissima"), Bp. 1937; and "Documenta Koriatovicsiana et fundatio monasterii Munkacsiensis," *AOSBM*, 7 (1950), 339-359, (1953), 525-551, and 8 (1954), 165-189. Hodinka's works on the South Slavs and the Balkans include several volumes in the *Monumenta* series (see Appendix). A number of his studies also deal with the city and the university of Pécs.

28.) On Holub see Miklós Komjáthy, "Holub József," *LK*, 33 (1962), 304-305; Andor Csizmadia, *Jogtörténeti oktatás*, 118-125; and Szabó, *Erzsébet Tudományegyetem*, Pt. II, 388-396.

29.) See Ch. XVIII.

30.) *A magyar alkotmánytörténelem vázlata. I. A legrégibb időktől 1526-ig* (An Outline of Hungarian Constitutional History. Vol. I. From the Most Ancient Times to 1526), Pécs, 1944. Vol. II of this work did not appear until 1947, and than only in a lithographed form. It covered the period between 1526 and 1867. For an assessment of this work see Alajos Degré's review in *Sz*, 81 (1947), 242-244.

31.) *Zala megye története a középkorban. I. A megyei és egyházi közigazgatás története* (The History of Zala County in the Middle Ages. Vol. I. The History of County and Church Administration), Pécs. 1929. Vol. II of this work, containing the history of the municipalities and villages, was finished, but remained in a manuscript form. Vol. III on the county's economic life and settlement pattern was finished only in an outline form; while Vol. IV on the history of the families of the county has reached the point of a rough draft. Cf. Csizmadia, *Jogtörténeti oktatás*, 119.

32.) Holub's other major works include: *Istvánffy Miklós históriája hadtörténeti szempontoból* (The History of M. Istvánffy from the Viewpoint of Military History), Szekszárd, 1909; *A tolnai reformáció történetének vázlata* (The Outline History of the Reformation in Tolna), Szekszárd, 1911; *A föispán és alispán viszonyának jogi természete* (The Legal Relationship Between the Vice Sheriff and the Lord High Sheriff), Bp. 1917; *Az életkor szerepe a középkori jogunkban* (its French version, *Le rôle de l'âge dans le droit hongrois du moyen âge*, Paris, 1922); *A leánynegyedről* (On the Daughters' Quarter Inheritance), Bp. 1928 (its French version, La 'Quarta Puellaris' dans l'ancien droit hongrois, Padua, 1935); *A királyi vármegyék eredete* (The Origin of the Royal Counties), Bp. 1938; *A kormányzói méltóság a magyar alkotmányban* (The Office of Regent in the Hungarian Constitution), Pécs, 1940; *La représentation politique en Hongrie au moyen âge*, Louvain-Paris, 1958; *La formation des deux Chambres de l'assemblée nationale hongroise*, Louvain-Paris, 1961; and *Zala megye középkori vízrajza* (The Hydrography of Zala County in the Middle Ages), Zalaegerszeg, 1963.

33.) On the historian Dezső Szabó see Varga, *Debreceni Tudományegyetem*, 202-204, 302; and *MÉL*, II, 675.

34.) *A magyar országgyűlések története II. Lajos korában*, Bp. 1909.

35.) For Szekfű's criticism see *Sz*, 45 (1911), 451. For Szabó's reply and Szekfű's answers see *ibid.*, 553 and 655.

36.) On Szekfű see Chs. VI, VIII, IX and X.

37.) *Küzdelmeink a nemzeti királyságért 1505-1526*, Bp. 1917.

38.) *A magyarországi úrbérrendezés története Mária Terézia korában*, Bp. 1933, vol. I.

39.) The information on the possible publication of the second volume of the above work comes from Prof. G. Ránki of the Institute of History of the Hungarian Academy of Sciences. Szabó's other works include: *A magyar országgyűlések története, 1519-1524* (The History of the Hungarian Diets, 1519-1524), Makó, 1904; *Az állandó hadsereg becikkelyezésének története II. Károly korában* (The History of the Enactment of the Law for a Standing Army in the Age of Charles III), Bp. 1911; and *A megyék ellenállása Mária Terézia úrbéri rendeletével szemben* (The County Opposition Against Maria Theresa's Peasant Reforms), Bp. 1934.

Chapter XVI

EAST EUROPEAN STUDIES IN INTERWAR HUNGARY

1.) On Lukinich, see below. No acceptable summary is available on Hungarian East European studies. For some fragmentary information see Tibor Baráth, "Kelet-Európa fogalma a modern történetírásban" (The Concept of Eastern Europe in Modern Historiography), in *Domanovszky-Emlékkönyv*, 23-43; B. Gunda, "Slavische ethnographische Forschungen in Ungarn zwischen 1945-1955," *SS*, 2 (1956), 467-470; Emil Niederhauser, "Geschichtswissenschaftlichen Arbeiten in Ungarn über die Beziehungen zu den Slawischen Völkern," *SS*, 2 (1956), 437-441; *idem*, "Beiträge zur Bibliographie der Geschichte der Slawischen Völkern in der ungarischen bürgerlichen Geschichtsschreibung," *SS*, 6 (1960), 457-473; *idem*, "L'histoire des peuples slaves et de l'Europe Orientale dans l'historiographie hongroise récente," *CSS*, 5 (1971), 410-419; István Kniezsa, "A magyar szlavisztika problémai és feladatai" (The Problems and Goals of Hungarian Slavistics), *MTA-NIOK*, 12 (1958), 69-124; József Perényi, "Hol élünk? Közép- vagy Kelet-Európában?" (Where do we Live? In Central or Eastern Europe?), *ET*, 21 (1966), 2092-2096; and Pál Horváth, "A közép- és kelet-európai népek jogfejlődése iránti érdeklődés a magyar burzsoá jogtörténetírásban" (The Interest of Hungarian Bourgeois Legal Historiography in the Constitutional Development of Central and East European Peoples), *JK*, 22 (1967), 341-353. See also Vardy, *Historiography*, 35-36, 69.

2.) Szentpétery, *Bölcsészeti kar*, 422, 458, 585, 618, 672-673. See also Béla Nagy, "A szomszéd népek nyelve és irodalma" (The Languages and Literatures of the Neighboring Peoples), in *ELTE története*, 510-517.

3.) On Kállay see Lajos Thallóczy, "Kállay Béni emlékezete" (Remembering B. Kállay), *AkE*, 20 (1909), 307-337; and Thallóczy's preface to Kállay, *A szerb felkelés története, 1807-1810* (The History of the Serbian Revolution, 1807-1810), ed. and intr. by Lajos Thallóczy, 2 vols., Bp. 1909; I, 1-38.

4.) Kállay, *A szerbek története, 1780-1815*, Bp. 1877 (German version: *Geschichte der Serben*, Wien-Leipzig, 1878); and *idem*, *A szerb felkelés története, 1807-1810*, Bp. 1909 (German version: *Die Geschichte des serbischen Aufstandes, 1807-1810*, Wien, 1910).

5.) On the Károlyi-Thallóczy Circle see Chs. V and XV. From among the numerous studies on Thallóczy see Árpád Karolyi, *Thallóczy Lajos emlékezete* (Remembering L. Thallóczy), Bp. 1937; *idem*, *Thallóczy Lajos élete és működése* (The Life and Activities of L. Thallóczy), Bp. 1937; Ferenc Eckhart, *Thallóczy Lajos a történetíró* (L. Thallóczy, the Historian), Bp. 1938; Károly Németh, *Emlékezések Thallóczy Lajosról* (Reminiscences about L. Thallóczy), Bp. 1940; and Mária Tömöry's introductory study of a selection from Thallóczy's diary, "Bosznia-Hercegovina annektálásának történetéből" (From the History of the Annexation of Bosnia-Herczegovina), *Sz*, 100 (1966), 878-923.

6.) Thallóczy's source publications include seven volumes in the *Monumenta* series (see Appendix). He also edited such related volumes as the *Diplomatarium relationum Republicae Ragusanae cum Regno Hungariae* (Documents on the Relationship between the Republic of Ragusa and the Kingdom of Hungary), with József Gelchich, Bp. 1887; *Török-Magyar oklevéltár, 1539-1789* (Turkish-Hungarian Archives, 1539-1789), with János Krcsmarik and Gyula Szekfű, Bp. 1914; and *Illyrisch-Albanische Forschungen*, with Konstantin Jireček, Milan Šufflay and others, 2 vols., München-Leipzig, 1916. Thallóczy's significant monographic studies on the Balkans and on Hungarian influences in the Balkans include: *Horvát szokásjog* (Croatian Customary Law), Bp. 1896; *III. Béla és a magyar birodalom* (Béla III and the Hungarian Empire), Bp. 1898, 2nd ed. 1906; *Nagy Lajos és a bulgár bánság* (Louis the Great and the Bulgarian Banate), Bp. 1900; *Tanulmányok a bosnyák és szerb élet- és nemzedek-rajzi tanulmányok* (Studies on Bosnian and Serbian Life and Generational System), Bp. 1909; and its German version, *Studien zur Geschichte Bosniens und Serbiens im Mittelalter*, München, 1914.

7.) Thallóczy's works with an economic orientation include: *I. Apafy Mihály udvara* (The Court of Mihály Apafy I), Bp. 1878; *Abauj vármegye közgazdasági viszonya* (The Economic Conditions of Abauj County), Bp. 1879; and *A korona haszna (lucrum camerae) története, kapcsolatban a magyar adó- és pénzügy fejlődéssel* (The History of Camerial Profit *(Lucrum Camerae)* in Conjunction with the Development of Hungarian Taxation and Finances), Bp. 1879.

8.) On Hodinka see Ch. XV.

9.) On Lukinich see *AkE*, 1924, 1928, 1933 and 1936; Szabó, *Erzsébet Tudományegyetem*, Pt. II, 643-650; and Szentpétery, *Bölcsészeti kar*, 674.

10.) Most of Lukinich's publications are listed in Szabó, *Erzsébet tudományegyetem*, Pt. II, 643-650. The works mentioned in the text are: *Auer János Ferdinánd pozsonyi nemes polgárnak héttoronyi fogságában írt naplója 1664* (The Diary of J.F. Auer, a Noble Citizen of Pozsony, Written During his Captivity in the Seven Towers 1664), Bp. 1923; *II. Rákóczi Ferenc felségárulási perének története és okirattára*, 2 vols., Bp. 1935; and *A podmanini és aszódi Podmaniczky-család története* (The History of the Podmaniczky Family of Podmanin and Aszód), 10 vols., Bp. 1933-1943 (vols. V-IX contain the archives).

11.) Some of Lukinich's monographic studies include: *I. Rákóczi György és lengyel királysága* (George Rákóczi I and his Polish Kingship), Bp. 1907; *Az erdélyi hódoltság és végvárai* (The Turkish Rule in Transylvania and their Fortresses), Bp. 1912; *Az erdélyi fejedelmi cím kialakulása* (The Evolution of the Princely Office in Transylvania), Bp. 1913; *A Magyar Történelmi Társulat története, 1867-1917* (The History of the Hungarian Historical Association, 1867-1917), Bp. 1918; *Erdély területi változásai a török hódoltság korában, 1541-1711* (The Territorial Changes of Transylvania during the Turkish Rule, 1541-1711), Bp. 1918; *A bethleni gróf Bethlen-család története* (The History of the Count Bethlen Family of Bethlen), Bp. 1927; and *Stefan Bathory*, Cracow, 1934. Lukinich also edited such major collective works as the memorial volumes dedicated to Count Klebelsberg (1925), the Battle of Mohács (1926), King Matthias Corvinus (1940). His *Les editions des sources de l'histoire hongroise, 1854-1930*, Bp. 1931, contains an annotated list of most of the significant Hungarian source publications published between 1854 and 1930. Lukinish also co-edited with L. Gáldi, A. Fekete-Nagy and L. Makkai a significant collection of sources on the Roumanians, *Documenta historiam Valachorum in Hungaria illustrantia usque ad annum 1400 p. Christum*, Bp. 1941.

12.) Lukinich, *A magyar történelem életrajzokban*, Bp. 1930. An English translation appeared in London in 1937.

13.) On Biró see *Erdély Magyar Egyeteme*, 400; and *MÉL*, I, 217-218.

14.) Biró, *Erdély története*, Kolozsvár, 1944.

15.) Biró's significant monographs include: *Az erdélyi fejedelmi hatalom fejlődése, 1542-1690* (The Development of the Princely Power in Transylvania, 1542-1690), Kolozsvár, 1917; *Altorjai gróf Apor István és kora* (Count I. Apor of Altorja and his Age), Kolozsvár, 1935; *Székhelyi Mailáth G. Károly* (Károly G. Mailáth of Székhely), Kolozsvár, 1940; *Az erdélyi udvarház gazdasági szerepe a XVII. század második felében* (The Economic Role of the Transylvanian Manor in the Second Half of the 17th Century), Kolozsvár, 1945. Biró also edited the work *Az erdélyi katolicizmus multja és jelene* (The Past and Present of Transylvanian Catholicism), Kolozsvár, 1925.

16.) Biró, *Erdély követei a portán*, Kolozsvár, 1921.

17.) On Divéky see Varga, *Debreceni Tudományegyetem*, 204; Endre Kovács, "Divéky Adorján, 1880-1964," *Sz*, 99 (1965), 1390-1391; and *MÉL*, I, 381.

18.) Divéky's significant works include: *Felsőmagyarország kereskedelmi összeköttetései Lengyelországgal, főleg a XVI-XVII. században* (Upper Hungary's Economic Connections with Poland, Especially in the 16th and 17th Centuries), Bp. 1905; *Magyarok és lengyelek a XIX. században* (Hungarians and Poles in the 19th Century), Bp. 1919; *A Lengyelországnak elzálogosított 16. szepesi város visszacsatolása 1770-ben* (The Reannexation in 1770 of the

Sixteen Zipser Towns Pawned to Poland), Bp. 1929; and *Az aranybulla és a Jeruzsálemi királyság alkotmánya* (The (Hungarian) Golden Bull and the Constitution of the Kingdom of Jerusalem), Bp. 1932.

19.) On Miskolczy see Hans Wagner, "Julius Miskolczy, 1892-1962," *MÖS*, 15 (1962), 697-700; and *MÉL*, II, 221-222.

20.) Miskolczy, *A horvát kérdés története és iromdnyai a rendi állam korában*, 2 vols., Bp. 1927-1928.

21.) On Sufflay see Gyula Szekfű, "Sufflay Milán tragédiája" (M. Sufflay's Tragedy), *MSz*, 11 (1931), 377-383, reprinted in Szekfű's *Állam és nemzet*, 265-275; József Bajza, "Sufflay Milán, 1879-1931," in his *A horvát kérdés*, 255-261; J(ózsef) D(eér), "Sufflay Milán, 1879-1931." in *Jancsó-Emlékkönyv*, 410-413; and Szentpétery, *Bölcsészeti kar*, 674.

22.) Miskolczy, *A magyar nép történelme a mohácsi vésztől az első világháborúig* (The History of the Hungarian People from the Battle of Mohács till the First World War), Rome, 1956.

23.) *Ibid.*, 299.

24.) Julius Miskolczy, *Ungarn in der Habsburger-Monarchie*, Wien, 1959. Miskolczy's other major work is his *A kamarilla a reformkorszakban* (The "Kitchen Cabinet" in the Reform Period), Bp. 1938.

25.) Miskolczy, *A magyar nép történelme*, 298.

26.) On Thim see József Perényi, "Thim József, 1864-1959," *Sz*, 94 (1960), 454-455; and *MÉL*, II, 856.

27.) Thim, *A szerbek története a legrégebbi kortól 1848-ig*, 3 vols., Nagy-Becskerek, 1892.

28.) Thim, *A magyarországi 1848-49-iki szerb fölkelés története*, 3 vols., Bp. 1930-1940. An earlier work by Thim on this same topic is his *Az 1848-49. szerb fölkelés* (The Serbian Uprising of 1848-49), Nagy-Becskerek, 1894.

29.) On Steier see Pál Török, "Steier Lajos, 1885-1938," *Sz*, 72 (1938), 135-136; and *MÉL*, II, 655.

30.) Steier, *A tót kérdés*, Liptószentmiklós, 1912.

31.) Steier's works in the *Fontes* series include: *Beniczky Lajos bányavidéki kormánybiztos és honvédezredes visszaemlékezései és jelentései az 1848-49-iki szabadságharcról és a tót mozgalomról* (The Reminiscences and Reports of Colonel L. Beniczky, State Commissioner of the Mining Region (of Upper Hungary), about the Revolution and about the Slovak Movement of 1848-49), Bp. 1924; and *A tót nemzetiségi kérdés 1848-49-ben*, 2 vols., Bp. 1937.

32.) Steier's cited monographs include: *Görgely és Kossuth*, Bp. 1924; and *Haynau és Paskievics*, 2 vols., Bp. 1925.

33.) Steier, *Ungarns Vergewaltigung*, Bp., c. 1930.

34.) On Veress see Dániel Csatári, *Veress Endre emlékezete* (Remembering E. Veress), Gyula, 1960; and *MÉL*, II, 987-988.

35.) *Fontes rerum Transylvanicarum*, ed. Endre Veress, 5 vols., Bp. 1911-1921; and *Documente privitoare la istoria Ardealului, Moldavei şi Tării Româneşti*, ed. Andrei Veress, 11 vols., Bucharest, 1929-1939.

36.) For Veress's works in the *Monumenta* series, see Appendix.

37.) Veress, *Bibliografia română-ungară, 1473-1838*, 3 vols., Bucharest, 1931-1935.

38.) On Melich see Jolán Berrár, "Johann Melich," *ALi*, 15 (1965), 135-142. His most significant works include: *Deutsche Ortsnamen und Lehnworter des ungarischen Sprachschatzes,* Innsbruck, 1900; *Szláv jövevényszavaink* (Our Slavic Loan Words), Bp. 1903; *A honfoglaláskori Magyarország* (Hungary at the Time of the Magyar Conquest), Bp. 1925; and *Magyar Etymológiai Szótár* (Hungarian Etymological Dictionary), with Zoltán Gombócz, pts. I-XVI (A-G), Bp. 1914-1944.

39.) On Kniezsa see the study by L. Kiss, "Stefan Kniezsa," *ALi,* 16 (1966), 337-362. Kniezsa's works on geographic names and ethnic-linguistic frontiers include: *Pseudo-rumänen in Pannonien in den Nordkarpathen,* Bp. 1936; *Ungarns Völkerschaften im XI. Jahrhundert,* Bp. 1938; *Zur Geschichte der ungarisch-slowakischen ethnischen Grenze,* Bp. 1941; *Erdély víznevei* (The River Names of Transylvania), Kolozsvár, 1943; *Keletmagyarország helynevei* (The Geographic Names of Eastern Hungary), Bp. 1943; *A párhuzamos helynévadás* (Bilingualism in Geographic Names), Bp. 1944; *A honfoglalás előtti szlávok nyelve a Dunántúlon* (The Language of the Pre-Conquest Slavs in Trans-Danubia), Bp. 1952; and *A magyar nyelv szláv jövevényszavai. Die Slawischen Lehnwörter der ungarischen Sprache,* Vol. I, prts. 1-2, Bp. 1955-1956.

40.) On Bonkáló see *MÉL,* I, 244. His significant works include: *A magyar rutének* (The Hungarian Ruthenians), Bp. 1920; *Az ukrán mozgalom története, 1917-22* (The History of the Ukrainian Movement, 1917-22), Bp. 1922; *A kárpátaljai rutén irodalom és művelődés* (The Ruthenian Literature and Culture of Sub-Carpathia), Bp. 1935; and *A rutének (ruszinok)* (The Ruthenians), Bp. 1940.

41.) On Bajza see László Tóth, "Bajza József és a horvát kérdés" (J. Bajza and The Croatian Question) in József Bajza, *A horvát kérdés. Válogatott tanulmányok* (The Croatian Question. Selected Studies), ed. by László Tóth, Bp. 1941, 5-22; and Ervin Supka, "Bajza József irodalmi munkássága" (The Bibliography of J. Bajza), in *ibid.,* 511-527. In addition to the above posthumous volume on the Croatian Question, Bajza has also authored the following relevant works: *Horvátország népessége* (The Population of Croatia), Bp. 1916, which he wrote under the pseudonym of József Szűcs; *A magyar-horvát unió felbomlása* (The Dissolution of the Hungarian-Croatian Union), Bp. 1925; and *Podmaniczky-Magyar Benigna a horvát költészetben* (Benigna Podmaniczky-Magyar in Croatian Literature), Bp. 1935.

42.) On Roumanian studies at the University of Budapest see Szentpétery, *Bölcsészeti kar,* 458, 459, 586, 587, 672; and *ELTE története,* 510-525. On L. Tamás see *MIL,* III, 299. Tamás's significant works include: *Der dynamische Wortakzent der ungarischen Lehnwörter im Rumänischen,* Paris-Bucharest, 1932; *Rómaiak, románok és oláhok Dácia Trajánában* (Romans, Roumanians and Vlachs in Dacia Trajana), Bp. 1935; *Az erdélyi oláhság* (The Transylvanian Roumanians), Bp. 1936; *A magyar eredetű rumén kölcsönszavak művelődéstörténeti értékelése* (The Cultural-Historical Assessment of Roumanian Loan Words of Magyar Origin), Kolozsvár, 1942; *La formation de la langue et du peuple roumains,* Bp. 1943; *Ugocsai magyar-rumén kapcsolatok* (Magyar-Roumanian Relations in Ugocsa), Kolozsvár, 1944; *Albán-magyar szótár* (Albanian-Hungarian Dictionary), Bp. 1953; and *Általános nyelvészet és a magyar nyelvtudomány* (General Linguistics and Hungarian Linguistic Sciences), Bp. 1956.

43.) On Roumanian studies at the University of Kolozsvár (Cluj) before 1919 and between 1940 and 1945 see László Gáldi, "Az erdélyi magyar tudományosság és a kolozsvári egyetem hatása a román tudományra'' (The Influence of the Transylvanian Hungarian Scholarship and of the University of Kolozsvár upon Roumanian Scholarship), in *Erdély Magyar Egyeteme,* 285-304, where the roles of Moldován and Siluca are both treated. Moldován's significant works include: *Román népdalok és balladák* (Roumanian Folksongs and Ballads), Kolozsvár, 1872; *Román közmondások* (Roumanian Proverbs), Kolozsvár, 1882; *Román nyelvtan*(Roumanian Grammar), Kolozsvár, 1888; *A románság*(The Roumanians), 2 vols., Nagy-Becskerek, 1895-1896; and *A magyarországi románok* (The Roumanians of Hungary), Bp. 1913.

44.) On Russian studies at the University of Budapest see Kálmán Bolla, ''Orosz nyelv és irodalom'' (Russian Language and Literature), in *ELTE története,* 499-509.

45.) Oszkár Asbóth, *Gyakorlati orosz nyelvtan*(Practical Russian Grammar), Bp. 1888; *Kurze russische Grammatik,* Leipzig, 1889; *Szlávság a magyar keresztény terminológiában* (Slavisms in Hungarian Christian Terminology), Bp. 1884; *A hangsúly a szláv nyelvekben*(Intonation in the Slavic Languages), Bp. 1891; and *Szláv jövevény-szavaink* (Our Slavic Loan Words), vol. I., Bp. 1907.

46.) Sándor Bonkáló, *Az orosz irodalom története* (The History of Russian Literature), 2 vols., Bp. 1926.

47.) On Hungarian Oriental studies and Byzantinology see Károly Czeglédi, ''Oriental Studies,'' *Science in Hungary,* 283-305; *idem,* ''Orientalisztika'' (Orientalistics), in *ELTE története,* 554-569; and Gyula Moravcsik, ''A magyar bizantinológia'' (Hungarian Byzantinology), in his *Bevezetés a bizantinológiába* (Introduction to Byzantinology), Bp. 1966, 155-164.

48.) On the *Universal History* see Ch. XIX.

49.) On Klebelsberg's and Hóman's cultural policy see Ch. VII.

50.) On the Teleki Institute and on its three component institutes see Bálint Hóman's presidential address to the Hungarian Historical Association in *Sz,* 75 (1941), 225-235; and Béla T. Kardos's unpublished paper, ''Tudósaink védelmében'' (In defense of Our Scholars), delivered at the plenary session of the American Hungarian Philosophical and Scientific Society, New Brunswick, New Jersey, September 29, 1973.

51.) On Gál and on the significance of the *Apollo* movement, see Jaroslava Pašiaková, ''Apollo'' in *Tanulmányok a csehszlovák-magyar irodalmi kapcsolatok köréből* Studies on Czechslovak-Hungarian Literary Connections, Bp. 1965, pp. 439-450. One of the most significant works edited by Gál is *Ungarn und die Nachbarvolker,* Bp. 1943.

Chapter XVII

DOMANOVSZKY AND THE HUNGARIAN CIVILIZATION OR KULTURGESCHICHTE SCHOOL

1.) On this young generation see sections of Chs. XI, XVI, XVIII and XXI. On the *Magyar Szemle* see Ch. X, and on *Magyarságtudomány* (1935-1937, 1942-1943) cf. *MIL,* II. 154.

2.) Not counting church historians, art historians and various philologists (classical, Semitic, Turkic, etc.), most of whom also taught history courses, there were generally at least a dozen chairs of history at the University of Budapest during the interwar period. In contrast, there were only four chairs at Szeged, and three each at Pécs and Debrecen. During the 1930's the holders of the Budapest chairs of history were: E. Mályusz (medieval Hungarian), G. Szekfű (modern Hungarian), S. Domanovszky (Hungarian *Kulturgeschichte),* I. Heinlein (ancient), A. Áldásy (medieval), I. Hajnal (modern), J. Illés (constitutional), F. Eckhart (constitutional), I. Lukinich (East European), G. Miskolczy (Balkans), L. Ligeti (Oriental) and I. Szentpétery (auxiliary sciences).

3.) During the 1930's the incumbents of the history chairs at Szeged were: J. Deér (Hungarian), L. Erdélyi (Hungarian *Kulturgeschichte),* J. Fógel (European) and B. Iványi (constitutional); at Pécs: J. Holub (Hungarian), Z. Kérészy (constitutional) and A. Hodinka (European); at Debrecen: I. Rugonfalvi-Kiss (Hungarian), B. Baranyai (constitutional) and D. Szabó (European).

4.) See Ch. XVI.

5.) On Hungarian *Kulturgeschichte* see Steven Bela Vardy, "The Birth of the Hungarian *Kulturgeschichte* School: A Study in the History of Hungarian Historical Studies," in *Sinor-Festschrift* (Bonn, Germany), in press; and *idem, Historiography,* 38-39, 71-72.

6.) On A.A. Kerékgyártó see Remig Békefi, *Kerékgyártó Alajos Árpád emlékezete* (Remembering A.A. Kerékgyártó), Bp. 1904; and Szentpétery, *Bölcsészeti kar,* 453-454. Kerékgyártó's significant works include: *Magyarország művelődésének története* (History of Hungarian Civilization), 2 vols., Pest, 1856-1858; *Magyarország történetének kézikönyve* (A Handbook of Hungarian History), 7 vols., Pest, 1867-1874; *Hazánk évlapjai, 884-1849; and A miveltség fejlődése Magyarországon, 889-1301* (The Development of Civilization in Hungary, 889-1301), Bp. 1880. Although outwardly impressive, Kerékgyártó's works were rather simplicistic accounts, with only few signs of a critical approach.

7.) See Ch. V.

8.) The first chair of Hungarian *Kulturgeschichte* was established at the University of Kolozsvár in 1883 which was held for the next two and half decades (1883-1909) by Gyula Vajda (1843-1909). But Vajda proved to be an historian of modest capacities and he wrote very little. His most important work is *Erédly viszonya a portához és a római császárhoz mint magyar királyhoz a nemzeti fejedelemség korszakában* (Transylvania's Relationship to the Porte and to the Holy Roman Emperors as kings of Hungary, during the Age of the Hungarian National Princes), Kolozsvár, 1891.

9.) For a complete list of the published dissertations written under Békefi see the *Békefi-Emlékkönyv,* 35-37. These dissertations are discussed and analyzed by István Prepatits in *ibid.,* 23-35.

10.) Békefi's significant works on the Hungarian religious orders include: *A pilisi apátság története* (The History of the Abbey of Pilis), 2 vols., Pécs, 1891-1892; *A czikádori apátság története* (The History of the Abbey of Czikádor), Pécs, 1894; *A pásztói apátság története* (The History of the Abbey of Pásztó), 3 vols., Bp. 1898-1902; and *A ciszterci rend története Magyarországon* (The History of the Cistercian Order in Hungary), Bp. 1896. Some of his works on the history of Hungarian education are: *A népoktatás Magyarországon 1540-ig* (Public Education in Hungary till 1540), Bp. 1906; *Az iskolázás története Magyarországon, 1000-1883* (The History of Education in Hungary, 1000-

1883), Bp. 1907; *A pécsi egyetem* (The University of Pécs), Bp. 1909; and *A káptalani iskolák története Magyarországon 1540-ig* (The History of the Chapter Schools in Hungary till 1540), Bp. 1910. Békefi's other significant works include: *Vallásos és erkölcsi élet Magyarországon az Árpádházi királyok korában* (Religious and Moral Life in Hungary in the Age of the Árpádian Kings), Bp. 1896; *A rabszolgaság Magyarországon az Árpádok alatt* (Slavery in Hungary Under the Árpáds), Bp. 1901; *A Balaton környékének egyházai és várai a középkorban*, Bp. 1907 (German version: *Kirchen und Burgen in der Umgebung des Balaton im Mittelalter*, tr. Milan v. Šufflay); and *Veszprém a középkorban* (Veszprém in the Middle Ages), Veszprém, 1912.

11.) On Acsády see Ch. V. This view was expressed by Hóman in the *New Paths*, 35.

12.) Erdélyi was Gyula Vajda's successor at the University of Kolozsvár. On Erdélyi see Lajos J. Csóka, "Erdélyi László," *Sz*, 81 (1947), 356-357; and Ferenc Rottler, "Beiträge zur Kritik der Historiographie des frühen Mittelalters. Über die Geschichtsanschauung László Erdélyis," *AUSB, Sec. Hist.*, 3 (1961), 121-152.

13.) Erdélyi's syntheses of Hungarian *Kulturgeschichte* include: *Magyar művelődéstörténet* (History of Hungarian Civilization), 2 vols., Kolozsvár, 1913-1918; *Árpádkor* (The Árpádian Age), Bp. 1922; *Magyar történelem uj rendszerben* (Hungarian History According to a New System), Bp. 1931; *A magyar lovagkor társadalma és művelődése* (Society and Culture of the Age of Hungarian Knighthood), Bp. 1932; and *Magyar történelem: Művelődés és államtörténet* (Hungarian History: Civilization and State History), 2 vols., Bp. 1936. Erdélyi's other significant works are: *A pannonhalmi Szent-Benedek-rend története* (The History of the Saint Benedictine Order of Pannonhalma), vols. I-V and VII-XI ed. by Erdélyi (Erdélyi also wrote the volumes on the history of the monasteries of Pannonhalma and Tihany), Bp. 1902-1916; *Egyházi földesúr és szolgái a középkorban* (Ecclesiastical Lord and His Servants in the Middle Ages), Bp. 1907; *Magyarország társadalma a XI. szdzad törvényeiben* (Hungary's Society in Light of the Laws of the 11th Century), Bp. 1907; *Az egyházi vagyon eredete és jellege Magyarországon* (The Origins and Nature of Ecclesiastical Property in Hungary), Bp. 1913; *A magyar lovagkor nemzetségei* (The Clans of the Age of Hungarian Knighthood), Bp. 1932; and *Magyarország törvényei Szent Istvántól Mohácsig* (Hungary's Laws from St. Stephen till Mohács), Bp. 1942.

14.) On Erdélyi's strange system of Hungarian historical evolution, which divided Hungarian history into cycles of approximately forty years each, see his "Művelődéstörténeti rendszerem és a szellemtörténet" (My System of *Kulturgeschichte* and the *Geistesgeschichte* School), *ETA*, 134-138; and the preface to his *Magyar történelem*, I, 5-9.

15.) Erdélyi's most bitter scholarly controversy was with K. Tagányi on the nature of medieval Hungarian society. This controversy took place on the pages of the *Történeti Szemle* (vols. III-V, 1914-1916). Tagányi's contribution to this debate consists of about 150 pages in the 1914 and 1916 issues of this journal, and Erdélyi's of about 340 pages. Of Erdélyi's contribution, the first half appeared in the 1914-1915 issues (subsequently reprinted under the title *Árpádkori társadalomtörténetünk legkritikusabb kérdései* (The Most Critical Questions of the Social History of the Árpádian Age), Bp. 1915); while the second half appeared only as an independent volume, entitled *A tizenkét legkritikusabb kérdés* (The Twelve Most Critical Questions), Kolozsvár, 1917.

16.) On Domanovszky see István Hajnal, "Domanovszky Sándor hetven éves" (S. Domanovszky is Seventy Years Old), *Sz*, 81 (1947), 355; Emma Lederer, "Domanovszky Sándor, 1877-1955," *Sz*, 89 (1955), 522-523; Harold Steinacker, "Alexander Domanovszky," *AÖAW* (1955), 368-377; and Lederer, *Történetírás*, 149-152.

17.) On Domanovszky's resistance to the *Geistesgeschichte* School see his reviews of Hóman's and Szekfű's *Magyar History* in *Sz*, 63-64 (1929-1930), 423-429, 881-903; and *ibid.*, 67 (1933), 308-315. See also Domanovszky's review of Hóman's *New Paths* in *Sz*, 65 (1931), 273-279.

18.) *József nádor élete és iratai*, 4 vols. in 5, Bp. 1925-1944.

19.) For a list of Domanovszky's publications up to 1937 see *Domanovszky-Emlékkönyv*, 715-723.

20.) *Die historische Entwicklung Ungarns mit Rücksicht auf seine Wirtschaftsgeschichte*, Bp. 1913; and *Társadalmi alapismeretek és gazdaságtörténelem*, Bp. 1922.

21.) *Die Geschichte Ungarns*, München-Leipzig, 1923.

22.) Some of Domanovszky's major monographic publications include: *A Dubnici Krónika* (The Chronicle of Dubnic), Bp. 1899; *A Budai Krónika* (The Chronicle of Buda), Bp. 1902; *A Pozsonyi Krónika* (The Chronicle of Pozsony), Bp. 1905; *Kézai Simon Mester Krónikája* (The Chronicle of Magister Simon de Kéza), Bp. 1906; *Mügeln Henrik német nyelvű krónikája és a Rímes Krónika* (The German Language Chronicle of Heinrich Mügeln and the Rhyming Chronicle), Bp. 1907; *Trónöröklés kérdése az Árpádok Korában* (The Question of the Succession to the Throne in the Age of the Árpáds), Bp. 1913; *A harmincad-vám eredete* (The Origins of the Thirtieth Tariff), Bp. 1916; *Duna-Fekete-tengeri kereskedelmi hajózásunk multjáról* (On the History of the Danube-Black Sea Trade), Bp. 1918; *A szepesi városok árumegállító joga, 1358-1570* (The Staple Rights of the Zipser Towns, 1358-1570), Bp. 1922; *Anonymus és a II. Géza-korabeli Gesta* (Anonymous and the Geste of the Age of Géza II), Bp. 1933; *Kézai és a Húnkrónika* (Kézai and the Hunnic Chronicle), Bp. 1933; and *La methode historique de M. Nicolas Jorga*, Bp. 1938.

23.) *Tanulmányok a magyar mezőgazdaság történetéhez*, ed. Sándor Domanovszky, Bp. 1930-1943. Altogether fifteen volumes appeared in the series. For a list see the rear covers of the later volumes

24.) See Jenő Berlász, *A magyar gazdaság- és társadalomtörténetírás kialakulása* (The Development of Hungarian Agricultural and Social Historiography), Bp. 1943; Imre Wellmann, "Mezőgazdaságtörténetünk új utjai" (The New Paths of Our Agricultural History Studies), in *Domanovszky-Emlékkönyv*, 664-715; *idem*, "Néprajz és gazdaságtörténet" (Ethnography and Agricultural History), *Et*, 58 (1947), 8-18; and *idem*, "Agrártörténetírásunk feladatai" (The Tasks of Our Agricultural History Studies), *ASz* (1947), 425-438.

25.) *Magyar művelődéstörténet*, ed. Sándor Domanovszky, György Balanyi, Elemér Mályusz, Imre Szentpétery and Elemér Varjú, Bp. (1939-1942).

26.) Information concerning Varjú's role in this project came from Professor E. Mályusz. See also Gabriella Tápay-Szabó, "Varjú Elemér, 1873-1945," *Sz*, 79-80 (1945-1946), 310-311.

27.) See Domanovszky's preface to the *Magyar művelődéstörténet,* I, 15.
28.) *Ibid.,* 5-20.
29.) Imre Lukinich, "A három részre szakított ország" (The Trisected Country), *ibid.,* III, 5-68.
30.) Elemér Mályusz, "A magyar állam a középkor végén" (The Hungarian State at the End of the Middle Ages), *ibid.,* II, 5-82.
31.) Imre Wellmann, "Barokk és felvilágosodás" (Baroque and Enlightenment), *ibid.,* IV, 5-108.
32.) Gyula Miskolczy, "A modern államszervezés kora" (The Age of Modern State Formation), *ibid.,* V, 5-98.
33.) Péter Váczy, "A magyarság a román és gót stílus korában" (The Magyars in the Age of the Romanesque and Gothic Styles, *ibid.,* I, 91-160.
34.) József Deér, "A magyarság a nomád kultúrközösségben" (The Magyars in the Nomadic Cultural World), *ibid.,* I, 21-90.
35.) *Ibid.,* I, 8.
36.) *Ibid.,* 11.
37.) For contemporary assessments on the *History of Hungarian Civilization* see István Hajnal's reviews in *Sz,* 73 (1939), 239-247; *Sz,* 75 (1941), 68-78; *Sz,* 77 (1943), 501-505; and Egyed Herman's review of the last volume in *Sz,* 78 (1944), 273-278.
38.) See the discussion on the *Magyar History* in Ch. X.
39.) On Mályusz and on his views see Ch. XII.
40.) See particularly Vardy's and Izsépi's studies cited in Ch. V, n. 26. See also *MÉL,* I, 994-995.
41.) Some of Kováts's important monographic works include: *Városi adózás a középkorban* (Urban Taxation in the Middle Ages), Pozsony, 1900; *Adalékok a dunai hajózás és dunai vámok történetéhez az Anjou korban* (On the History of Shipping and Tariffs on the Danube in the Age of the Anjous), Bp. 1901; *A középkori magyar pénztörténet vázlata* (An Outline of Medieval Hungarian Monetary History), Bp. 1901; *Nyugatmagyarország áruforgalma a XV. században* (West Hungary's Commerce in the 15th Century), Bp. 1902; *A pozsonyi városgazdaság a középkor végén* (The Urban Economy of Pozsony at the End of the Middle Ages), Pozsony, 1918; and *Adalékok a pozsonyi zsidóság későközépkori gazdaságtörténetéhez* (On the Late Medieval Economic History of the Jews of Pozsony), Bp. 1938. For Kováts's other published works see Szabó, *Erzsébet Tudományegyetem,* Pt. II, 557-562.
42.) *Közgazdasági Lexikon,* ed. Sándor Halász and Gyula Mandelló, 3 vols., Bp. 1898-1901.
43.) Kováts was to write the volume provisionally entitled *Magyar pénztörténet és numizmatika* (The History of Hungarian Money and Numismatics) for the series *Handbook of Hungarian Historical Sciences.*
44.) See Chs. IX-X. Dékány's essay, "Gazdaság- és társadalomtörténet," *New Paths,* 183-236, has already been cited in Ch. X, n. 41. See also *MÉL,* I, 362.
45.) See Dékány's above-cited essay in *New Paths,* 188-194, 219-222.
46.) István Dékány, *A történettudomány módszertana,* Bp. 1925. See also Ch. VII. Some of his other works are listed in Ch. IX, n. 27.

Chapter XVIII

LEGAL AND CONSTITUTIONAL HISTORY AND THE "DOCTRINE OF THE HOLY CROWN"

1.) On Eckhart see György Székely, "Eckhart Ferenc, 1885-1957," *Sz,* 91 (1957), 883-885; W.A., "Eckhart Ferenc," *JK,* 12 (1957), 224; Vardy, *Historiography,* 36-38, 69-71; Sarlós, "A szellemtörténeti irány," 87-103; Csizmadia, *Jogtörténeti oktatás,* 107-128; Degré, "Jogtörténetírás a Horthy-korban," 77-99; and Glatz, "Jogtörténetírás," 911-917.

2.) Eckhart, "Jog- és alkotmánytörténet," *New Paths,* 269-320. For the "Doctrine of the Holy Crown" see below.

3.) *Ibid.,* 271.

4.) *Ibid.,* 270.

5.) For Király and Hajnik see below.

6.) See below.

7.) See below.

8.) On the history of Hungarian legal and constitutional history studies see Csizmadia, "Jogtörténet-tudomány," 28-51; Eckhart, *Jog- és állam-tudományi kar;* and Pál Horváth, *A kelet- és közép- európai népek jogfejlődésének főbb irányai* (The Main Trends of the Constitutional Development of the Peoples of Eastern and Central Europe), Bp. 1958, 5-74.

9.) On M.G. and J.M. Kovachich see Ch. IV.

10.) On Fejér see Ch. IV, n. 23 and the relevant text.

11.) On Wenzel and Hungarian constitutional historical studies of the dualist period see Degré, "Jogtörténetírás a dualizmus korában," 285-315; and Pál Horváth, "Dualizmuskori jogtörténetírásunk," 3-16.

12.) *Árpádkori új okmánytár,* ed. Gusztáv Wenzel, 12 vols., Pest, 1860-1875.

13.) Some of Wenzel's significant syntheses and monographs include: *A magyar és erdélyi magánjog rendszere* (The Hungarian and Transylvanian System of Private Law), 2 vols., Pest, 1863-1864; *Egyetemes európai jogtörténet* (Universal European Constitutional History), Pest, 1869; *Magyarország jogtörténetének rövid vázlata* (A Short Outline of Hungarian Constitutional History), Pest, 1872; *Magyarország városai és városjogai* (Hungarian Cities and Urban Law Codes), Bp. 1877; *Magyar és erdélyi bányajogrendszer*(The System of Hungarian and Transylvanian Mining Laws), 2 vols., Bp. 1879; *Magyarország bányászatának kritikai története* (A Critical History of Hungarian Mining), Bp. 1880; and *Magyarország mezőgazdaságának története*(The History of Hungarian Agriculture), Bp. 1887.

14.) On Hajnik see Illés, *Hajnik Imre és a magyar jogtörténet* (I. Hajnik and Hungarian Constitutional History), Bp. 1928; Degré, "Jogtörténetírás a dualizmus korában," 299-306; and Horváth, "Dualizmuskori jogtörténetírásunk," 3-16.

15.) Hajnik, *Magyar alkotmány és jog az Árpádok alatt* (Hungarian Constitution and Law Under the Árpáds), vol. I of his incomplete *Magyar alkotmány- és jogtörténet*(Hungarian Constitutional and Legal History), Bp. 1872; and *idem, Alkotmány és jogfejlődés a középkorban* (Constitutional and Legal Developments in the Middle Ages), vol. I of his incomplete *Egyetemes európai jogtörténet* (Universal European Constitutional History), Bp. 1874.

16.) Hajnik, *Magyarország az Árpád királyoktól az ősiség megalapításáig és a hűbéri Európa* (Hungary from the Árpádian Kings to the Foundation of Entail and Feudal Europe), Pest, 1867; *A nemesség országgyűlési fejenként való magjelenésének magszűnése* (The Cessation of the Right of the Nobility for Personal Appearance at the Diet), Bp. 1873; *Az örökös főispánság a magyar alkotmánytörténetben* (The Office of the Hereditary High Sheriff in Hungarian Constitutional History), Bp. 1886; *A magyar bírósági szervezet és perjog az Árpádok és a vegyes-házi királyok alatt* (Hungarian Court System and the Right of Law Suit Under the Kings from the Árpádian and the Mixed Dynasties), Bp. 1899; and others.

17.) On Hajnik's achievements at the University of Budapest see Eckhart, *Jog- és államtudományi kar,* 532, 537-538, 609-610, 613-614.

18.) On the Doctrine of the Holy Crown see Ernő Nagy's traditional essay in *MJL,* V, 35-38; the Marxist summary in *UML,* VI, 212; Eckhart's yet to be discussed *A szentkorona-eszme története;* and the Marxist analysis by Márton Sarlós, "A 'szentkorona tan' kialakulásához" (On the Evolution of the 'Doctrine of the Holy Crown'), *JK,* 15 (1960), 557-600.

19.) Stephanus de Werbewcz (István Werbőczi), *Tripartitum Juris Consuetudinarii Regni Hungariae* (The Tripartite Book of Hungary's Customary Laws), Vienna, 1517. For a good and relatively modern version of these works see the annotated bilingual edition by Kálmán Csiky, Bp. 1894.

20.) For a critical assessment of the "Regnum Mariannum" concept see Béla Beller, " 'Regnum Mariannum'," *Vil,* 7 (1966), 37-43.

21.) Hajnik, *Egyetemes európai jogtörténet,* I, 209.

22.) József Kardos, "Az Eckhart-vita," 1108.

23.) In addition to the above mentioned studies see also Imre Szabó, *A burzsoá állam- és jogbölcselet Magyarországon* (The Bourgeois State and Legal Philosophy in Hungary), Bp. 1955. Concha's major works include: *Újkori alkotmányok* (Constitutions of the Modern Age), 2 vols., 1884-1888; *Politika I: Alkotmánytan* (Politics I: Constitutional Law), Bp. 1894; *Politika II: Közigazgatástan* (Politics II: Administrative Law), Bp. 1905; and *Hatvan év tudományos mozgalmai között* (Amidst Sixty Years of Scholarly Activities), 2 vols., Bp. 1928-1935. Kmety's major works, all of them handbooks, are: *A magyar közigazgatási jog kézikönyve* (A Handbook of Hungarian Administrative Law), Bp. 1897; *A magyar közjog tankönyve* (Textbook of Hungarian Public Law), Bp. 1900; and *A magyar közjog alapintézményei* (The Fundamental Institutions of Hungarian Public Law), Bp. 1902. Balogh's major works are also primarily handbooks, including *A magyar államjog alaptanai* (The Fundamental Principles of Hungarian Public Law), Bp. 1895; and *Az állam tudománya: Alkotmánytan* (The Science of State: Constitutional Law), Bp. 1909.

24.) See below.

25.) On Timon see Gyula Vargyas, "Adalékok a magyar nacionalista állam- és jogtörténet kritikájához. Timon Ákos állam- és jogtörténetírása" (Contributions to the Critique of Hungarian Nationalist Constitutional and Legal History. The Constitutional and Legal Historical Scholarship of A. Timon), *TSz,* 13 (1970), 451-482; Eckhart, "Jog- és alkotmánytörténet," 269-320; *idem, A szentkorona eszme;* Degré, "Jogtörténetírás a dualizmus korában," 303-306; and Horváth, Dualizmuskori jogtörténetírásunk."

26.) See particularly Timon's following studies: *A szent korona 'es a koronázás közjogi jelentősége* (The Holy Crown and the Significance of Coronation in Public Law), Bp. 1907; *Die Entwicklung und Bedeutung des Begriffs der Heiligen Krone in der ungarischen Verfassung*, Berlin, 1910; *A szent korona elmélete* (The Doctrine of the Holy Crown), Bp. 1912; and his oft-reprinted textbook, *Magyar alkotmány- és jogtörténet különös tekintettel a nyugati államok jogfejlődésére*, Bp. 1902, 6th ed., 1923; and its German version: *Ungarische Verfassungs- und Rechtsgeschichte mit Bezug auf die Rechtsentwicklung der westlichen Staaten*, Berlin, 1904; 2nd ed., 1909.

27.) Paraphrased by Kardos, "Eckhart-vita," 1109.

28.) Timon, *A szent korona*, 5.

29.) *Ibid.*, 13.

30.) Marczali, *Ungarische Verfassungsgeschichte*, Tübingen, 1910; and *idem*, *Ungarisches Verfassungsrecht*, Tübingen, 1911. See also Ch. XV.

31.) On Óvári and Kolosvári see respectively Bálint Kolosvári, *Óvári Kelemen emlékezete* (Remembering K. Óvári), Bp. 1931; and József Illés, *Kolosvári Sándor emlékezete* (Remembering S. Kolosvári), Bp. 1929. Their significant works include: *Corpus Statutorum Hungariae Municipalium* (A Collection of Hungarian Municipal Laws), 8 vols. Bp. 1885-1904. They also translated and edited a new version of Werbőczi's *Tripartitum (Werbőczy István Hármaskönyve*, Bp. 1894); and participated in the editing of a new collection of Hungarian laws on the occasion of Hungary's "Millennium" in 1896, *Corpus Juris Hungarici — Magyar Törvénytár 1000-1895*, 2 vols., Bp. 1899-1900.

32.) On Király see Eckhart, *Jog- és államtudományi kar*, 609-610, 616, 618-620. Király's major works include: *Pozsony város joga a középkorban* (The Law Code of the City of Pozsony in the Middle Ages), Bp. 1894; and *Magyar alkotmány és jogtörténet* (Hungarian Constitutional and Legal History), Bp. 1908.

33.) On all of these historians see below.

34.) On Ferdinándy see Ödön Polner, *Három magyar közjogász* (Three Hungarian Scholars of Public Law), Bp. 1941. Ferdinándy's most relevant study, alluded to in the text, is his "A szent korona" (The Holy Crown), *BpSz*, 169 (1917), 161-198. His other significant works include: *A királyi méltóság és hatalom Magyarországon* (Royal Dignity and Power in Hungary), Bp. 1896; *Az aranybulla* (The Golden Bull), Bp. 1899; *A magyar alkotmány történelmi fejlődése* (The Historical Evolution of the Hungarian Constitution), Bp. 1907; *Staats und Verwaltungsrecht des Königreichs Ungarn*, Hanover, 1909; *A magyar alkotmányjog tankönyve* (A Textbook of Hungarian Constitutional Law), Bp. 1911; and *Magyarország közjoga* (Hungarian Public Law), Bp. 1912.

35.) See the various essays in Mihály Samu, *et al.*, *Tanulmányok a Horthy-korszak államáról és jogáról* (Studies on the State and Legal System of the Horthy Period), Bp. 1958; and Ilona Pándi, *Osztályok és pártok a Bethlen-konszolidáció időszakában* (Classes and Parties in the Period of Bethlen's Consolidation), Bp. 1966.

36.) *Emlékkönyv Szent István király halálának kilencszázadik évfordulójára* (Memorial Album for the Occasion of the 900th Anniversary of Saint Stephen's Death), 3 vols., ed. Justinián György Serédi, Bp. 1938. See also Lederer, *Történetirás*, 136-138.

37.) Serédi's preface in *Szent István-Emlékkönyv.*

38.) Bálint Hóman, "Szent István király," in *ibid.*, as quoted by Lederer, *Történetírás*, 137.

39.) On Széchenyi see George Bárány, *Stephen Széchenyi and the Awakening of Hungarian Nationalism, 1791-1841,* Princeton, 1968; Domokos Kosáry, "Széchenyi in Recent Western Literature," *AH,* 9 (1963), 255-278; Gyula Ortutay, "The Living Széchenyi," *NHQ,* 1 (1960), 36-49; and Francis S. Wagner, "Széchenyi and the Nationality Problems in the Habsburg Empire," *JCEA*, 20 (1960), 289-311.

40.) On Eötvös see the studies listed in Ch. V, n.7.

41.) Szekfű as quoted in Lederer, *Történetírás,* 141. See also Szekfű, "A szent korona-eszme" (The Doctrine of the Holy Crown), in his *Állam és nemzet,* 304-311.

42.) Miklós Nagy, "A szent korona eszméje" (The Doctrine of the Holy Crown), in *Szent István-Emlékkönyv,* II, 267-307.

43.) Eckhart, *A szentkorona eszme,* 4.

44.) For additional relevant studies see Ervin Pamlényi, "A szentistváni gondolat" (The Ideology of St. Stephen), *ÉT,* 17 (1962), 1507-1710; Görgy Balázs, "A szentistváni gondolat útja" (The Path of the Ideology of St. Stephen), *Vil,* 5 (1964), 432-437; and Sarlós, "A 'szentkorona tan'," 557-600.

45.) Eckhart, "Jog- és alkotmánytörténet," 278.

46.) *Ibid.,* 305.

47.) *Ibid.,* 286.

48.) *Ibid.,* 298. On this question of the alleged similarity between English and Hungarian constitutional developments see also Sándor Fest, "Magna Charta — Aranybulla" (Magna Charta — Golden Bull), *BpSz,* 234 (1934), 273-289 and 235 (1934), 41-63, which affirms this similarity; and Béla Handel, "Volt-e párhuzam az angol és a magyar alkotmány fejlődése között?" (Was there a Parallel Between the Evolution of the English and the Hungarian Constitutions?), *Sz,* 76 (1942), 123-128, which denies it.

49.) Eckhart, "Jog- és alkotmánytörténet," 301-304.

50.) Kardos, "Az Eckhart-vita," 1112-1113. Kardos also lists some of Eckhart's most vocal opponents.

51.) Zoltán Kérészy, *Hűbéri eszmék és magyar jogfejlődés. Észrevételek Eckhart Ferencnek "Jog- és alkotmánytörténet" cimű dolgozatára* (Feudal Concepts and Hungarian Constitutional Developments. Observations on F. Eckhart's Study entitled "Legal and Constitutional History), Bp. 1931.

52.) On Klebelsberg and on his support of Eckhart see the studies listed in Ch. VII, n. 2-3.

53.) See Sándor Domanovszky's review of the *New Paths* in *Sz,* 65 (1931), 273-279; and Elemér Mályusz's study, "Az Eckhart-vita" (The Eckhart Controversy), *Sz,* 65 (1931), 406-419, which is the first scholarly summary and critical commentary of the question.

54.) Mályusz, "Az Eckhart-vita," 417.

55.) Eckhart, *A szentkorona eszme története,* Bp. 1941. For another contemporary observation on this question by a prominent, but isolated historian see László Erdély, *Az ezer éves magyar alkotmány* (The Millennial Hungarian Constitution), Szeged, 1931.

56.) Eckhart's works in question are: *A bécsi udvar gazdaságpolitikája Magyarországon Mária Terézia Korában*, Bp. 1922; *A bécsi udvar gazdaságpolitikája Magyarországon, 1780-1815*, Bp. 1958; "A bécsi udvar jobbágypolitikája, 1761-1790," *Sz*, 90 (1956), 69-125; and *A földesúri büntetőbíráskodás a XVI-XVII. században*, Bp. 1954.

57.) Eckhart, *A magyar közgazdaság száz éve. 1841-1941*, Bp. 1941.

58.) Iván Berend and György Ránki, *A magyar gazdaság száz éve*, Bp. 1972. Its English version: *Hungary: A Century of Economic Development*, New York 1974.

59.) Eckhart, *Magyar alkotmány- és jogtörténet*, Bp. 1946. For the other contemporary synthesis of Hungarian constitutional developments see Holub's work mentioned in Ch. XV, n. 30, and below, this chapter.

60.) *MÉL*, I, 771. On Illés see also Alajos Degré, "Illés József, 1871-1944," *Sz*, 78 (1944), 157-158; *idem*, "Jogtörténetírás a dualizmus korában," 307; *idem*, "Jogtörténetírás a Horthy-korban," 80-81, 89 ff; and Csizmadia, "Jogtörténet-tudomány," 37-38.

61.) Illés's significant works include: *Az újkori alkotmányfejlődés elemei* (Elements of Modern Constitutional Developments), Bp. 1899; *Az Anjou-kori társadalom és az adózás* (Society and Taxation in the Anjou Period), Bp. 1900; *Magyar házassági vagyonjog az Árpádok korában* (Hungarian Property Rights in Marriage in the Age of the Árpads), Bp. 1900; *A magyar szerződési jog az Árpádok korában* (Hungarian Law of Contracts in the Age of the Árpáds), Bp. 1901; *A törvényes öröklés rendje az Árpádok korában* (The System of Legal Inheritance in the Age of the Árpáds), Bp. 1904; *Öröklés a női vagyonban az Árpádok korában* (Inheritance of Female Property in the Age of the Árpáds), Bp. 1906; and *A jobbágyság társadalmi és jogi helyzetének megalakulása* (The Development of the Social and Legal Position of the Serfs), Bp. 1908.

62.) Illés, *Bevezetés a magyar jogtörténetbe*, Bp. 1910; rev. ed., Bp. 1930. This work was not so much a synthesis of Hungarian constitutional evolution, as a history of the significant sources of Hungarian constitutionalism, with emphasis on the *Tripartitum*.

63.) See particularly Degré, "Jogtörténetírás a Horthy-korban;" and Ferenc Glatz's summary of the debate on the above study in *Sz*, 103 (1969), 911-917. I have also relied on Dr. Degré's letter to me, dated April 2, 1974.

64.) On Kérészy see Csizmadia, *Jogtörténeti oktatás*, 107-118; Szabó, *Erzsébet Tudomdnyegyetem*, Pt. I, 137, Pt. II, 467-472; and Degré's and Glatz's above-cited studies (n. 63).

65.) Kérészy, *Katholikus Egyházi jog a Codex Juris Canonici alapján* (Catholic Ecclesiastical Law on the Basis of the Codex Juris Canonici), 4 vols., Pécs, 1927.

66.) Kérészy, *Az egyházjog tankönyve*, Bp. 1903.

67.) Kérészy's related works include: *A ius exclusivae (vétójog) a pápaválasztásoknál* (The Ius Exclusiviae (Right of Veto) in Papal Elections), Bp. 1904; *A katolikus autonómia közreműködése a főkegyúri jog gyakorlásában* (The Catholic Autonomy's Cooperation in the Exercise of Patrimonial Rights), Bp. 1912; and *A papi rend törvénykezési kiváltsága az egyházi jog és régi magyar büntetőjog szerint* (The Juridical Privileges of the Ecclesiastical Order in Accordance with Canon Law and the Ancient Hungarian Penal Code), Pécs, 1936.

68.) Kérészy's studies on the dietary system include: *A vármegyék szereplése a magyar politikai élet terén, 1526-1848* (The Participation of the Counties in Hungarian Political Life, 1526-1848), Debrecen, 1896; *A magyar országgyűlések eredete és szervezetük fejlődése a rendi országgyűlések alakulásának kezdetén* (The Origins and Organizational Development of Hungarian Diets in the Age of the Beginnings of Feudal Diets), Debrecen, 1898; *Rendi országgyűlések tanácskozási módja* (The System of Debate at Feudal Diets), Kassa, 1906; *Receptió, paritás és főrendházi képviselet* (Reception, Parity and Representation in the House of Lords), Bp. 1907; and *A magyar rendi országgyűlés két táblájának kialakulása* (The Development of the Two Houses in the Hungarian Feudal Diet), Bp. 1925.

69.) See n. 51. Some of Kérészy's other noteworthy publications include: *Adalékok a magyar kamarai pénzügyigazgatás történetéhez* (Contributions to the History of the Financial Administration of the Hungarian Treasury), Bp. 1916; and *Politika mint művészet és tudomány* (Politics as Art and Science), Bp. 1926.

70.) For Somogyi see below.

71.) Vinkler, *A magyar igazságszolgáltatási szervezet és polgári eljárás a mohácsi vésztől 1848-ig*, 2 vols., Pécs, 1921-1927. On Vinkler see Szabó, *Erzsebét Tudományegyetem*, Pt. II, 1038-1041; and Degré, "Jogtörténetírás a Horthy-korban," 86-87.

72.) On Iványi see Varga, *Debreceni Tudományegyetem*, I, 205; Csizmadia, "Jogtörténet-tudomány," 42-43; and Degré, "Jogtörténetírás a Horthy-korban," 83-84.

73.) For a list of Iványi's related publications see *MÉL*, I, 785; and *RNL, XX, 419, XXI, 464.*

74.) Iványi, *A városi polgárjog keletkezése, figyelemmel Buda és Pest városokra* (The Origins of Urban Citizenship Rights, with Special Attention to the Cities of Buda and Pest), Bp. 1936; and *Magyar alkotmány- és jogtörténeti jegyzet*, 2 vols., Debrecen, 1925 (mimeographed).

75.) On Baranyai see Varga, *Debreceni Tudományegyetem*, 205-206, 303; Endre Varga, "Baranyai Béla, 1881-1945," *Sz, 79-80 (1945-1946), 302; Csizmadia, "Jogtörténet-tudomány," 43; and Degré, "Jogtörténetírás a Horthy-korban," 82-83.*

76.) On this unpublished work see Ch. VII, n. 22, and the relevant text.

77.) Baranyai's most important studies include: *Somogy vármegye nemes családai* (The Noble Families of Somogy County), Bp. 1914; *Zsigmond király úgynevezett sárkányredje* (The So-called Dragon Order of King (Emperor) Sigismund), reprinted from *Sz*, 59-60 (1925-1926); and *Lengyel királykoronázás* (Polish Royal Coronation), Karcag, 1927.

78.) See Ch. XV.

79.) On Holub's publicatons see Ch. XV n. 30-32.

80.) On Ferenc Somogyi see Szabó, *Erzsébet Tudományegyetem*, Pt. 1, 137, Pt. II, 864-868; *Krónika*, IV-V, 259-260; Várdy, *Magyarságtudomány*, 10; *idem*, "Dr. Somogyi Ferenc, magyar jog- és művelődestörténész" (Dr. F. Somogyi, Legal and Cultural Historian), *Magyarság* (Pittsburgh), March 27, 1973; Csizmadia, "Jogtörténet-tudomány," 41-42; and *idem*, *Jogtörténeti oktatás*, 114. Somogyi's most significant works include: *Az ősiség intézménye és a hűbéri vagyonjog* (The Institution of Entail and Feudal Property Rights), Pécs, 1931; *Zsidójogunk fejlódésének áttekintése* (A Summary of Our Jewish

Law Codes), Pécs, 1936; *Végrendelkezés nemesi magánjogunk szerint 1000-től 1715-ig* (Testamentary Disposition According to Our Noble Civil Law from 1000 to 1715), Pecs, 1938; *Családiság és ősiség* (Family Inheritance and Entail), Pécs, 1938 (the latter being a polemical study against Eckhart's criticism of Somogyi's previous work); *Társadalompolitikai törvényalkotás Werbőczy előtt* (Social Legislation Before Werbőczy), Kassa, 1943; and *Társadalompolitikai törvényalkotás Werbőczy után* (Social Legislation After Werbőczy), Kassa, 1944. Somogyi's recently published *Küldetés: A magyarság története* (Mission: The History of the Hungarians), Cleveland, 1973, is his major synthesis and interpreation of Hungarian historical evolution. The first volume of his accompaning history of Hungarian literary culture, *Magyar nyelv és irodalom 1825-ig* (Hungarian Language and Literature to 1825), Cleveland, 1975, has just appeared in print, with two additional volumes to follow.

81.) On Degré see his own study, "Jogtörténetírás a Horthy-korban," 98-99; Csizmadia, "Jogtörténet-tudomány," 41; and Glatz, "Jogtörténetírás." I have also relied on Dr. Degré's letter to me, dated January 19, 1974. Degré's most significant works include: *A négyeskönyv perjogi anyaga* (The Law Suit Aspects of the Quadripartitum), Bp. 1936; *A négyeskönyv büntetőjogi elve* (The Principles of Penal Law in the Quadripartitum), Bp. 1936; *Magyar halászati jog a középkorban* (Hungarian Fishing Laws in the Middle Ages), Bp. 1939; *A XVI-XVII. századi erdélyi büntetőjog vázlata* (An Outline of 16th-17th Century Transylvanian Criminal Law), with Pál Angyal, Bp. 1943; *Feudalis gyámsági jog Magyarországon* (Feudal Guardianship Law in Hungary), Bp. 1955 (Academy Dissertation); *Megyei közgyűlésk a XVI-XVII. században* (County Assemblies in the 16th-17th Centuries), Bp. 1971; *Elemente des römischen Rechtes im Vermögensrecht der ungarischen Leibeigenen,* Szeged, 1970; and others.

82.) On György Bónis see Degré, "Jogtörténetírás a Horthy-korban," 96-97; Csizmadia, "Jogtörténet-tudomány," 43; and *Erdély Magyar Egyeteme,* 395. I have also relied on Dr. Degré's letter to me, dated January 19, 1974. Bónis is one of the most prolific scholars of Hungarian constitutional history. His significant works include: *Birósági szervezetünk megújitása* (The Revival of Our Court System), Bp. 1935; *Magyar jog — Székely jog* (Hungarian Law — Székely Law), Kolozsvár, (1942); *Hűbériség és rendiség a középkori magyar jogban* (Estatism and Feudalism in Medieval Hungarian Law), Bp. 1947; *Hajnóczy József a jogtudós* (J. Hajnóczy the Legal Scholar), Bp. 1952; *István Király* (King (St.) Stephen), Bp. 1956; *Buda és Pest birósági gyakorlata a török kiűzése után* (The Court System of Buda and Pest after the Expulsion of the Turks), Bp. 1962; *A jogtudó értelmiség a középkori nyugat és középeurópában* (Legal Intelligentsia in Medieval Western and Central Europe), Bp. 1972; *Középkori jogunk elemei* (Elements of Our Medieval Law), Bp. 1972; *A jogtudó értelmiség a Mohács előtti Magyarországon* (Legal Intelligentsia in Hungary Prior to Mohács), Bp. 1971; and many others, including numerous shorter studies in Western languages. Bónis has also co-authored, with Márton Sarlós, the first Marxist synthesis of Hungarian constitutional history, *Egyetemes állam- és jogtörténet* (Universal State and Constitutional History), Bp. 1957.

83.) On these young scholars see Degré, "Jogtörténetírás a Horthy-korban," 95-99. I have also relied on Dr. Degré's letter to me, dated January 19, 1974.

84.) Andor Csizmadia, Kálmán Kovács and László Asztalos, *Magyar állam- és jogtörténet,* ed. Andor Csizmadia, Bp. 1972. Some of Csizmadia's other major works include: *Magyar városok kegyurasága* (Patrimonial Rights of Hungarian Cities), Győr, 1937; *Magyar városi jog. Reformtörekvések a magyar városi közigazgatásban* (Hungarian Urban Law. Reform Tendencies in Hungarian Urban Administration), Kolozsvár, 1941; *A feudális jogintezmenyek továbbélése a Horthy-korban* (The Continued Existence of Fuedal Institutions in the Horthy Period), Bp. 1961; *Az egyházi mezővárosok jogi helyzete és küzdelmük a felszabadulásért a XVIII. században* (The Legal Position of Ecclesiastical Oppidums and their Struggles for Emancipation in the 18th Century), Bp. 1962; *A magyar választási rendszer 1848-1849-ben* (Hungarian Election System in 1848-1849), Bp. 1963; *A pécsi egyetem a középkorban* (The University of Pécs in the Middle Ages), Bp. 1965; and *A nemzeti bizottságok állami tevékenysége (1944-1945)* (The Political Activities of the National Committees (1944-2945)), Bp. 1968. Csizmadia has also edited a number of major source and essay collections in constitutional history, and has authored an English language study, "The Origins of University Education in Hungary," *AJ,* 9 (1967), 127-160.

Chapter XIX

EUROPEAN AND WORLD ("UNIVERSAL") HISTORY STUDIES

1.) For a short summary of this question see Vardy, *Historiography,* 44-45, 75-76.

2.) The first incumbent of the Budapest chair of world history was Ferenc Somhegyi (1813-1879), who held his chair from 1866 to 1879. Cf. Szentpétery, *Bölcsészeti kar,* 452-454, 673.

3.) *Erdély Magyar Egyeteme,* 185. The first incumbent of the chair of world history at Kolozsvár (later Szeged) was Gedeon Ladányi (1824-1886), who held his chair between 1872 and 1886. For the next five years (1886-1891) it was held by Gyula Lánczy (1850-1911), and then for over three decades (1892-1925) by Sándor Márki, followed by József Fógel (1926-1941) and László Tóth (1942-1950).

4.) The trisection of the Budapest chair of world history in 1879 resulted in separate chairs for ancient, medieval and modern history. The chair of ancient history was held in succession by Ferenc Ribáry (1878-1880), József Hampel (1881-1891), Gyula Schwarcz (1894-1900), Bálint Kuzsinszky (1901-1914), István Heinlein (1915-1941), and Aurél Förster (1942-1947); the chair of medieval history by Henrik Marczali (1878-1879), Ferenc Salamon (1880-1891), Gyula Lánczy (1891-1911), Antal Áldásy (1912-1932), and after a period of vacancy by Péter Váczy (1942-1961); and the chair of modern history by Aladár Ballagi (1880-1924), Dávid Angyal (1925-1929), and István Hajnal (1930-1956). Cf. Szentpétery, *Bölcsészeti kar,* 527-529, 673-674.

5.) The world history chair at Pozsony (later Pécs) was held in succession by Imre Lukinich (1918-1923), Antal Hodinka (1923-1935), and László Tóth (1935-1940), when the whole Faculty of Philosophy was terminated. Its counterpart at Debrecen was held by József Pokoly (1914-1922), and Dezső Szabó (1924-1959). Cf. Szabó, *Erzsébet Tudományegyetem*, Pt. II, 382-388, 643-650, 971-973; and Varga, *Debreceni Tudományegyetem*, 197-198, 202-204.

6.) Ferenc Somhegyi (Schröck), *Egyetemes világtörténet*, 3 vols., Pest, 1851-1856.

7.) *Ribáry Képes Világtörténete*, 8 vols., 1878-1886. The three volumes on the middle ages were authored by H. Marczali. See Ch. XV.

8.) Sándor Márki's world history consists of two parts: *Az ó- és középkor története* (Ancient and Medieval History), 2 vols., Bp. 1910; and *Az újkor és legújabb kor története* (History of the Modern and Recent Age), 2 vols., Bp. 1911. On Márki see Ch. V, n. 16.

9.) See Ch. V, n. 23.

10.) *Világtörténet* (World History), by the Historical Institute, the Oriental Institute and the Institute of the History of Material Culture of the Soviet Academy of Sciences, 10 vols., Bp. 1963-1967.

11.) On the tenures of these scholars see n. 4 above. On Ballagi and Áldásy see György Balanyi, "Ballagi Aladár, 1853-1928," *Sz*, 61-62 (1927-1928), 845-847; Béla Zolnai, "Thaly, Ballagi, Riedl," *IT*, 43 (1961), 318-319; József Holub, "Áldásy Antal, 1869-1939," *Sz*, 66 (1932), 366-367; István Miskolczy, *Áldásy Antal emlékezete* (Remembering A. Áldásy), Bp. 1935; and Bálint Hóman, "Áldásy Antal," in his *Történetírás*, 521-522. On David Angyal see Ch. XV; on Heinlein see Endre Fischer, "Heinlein István, 1874-1945," *Sz*, 79-80 (1945-1946), 304-305; and on Förster see Egon Maróti, *Ho koinos polemos. In memoriam Aurelii Förster*, Berlin, 1962.

12.) On Márki see Ch. V; and on Fógel see György Balanyi, *Fógel József emlékezete* (Remembering J. Fógel), Bp. 1941.

13.) On Tóth see Szabó, *Erzsébet Tudományegyetem*, Pt. II, 971-973; and *Erdély Magyar Egyeteme*, 401.

14.) On Lukinich and Hodinka see Chs. XV and XVI.

15.) On Pokoly see Varga, *Debreceni Tudományegyetem*, 197-198.

16.) On Szabó see Ch. XV.

17.) On Horváth see *MÉL*, I, 748.

18.) Horváth's works which deal with the origins and consequences of Trianon include: *A háboru diplomáciai előkészitése 1901-1914* (The Diplomatic Background to the War, 1901-1914), Bp. 1914; *Hungary and Servia. The Fate of Southern Hungary*, Bp. 1919; *A Balkán-kérdés utolsó fázisa, 1895-1920* (The Last Phase of the Balkan Question, 1895-1920), Bp. 1922; *A trianoni béke megalkotása, 1915-1920-ig* (The Manufacturing of the Treaty of Trianon, 1915-1920), Bp. 1924; *Responsibility for the War and for the Treaty of Trianon*, Bp. 1928; *The Banate*, Bp. 1931; *Ungarn und der Weltkrieg*, Bp. 1931; *Transylvania and the History of the Rumanians. A Reply to Professor R.W. Seton-Watson*, Bp. 1935; and *The Hungarian Question. A Bibliography on Hungary and Central Europe*, Bp. 1938.

19.) Horváth's significant works on Hungarian diplomacy include: *A magyar kormány adriai politikája, 1848-49* (The Adriatic Policy of the Hungarian Government, 1848-49), Bp. 1927; *Magyar diplomácia, 1815-1918* (Hungarian Diplomacy, 1815-1918), Bp. 1928; *Magyarország útja az Adriához* (Hungary's Road to the Adriatic), Bp. 1932; and *Magyar diplomácia — magyar diplomaták* (Hungarian Diplomacy — Hungarian Diplomats), Bp.

1941. Some of Horváth's major syntheses of European history include: *A legújabb kor politikai története, 1815-1910*(The Political History of the Recent Age, 1815-1910), Bp. 1913; *Diplomáciai történelem, 1815-1920-ig* (Diplomatic History, 1815-1920), 2 vols., Bp. 1921; and an accompanying collection of documents, *Szövegek a diplomáciai történelemhez, 1815-1920-ig* (Texts for Diplomatic History, 1815-1918), 4 parts, Bp. 1921-1922. Horváth also authored books on America, Asia the Near East and Africa.

20.) On Balanyi see Mihály Medvigy. "Balanyi György emlékezete" (Remembering G. Balanyi), *Vig,* 28 (1963), 360-361; and *MÉL,* I, 80.

21.) Balanyi had authored or edited fifty-one independent works and over two hundred articles. Some of his most significant political histories are: *Világpolitika* (World Politics), Bp. 1918; *A Balkán-probléma fejlődése, 1856-1914*(The Development of the Balkan Problem, 1856-1914), Bp. 1920; and *A római kérdés* (The Roman Question), Bp. 1929. His significant works on religious history include: *A szerzetesség története* (The History of Monasticism), Bp. 1923; *Magyar piaristák a XIX. és XX. században* (The Hungarian Piarists in the 19th and the 20th Century), Bp. 1942; and *A magyar piarista rendtartomány története* (The History of the Hungarian Piarist Province), Bp. 1943.

22.) On Alföldi see Varga, *Debreceni Tudományegyetem,* 196; *ELTE története,* 584-585; *Hungarians in America,* 2nd ed., 5, 3rd ed., 4; and *Prominent Hungarians,* 10.

23.) Some of Alföldi's monographic studies published before 1945 include: *Pannóniai agyagminták és vonatkozásai a császárkorra* (Pannonian Clay Moulds and their Implications on the Imperial Age), Bp. 1918; *Der Untergang der Römerherrschaft in Pannonien,* Berlin and Leipzig, 1924; *Magyarország népei és a Római Birodalom* (Hungary's Peoples and the Roman Empire), Bp. 1934; and *Zu den Schicksalen Siebenbürgen im Altertum,* Bp. 1944. For a complete list of Alföldi's publications until 1964 see *Bonner Historia — Augusta Colloquium 1964-1965* (Antiquitas ser. 4, vol. 3), 66. See also *Directory of American Scholars,* 6th ed., New York and London, 1974, 9.

24.) On Hajnal see Imre Wellmann, "Hajnal István, 1892-1956," *Sz,* 90 (1956), 830-833; and *MÉL,* I, 657-658.

25.) Hajnal, *IV. Béla Király kancelláriájáról* (On the Chancery of King Béla IV.), Bp. 1914.

26.) Hajnal's related works include: *Irástörténet az írásbeliség felújulása korából* (The History of Writing in the Period of the Revival of Literacy), Bp. 1921; *Le rôle sociale de l'écriture et l'evolution Europeenne,* Brussels, 1934; *Vergleichende Schriftproben zur Entwicklung und Verbreitung der Schrift im 12-13. Jahrhundert,* Bp. 1943; and *L'enseignement de l'écriture aux universités médiévales,* Bp. 1954.

27.) Hajnal, "Történelem és szociológia" (History and Sociology), *Sz,* 73 (1939), 1-32, 137-166; *idem,* "A kis nemzetek történetírásának munkaközösségéről" (About the Collaboration of the Historiographies of Small Nations), *Sz,* 76 (1942), 1-42, 133-165; and *idem,* "Külföldi kritikák egy magyar írástörténeti munkáról" (Foreign Critiques about a Hungarian Work on the History of Writing), *Sz,* 90 (1956), 470-473.

28.) Hajnal, *Az újkor története* (History of the Modern Age), Bp. 1936. The philosophical-bibliographical essay is on pp. 662-667. For a contemporary assessment see István Dékány's review, *Sz,* 78 (1944), 510-511.

29.) Hajnal, *Az újkor története,* 662.
30.) *Ibid.*
31.) *Ibid.,* 663.
32.) All quotations on this and the next four pages are from *ibid.*
33.) For additional analyses on Hajnal's philosophy of history see Károly Irinyi, "Hajnal István szociológiai történetszemléletéről" (About I. Hajnal Sociological View of History), *AIHUSD,* I (1962), 167-183; and Lederer, *Történetírás,* 154-159.
34.) Hajnal, "Osztálytársadalom" (Class Society), in *Magyar művelődéstörténet,* V, 167-200. Hajnal's other significant works include: *A Kossuth-emigráció Törökországban* (The Kossuth Emigration in Turkey), Bp. 1927; *Esterházy Miklós nádor lemondása* (The Resignation of Palatinate M. Esterházy), Bp. 1929; *Esterházy Miklós nádor iratai. I.* (The Papers of Palatinate M. Esterházy. I.), Bp. 1930; and *A Batthyány-kormány külpolitikája* (The Foreign Policy of the Batthyany Government), Bp. 1957.
35.) *Egyetemes történet,* ed. by Bálint Hóman, Gyula Szekfű and Károly Kerényi, 4 vols., Bp. 1935-1937.
36.) See n. 28.
37.) *Az ókor története,* ed. by Károly Kerényi, Bp. 1935. On Kerényi see Mihály Ferdinándy, "Kerényi Károly," *Nemzetőr* (München), 18 (May 1973); *idem,* "Kerényi Karóly humanista tanítása" (The Teachings of K. Kerényi, the Humanist), *Nemzetőr*(July-August 1973); and *MIL,* I, 626.
38.) Besides Kerényi himself, the authors of this volume include Franz Altheim (Frankfurt), Antal Dávid (Budapest), Sándor Gallus (Budapest), Gyula Hornyánszky (Budapest), Ulrich Kahrstedt (Göttingen), Ernst Kronemann (Breslau) and Kenneth Scott (Cleveland-Western Reserve University).
39.) Váczy, *A középkor története* (The History of the Medieval Age), Bp. 1936; and Iványi-Grünwald, *A legújabb kor története*(The History of the Most Recent Age), Bp. 1937.
40.) On Váczy and his publications see Ch. XI.
41.) On Deér and his publications see Ch. XI.
42.) On Iványi-Grünwald and his publications see Ch. XI.
43.) Quotations from Iványi-Grünwald, *A legújabb kor története,* 651.

Chapter XX

AUXILIARY AND ALLIED SCIENCES OF HISTORY

1.) The teaching of the auxiliary sciences at the University of Budapest began in 1777, when two separate chairs were established in this area: One for diplomatics, and one for heraldry and sfragistics. In 1790 the two chairs were merged into the chair of diplomatics and heraldry, and in 1950 were renamed the chair of auxiliary sciences. The incumbents of this chair during the past century were Árpád Horvát (1846-1894) with various titles, László Fejérpataky (1895-1923), Imre Szentpétery (1923-1950), Emma Lederer (1950-1969) and István Sinkovics (1969-). Cf. Szentpétery, *Bölcsészeti kar,* 293-297, 675; and *ELTE története,* 529-535. See also Szentpétery's summary in Hóman, *New Paths,* 321-352.

2.) On Árpád Horvát see Árpád Károlyi, *Horvát Árpád emlékezete* (Remembering Á. Horvát), Bp. 1904. Horvát's significant works include: *Oklevéltani jegyzetek* (Notes on Diplomatics), 3 vols., Bp. 1880-1884; and *Mabillion János, a diplomatica megalapítója* (Jean Mabillion, the Founder of Diplomatics), Bp. 1885.

3.) On these developments during the dualist period see Ch. V. Of the enumerated historians all but János Karácsonyi had already been mentioned. On Karácsonyi see Dezső Csánki, "Karácsonyi János, 1858-1929," *Sz,* 63-64 (1929-1930), 1-4. Karácsonyi's significant works include: *Szent István király oklevelei és a Szilveszter-Bulla* (St. Stephen's Charters and the Bull of Sylvester II), Bp. 1891; *Az aranybulla* (The Golden Bull), Bp. 1899; *Magyar nemzetségek a XIV. század közepéig* (Hungarian Clans up to the Middle of the 14th Century), 3 vols., Bp. 1900-1902; and *Hamis, hibáskeltű és keltezétlen oklevelek jegyzéke 1400-ig* (A Register of Forged, Misdated and Undated Charters up to 1400), Bp. 1902. Among his synthesizing works, those that deal with the history of the Catholic Church are the most important: *Magyarország egyháztörténete 970-től 1900-ig* (Hungary's Church History from 970 to 1900), Nagyvárad, 1906; and *A görög-katólikus magyarok eredete* (The Origins of the Greek Catholic Hungarians), Bp. 1924.

4.) See Chs. V and XV.

5.) See Ferenc Donászy, "A magyar heraldika múltja, jelene és jövője" (The Past, Present and Future of Hungarian Heraldry), in *Szentpétery-Emlékkönyv,* 130-141. On the Hungarian Heraldic and Genealogical Association see also Magyary, *Tudománypolitika,* 492-493.

6.) In addition to Horvát's and Karácsonyi's above-mentioned relevant works, these handbooks include: the *Monumenta Hungariae Heraldica,* vols. I-II, ed. László Fejérpataky, Bp. 1901-1902; vol. III, ed. Antal Áldásy, Bp. 1926, which contains the description of close to 100 Hungarian coats of arms; the Hungarian Heraldic and Genealogical Association's *Magyar nemzetségi zsebkönyv* (Handbook of Hungarian Genealogy), 2 vols., Bp. 1888-1905, which contains the genealogies of Hungary's aristocratic families (vol. I) and some of the non-titled familes as well (vol. II); Albert Nyáry, *A heraldika vezérfonala* (An Outline of Heraldry), Bp. 1886; Oszkár Bárczay, *A heraldika kézikönyve* (A Handbook of Heraldry), Bp. 1897; József Csoma, *Magyar nemzetségi cimerek* (Coats of Arms of the Hungarian Clans), Bp. 1903; *idem, A magyar heraldika korszakai* (The Epochs of Hungarian Heraldry), Bp. 1913; Béla Kempelen, *Nemesség* (Nobility), Bp. 1907; and Imre Szentpétery, *Oklevéltani naptár* (Calendar of Diplomatics), Bp. 1912.

7.) In addition to the above handbooks, there are such related compilations in the area of heraldry and genealogy as Iván Nagy's *Magyarország csalddai címerekkel és nemzetségrendi táblákkal* (Hungary's Families, with Coat of Arms and Genealogical Tables), 13 vols., Pest, 1857-1868; Béla Kempelen, *Magyar nemes családok címerei* (Coats of Arms of Hungarian Noble Families), Bp. 1914. Kempelen's compilations are less than fully reliable.

8.) See Ch. VII and Appendix.

9.) The traditional auxiliary sciences generally included diplomatics, palaeography, epigraphy, sfragistics, heraldry, numismatics, genealogy and chronology. The examination of the above handbooks reveal that half of them are not even represented. Numismatics, however, was well represented by the Hungarian Numismatic Association, founded in 1901. The society's most significant publication was László Réthy's *Corpus Nummorum Hungariae*, 2 vols., Bp. 1899-1907, which can also be added to the list of the relevant handbooks. Cf. Szentpétery, *Bölcsészeti kar*, 297-301; *idem*, "Történelmi segédtudományok," in Hóman, *New Paths*, 346-347; and Magyary, *Tudománypolitika*, 492-493.

10.) See Ch. VII.

11.) Gyula Kornis, *Történetfilozófia*, Bp. 1924; and István Dékány, *A történettudomány módszertana*, Bp. 1925. See also Chs. VII and IX.

12.) Hungarian historians are now engaged in the writing of the history of Hungarian historiography in conjunction with the ten-volume history of Hungary now under preparation. On this proposed synthesis see Varga, *Vita;* Ervin Pamlényi, "A Magyarország története szerkesztésének módszeréről" (On the Editorial Methodology of the (Proposed) History of Hungary), *TSz*, 12 (1969), 66-82; Emil Niederhauser-Tibor Kolossa-László Márkus, "Az újkori magyar történet kritikai-históriográfiai áttekintése" (The Critical-Historiographical Review of Modern Hungarian History), *TSz*, 12 (1969), 283-336; and Ferenc Glatz, "A Magyarország története munkálatainak helyzetéről" (On the (Proposed) History of Hungary), *TSz*, 14 (1971), 239-253.

13.) Flegler, *A magyar történetírás történelme*, tr. József Szinnyei Jr., Bp. 1877.

14.) Lederer, *A Magyar polgári történetírás rövid története*, Bp. 1969. Both Flegler's and Lederer's works have been cited many times.

15.) On Flegler and on his relationship to Szalay see Ágnes R. Várkonyi, "Históriográfiai törekvések Magyarországon a XIX. században" (Historiographical Tendencies in Hungary in the 19th Century), *Sz*, 103 (1969), 939-989, especially pp. 965-971. See also S(ándor) Sz(ilágyi), "Flegler Sándor," *Sz*, 27 (1893), 80-81.

16.) Alexander Flegler, *Erinnerungen an Ladislaus von Szalay und seine Geschichte des ungarischen Reiches*, Leipzig, 1866.

17.) Lederer's work is divided into two parts (Pt. I to 1917, and Pt. II between 1917 and 1945). She prefaced each section with a summary of contemporary historiographical developments in Western Europe. European and Hungarian developments, however, are not integrated.

18.) Many of the relevant studies of these scholars have been cited in the footnotes of this work.

19.) *A magyar irodalom története*, ed. Zsolt Beöthy, 2 vols., Bp. 1899-1900.

20.) Bálint Hóman, *Történetírás és forráskritika*, Bp. 1938. Both Beöthy's and Hóman's work has been cited often.

21.) Bálint Hóman, *A magyar történetírás első korszaka*, Bp. 1923; *idem*, *Tudományos történetírásunk megalapítása a XVIII. században*, Bp. 1920-1921; and *idem*, *A forráskutatás és forráskirtika története Magyarországon*, Bp. 1925. All three of these works were reprinted in Hóman's *Történetírás*, 251-282, 353-437.

22.) See Ch. VII.

23.) Elemér Mályusz, *Thuróczy János krónikája*, Bp. 1944; and *idem*, *A magyar történettudomány*, Bp. 1942.

24.) Elemér Mályusz, *A Thuróczy-krónika és forrásai*, Bp. 1967. On Mályusz and his scholarship see Ch. XII.

25.) C.A. Macartney, *Studies in the Early Hungarian Historical Sources*, vols. I-II, Bp. 1938; vol. III, Bp. 1941; vols. IV-V (printed as III-IV), Bp. 1940 (1942); vols. VI-VII, Oxford, 1951.

26.) C.A. Macartney, *Medieval Hungarian Historians. A Critical and Analytical Guide*, Cambridge, 1953.

27.) C.A. Macartney, *Magyars in the Ninth Century*, Cambridge, 1930.

28.) Macartney's other related studies include: "Pascua Romanorum," *Sz*, 74 (1940), 1-11; "Dlugosz et la Chronica Budense," *RHC*, 24 (1946), 301-308; and "The Hungarian National Chronicle," *MH*, 16 (1964), 3-10. His works of non-historiographical nature are: *The Social Revolution in Austria*, Cambridge, 1926; *National States and National Minorities*, Oxford, 1934; *Hungary*, London, 1934 (Hungarian version, Bp. 1935); *Hungary and Her Successors*, Oxford, 1937; *Problems of the Danubian Basin*, Cambridge, 1942; *October Fifteenth: A History of Modern Hungary, 1929-1945*, 2 vols., Edinburgh, 1957; *Independent Eastern Europe*, with A.W. Palmer, New York, 1962; and *Hungary: A Short History*, Edinburgh, 1962.

29.) Albert Gárdonyi, *A segédtudományok története*, Bp. 1926.

30.) On Imre Szentpétery see Lajos Elekes, "Szentpétery Imre, 1878-1950," *Sz*, 86 (1950), 471; and Győző Ember, "Szentpétery Imre," *AkÉ* (1950), 99.

31.) Imre Szentpétery, *Magyar oklevéltan*, Bp. 1930.

32.) *Scriptores rerum Hungaricarum tempore ducum regumque stirpis Arpadianae gestarum*, ed. Emericus Szentpétery, 2 vols., Bp. 1937-1938.

33.) For Szentpétery's *Chronologia* and *Magyar okleveltan* see Ch. VII and Appendix.

34.) For a list of Szentpétery's publications see *Szentpétery-Emlékkönyv*, 572-579. In addition to his already mentioned works Szentpétery's major monographs include: *Az újkor kezdete* (The Start of the Modern Age), Marosvásárhely, 1901; *A borsmonostori apátság árpádkori oklevelei* (The Árpádian Diplomas of the Abbey of Borsmonostor), Bp. 1916; *Szent István király pécsváradi és pécsi alapítólevele* (King St. Stephen's Founding Charters of Pécs and Pécsvárad), Bp. 1918; and *Az árpádházi királyok okleveleinek kritikai jegyzéke — Regesta Regum Stirpis Arpadianae Critico-Diplomatica* (A Critical Register of the Diplomas of the Árpádian Kings), I/1, Bp. 1923; I/2, Bp. 1927; I/3, Bp. 1930; II/1, Bp. 1943. This work was continued by István Borsa, based on Szentpétery's manuscripts, II/2-3, Bp. 1961.

35.) See his cited essay in Hóman, *New Paths*, 325-326.

36.) Varga, *Debreceni Tudományegyetem*, 196. During the dualist period for a while the University of Kolozsvár also had a special chair for the historical auxiliary sciences. But after the death of the first incumbent, Henrik Finály (1825-1898), that chair remained empty until 1940, when Loránd Szilágyi (b. 1908) was appointed to it. After only four years at Kolozsvár (1940-1944), Szilágyi was obliged to transfer to Budapest. Cf. *Erdély Magyar Egyeteme*, 185, 403; and *ELTE története*, 526-541. On Finály see Sándor Márki, *Finály Henrik emlékezete* (Remembering H. Finály), Bp. 1899.

Chapter XXI

CONCLUSIONS AND THE BEGINNINGS OF MARXIST HISTORIOGRAPHY

1.) See end of Ch. V.

2.) On Ervin Szabó see the introductory essay to his selected works, *Szabó Ervin válogatott írásai* (The Selected Writings of E. Szabó), ed. Piroska R. Török, Bp. 1958, 5-10. See also Révai, *Válogatott írások*, I, 85-123; and Zoltán Horváth, *Magyar századforduló* (Hungarian Fin de Siècle), Bp. 1961, 388-405. For additional studies on Szabó see the list in his *Selected Writings*, 501-505.

3.) Szabó, *Társadalmi és pártharcok az 48-49-es magyar forradalomban*, with an introductory study on E. Szabó by Oszkár Jászi, Vienna 1921; 2nd ed., Bp. 1946. For a complete list of Szabó's works, see his *Selected Writings*, 483-500.

4.) On Erik Molnár see György Ránki's introductory essay to Molnár's selected writings, *Válogatott tanulmányok (Selected Studies)*, ed. György Ránki, Bp. 1969, 7-41, which later also appeared separately in a booklet form. See also Ervin Pamlényi, "Molnár Erik történetírásáról" (About E. Molnár's Historical Writings), *Sz*, 98 (1964), 931-942; and Zsigmond Pál Pach, "Molnár Erik társadalomtörténet-írásáról" (About E. Molnár's Writings as a Social Historian), *Sz*, 101 (1967), 1119-1125.

5.) Molnár, *Az Árpádkori társadalom*, 2 vols., Bp. 1943. Both volumes appeared under the pseudonym Lajos Szentmiklósy. For a complete list of Molnár's works see his *Válogatott tanulmdnyok*, 497-513, mentioned above.

6.) On József Révai see Mihály Bimbó, "Révai József és a 'népi írók' történetszemléletének értékelése" (J. Révai and the Evaluation of the Philosophy of History of the 'Populist Writers'), *SSS*, 4 (1967, 116-124; Erik Molnár, "Révai József történetszemléletéről" (About J. Révai's Philosophy of History), *Kr*, 4 (1966), no. 3-8; and Aladár Mód, "Révai József történetszemléletéről" (About J. Revai's Philosophy of History), in Mód, *Sors*, 315-339.

7.) On Aladár Mód see *MIL*, II, 257-258. In light of his recent death some analytical studies on Mód should soon be forthcoming.

8.) On the populists see Ch. XIV.

9.) Mód, *Négyszáz év küzdelem az önálló Magyarországért*, Bp. 1943; 7th ed., Bp. 1955.

10.) On the scholarly achievements of the members of this young generation see *A magyar történettudomány válogatott bibliográfidja, 1945-1968* (The Selected Bibliography of Hungarian Historical Sciences, 1945-1968), ed. Institute of History, Hungarian Academy of Sciences, Bp. 1971.

11.) For some standard summaries on the achievements of post-1945 Hungarian Marxist historiography see Molnár, "Historical Sciences," 169-178; *idem*, "A magyar történetírás tíz esztendeje" (Ten Years of Hungarian Historiography), *Sz*, 89 (1955), 169-190; *idem*, "A magyar történetírás fejlődése az elmult évtizedben" (The Development of Hungarian Historiography During the Past Decade), *Sz*, 94 (1960), 45-81; Ervin Pamlényi, "A magyar történetírás fejlődése a felszabadulás óta" (The Development of Hungarian Historiography Since the Liberation), *Sz*, 101 (1967), 1191-1204; Zsigmond Pál Pach, "A magyar történettudomány 25 éve'' (Twenty-Five Years of Hungarian Historical Sciences), *TSz,* 13 (1970), 131-146; and István Sinkovics, ''Történelem'' (History), in *ELTE története,* 526-541. For some non-Marxist assessments see Ferenc Wagner, *A magyar történetírás új útjai, 1945-1955*(The New Paths of Hungarian Historiography, 1945-1955), Washington, D.C. 1956; and Szendrey, *Historiography,* 363-406.

ABBREVIATIONS

AA, *Acta Antiqua Academiae Scientiarum Hungaricae* (Bp. 1953-).
AAr, *Acta Archeologica Academiae Scientiarum Hungaricae* (Bp. 1952-).
AH, *Acta Historica Academiae Scientiarum Hungaricae* (Bp. 1951-).
AHA, *Acta Historiae Artium Academiae Scientiarum Hungaricae* (Bp. 1953-).
AIHUSD, *Annales Instituti Historici Universitatis Scientiarum Debreceniensis de Ludovico Kossuth Nominatae* (Bp. 1962-).
AJ, *Acta Juridica Academiae Scientiarum Hungaricae* (Bp. 1959-).
AkÉ, *Akadémiai Értesítő* (Academy Journal) (Bp. 1890-1955). Title changed to *Magyar Tudomány* (Hungarian Science) in 1956.
AL, *Acta Litteraria Academiae Scientiarum Hungaricae* (Bp. 1957-).
ALi, *Acta Linguistica Academiae Scientiarum Hungaricae* (Bp. 1951-)
Al, *Alföld* (Lowland) (Debrecen 1950-).
AÖAW, *Almanach der Österreichischen Akademie der Wissenschaften* (Vienna).
AOSBM, *Analecta Ordinis Sancti Basilii Magni* (Rome).
Ar, *Arrabona. A Győri Múzeum Évkönyve* (Arrabona. The Yearbook of the Győr Museum)(Győr 1959-).
ASEER, *American Slavic and East European Review* (Since 1961 *Slavic Review;* between 1941 and 1944 American Series of *Slavonic and East European Review)* (New York - Bloomington - Seattle - Urbana 1941-).
ASz, *Agrártudományi Szemle* (Agricultural Review), (Bp. 1947-)
At, *Athenaeum* (Bp. 1915-1944).
AtSz, *Agrártörténeti Szemle* (Agricultural History Review), (Bp. 1959-).
AUD, *Acta Universitatis Debreceniensis de Ludovico Kossuth Nominatae* (Bp. 1962-).
AUSAH, *Acta Universitatis Szegediensis. Acta Historica* (Szeged 1957-).
AUSB, *Annales Universitatis Scientiarum Budapestiensis de Rolandó Eötvös Nominatae* (Bp. 1957-).
BMTIÉ, *Bécsi Magyar Történettudományi Intézet Évkönyve - Jahrbuch des Instituts für Ungarische Geschichtsforschung in Wien* (Vienna 1930-1940).

Bp, Budapest
BpSz, *Budapesti Szemle* (Budapest Review) (Pest-Bp. 1840-1841, 1857-1869, 1873-1944).

CSS, *Canadian Slavic Studies-Revue Canadienne D'Etudes Slaves* (Montreal, 1967-1971).

DN, *Dunantúli Napló* (Transdanubian Daily) (Pécs).
DR, *Duquesne Review* (Pittsburgh, Pa. 1956-).

EhT, *Egyháztörténet* (Church History) (Bp. 1943-1945, 1958-).
EKÉ, *Egyetemi Könyvtár Évkönyve* (Yearbook of the University Library), (Bp. 1962-).
EKL, *Esztétikai Kislexikon* (A Short Lexicon of Aesthetics), ed. I. Szerdahelyi and D. Zoltai, 2nd ed., Bp. 1972.

ELTE, Eötvös Loránd Tudományegyetem (Eötvös Loránd University of Budapest).
ELTE-A, *Eötvös Loránd Tudományegyetem Állam- és Jogtudományi Karának Aktái* (Actas of the School of Political and Legal Sciences of the Eötvös Loránd University of Budapest) (Bp. 1959-).
EM, *Erdélyi Múzeum* (Transylvanian Museum) (Pest 1815-1818, Kolozsvár 1874-1917, 1930-1945).
EPhK, *Egyetemes Philólógiai Közlöny* (Universal Philological Review), (Bp. 1887-1948).
Est, *Az Est* (Evening) (Bp.).
ÉT, *Élet és Tudomány* (Life and Science) (Bp. 1946-).
Et, *Ethnographia* (Bp., 1890-).
ETA, *Erdélyi Tudósító Almanachja* (Almanach of the Transylvanian Informer) (Kolozsvár).
FK, *Filológiai Közlöny* (Philological Review) (Bp. 1955-).
FKL, *Filozófiai Kislexikon* (A Short Lexicon of Philosophy), (Bp. 1970).
FSz, *Felsőoktatási Szemle* (Review of Higher Education) (Bp. 1952-).
GJ, *Gazdaság- és Jogtudomány. A Magyar Tudományos Akadémia Gazdaság- és Jogtudományok Osztályának közleményei* (Economic and Legal Sciences. Proceedings of the Section on Economic and Legal Sciences of the Hungarian Academy of Sciences) (Bp. 1967-).
HHR, *Hungarian Historical Review - Magyar Történelmi Szemle* (New York, Buenos Aires 1969-).
Hi, *The Historian* (Albuquerque, N.M. 1938-).
IMITE, *Az Izraelita Magyar Irodalmi Társulat Évkönyve* (Yearbook of the Jewish Hungarian Literary Society) (Bp. 1895-).
IT, *Irodalomtortenet* (Literary History) (Bp. 1912-).
ITK, *Irodalomtörténeti Közlemények* (Studies in Literary History) (Bp. 1891-).
JAAC, *The Journal of Aesthetics and Art Criticism* (New York 1942-).
JCEA, *Journal of Central European Affairs* (Boulder, Col., 1941-1964).
Je, *Jelenkor* (Present) (Pécs 1958-).
JEEH, *The Journal of European Economic History* (Rome 1972-).
JK, *Jogtudományi Közlöny* (Review of Legal Sciences) (Bp. 1946-).
JKö, *Jogtudományi Közlemények* (Studies in Legal Sciences) (Bp. 1947-).
JT, *Jubileumi Tanulmányok* (Anniversary Studies), 2 vols., Pécs, 1967. (Vol. I. *A pécsi egyetem történetéből* (From the History of the University of Pécs), ed. Andor Csizmadia. Vol. II, ed. Tibor Pap).
KL, *Közgazdasági Lexikon* (Economics Lexicon), 3 vols., ed. Sándor Halász and Gyula Mandelló, Bp. 1898-1901.
Kr, *Kritika* (Bp. 1963-).
LK, *Levéltári Közlemények* (Archival Proceedings) (Bp. 1923-1946, 1954-).
M, *Minerva* (Bp. 1922-1940).
MÉL, *Magyar Életrajzi Lexikon* (Hungarian Biographical Lexicon), 2 vols., ed. Ágnes Kenyeres, Bp. 1967-1969.
MGSz, *Magyar Gazdák Szemléje* (Hungarian Farmers' Review) (Bp.).
MH, *Medievalia et Humanistica* (Boulder, Colorado 1949-).
MHH, *Monumenta Hungariae Historica* (Pest-Bp. 1857-).
MHHD, *Monumenta Hungariae Historica Diplomataria* (Pest-Bp. 1857-).

MHHS, Monumenta Hungariae Historica, Scriptores (Pest-Bp. 1857-).

MIL, Magyar Irodalmi Lexikon (Hungarian Literary Lexicon) ed. Marcell Benedek, 3 vols., Bp. 1963-1965.

MIÖG, Mitteilungen des Instituts für Österreichische Geschichtsforschung (Innsbruck 1880-1928, Gratz 1948-).

MJL, Magyar Jogi Lexikon (Hungarian Legal Lexicon), 6 vols., ed. Dezső Márkus, Bp. 1898-1907.

MK, Magyar Könyvszemle (Hungarian Book Review)(Bp. 1876-1892; Új Folyam 1893-1944, 1955-).

MKu, Magyar Kultúra (Hungarian Culture) (Bp. 1913-1944).

MMT, Magyar művelődéstörténet(History of Hungarian Civilization), 5 vols., ed. Sándor Domanovszky, György Balanyi, Elemér Mályusz, Imre Szentpétery and Elemér Varjú, Bp. (1939-1942).

MÖS, Mitteilungen des Österreichischen Staatsarchivs (Vienna 1948-).

MP, Magyar Pedagógia (Hungarian Education) (Bp. 1892-1950, 1961-).

MsT, Magyarságtudomány(Hungarian Studies) (Bp. 1936-1938, 1942-1943).

MSz, Magyar Szemle (Hungarian Review) (Bp. 1927-1944).

MT, Magyar Tudomány (Hungarian Science) (Bp. 1956-).

MTA, Magyar Tudományos Akadémia (Hungarian Academy of Sciences).

MTAAl, Magyar Tudományos Akadémiai Almanach MCMXXXIII-ra (Almanach of the Hungarian Academy of Sciences for 1933), Bp. 1933.

MTA-NIOK, A Magyar Tudományos Akadémia Nyelv- és Irodalomtudományok Osztályának Közleményei (Proceedings of the Section on Language and Literary Sciences of the Hungarian Academy of Sciences) (Bp. 1951-).

MTAT, Magyar Tudományos Akadémia Tagajánlások 1941-ben(Proposals for Membership in the Hungarian Academy of Sciences in 1941), Bp. 1941.

NHQ, The New Hungarian Quarterly (Bp. 1960-).

Ny, Nyugat (West) (Bp. 1908-1941).

NyKu, Nyelvünk és Kultúránk. Az Anyanyelvi Konferencia Védnökségének Tájékoztatója(Our Language and Our Culture. The Journal of the Board of Directors of the Mother Language Conference) (Bp. 1970-).

OSZKE, Az Országos Széchényi Könyvtár Évkönyve(Yearbook of the National Széchényi Library) (Bp. 1957-).

PEIL, Protestáns Egyházi és Iskolai Lap(Protestant Church and School Review) (Pest-Bp. 1842-1848, 1858-1919).

PeSz, Pedagógiai Szemle (Educational Review) (Bp. 1951-).

PN, Pesti Napló (Pest Diary) (Pest-Bp. 1850-1939).

PSz, Protestáns Szemle (Protestant Review) (Bp. 1889-1944).

REHFO, Revue des Etudes Hongroises et Finno-Ougriennes (Paris 1923-1938).

RHC, Revue d'Histoire Comparée (Bp. 1923-1948).

RNL, Révai Nagy Lexikona(Révai's Great Lexicon), 21 vols., Bp. 1911-1935.

Sec. Hist., Sectio Historica.

Ser. M-L, Series Marxistica-Leninica.

Ser. Ped., Series Pedagogica.

SNCE, Studies for a New Central Europe(New York 1963-).

SS, Studia Slavica Academiae Scientiarum Hungaricae (Bp. 1955-).

SSS, Szabolcs-Szatmári Szemle (Szabolcs-Szatmár Review) (Nyiregyháza 1966-).

Sz, *Századok* (Centuries) (Pest-Bp. 1867-).
Szo, *Szocializmus* (Socialism) (Bp. 1906-1919, 1922-1939, 1945-1948).
TdSz, *Társadalmi Szemle* (Social Review) (Bp. 1945-).
TeTa, *Természet és Társadalom* (Nature and Society) (Pest-Bp. 1842-).
ThSz, *Theológiai Szemle* (Theological Review) (Bp. 1925-).
TöSz, *Történeti Szemle* (Historical Review) (Bp. 1912-1930).
TR, *Turkish Review* (Pittsburgh, Pennsylvania 1971-).
TSz, *Történelmi Szemle* (Historical Review) (Bp. 1958-).
UJ, *Ungarische Jahrbücher* (Berlin 1921-1944).
UML, *Új Magyar Lexikon* (New Hungarian Lexicon), 6 vols., Bp. 1959-1962. Supplement, Bp. 1972.
UMM, *Új Magyar Múzeum* (New Hungarian Museum) (Pest 1850-1860) (Included in it: *Magyar Académiai Értesítő* (Hungarian Academy Journal)).
UR, *Ungarische Rundschau* (Bp. 1912-1917).
URe, *Ungarische Revue* (Bp. 1882-1895).
Va, *Valóság* (Reality) (Bp. 1945-1948, 1958-).
Vi, *Világ* (World) (Pest-Bp. 1841-1844, 1910-1926, 1945-1949).
Vig, *Vigilia* (Bp. 1935-).
Vil, *Világosság* (Light) (Bp. 1904-1907, 1945-1952, 1960-).
VSz, *Vasi Szemle* (Vas Review) (Szombathely 1958-).

BIBLIOGRAPHY

Angyal, *Emlékezések* — Angyal, Dávid: *Emlékezések* (Reminiscences), ed. Lóránt Czigány, intr. László Péter, London, 1971.

Bajza, *Horvát kérdés* — Bajza, József: *A horvát kérdés. Válogatott tanulmányok*(The Croatian Question. Selected Studies),ed. László Tóth, Bp. 1941.

Barnes, *Historical Writing* — Barnes, Harry Elmer: *A History of Historical Writing,* 2nd rev. ed., New York, 1963.

Békefi-Emlékkönyv — *Békefi-Emlékkönyv: Dolgozatok Békefi Remig egyetemi tanári működésének emlékére*(Békefi Memorial Album: Studies in Honor of Remig Békefi's University Professorship), írták tanitványai (by his students), Bp. 1912.

Beöthy, *MIT* — *A magyar irodalom története* (The History of Hungarian Literature), 2 vols., 2nd ed., ed. Zsolt Beöthy, Bp. 1899-1900.

Biró, *Történelemtanitásunk* — Biró Sándor: *Történelemtanitásunk a XIX. század első felében*(The Teaching of History in Hungary in the First Half of the 19th Century), Bp. 1960.

Borsody, "Historiography" — Borsody, Stephen: "Modern Hungarian Historiography," *Journal of Modern History,* 26 (1952), 398-405.

Collingwood, *Idea of History* —Collingwood, R.G.: *The Idea of History,* New York, 1956.

Csizmadia, *Jogtörténeti oktatás* —Csizmadia Andor: *A jogtörténeti oktatás a pécsi tudományegyetemen a két világháború között* (Instruction of Legal History at the University of Pécs in the Interwar Period), Pécs, 1967. Reprinted from *JT,* II, 107-128.

Csizmadia, "Jogtörténet-tudomány" — Csizmadia, Andor: "A magyar állam- és jogtörténet-tudomány" (Hungarian State and Legal Historical Scholarship), in *Magyar állam- és jogtörténet* (Hungarian State and Legal History), ed. Andor Csizmadia, Bp. 1972, 28-51.

Csóka, *Történeti irodalom* —Csóka Lajos J.: *A latin nyelvű történeti irodalom kialakulása Magyarországon a XI-XIV. században* (The Development of Latin Historical Literature in Hungary in the 11th-14th Centuries), Bp. 1967.

Degré, "Jogtörténetirás a dualizmus korában" — Degré, Alajos: "A magyar jogtörténetirás keletkezése és fejlődése a dualizmus korában" (The Beginnings and Development of Hungarian Legal Historical Scholarship in the Dualist Period), in *Értekezések* (1967-1968), 285-313.

Degré, "Jogtörténetirás a Horthy-korban" — Degré, Alajos: "Magyar jogtörténetirás a Horthy-korban" (Hungarian Legal Historical Scholarship in the Horthy Period), *GJ,* 3 (1969), 77-99.

Domanovszky-Emlékkönyv — *Emlékkönyv Domanovszky Sándor születése hatvanadik fordulójának ünnepére* (Memorial Album for the Occasion of the Sixtieth Anniversary of Sándor Domanovszky's Birth), Bp. 1937.

Eckhart, "Jog- és alkothmánytortenet" — Eckhart, Ferenc: "Jog- és alkotmánytortenet" (Legal and Constitutional History), in Hóman, *New Paths,* 269-320.

Eckhart, *Jog- és államtudományikar* — Eckhart, Ferenc: *A jog- és államtudományi kar története,* 1667-1935 (The History of the School of Legal and Political Sciences, 1667-1935), Bp. 1936 (Vol. II of *Pázmány Péter-Tudományegyetem.)*

Eckhart, *A szentkorona eszme* — Eckhart, Ferenc: *A szentkorona eszme története* (The History of the Doctrine of the Holy Crown), Bp. 1941.

ELTE története — Az Eötvös Loránd Tudományegyetem története, 1945-1970 (The History of the Eötvös Loránd University of Budapest, 1945-1970), editor-in-chief István Sinkovics, Bp. 1970.

Ember, "MTT" — Ember, Győző: "A Magyar Történelmi Társulat száz éve" (Hundred Years of the Hungarian Historical Association), *Sz,* 101 (1967), 1140-1169.

Erdély Magyar Egyeteme — Erdély Magyar Egyeteme. Az erdélyi egyetemi gondolat és a M. Kir. Ferenc József Tudományegyetem törtenete (Transylvania's Hungarian University. The History of the Idea of a Transylvanian University and of the Hung. Roy. Francis Joseph University), eds. Gyula, Bisztray, Attila T. Szabó and Lajos Tamás, Kolozsvár, 1941.

Értekezések — A Magyar Tudományos Akadémia Dunántúli Tudományos Intézete (The Transdanubian Research Institute of the Hungarian Academy of Sciences): *Értekezések* (Studies), Bp. 1961- .

Études — Études historiques, 2 vols., Publiées par la Commission Nationale des Historiens Hongrois, Bp. 1960.

Flegler, *Történetírás* — Flegler, Sándor (Alexander): *A magyar történetírás történelme* (The History of Hungarian Historiography), Bp. 1877.

Glatz, "Eötvös Kollégium" — Glatz, Ferenc: "Gondolatok az Eötvös Kollégium történészképzéséről" (Thoughts About the Education of Historians at Eötvös College), *Sz,* 104 (1970), 799-805.

Glatz, "Historiography" — Glatz, Ferenc: "Historiography, Cultural Policy, and the Organization of Scholarship in Hungary in the 1920's," *AH,* 16 (1970), 273-293.

Glatz, "Jogtörténetirás" — G(latz, Ferenc): "Magyar jogtörténetirás a Horthy-korban" (Hungarian Legal Historical Scholarship in the Horthy Period), *Sz,* 103 (1969), 911-917.

Glatz, "Klebelsberg" — Glatz, Ferenc: "Klebelsberg tudománypolitikai programja és a magyar történettudomány" (Klebelsberg's Scientific Program and the Hungarian Historical Sciences), *Sz,* 103 (1969), 1176-1200.

Glatz, "Történelmi Társulat" — Glatz, Ferenc: "A Magyar Történelmi Társulat megalakulásának története" (The History of the Foundation of the Hungarian Historical Association), *Sz,* 101 (1967), 233-267.

Gunst, *Acsády* — Gunst, Péter: *Acsády Ignác történetírása* (Ignác Acsády's Historical Writings), Bp. 1961.

Győrffy, *Krónikáink* — Győrffy, György: *Krónikáink és a magyar őstörténet* (Our Chronicles and Ancient Hungarian History), Bp. 1948.

Hatvany, *Emberek* — Hatvany, Lajos: *Emberek és korok* (People and Ages), 2 vols., Bp. 1964.

Hatvany, *Öt évtized* — Hatvany, Lajos: *Öt évtized* (Five Decades), Bp. 1961.

Histoire et historiens — Histoire et historiens depuis cinquante ans. Méthodes, organisation et résultats du travail historique de 1876 à 1926. Recueile publié à l'occasion du cinquantenaire de la "Revue Historique", 2 vols., Paris, 1927-1928. Reprinted in New York, 1971, 2 vols. in 1.

Hóman, *Forráskritika* — Hóman, Bálint: *A forráskutatás és forráskritika története Magyarországon* (The History of Source Research and Source Criticism in Hungary), Bp. 1925. (Vol. I/1.a. of *A magyar történettudomány kézikönyve* (The Handbook of Hungarian Historical Studies)).

Hóman, *Művelődéspolitika* — Hóman, Bálint: *Művelődéspolitika* (Cultural Policy), Bp. 1938. (Vol. III of his *Munkái*(Works)).

Hóman, *New Paths* — *A magyar történetírás új útjai* (The New Paths of Hungarian Historiography), ed. Bálint Hóman, Bp. 1931.

Hóman-Szekfű (1927-1934) — Hóman, Bálint and Szekfű, Gyula: *Magyar történet*(Magyar History), 8 vols., Bp. 1927-1934. (First edition).

Hóman-Szekfű (1941-1943) — Hóman, Bálint and Szekfű, Gyula: *Magyar történet*(Magyar History), 5 vols., 7th ed., Bp. 1941-1943.

Hóman, *Történetírás* — Hóman, Bálint: *Történetírás és forráskritika* (Historiography and Source Criticism), Bp. 1938. (Vol. II of his *Munkái* (Works)).

Hóman, *Tudományos történetírásunk* — Hóman, Bálint: *Tudományos történetírásunk megalapítása a XVIII. században* (The Foundation of Our Scientific Historiography in the 18th Century), Bp. 1920.

Horváth, "Dualizmuskori jogtörténetírásunk" — Horváth, Pál: "Dualizmuskori jogtörténetírásunk főbb irányai" (The Main Trends of Our Legal Historical Scholarship of the Dualist Period), *ELTE-A*, 10 (1968), 3-16.

Horváth, *Kezdetei* — Horváth, János: *A magyar irodalmi műveltség kezdetei* (The Beginnings of Hungarian Literary Culture), Bp. 1931.

Horváth, *Kisebb munkái* — Horváth, Mihály: *Kisebb történelmi munkái* (Short Historical Studies), 4 vols., Pest, 1868.

Horváth, *Megoszlása* — Horváth, János: *Az irodalmi műveltség megoszlása. Magyar humanizmus* (The Diffusion of Literary Culture. Hungarian Humanism), Bp. 1935.

Horváth, *Reformácio* — Horváth, János: *A reformáció jegyében* (In the Sign of the Reformation), Bp. 1953; 2nd ed., Bp. 1957.

Hungarians in America — *Hungarians in America. A Biographical Directory of Professionals of Hungarian Origin in the Americas,* 1st and 2nd ed. by Tibor Szy, New York 1963 and 1966; 3rd ed. by Desi K. Bognar, Mt. Vernon, N.Y., 1972.

Ignotus, *Hungary* — Ignotus, Paul: *Hungary,* New York, 1972.

Illés-Emlékkönyv — *Emlékkönyv Illés József tanári működésének 40. évfordulójára* (Memorial Album for the Occasion of the 40th Anniversary of Joseph Illés's Professorship), ed. Ferenc Eckhart and Alajos Degré, Bp. 1942.

Jancsó-Emlékkönyv: Jancsó Benedek Emlékkönyv (Benedek Jancsó Memorial Album), ed. Miklós Asztalos, Bp. 1931.

Joó, *Bevezetés* — Joó, Tibor: *Bevezetés a szellemtörténetbe* (Introduction to *Geistesgeschichte),* Bp. 1935.

Juhász, *Népi írók* — Juhász, Géza: *Népi írók* (Populist Writers), Bp. 1943.

Kardos, "Eckhart-vita" — Kardos, József: "Az Eckhart-vita és a szentkorona-tan" (The Eckhart Controversy and the Doctrine of the Holy Crown), *Sz,* 103 (1969), 1104-1117.

Kardos, *Humanizmus* —Kardos, Tibor: *A magyarországi humanizmus kora* (The Age of Hungarian Humanism), Bp. 1955.

Kardos, *Középkori kultúra* — Kardos, Tibor: *Középkori kultúra, középkori költészet* (Medieval Culture, Medieval Literature), Bp. 1941.

Károlyi-Emlékkönyv — *Emlékkönyv Károlyi Árpád születése nyolcvanadik fordulójának ünnepére* (Memorial Album for the Occasion of the Feast of the Eightieth Anniversary of A. Károlyi's Birth), Bp. 1933.

Katólikus írók — *Katólikus írók új magyar kalauza* (Catholic Writers' New Hungarian Guide), Bp. (1931).

Keresztúry, *Örökség* — Keresztúry, Dezső: *Örökség: Magyar írói-arcképek* (Heritage: Hungarian Literary Portraits), Bp. 1970.

Klaniczay, *Marxizmus* —Klaniczay, Tibor: *Marxizmus és irodalomtudomány* (Marxism and Literary Scholarship), Bp. 1964.

Klaniczay *Reneszánsz és barokk* — Klaniczay, Tibor: *Reneszánsz és barokk* (Renaissance and Baroque), Bp. 1961.

Klebelsberg-Emlékkönyv — *Emlékkönyv dr. gróf Klebelsberg Kunó negyedszázados kultúrpolitikai működésének emlékére* (Memorial Album for the Occasion of the Quarter Centennial of Activities of dr. Count Kunó Klebelsberg as a Cultural Politician), Bp. 1925.

Kosáry, *Bevezetés* — Kosáry, Domokos: *Bevezetés a magyar történelem forrásaiba és irodalmába* (Introduction into the Sources and Literature of Hungarian History), 3 vols., Bp. 1951-1958.

Kosáry, *Bevezetés Magyarország* — Kosáry, Domokos: *Bevezetés Magyarország történetének forrásaiba és irodalmába* (Introduction into the Sources and Literature of the History of Hungary), projected 5 vols., Vol. I, Bp. 1970.

Kosáry, *History* —Kosáry, Dominic G.: *A History of Hungary,* Cleveland-N.Y., 1941.

Kosáry-Várdy, *History* — Kosáry, Dominic G. and Várdy, Steven Béla: *History of the Hungarian Nation,* Astor Park, Flo., 1969.

Kovács, "Divéky" — Kovács, Endre: "Divéky Adorján, 1880-1965," *Sz,* 99 (1965), 1390-1391.

Krónika — *A . . . Magyar Találkozó Krónikája* (Proceedings of the . . . th Hungarian Congress), Vols. I-XIII, ed. János Nádas and Ferenc Somogyi, Cleveland, Oh., 1962-1974. (Vols. II-III and IV-V are combined.)

Lederer, *Bevezetés* —Lederer, Emma: *Bevezetés a történettudományba* (Introduction into Historiography), Bp. 1958.

Lederer, "Marczali" — Lederer, Emma: "Marczali Henrik helye a magyar polgári történettudományban" (H. Marczali's Place in Bourgeois Hungarian Historiography) *Sz,* 96, 440-469.

Lederer, *Történetírás* —Lederer, Emma: *A magyar polgári történetírás rövid története* (A Short History of Hungarian Bourgeois Historiography), Bp. 1969. Lekai, "Historiography" — Lekai, Louis J.: "Historiography in Hungary, 1790-1848," *JCEE* 14 (1954), 3-18.

Lékai, *Történetírás* —Lékai, Lajos (Louis J.): *A magyar történetírás, 1790-1830* (Hungarian Historiography, 1790-1830), Bp. 1942.

Lukács, *Magyar irodalom* — Lukács, György: *Magyar irodalom — Magyar kultúra* (Hungarian Literature — Hungarian Culture), Bp. 1970.

Lukács, *Szellemtörténet* — Lukács, H. Borbála: *Szellemtörténet és irodalomtudomány (Geistesgeschichte* and Literary Scholarship), Bp. 1971.

Lukinich, *Történelmi Társulat* — Lukinich, Imre: *A Magyar Történelmi Társulat története* (The History of the Hungarian Historical Association), Bp. 1918.

Lukinich, "Történettudomány" — Lukinich, Imre: "A Magyar Tudományos Akadémia és a magyar történettudomány" (The Hungarian Academy of Sciences and Hungarian Historiography), in *MTA első évszázada,* I, 127-142.

Macartney, *Historians* — Macartney, C.A.: *The Medieval Hungarian Historians: A Critical and Analytical Guide,* Cambridge, 1955.

Macartney, *History* — Macartney, C.A.: *Hungary: A Short History,* Edinburgh, 1962.

Macartney, *Studies* — Macartney, C.A.: *Studies in the Early Hungarian Historical Sources,* I-II, Bp. 1938; III, Bp. 1941; IV-V (printed as III-IV), Bp. 1940, VI-VII, Oxford 1951.

Magyar history — Magyar történet (see Hóman-Szekfű).

Magyar humanisták — Magyar humanisták levelei, XV-XVI. század (Letters of Hungarian Humanists, 15-16th Centuries), ed. Sándor V. Kovács, Bp. 1971.

Magyar művelődéstörténet (also: *MMT) – Magyar művelődéstörténet* (History of Hungarian Civilization), 5 vols., ed. Sándor Domanovszky, György Balanyi, Elemér Mályusz, Imre Szentpétery and Elemér Varjú, Bp. (1939-1942).

Magyar történet — Magyar history (see Hóman-Szekfű)

Magyarság néprajza — A magyarság néprajza (Hungarian Ethnography), 4 vols., Bp. 1933-1937. (Hungarological Series).

Magyary, *Tudománypolitika — A magyar tudománypolitika alapvetése* (The Foundations of Hungarian Scientific Policy), ed. Zoltán Magyary, Bp. 1927.

Mályusz, "A népiség története" — Mályusz, Elemér: "A népiség története" (The History of Ethnicity), in Hóman, *New Paths,* 237-268.

Mályusz, "Eckhart-vita" — Mályusz, Elemér: "Az Eckhart-vita" (The Eckhart Controversy), *Sz,* 65 (1931), 406-419.

Mályusz, *Magyar renaissance — Magyar renaissance* (Hungarian Renaissance), ed. Elemér Mályusz, Bp. (1940). (Vol. II of *Magyar művelődéstörténet.)*

Mályusz, *Thuróczy-krónika* — Mályusz, Elemér: *A Thuróczy-krónika és forrásai* (The Thuróczy Chronicle and its Sources), Bp. 1967.

Mályusz, *Történettudomány*—Mályusz, Elemér: *A magyar történettudomány* (Hungarian Historical Sciences), Bp. (1942).

Márki-Emlékkönyv — Márki Sándor Emlékkönyv (Sándor Márki Memorial Album), ed. Lajos György, Kolozsvár, 1927.

Mátyás-Emlékkönyv — Mátyás király emlékkönyv születésének ötszázéves fordulójára (King Matthias Memorial Album on the Occasion of the 500th Anniversary of His Birth), 2 vols., ed. I. Lukinich, Bp. (1940).

Mérei, "Szekfű" — Mérei, Gyula: "Szekfű Gyula történetszemléletének bírálatához" (On the Critique of Gyula Szekfű's Philosophy of History), *Sz,* 94 (1960), 180-256.

Mód, *Sors:* —Mód, Aladár: *Sors és felelősség* (Fate and Responsibility), Bp. 1967

Mohácsi Emlékkönyv — Mohácsi Emlékkönyv 1526 (Mohács Memorial Album 1526), ed. Imre Lukinich, Bp. 1926.

Molnár, "Historical Sciences" — Molnár, Erik: "Historical Sciences," *Science in Hungary,* 161-178.

Molnár, *Magyarország* — *Magyarország története* (History of Hungary), ed. Erik Molnár, Bp. 1964, 2nd ed., 1967, 3rd ed., 1973.

MTA első évszázada — *A Magyar Tudományos Akadémia első évszázada* (The First Century of the Hungarian Academy of Sciences), 2 vols., Bp. 1926-1928.

Nemeskürty, *Széppróza* —Nemeskürty, István: *A magyar széppróza születése* (The Birth of Hungarian Prose), Bp. 1963.

Németh, *Katedrám* — Németh, László: *Az én katedrám* (My University Chair), Bp. 1969.

Németh, *Két nemzedék* —Németh, László: *Két nemzedék* (Two Generations), Bp. 1970.

Németh, *Kiadatlan tanulmányok* —Németh, László: *Kiadatlan tanulmányok* (Unpublished Studies), 2 vols., Bp. 1968.

New Paths (also: Hóman, *New Paths)* — *A magyar történtírás új útjai* (The New Paths of Hungarian Historiography), ed. Bálint Hóman, Bp. 1931.

Nouvelles études — *Nouvelles études historiques,* 2 vols., publiées à l'occasion du XIIe Congrès International des Sciences Historiques par la Commission Nationale des Historiens Hongrois, Bp. 1965.

Ortutay, *Írók* — Ortutay, Gyula: *Írók, népek, századok* (Writers, People, Centuries), Bp. 1960.

Pamlényi, *Horváth* — Pamlényi, Ervin: *Horváth Mihály* (Mihály Horváth), Bp. 1954.

Pázmány Péter-Tudományegyetem — *A Királyi Magyar Pázmány Péter-Tudományegyetem története* (The History of the Royal Hungarian Pázmány Péter University (of Budapest)), 4 vols., Bp. 1935-1937.

Pintér, *MIT* —Pintér, Jenő: *A magyar irodalom története a legrégibb időktől Kazinczy Ferenc haláláig* (The History of Hungarian Literature from the Most Ancient Times to the Death of Ferenc Kazinczy (1831)), 4 vols., Bp. 1909-1913.

Pintér, *MI* — Pintér, Jenő: *Magyar irodalomtörténet. Tudományos rendszerezés* (Hungarian Literary History. A Scientific Systematization), 8 vols., Bp. 1930-1941.

Prominent Hungarians — *Prominent Hungarians Home and Aborad,* ed. Márton Fekete, London 1973.

Ravasz, *Tanulmányok* — *Tanulmányok a magyar nevelés történetéből, 1849-1944* (Studies in the History of Hungarian Education, 1849-1944), ed. János Ravasz, Bp. 1957.

Renaissance et Réformation — *La Renaissance et la Réformation en Pologne et en Hongrie. Conférence Budapest-Eger, 10-14 oct. 1961,* ed. Gy. Székely and E. Fügedi, Bp. 1963.

Révai, *Válogatott írások* —Révai, József, *Válogatott történelmi írások* (Selected Historical Essays), 2 vols., Bp. 1966.

Révész, *Sinai Miklós* —Révész, Imre: *Sinai Miklós és kora* (Miklós Sinai and His Age), Bp. 1959.

Sándor, *Magyar filozófia* —Sándor, Pál: *A magyar filozófia története, 1900-1945* (The History of Hungarian Philosophy, 1900-1945), 2 vols., Bp. 1973.

Sarlós, "A 'szentkorona tan' " — Sarlós, Márton: "A 'szentkorona tan' kialakulásához" (On the Development of the Doctrine of the Holy Crown), *JK* 15 (1960), 557-600.

Sarlós, "A Szellemtörténeti irány" — Sarlós, Márton: "A szellemtörténeti irány és a magyar jogtörténetírás" (The *Geistesgeschichte* Orientation and Hungarian Constitutional History), *JK*, 11 (1956), 87-103.

Science in Hungary — *Science in Hungary*, ed. Tibor Erdey-Grúz and Imre Trencsényi-Waldapfel, Bp. 1965.

Sinor, *History* —Sinor, Denis: *History of Hungary*, London and New York, 1959.

Sőtér, *MIT* — *A magyar irodalom története* (The History of Hungarian Literature), 6 vols., editor-in-chief István Sőtér, Bp. 1964-1966.

Studium Generale — *Studium Generale. Studies Offered to Astrik L. Gabriel.* (Vol. XI of *Texts and Studies in the History of Mediaeval Education),* ed. L.S. Domonkos and others, Notre Dame, Ind., 1967.

Szabó, *Erzsébet Tudományegyetem* — Szabó, Pál: *A M. Kir. Erzsébet Tudományegyetem és irodalmi munkássága* (The Hung. Roy. Erzsébet University and its Scholarly Activities), Pts. I and II in one vol., Pécs. 1940.

Szabolcsi, *Magyar zene*—Szabolcse, Bence: *A magyar zene századai* (Centuries of Hungarian Music) 2 vols., Bp. 1959-1961.

Szabolcsi, *Változó világ* — Szabolcsi, Miklós: *Változó világ — Szocialista irodalom* (Changing World — Socialist Literature), Bp. 1973.

Szekfű, *Állam es nemzet* —Szekfű, Gyula: *Állam és nemzet. Tanulmányok a nemzetiségi kérdésről* (State and Nation. Studies on the Nationality Question), Bp. 1942. (Not identical with Szekfű's *État et nation,* Paris, 1945, as commonly assumed.)

Szekfű-Emlékkönyv — *Szekfű Gyula a történetíró és nemzetnevelő* (Gyula Szekfű, Historian and Sage of the Nation), Bp. 1943. (A collection of essays for Szekfű's 60th birthday.)

Szekfű, *Három nemzedék* —Szekfű, Gyula: *Három nemzedék. Egy hanyatló kor története* (Three Generations. The History of a Declining Age), Bp. 1920.

Szekfű, *Három nemzedék II* —Szekfű, Gyula: *Három nemzedék és ami utána következik* (Three Generations and What Follows), Bp. 1934.

Szekfű, "Károlyi" — Szekfű, Gyula: "Károlyi Árpád, a történetíró" (Árpád Károlyi the Historian), in *Károlyi-Emlékkönyv,* 5-27.

Szekfű, *Mai Széchenyi* — *A mai Széchenyi. Eredeti szövegek Széchenyi István munkáiból* (Today's Széchenyi. Original Selections from István Széchenyi's Works), ed. Gyula Szekfű, Bp. 1935.

Szekfű, *Mi a magyar?* — *Mi a magyar?* (What is a Magyar?), ed. Gyula Szekfű, Bp. 1939.

Szekfű, *Széchenyi igéi* — *Széchenyi igéi* (The Teachings of Széchenyi), ed. Gyula Szekfű, Bp. 1921.

Szekfű, *Történetpolitikai tanulmányok* — Szekfű, Gyula: *Történetpolitikai tanulmányok* (Studies in Historical Politics), Bp. 1924.

Szendrey, *Historiography* — Szendrey, Thomas L.: *The Ideological and Methodological Foundations of Hungarian Historiography, 1750-1970,* Ph.D. Diss., St. John's University, Jamaica, N.Y., 1972.

Szent István-Emlékkönyv — *Emlékkönyv Szent István király halálának kilencszázadik évfordulóján* (Memorial Album on the Occasion of the Nine-

Hundredth Anniversary of King Saint Stephen's Death), 3. vols., ed. Jusztinian György Serédi, Bp. 1938.

Szentpétery, *Bölcsészeti kar* —Szentpétery, Imre: *A bölcsészettudományi kar története, 1635-1935* (The History of the School of Philosophy, 1635-1935), Bp. 1935. (Vol. I of *Pázmány Péter-Tudományegyetem.)*

Szentpétery-Emlékkönyv — Emlékkönyv Szentpétery Imre születése hatvanadik évfordulójának ünnepére (Memorial Album on the Occasion of the Feast of the Sixtieth Anniversary of Imre Szentpétery's Birth), írták tanítványai (by his students), Bp. 1938.

Szentpétery, *Scriptores rerum — Scriptores rerum Hungaricarum tempore ducum regumque stirpis Arpadianae gestarum,* 2 vols., ed. Emericus Szentpétery, Bp. 1937-1938.

Szigeti, *Szellemtörténet* — Szigeti, József: *A magyar szellemtörténet bírálatához* (On the Critique of Hungarian *Geistesgeschichte),* Bp. 1964.

Timon, *A szent korona* — Timon, Ákos: *A szent korona és a koronázás közjogi jelentősége* (The Holy Crown and the Significance of the Coronation in Public Law), Bp. 1907.

Tiszti névtár — Magyarország tiszti cím- és nevtára (Address and Name Index of Hungary's Public Servants), vol. 48, Bp. 1941.

Tolnai, *Vázlatok* —Tolnai, Gábor: *Vázlatok és tanulmányok* (Sketches and Studies), Bp. 1955.

Turóczi-Trostler, *Magyar-Világ* —Turóczi-Trostler, József: *Magyar irodalom — Világirodalom* (Hungarian Literature — World Literature), 2 vols., Bp. 1961.

Vardy, "Economic History" — Vardy, Steven Bela: "The Hungarian Economic History School: Its Birth and Development," *JEEH,* 4 (1975), in PP. 121-136.

Vardy, *Historiography* —Vardy, Steven Bela: *Hungarian Historiography and the Geistesgeschichte School — A magyar történettudomány ès a szellemtörténeti iskola,* Cleveland, 1974.

Várdy, "Történetírás" — Várdy, (Steven) Béla: "A magyar történetírás multja. A szellemtörténeti iskola előzményei" (The Past of Hungarian Historiography. The Precedents of *Geistesgeschichte),* in *Krónika,* XIII (1974), 154-168.

Vardy, "Kulturgeschichte" — Vardy, Steven Bela: "The Birth of the Hungarian *Kulturgeschichte* School: A Study in the History of Hungarian Historical Studies," *Sinor-Festschrift* (Bonn, Germany 1976).

Várdy, *Magyarságtudomány* —Várdy, (Steven) Béla: *Magyarságtudomány az észak-amerikai egyetemeken és föiskolákon* (Hungarian Studies at North American Colleges and Universities), Cleveland, 1973. Reprinted from *Krónika,* XII, 102-132.

Varga, *Debreceni Tudományegyetem* — Varga, Zoltán: *A debreceni tudományegyetem története, 1914-1944* (The History of the University of Debrecen, 1914-1944), Debrecen, 1967.

Varga, *Vita — Vita a feudális kori magyar történelem periodizációjáról* (Debate on the Periodization of Hungarian History of the Feudal Age), ed. János Varga, Bp. 1968.

Várkonyi, "Históriográfiai törekvések" — Várkonyi, R. Ágnes: "Históriográfiai törekvések Magyarországon a XIX. században" (Historiographical Tendencies in Hungary in the 19th Century), *Sz,* 103 (1969), 939-989.

Várkonyi, *Pozitivista történetszemlélet* —Várkonyi, R. Ágnes: *A pozitivista történetszemlélet a magyar történetírásban* (Positivist Philosophy of History in Hungarian Historiography), 2 vols., Bp. 1973.

Várkonyi, "Scientific Thinking" — Várkonyi, R. Ágnes: "The Impact of Scientific Thinking on Hungarian Historiography about the Middle of the 19th Century," *AH*, 14 (1968), 1-20.

Várkonyi, *Thaly* — Várkonyi, R. Ágnes: *Thaly Kálmán és történetírása* (Kálmán Thaly and his Historiography), Bp. 1961.

Waldapfel, *Tanulmányok*—Waldapfel, József: *Irodalmi tanulmányok* (Literary Studies), Bp. 1957.

APPENDIX

SIGNIFICANT SOURCE PUBLICATION SERIES SINCE 1857 MONUMENTA HUNGARIAE HISTORICA — MAGYAR TÖRTÉNELMI EMLÉKEK

1.) Section One: *Diplomataria — Okmánytárak* (— MHHD)

Volumes: I-IV. Hatvani (Horváth), Mihály: *Magyar történelmi okmánytár: a brüsszeli országos levéltárból és a burgundi könyvtárból* (Hungarian Historical Documents from the National Archives of Brussels and from the Library of Burgundy), 4 vols., Pest 1857-1859.

V. Simonyi, Ernő: *Magyar történelmi okmánytár londoni könyvés levéltárakból, 1521-1717* (Hungarian Historical Documents from the Libraries and Archives of London, 1521-1717), Pest 1859. Continued as no. XVI; later removed from circulation.

VI-XIII. Wenzel, Gusztáv: *Codex diplomaticus Arpadianus continuatus — Árpád-kori új okmdnytár,* 8 vols., Pest 1860-Bp. 1878. Continued as supplmentary volumes under nos. XVII, XVIII, XX and XXII.

XIV-XV. Szilágyi, Sándor: *Alvinczi Péter okmánytára* (The Archives of Péter Alvinczi), 2 vols., Pest 1870. Continued as no. XXVII.

XVI. Simonyi, Ernő: *Magyar történelmi okmdnytár londoni könyv- és levéltárakból, 1517-1629* (Hungarian Historical Documents from the Libraries and Archives of London, 1517-1717), Bp. 1875. This work was subsequently removed from circulation by the Hungarian Academy of Sciences. Consequently the next volume is also numbered XVI.

XVI. Ováry, Lipót: *III. Pál pápa és Farnese Sándor bíbornok Magyarországra vonatkozó diplomácziai levelezései, 1535-1549* (The Correspondences of Pope Paul III and Cardinal Alexander Farnese Relative to Hungary, 1535-1549), Bp. 1879.

XVII-XVIII. Wenzel, Gusztáv: *Codex diplomaticus Arpadianus continuatus,* vols. 9-10, Pest 1871-Bp. 1873. Continuation of nos. VI-XIII.

XIX. Frankl (Fraknói), Vilmos: *Pázmdny Péter levelezése, 1605-1625* (The Correspondence of Péter Pázmány, 1605-1625), Bp. 1873.

XX. Wenzel, Gusztáv: *Codex diplomaticus Arpadianus continuatus,* vol. 11 Bp. 1873. See also nos. VI-XIII, XVII-VII-XVIII and XXII.

XXI. Szilágyi, Sándor: *Okmánytár I. Rákóczy György svéd és franczia összeköttetéseinek történetéhez, 1632-1648* (Documents on the Swedish and French Connections of György Rákóczy I), Bp. 1873.

XXII. Wenzel, Gusztáv: *Codex diplomaticus Arpadianus continuatus,* vol. 12, Bp. 1874. See also nos. VI-XIII, XVII-XVIII and XX.

XXIII. Szilágyi, Sándor: *Okmánytár II. Rákóczy György diplomáciai összeköttetéseihez* (Documents on the Diplomacy of György Rákóczy II), Bp. 1874.

XXIV. Szilágyi, Sándor: *A két Rákóczy György fejedelem családi levelezése* (The Family Correspondences of the two Princes Gyorgy Rákóczy) Bp. 1875.

XXV. Ipolyi, Arnold: *Oláh Miklós esztergomi érsek-prímás és kir. helytartó levelezése* (The Correspondence of Miklós Oláh, the Primate Archbishop of Esztergom and Roy. Governor), Bp. 1875.

XXVI. Szilágyi, Sándor: *Okirattár Strassburg Pál 1631-33-iki követsége és I. Rákóczy György első diplomácziai összeköttetései történetéhez* (Documents on Pál Strassburg's Embassy of 1631-33, and on the Initial Diplomatic Connections of György Rákóczy I), Bp. 1882.

XXVII. Gergely, Samu and Pettkó, Béla: *Alvinczi Péter okmánytára* (The Archives of Péter Alvinczi), vol. III Bp. 1887. Continuation of nos. XIV-XV.

XXVIII. Thallóczy, Lajos and Barabás, Samu: *Codex diplomaticus de Blagay — A Blagay család oklevéltára, 1260-1578,* Bp. 1897.

XXIX-XXX. Barabás, Samu: *Codex epistolaris et diplomaticus Comitis Nicolai de Zrinio — Zrínyi Miklós a szigetvári hős életére vonatkozó levelek és okiratok, 2 vols., Bp. 1898-1899.*

XXXI. Thallóczy, Lajos and Hodinka, Antal: *Codex diplomaticus partium Regno Hungariae adnexarum — Magyarország melléktartományainak oklevéltára,* vol. I: *A horváth véghelyek oklevéltára, 1490-1527* (Documents on the Croatian Frontier, 1490-1527), Bp. 1903. Continued as nos. XXXIII, XXXVI and XL.

XXXII. Veress, Endre: *Carillo Alfonz jezsuita atya levelezése és iratai, 1591-1618* (The Correspondence and Papers of the Jesuit Father Alfons Carillo, 1591-1618), Bp. 1906. Continued as no. XLII.

XXXIII. Thallóczy, Lajos and Áldásy, Antal: *Codex diplomaticus partium Regno Hungariae adnexarum,* vol. II: *A Magyarország és Szerbia közti összeköttetések oklevéltara, 1198-1526* (Documents on the Inter-Relations Between Hungary and Serbia, 1198-1526), Bp. 1907. See also nos. XXXI, XXXVI and XL.

XXXIV. Veress, Endre: *Básta György hadvezér levelezése és iratai* (The Correspondence and Papers of General George Basta), vol. I (1597-1602), Bp. 1909. Continued as no. XXXVII.

XXXV. Thallóczy, Lajos and Barabás, Samu: *Codex diplomaticus Comitum de Frangepanibus,* vol. I (1133-1453), Bp. 1910. Continued as no. XXXVIII.

XXXVI. Thallóczy, Lajos and Horváth, Sándor: *Codex diplomaticus partium Regno Hungariae adnexarum,* vol. III: *Alsószlavóniai okmánytár* (Documents on Lower Slavonia), Bp. 1912. See also nos. XXXI, XXXIII and XL.

XXXVII. Veress, Endre: *Básta György hadvezér levelezése és iratai* (The Correspondence and Papers of General George Basta), vol. II (1602-1607), Bp. 1913. Continuation of no. XXXIV.

XXXVIII. Thallóczy, Lajos and Barabás, Samu: *Codex diplomaticus Comitum de Frangepanibus,* vol. II (1454-1527), Bp. 1913. Continuation of no. XXXV.

XXXIX. Berzeviczy, Albert: *Acta vitam Beatricis reginae Hungariae illustrantia,* Bp. 1914.

XL. Thallóczy, Lajos and Horváth, Sándor: *Codex diplomaticus partium Regno Hungariae adnexarum,* vol. IV: *Jajcza (bánság, vár és város) története,*

1450-1527 (The History of the Banate, Castle and City of Jajcza, 1450-1527), Bp. 1915. See also nos. XXXI, XXXIII and XXXVI.

XLI. Veress, Endre: *Carillo Alfonz jezsuita atya levelezése és iratai, 1591-1618* (The Correspondence and Papers of the Jesuit Father Alfons Carillo, 1591-1618), vol. II, Bp. 1943. Continuation of no. XXXII.

XLII. Veress, Endre: *Báthory István király levélváltása az erdélyi kormánnyal, 1581-1585* (King Stephen Báthory's Correspondence with the Government of Transylvania, 1581-1585), Bp. 1948.

2.) Section Two: *Scriptores -Írók* (— MHHS):

I. Wenzel, Gusztáv (ed.): *Szerémi György, II. Lajos és János királyok házi káplánja Emlékirata Magyarország romlásáról, 1484-1543* (The Memoires on Hungary's Fall by György Szerémi, the House Chaplain of Kings Louis II and John, 1484-1543), Pest 1857.

II-VI. Szalay, László (ed.): *Verancsics Antal m. kir. helytartó, esztergomi érsek összes munkái* (The Complete Works of Antal Verancsics, Roy. Hung. Governor, Archbishop of Esztergom), 5 vols., Pest 1857-1860. Continued as IX-X, XIX-XX, XXV-XXVI and XXXII.

VII. Kazinczy, Gábor (ed.): *Gr. Illésházy István nádor följegyzései, 1592-1603 és Hidvégi Mikó Ferenc históriája, 1594-1613, Bíró Sámuel folytatásával* (The Memoire Notes of Palatinate Count István Illésházy, 1591-1603, and the History of Ferenc Hidvégi-Mikó, 1594-1613, with a Continuation by Sámuel Bíró), Pest 1863.

VIII. Szilágyi, Sándor (ed.): *Rozsnyay Dávid, az utolsó török deák, történeti maradványai* (The Historical Notes of Dávid Rozsnyay, the Last Turkish Scribe), Pest 1867.

IX-X. Szalay, László (ed.): *Verancsics Antal . . . összes munkái* (The Complete Works of Antal Verancsics . . .), vols. VI-VII, Pest 1860-1865. See also II-VI, XIX-XX, XXV-XXVI, XXXII.

XI. Kazinczy, Gábor (ed.): *Altorjai br. Apor Péter munkái* (The Works of Baron Péter Altorjai), Pest 1863.

XII-XIV. Toldy, Ferenc (for vol. III, Iván Nagy) (eds.): *Brutus János Mihály m. kir. történetíró magyar históriája, 1490-1552* (The Hungarian History of the Hung. Roy. Historian Gian Michele Bruto), 3 vols., Pest 1863-Bp. 1876.

XV. Nagy, Iván (ed.): *Késmárki Thököly Imre naplója, 1693-1694* (The Diary of Imre Thököly of Késmark, 1693-1694), Pest 1863. Continued as no. XVIII. See also XXIII, XXIV and XXXIV.

XVI. Majer, Fidel (ed.): *Ghymesi Forgách Ferencz nagyváradi püspök magyar históriája, 1540-1572. Forgách Simon és Istvánfi Miklós jegyzéseikkel együtt* (The Hungarian History of Ferencz Forgách of Ghymes, 1540-1572, with the Notes of Simon Forgách and Miklós Istvánfi), intr. by Ferenc Toldy, Pest 1866.

XVII. Toldy, Ferenc (ed.): *Baronyay Décsi János magyar históriája, 1592-1598* (The Hungarian History of János Décsi of Baronya, 1592-1598), Pest 1866.

XVIII. Torma, Károly (ed.): *Késmárk Thököly Imre naplója, 1676-1678* (The Diary of Imre Thököly of Késmárk, 1676-1678), Pest 1866. Continuation of XV and XVIII. See also XXIII, XXIV, XXXIV.

XIX-XX. Szalay, Laszlo and Wenzel, Gusztav (eds.): *Verancsics Antal összes munkái* (The Complete Works of Antal Verancsics), vols. VIII-IX,

Pest 1868-1870. See also II-VI, IX-X, XXV-XXVI, XXXII.

XXI. Szilágyi, Sándor (ed.): *Szamosközy István történeti maradványai, 1566-1603* (The Historical Writings of István Szamosközy, 1566-1603), vol. I, Bp. 1876. Continued as nos. XXVIII-XXX.

XXII. Szabó, Károly (tr.): *Kritobulosz, II. Mehmet élete* (The Life of Mehmet II by Kritobulos), Bp. 1876.

XXIII. Thaly, Kálmán (ed.): *Késmárki Thököly Imre és némely főbb hívének naplói és emlékezetes írásai, 1686-1705* (The Diaries and Memorable Writings of Imre Thököly of Késmárk and of a Number of His Chief Supporters, 1686-1705), Pest 1868. See also nos. XV, XVIII, XXIV and XXXIV.

XXIV. Thaly, Kálmán (ed.): *Késmárki Thököly Imre naplói, leveleskönyvei és egyéb emlékezetes írásai* (The Diaries, Letters and Other Memorable Writings of Imre Thököly of Késmárk), Bp. 1873. See also XV, XVIII, XXIII and XXXIV.

XXV-XXVI. Wenzel, Gusztáv (ed.): *Verancsics Antal . . . összes munkái* (The Complete Works of Antal Verancsics . . .), vols. X-XI, Pest 1871-Bp. 1873. See also II-VI, IX-X, XIX-XX and XXXII.

XXVII. Thaly, Kálmán (ed.): *Történelmi naplók, 1663-1719* (Historical Diaries, 1663-1719), Bp. 1875. Included are: György Ottlyk's autobiography, the notes of the representatives of Bártfa at the diet of Onód, the diaries of Count Mihály Teleki and of János Pápai about their embassy to Belgrad, the chronicle of János Tétsi, Jr., the diary fragments of István Bivolinyi, and the memoires of János György Ritter.

XXVIII-XXX. Szilágyi, Sándor (ed.): *Szamosközy István történeti maradványai* (The Historical Writings of István Szamosközy), vols. II-IV, Bp. 1876-1880. Continuation of no. XXI.

XXXI. *Magyar történelmi évkönyvek és naplók a XVI-XVIII. századból,* (Hungarian Historical Yearbooks and Diaries from the 16th-18th Centuries), Vol. I: Károly Szabó, ed., *Gyulafy Lestár följegyzései, 1565-1605* (The Diaries of Lestár Gyulafy, 1565-1605); Imre Szopori-Nagy, ed., *Mártonfalvi Imre Deák emlékirata, 1528-1585)* (The Memoires of Scribe Imre of Mártonfalva, 1528-1585); *A Pálóczi Horvát család naplója,* 1622-1790),(The Diaries of the Pálóczi-Horvát Family, 1622-1790) Bp. 1881. See also XXXIII, XXXV and XXXVIII.

XXXII. Szalay, László (ed.): *Verancsics Antal . . összes munkái. Pótlékok s név- és tárgymutató a 12 kötethez* (The Complete Works of Antal Verancsics . . . . Supplement and Name and Subject Index to the Twelve Volumes), Bp. 1875. See also II-VI, IX-X, XIX-XX, and XXV-XXVI.

XXXIII. *Magyar történelmi évkönyvek és naplók a XVI-XVIII. századból* (Hungarian Historical Yearbooks and Diaries from the 16th-18th Centuries), vol. II: Sándor Szilágyi, ed., *Gyulafy Lestár följegyzései* (The Diaries of Lestár Gyulafy); Gyula Tasnádi-Nagy, ed., *Keczer Ambrus naplója, 1663-1669* (The Diary of Ambrus Keczer, 1663-1669); Ferdinánd Mencsik and János Kulich, eds., *Krman Dániel superintendens 1708-1709-iki oroszországi útjának leírása* (The Travel Notes of Superintendent Dániel Krman on his Trip to Russia in 1708-1709), Bp. 1894. Continuation of no. XXXI.

XXXIV, Thaly, Kálmán (ed.): *Thököly Imre fejedelem 1691-1692-iki leveleskönyve* (Prince Imre Thököly's Letters of 1691-1692), Bp. 1896. See also XV, XVIII, XXIII and XXIV.

XXXV. *Magyar történelmi évkönyvek és naplók a XVI-XVIII. századokból* (Hungarian Historical Yearbooks and Diaries from the 16th-18th Centuries), vol. III: Gyula Nagy, ed., *Czegei Vass György és Vass László naplói, 1659-1739* (The Diaries of György Vass and László Vass of Czege, 1659-1739), Bp. 1896. See also XXXI, XXXIII and XXXVIII.

XXXVI-XXXVII. Szádeczky, Lajos (ed.): *Br. Apor Péter verses művei és levelei, 1676-1752* (The Lyrical Works and Letters of Baron Péter Apor, 1676-1752), 2 vols., Bp. 1903.

XXXVIII. *Magyar történelmi évkönyvek és naplók a XVI-XVIII. századokból* (Hungarian Historical Yearbooks and Diaries from the 16th-18th Centuries), vol. IV: Lajos Szádeczky, ed., *Halmágyi István naplói, 1752-1753, 1762-1769 és iratai, 1669-1785* (The Diaries (1752-1753, 1762-1769) and Papers (1669-1785) of István Halmágyi), Bp. 1906. See also XXXI, XXXIII and XXXV.

3.) Section Three: *Monumenta Comitialia — Országgyűlési emlékek:*

A.) *Monumenta comitialia regni Hungariae — Magyar országgyűlési emlékek* (Papers of the Hungarian Diets), 12 vols. (1526-1606), vols. I-VIII ed. Vilmos Fraknói; vols. IX-X ed. by Vilmos Fraknói and Árpád Károlyi; and vols. XI-XII ed. by Árpád Károlyi, Bp. 1874-1917. Series to be continued under the direction of the Hungarian Academy of Sciences.

B.) *Monumenta comitialia regni Transsylvaniae — Erdélyi országgyűlési emlékek* (Papers of the Diets of Transylvania), 21 vols. (1540-1699), ed. by Sándor Szilágyi, Bp. 1875-1898. Several volumes also include various related documents. The series lacks an index.

4.) Section Four: *Acta extere — Diplomácziai emlékek:*

A.) Wenzel, Gusztáv (ed.): *Magyar diplomácziai emlékek az Anjou-korból* (Hungarian Diplomatic Documents from the Anjou Period), 3 vols., Bp. 1875-1878. The period covered is from 1268 till 1420.

B.) Nagy, Iván and br. Nyáry, Albert (eds.): *Magyar diplomácziai emlékek Mátyás korából, 1458-1490* (Hungarian Diplomatic Documents from the Age of Matthias (Corvinus), 1458-1490), 4 vols., Bp. 1875-1878.

MAJOR SOURCE PUBLICATIONS OUTSIDE THE "MONUMENTA" SERIES:

1.) *Kodex diplomaticus Hungaricus Andegavensis — Anjou-kori okmánytár* (Documents on the Anjou Period), 7 vols.; vols. I-VI ed. by Imre Nagy, vol. VII ed. by Gyula Nagy, Bp. 1878-1920. It covers the period between 1301 and 1359. This series remained incomplete.

2.) *Török-magyarkori történelmi emlékek* (Historical Sources on the Turkish-Hungarian Period).

a.) Section One: *Diplomataria — Okmánytár:*

I-II. Szilády, Áron and Szilágyi, Sándor (eds.): *Okmánytár a hódoltság történetéhez Magyarországon. Nagy-Kőrös, Czegléd, Dömsöd, Halas levéltáraiból* (Documents on the History of the (Turkish) Conquest. From the Archives of Nagy-Kőrös, Czegléd, Dömsöd, and Halas), 2 vols., Pest 1863.

III-IX. Szilády, Áron and Szilágyi, Sándor (eds.): *Török-magyarkori állam-okmánytár* (Governmental Documents of the Turkish-Hungarian Age), 7 vols., Pest 1868-1872. A separate *Név- és tárgymutató* (Name and Subject Index), Bp. 1874. It covers the period between 1540 and 1699.

b.) Section Two: *Scriptores — Írók:*

I-II. Thury, József (tr.): *Török történetírók* (Turkish Historians), 2 vols., Bp. 1893-1896.

III. Karácson, Imre (tr.) and Szekfű, Gyula (ed.): *Török történetírók* (Turkish Historians), vol. III, Bp. 1916.

IV. Karácson, Imre (tr.): *Evlia Cselebi világutazó magyarországi utazásai, 1660-1664* (The World Traveler Evliya Chelebi's Travels in Hungary, 1660-1664), Bp. 1904.

V. Karácson, Imre (tr.): *Evlia Cselebi magyarországi utazásainak folytatólagos leírása az 1664-1666 közti években* (The Continuous Description of Evliya Chelebi's Travels in Hungary Between the Years 1664-1666), Bp. 1908.

3.) *Other Works on the Turkish Period:*

a.) *Magyarországi török kincstári defterek* (Turkish Government Tax Rolls in Hungary), tr. by Antal Velics, ed. by Ernő Kammerer, 2 vols., Bp. 1886-1890. This work covers the period between 1543 and 1639.

b.) *A budai basák magyarnyelvű levelezése, 1553-1589* (The Magyar Language Correspondences of the Pashas of Buda, 1553-1589), ed. by Sándor Takáts, Ferenc Eckhart and Gyula Szekfű. This unfinished work was recently continued by Gustav Bayerle in his *Ottoman Diplomacy in Hungary: Letters from the Pashas of Buda, 1590-1593* (Indiana University Uralic and Altaic Series 101), Bloomington, Ind. 1972.

4.) *Archivum Rákóczianum — II. Rákóczi Ferencz levéltára:*

a.) Section One: *Had- és belügy* (Military and Internal Affairs):

I-III. Thaly, Kálmán (ed.): *II. Rákóczi Ferenc fejedelem leveleskönyvei, levéltárának egykorú lajstromaival, 1703-1712* (The Correspondences of Prince Ferenc Rákóczi II, with the Contemporary Index of His Archives, 1703-1712), 3 vols., Pest 1873-Bp. 1879.

IV-VII. Thaly, Kálmán (ed.): *Székesi gr. Bercsényi Miklós főhadvezér és fejedelmi helytartó levelei Rákóczi fejedelemhez, 1704-1712* (The Letters of the Commanding General and Princely Governor Count Miklós Bercsényi of Székes to Prince Rákóczi, 1704-1712), 4 vols., Bp. 1875-1879.

VIII. Thaly, Kálmán (ed.): *Székesi gr. Bercsényi Miklós főhadvezér és fejedelmi helytartó leveleskönyvei és más emlékezetre méltó iratai, 1705-1711* (The Correspondence and Other Notable Documents of the Commanding General and Princely Governor Count Miklós Bercsényi of Székes, 1705-1711), Bp. 1882.

IX. Thaly, Kálmán (ed.): *Bottyán János vezénylő tábornok levelezése s róla szóló más emlékezetre méltó iratok, 1685-1716* (The Correspondence of the Commanding General János Bottyán, and Other Noteworthy Documents About Him, 1685-1716), Bp. 1883.

X. Thaly, Kálmán (ed.): *Pótlék s betűrendes név- és tárgymutató II. Rákóczi*

Ferenc levéltára I. osztály I-IX. kötetéhez (Supplement and an Alphabetical Name and Subject Index to Volumes I-IX of Ferenc Rákóczi II's Archives), Bp. 1889.

XI-XII. Lukinich, Imre: *II. Rákóczi Ferenc felségárulási perének története és okirattára* (The History and Archives of the High Treason Trial of Ferenc Rákóczi II), 2 vols., Bp. 1935.

b.) Section Two: *Diplomatia:*

I-III. Simonyi, Ernő (ed.): *Angol diplomátiai iratok II. Rákóczi Ferenc korára* (English Diplomatic Documents Concerning the Age of Ferenc Rákóczi II), 3 vols., Pest 1871- Bp. 1877.

FONTES HISTORIAE HUNGARICAE AEVI RECENTORIS— MAGYARORSZÁG UJABBKORI TÖRTÉNETÉNEK FORRÁSAI (FONTES)

A.) *Gr. Széchenyi István összes munkái* (The Complete Works of Count István Széchenyi).

1.) As yet unpublished

2.) *Hitel. A Taglalat és a Hitellel foglalkozó kisebb iratok* (Credit. Analysis and Various Lesser Studies Dealing with the Credit), ed. and intr. by Béla Iványi-Grünwald, Bp. 1930.

3.) As yet unpublished.

4.) As yet unpublished.

5.) *A Kelet Népe* (The People of the East), ed. and intr. by Zoltán Ferenczi, Bp. 1925.

6.) *Gr. Széchenyi István iroi és hírlapi vitája Kossuth Lajossal* (Count István Széchenyi's Literary and Publicistic Debate With Lajos Kossuth), 2 parts, pt. I (1841-1843), pt. II (1843-1848), ed. and intr. by Gyula Viszota, Bp. 1927-1930.

7-9.) *Gr. Széchenyi István döblingi irodalmi hagyatéka* (Count István Széchenyi's Legacy of Döbling), 3 vols., vol. I-II ed. by Árpád Károlyi, vol. III ed. by Vilmos Tolnai, Bp. 1921-1925.

10-15.) *Gr. Széchenyi István naplói* (The Diaries of Count István Széchenyi), ed. and intr. by Gyula Viszota, Bp. 1925-1939.

B.) *A nemzeti szinház százéves története* (The Centennial History of the National Theater).

1.) Kádár, Jolán (Pukánszkyné): *A nemzeti szinház százéves története* (The Centennial History of the National Theater), Bp. 1940.

2.) Kádár, Jolán (Pukánszkyné) (ed.): *Iratok a nemzeti színház történetéhez* (Documents on the History of the National Theater), Bp. 1938.

C.) *Personal Letters:*

1.) Angyal, Dávid (ed.): *Falk Miksa és Kecskeméthy Aurél elkobzott levelezése* (The Confiscated Correspondences of Miksa Falk and Aurél Kecskeméthy), Bp. 1925.

D.) *Official Documents and Letters:*

1.) Lukinich, Imre: *A Szatmári béke története és okirattára* (The History and Papers of the Peace of Szatmár (1711), Bp. 1925.

2.) Csengery, Lóránt: *Csengery Antal hátrahagyott iratai és feljegyzései* (The Unpublished Papers and Notes of Antal Csengery), intr. by Gyula Wlassics, Bp. 1928.

3.) Károlyi, Árpád: *Németújvári gróf Batthyány Lajos első magyar miniszterelnök főbenjáró pöre* (The High Treason Trial of Count Lajos Batthyány of Németújvár, the First Hungarian Prime Minister), 2 vols., Bp. 1932.

a.) Vol. I: *A pör története* (The History of the Trial).

b.) Vol. II: *Pöriratok és államiratok* (Trial and Governmental Papers).

4.) Károlyi, Árpád: *Az 1848-diki Pozsonyi Törvénycikkek az udvar elött* (The Pozsony Statutes of 1848 at the Court), Bp. 1936.

E.) *Memoires:*

1.) Steier, Lajos: *Béniczky Lajos bányavidéki kormánybiztos és honvédezredes visszaemlékezései és jelentései az 1848-49-iki szabadságharcról és a tót mozgalomról* (The Reminiscences and Reports of Colonel Lajos Beniczky, State Commissioner at the Mining Region (of Upper Hungary), about the Revolution and the Slovak Movement of 1848-1849), Bp. 1924.

2.) Madzsar, Imre: *Farádi Vörös Ignác visszaemlékezései az 1778-1822. évekről* (The Reminiscences of Ignác Vörös of Farád About the Years 1778 to 1822), Bp. 1927.

3.) Czeke, Marianne: *Brunszvik Teréz grófnő naplói és feljegyzései* (The Diaries and Notes of Countess Teréz Brunszvik), Bp. 1938.

F.) *Documents on the National Minority Question:*

1.) Szekfű, Gyula: *Iratok a magyar államnyelv kérdésének történetéhez, 1790-1848* (Documents on the Question of the Magyar State Language, 1790-1848), Bp. 1926.

2.) Thim, József: *A magyarországi 1848-49-iki szerb fölkelés története* (The History of the Serbian Uprising in Hungary in 1848-1849), 3 vols., Bp. 1930-1940.

a.) Vol. I: The History of the Uprising with the above title, Bp. 1940.

b.) Vol. II: *Iratok: 1848 márc.-aug.* (Documents, March-August, 1848), Bp. 1930.

c.) Vol. III: *Iratok: 1848. szept-1949. aug.* (Documents, Sept. 1848-Aug. 1849), Bp. 1935.

3.) Steier, Lajos: *A tót nemzetiségi kérdés 1848-49-ben* (The Slovak Nationality Question in 1848-1849), 2 vols., Bp. 1937.

a.) Vol. I: *A kérdés története* (The History of the Question).

b.) Vol. II: *Okmánytár* (Documents).

4.) Miskolczy, Gyula: *A horvát kérdés története és irományai a rendi állam korában* (The History and Documents of the Croatian Question in the Age of the Feudal State), 2 vols., Bp. 1927-1928.

G.) *Documents on Hungarian Social and Economic History:*

1.) Szabó, Dezső: *A magyarországi úrbérrendezés története Maria Terézia korában* (The History of the Systematization of Feudal Obligations in Hungary in the Age of Maria Theresa), Bp. 1933. The projected second volume of this work is still in manuscript, with plans for its imminent publication.

H.) *Diaries and Autobiographies:*
1.) Gávai-Gál, Jenő: *Élmények és tanulmányok* (Experiences and Studies), Bp. 1940.

I.) *Governmental and Administrative Papers:*
1.) Domanovszky, Sándor: *József nádor élete és iratai* (The Life and Papers of Palatinate Joseph), 4 vols. in 6, Bp. 1925-1944.
a.) Vol. I: *József nádor élete* (The Life of Palatinate Joseph), parts I-II, Bp. 1944.
b.) Vol. II: *József nádor iratai, 1792-1804* (The Papers of Palatinate Joseph, 1792-1804), Bp. 1925.
c.) Vol. III: *József nádor iratai, 1805-1807,* Bp. 1929.
d.) Vol. IV: *József nádor iratai, 1807-1809,* Bp. 1935.
2.) Mályusz, Elemér: *Sándor Lipót főherceg nádor iratai, 1790-95* (The Papers of Palatinate Archduke Alexander Leopold, 1790-1795), Bp. 1926.

J.) *Documents on the History of the Emigration of 1848-1849:*
1.) Hajnal, István: A Kossuth-emigráció Torokországban The Kossuth Emigration in Turkey , Bp. 1927.
2.) Janossy, Denes: *A Kossuth-emigracio Angliában és Amerikában, 1851-52* (The Kossuth Emigration in England and in America, 1851-1852), 2 vols. in 3, Bp. 1944-1948. The documents are in the last part of vol. I, and in the two parts of vol. II.

A MAGYAR TÖRTÉNETTUDOMÁNY KÉZIKÖNYVE (THE HANDBOOK OF HUNGARIAN HISTORICAL SCIENCES)

Vol. I. *A TÖRTÉNETTUDOMÁNY ELMÉLETE ÉS FORRÁSAI — THE PHILOSOPHY AND SOURCES OF HUNGARIAN HISTORICAL SCIENCES:*

* 1.) *Történetfilozófia* (Philosophy of History), by Gyula Kornis, Bp. 1924.
* 2.) *A történettudomány módszertana* (The Methodology of Historiography), by István Dékány, Bp. 1925.
3.) * a.) *A forráskutatás és forráskritika története* (The History of Source Research and Source Criticism in Hungary), by Bálint Hóman, Bp. 1925.
b.) *Magyar történeti forráskiadványok* (Hungarian Historical Source Publications), by Emma Bartoniek, Bp. 1929.
4.) *Hazai elbeszélő források* (Hungarian Descriptive Sources).
a.) *Történetírás* (Historical Writing), to be written by Bálint Hóman and Dávid Angyal.
*b.) *Magyar történeti tárgyu szépirodalom* (Hungarian Belles Lettres with Historical Themes), by Lajos Dézsi, Bp. 1927.
5.) *Magyarország történetének forrásai a honfoglalásig* (The Sources of Hungary's History Until the Conquest (by the Magyars)).
a.) *Őskor* (Ancient Period), to be written by Lajos Bella.
b.) *Római és népvándorlási kor* (The Age of Rome and of the Barbarian Invasions), to be written by András Alföldi.
6.) *A magyar történet keleti elbeszélő forrásai* (The Oriental Narrative Sources of Hungarian History).

a.) *Arab-perzsa írók* (Arabian and Persian Writers), to be written by Count István Zichy.
* b) *A magyar történet bizánci forrásai* (The Byzantine Sources of Hungarian History), by Gyula Moravcsik, Bp. 1934.
c.) *Szláv írók* (Slavic Writers), to be written by Antal Hodinka.
d.) *Török írók* (Turkish Writers), to be written by Ferenc Zsinka.
7.) *A magyar történet nyugati elbeszélő forrásai* (The Western Narrative Sources of Hungarian History):
a.) *A IX-XIII. századig* (From the 9th to the 13th Century), to be written by Albin G. Gombos.
b.) *XIV, század* (The 14th Century), to be written by Ferenc Patek.
*c.) *A magyar történet nyugati elbeszélő forrásai, XV. század (1526-ig)* (The Western Narrative Sources of Hungarian History, 16th Century (till 1526)), by Antal Áldásy, Bp. 1927.
d.) *XVI-XVIII. század* (The 16th-18th Centuries), to be written by Imre Lukinich.
e.) *XIX. század* (1790-1918) (The 19th Century (1790-1918)) to be written by György Balanyi.
8.) *Történeti emlékek* (Other Historical Sources):
a.) *Oklevelek és más levéltari források* (Diplomas and Other Archival Sources), to be written by Bela Baranyay, Ferenc Eckhart and József Herzog.
b.) *Törvények és jogszabályok* (Laws and Regulations), to be written by Ferenc Dőry.
c.) *Jogszokások* (Legal Customs), to be written by József Holub.
d.) *Néprajzi emlékek* (Ethnographical Sources), to be written by László Madarassy.
e.) *Régészeti emlékek* (Archeological Sources), to be written by József Ernyey.
f.) *Irodalmi emlékek* (Literary Sources), to be written by Vilmos Tolnai.
g.) *Politikai és közgazdasági irodalom* (Political and Economic Sources), to be written by Albert Gárdonyi.

Vol. II.
A TÖRTÉNET SEGÉDTUDOMÁNYAI — AUXILIARY SCIENCES OF HISTORY:

*1.) *A segédtudományok története Magyorországon* (The History of the Auxiliary Sciences in Hungary), by Albert Gárdonyi, Bp. 1926.
2.) *Paleográfia* (Palaeography), to be written by László Fejérpataky and István Hajnal.
*3.) *Magyar oklevéltan* (Hungarian Diplomatics), by Imre Szentpétery, Bp. 1930.
*4.) *Pápai oklevelek* (Papal Diplomas), by László Fejérpataky and Antal Áldásy, Bp. 1926.
*5.) *Chronologia* (Chronology), by Imre Szentpétery, Bp. 1923.
*6.) *Címertan* (Heraldry), by Antal Áldásy, Bp. 1923.
7.) *Genealogia* (Genealogy), to be written by Antal Áldásy.
8.) *Epigráfika* (Epigraphy), to be written by Bálint Kuzsinszky.
9.) *Magyar penztortenet es numizmatica* (The History of Hungarian Money and Numismatics), to be written by Ference Kovaits.
10.) *Magyarország történeti föld- és néprajza* (The Historical Geography and Ethnography of Hungary), to be written by Elemér Mályusz.

11.) *Történeti statisztika* (Historical Statistics), to be written by Alajos Kovács.
12.) *A nyelvtudomány, mint történeti segédtudomany* (Linguistics as an Auxiliary Science of History), to be written by Zoltán Gombócz and János Melich.
13.) *A magyarországi latinság* (The Latin of Hungary), to be written by Jusztin Budó.

Vol. III,
A MAGYAR TÖRTÉNET RÉSZTUDOMÁNYAI —
THE SUB-DISCIPLINES OF HUNGARIAN HISTORY:

1.) *Magyar alkotmány- és közigazgatástörténet* (Hungarian Constitutional and Administrative History), to be written by István Ereky.
2.) *Magyar jogtörténet* (Hungarian Legal History), to be written by József Holub.
3.) *A magyar róm. kath. egyház története* (The History of the Hungarian Catholic Church), to be written by József Lukcsics.
*4.) *A magyarországi protestantizmus történelme* (The History of Protestantism in Hungary), by Imre Révész, Bp. 1925.
5.) *Magyar gazdaság- és társadalomtörténet* (Hungarian Economic and Social History), to be written by Sándor Domanovszky.
6.) *Magyar irodalomtörténet* (Hungarian Literary History), to be written by Jenő Pintér.
7.) *Magyar művészettörténet* (The History of Hungarian Art), to be written by Tibor Gerevich and Antal Hekler.
8.) *Magyar zenetörténet* (The History of Hungarian Music), to be written by Kálmán Isoz.

Only the thirteen volumes marked with an asterisk (+) have appeared in print.

INDEX

A

G

H

K

O

P

S

U

V